I0001031

House of Commons

Return of judicial Statistics of Ireland 1896

Part I. Police, Criminal Proceedings, Prisons

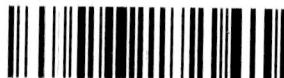

House of Commons

Return of judicial Statistics of Ireland 1896
Part I. Police, Criminal Proceedings, Prisons

ISBN/EAN: 9783742800053

Manufactured in Europe, USA, Canada, Australia, Japa

Cover: Foto ©Lupo / pixelio.de

Manufactured and distributed by brebook publishing software
(www.brebook.com)

House of Commons

Return of judicial Statistics of Ireland 1896

JUDICIAL STATISTICS, IRELAND, 1896.

PART I.—CRIMINAL STATISTICS.

STATISTICS

RELATING TO

Police—Crime and its Distribution—Modes of Procedure for Punishment of Crime—Proceedings in Criminal Courts—Persons under Detention in Prisons and other places of Confinement—for the year 1896.

Presented to both Houses of Parliament by Command of Her Majesty.

DUBLIN:
PRINTED FOR HER MAJESTY'S STATIONERY OFFICE,
BY ALEXANDER THOM & CO. (LIMITED).

And to be purchased, either directly or through any Bookseller, from
HODGES, FIGGIS, and Co. (LIMITED), 104, Grafton-street, Dublin; or
EYRE and SPOTTISWOODE, East Harding-street, Fleet-street, E.C., and
32, Abingdon-street, Westminster, S.W.; or
JOHN MENZIES and Co., 12, Hanover-street, Edinburgh and 90, West Nile-street, Glasgow.

1898.

Charlemont House, Dublin,

12th *August*, 1895.

Sir,

I have the honour to submit herewith, for the consideration of His Excellency the Lord Lieutenant, Part I. of the Judicial Statistics of Ireland for the year 1894, consisting of my Report on the Criminal Statistics for the year, with an Appendix of Comparative and Detailed Tables.

I remain, Sir,

Your obedient Servant,

THOS. W. GRIMSHAW,

Registrar-General.

The Under Secretary,

&c., &c., &c.,

Dublin Castle.

CONTENTS OF REPORT.

I.—INTRODUCTORY REMARKS.

Classification of Offences, ...
Grouping of Offences by Classes, ...
Quasi Criminal Cases, ...
Explanation regarding Comparative Tables, ...

II.—INCREASE AND DECREASE OF CRIME.

Standards by which to measure the prevalence of Crime, ...
Number of Offences in 1896 compared with those in 1895, ...
Indictable Offences of each Class to every 10,000 of the Estimated Population in 1896, and ten preceding years, ...

III.—NATURE OF CRIMES.

Number of Persons proceeded against under Crimes Acts in the years, 1882–6, and 1887–96,
Classification of Serious Crimes :—
Offences against the Person, ...
Offences against Property with Violence, ...
Offences against Property without Violence, ...
Malicious Injury to Property, ...
Forgery and Offences against the Currency, ...
Other Indictable Offences, ...
Offences disposed of Summarily, ...
Number of Persons proceeded against for Common Assaults and for Drunkenness in 1896, and in each of the ten years 1886–95, ...
Offences coming under the head of Quasi-Criminal Cases, ...

IV.—GEOGRAPHICAL DISTRIBUTION OF CRIME.

The distribution throughout Ireland of Criminal Offences of all kinds, distinguishing Indictable from Non-indictable Offences, with the Rate per 100,000 of the Population, represented by each of these two Classes of Offences, ...
Indictable Offences in each County in 1896 per 100,000 of Population, ...
Persons tried Summarily in each County for Non-Indictable Offences per 100,000 of Population, .
All Criminal Offences and Charges in each County per 100,000 of Population, . . .
Offences in Large Town Districts, ...
Offences in Large Town Districts compared with those in other Districts. . . .
Distribution of Crime, by Counties, for the five years 1892–96, ...
Relative proportion of Drunkenness in Town and Country Districts, ...

V.—PROCEDURE FOR THE PUNISHMENT OF CRIME.

	Page
Criminal Procedure, ...	18
Districts Proclaimed in 1894, ...	18
Statement giving the Number of Persons Tried by Jury in each of the years 1885–94, and how the Cases were Disposed of, ...	19
Cost of Criminal Proceedings at Assizes and Quarter Sessions for year ended 31st March, 1895, .	19
Court for Crown Cases reserved, ...	19
Number of Persons Tried in Courts of Summary Jurisdiction, ...	19
Appeals to Quarter Sessions, ...	20

VI.—CRIMINALS AND OTHERS IN CONFINEMENT, AND KNOWN CRIMINALS AT LARGE.

Character of Persons prosecuted, ...	20
Suspected Persons at Large and Houses of Bad Character, ...	20
Comparison of the Number of "Men and Boys," and "Women and Girls," admitted to Places of Detention, ...	20
Ages of Convicted Prisoners committed during 1894, ...	21
Habitual Criminals, ...	21
State of Education of Prisoners, ...	21
Previous Occupations of Prisoners, ...	22
Number of Children confined in Reformatory Schools, ...	22
Social condition of Children committed to Reformatories in 1894, ...	23
Degree of Education of Children committed to Reformatory Schools, ...	23
Children under Warrant of Detention in Industrial Schools in 1894 compared with 1893, . .	23
Ages of Children placed in Industrial Schools in 1894, ...	24
Criminal and Dangerous Lunatics in Confinement, ...	24
Number of Criminal and Dangerous Lunatics in Asylums, with the Judgments or Orders under which they were committed, ...	25

VII.—POLICE ESTABLISHMENTS.

Number of Police in 1894 compared with 1893, . . .	25
Proportion of Police to Population, ...	26
Detectives, ...	26
Cost of Police Establishments, ...	26

CONTENTS OF APPENDIX OF TABLES.

COMPARATIVE AND SUMMARY TABLES.

	Page
A.—Number of Persons Tried at Assizes and Quarter Sessions, 1877 to 1896,	28
B.—Number of Persons Tried Summarily, 1877 to 1896,	30
C.—Number of Crimes Committed, 1877 to 1896,	32
D.—Summary of the three preceding Tables, with proportions of Persons Tried and of Crimes to Population,	34
E.—Geographical distribution of Crime, Drunkenness, and Suicides in the Counties of Ireland:—	
Part I.—Counties arranged according to proportion of Crimes and Offences to Population,	38
Part II.—Counties arranged in Alphabetical Order by Provinces,	38

ANNUAL TABLES, 1896.

Assizes and Quarter Sessions.

1. Assizes.—Number of Persons for Trial, Nature of Offences, and Results of Proceedings,	41
2. Assizes.—Length of Sentences,	56
3. Quarter Sessions.—Number of Persons for Trial, Nature of Offences, and Results of Proceedings,	60
4. Quarter Sessions.—Length of Sentences,	54
5. Assizes and Quarter Sessions.—Number of Persons for Trial, Nature of Offences, and Results of Proceedings,	58
6. Assizes and Quarter Sessions.—Number of Persons for Trial for each Offence in each County,	63
7. Assizes and Quarter Sessions.—Number of Persons for Trial and Results of Proceedings in each Court,	64
8. Criminal Proceedings.—Cost of Prosecutions at Assizes, Quarter Sessions, &c.,	70
9. Supreme Courts of Appeal.—Cases for Crown Cases Reserved,	73
10. Districts subject to Proclamations in Council under 6 William IV., cap. 13, sec. 13,	74
11. Districts subject to Proclamations in Council prohibiting the carrying or having of Arms under the Peace Preservation (Ireland) Act, 1881,	74
12. Districts subject to Proclamations in Council prohibiting the carrying of Arms under the Peace Preservation (Ireland) Act, 1881,	74
13. Establishments, Royal Irish Constabulary,	76
14. Establishments, Dublin Metropolitan Police,	79

Courts of Summary Jurisdiction.

15. Courts of Summary Jurisdiction.—Number of Persons Tried, Nature of Offences, Results of Proceedings, and Length of Sentences,	83
16. Courts of Summary Jurisdiction.—Number of Persons Tried for each Offence in each County,	86
17. Courts of Summary Jurisdiction.—Age and Sex of Persons Convicted,	94
18. Courts of Summary Jurisdiction.—Proceedings in Quasi Criminal matters,	95
19. Courts of Summary Jurisdiction.—Appeals to Quarter Sessions,	96

POLICE RETURNS.

20. Indictable Offences.—Crimes Committed, Apprehensions, and Prosecutions,
21. Non-indictable Offences.—Apprehensions and Prosecutions, . .
Returns from the several Counties:—
22. Indictable Offences.—Crimes, Apprehensions, and Prosecutions in each County,
23. Non-indictable Offences.—Apprehensions and Prosecutions in each County, .
24. Indictable Offences.—Nature of Crimes committed in each County, . .
25. Character of Persons Prosecuted, ...
26. Numbers of Suspected Persons at Large, ...
27. Number of Houses of Bad Character, ...
28. Crimes (Indictable Offences) Committed, and Apprehensions in each month of the year, .
29. Persons Convicted for Drunkenness three times and upwards in the year, . .

PRISONS.

30. Prisoners.—Receptions of Prisoners in each Prison, ...
31. Prisoners.—Disposal of Prisoners in each Prison, ...
32. Convicted Prisoners.—Nature of Sentences of Prisoners received in each Prison, .
33. Convicted Prisoners.—Length of Sentence, ...
34. Convicted Prisoners.—Previous Convictions, ...
35. Convicted Prisoners.—Age and Sex, ...
36. Convicted Prisoners.—Birthplace, ...
37. Convicted Prisoners.—Degree of Instruction, ...
38. Convicted Prisoners.—Previous Occupations, ...
39. Criminal Prisoners.—Number received in Prison in each month of the year, .
40. Convicts.—Length of Sentences of Convicts under Detention on 31st December, 1896,

REFORMATORY AND INDUSTRIAL SCHOOLS.

41. Reformatory Schools.—Committals and Sentences, ...
42. Reformatory Schools.—Offences, ...
43. Reformatory Schools.—Age, Sex, State of Instruction, and Previous Commitments of Offenders,
44. Reformatory Schools.—Numbers under Detention, Committed, Discharged, and Removed,
45. Industrial Schools.—Numbers under Detention, Committed, Discharged, and Removed, .
46. Industrial Schools.—Discharges and Terms of Detention actually served, . . .
47. Industrial Schools.—Grounds of Committal, ...

CRIMINAL AND DANGEROUS LUNATICS.

48. Criminal Lunatics.—Receptions and Discharges during the year, . . .
49. Criminal Lunatics.—Numbers undergoing Detention on 31st December, 1896, .
50. Criminal Lunatics.—Offences, ...
51. Dangerous Lunatics.—Receptions and Discharges during the year, . .
52. Dangerous Lunatics.—Numbers undergoing Detention on 31st December, 1896, .

INDEX TO SUBJECTS

IN

REPORT AND TABLES.

Acquittals and Convictions in Ireland for a series of years compared,
Ages of Children received into Reformatories,
" Children received into Industrial Schools,
" Convicted Prisoners committed to Larger and Minor Prisons,
Appeals to Quarter Sessions, from Magistrates,
Apprehensions, Number of, for Indictable Offences,
Assizes, Commissions, and Quarter Sessions, Criminal Business at,
Asylums, Criminal and Dangerous Lunatics in,
Birthplaces of Convicted Criminals,
Bridewells,
Character of Persons proceeded against,
Common Assaults,
Constabulary, Royal Irish,
Convicts in State Prisons,
Coroners' Courts,
Cost of Police,
" of Criminal Prosecutions,
Counties, Distribution of Crime in,
Crime, Comparison of, with previous years,
" excess of, in Large Town Districts,
" Geographical Distribution of,
" Standards by which to measure Prevalence of,
Crimes Acts, Persons proceeded against under,
Criminal Classes known to Police,
" Law and Procedure (Ireland) Act, 1887,
" Lunatics,
" Offences, distribution of,
" " Comparison by Counties of number of, in 1896, with Number for the year 1895,
" Proceedings at Assizes, &c.,
" " Costs of,
Criminals, Habitual,
" in Confinement and at Large,
" Recommittments of Convicted,
Crown Cases Reserved, Court for Consideration of,
Dangerous Lunatics charged with Intent to Commit Crime,
Death, Sentence of,
Distribution of Criminal Offences,
Drunkards, Habitual,
Drunkenness,
Dublin Metropolitan Police Establishment,
Education, State of, of Convicted Prisoners,
" " " compared with state of Education of general Population,
" " Reformatory School Children,
" " Industrial School Children,

	Report. Page.	Tables. Page.
Habitual Criminals,	21	140
Habitual Drunkards, Re-commitments of,	–	126
Houses of Bad Character,	20	131
Indictable Offences,	9, 11, 16	24–65, 83–94, 100, 102, 108–117
" " compared with previous years,	11, 15	38
" " Distribution of, in Counties,	15	108, 110
Industrial Schools,	20, 23	154–161
Infanticide, Statistics of,	–	100, 110, 132
Intoxicating Liquor Laws, Offences against,	–	30, 62, 86, 90, 94, 101
Local Prisons—(1) Larger, (2) Minor,	20	130–147
Lunatics, Criminal and Dangerous,	24	164–171
Malicious Injuries to Property,	11, 13	26, 39, 34, 44, 18, 52, 56, 60, 66, 102, 112, 116, 124
Murder, Attempts to,	13	89, 100, 110, 133
Murders,	13	100, 110, 133
Non-indictable Offences,	11, 13, 15, 16	35, 68, 95
Occupations of Convicted Prisoners,	21	145
Offences determined Summarily,	13	50, 35, 65–95
" " Compared with previous years,	11, 15	30
" " Distribution of, in Counties,	–	66
Offences in each County, per 100,000 of Population,	15	–
Offences in Large Town Districts,	17	–
Offences not determined Summarily—(see Indictable Offences).		
Offences, Quasi-Criminal,	10, 14	95
Peace Preservation Act,	18	74
Police, Establishment, and Proportion of, to Population,	25	76–79
Prisons, Admissions to and Numbers in,	20	130–148
Proclaimed Districts, Proceedings as to, in 1898,	18	74
Quasi-Criminal Offences,	10, 14	93
Quarter Sessions, Criminal Proceedings,	16, 20	50–7
Re-commitments of Convicted Criminals,	21	140
" Habitual Drunkards,	–	119, 126
Reformatory Schools,	22	151–153
Thieves, &c., known to Police,	20	120
Town Crime, Excess of,	17	–

JUDICIAL STATISTICS OF IRELAND FOR THE YEAR 1896.

PART I.—CRIMINAL STATISTICS.

I.—INTRODUCTORY REMARKS.

I.—Introductory Remarks.

The tables appended to this Report have been compiled on the principles first adopted as regards Ireland in connection with the Criminal Statistics for the year 1895.

In the reports for years prior to 1895 all offences were in the first place separated into two great divisions under the heads—" Indictable offences not disposed of summarily" and " All cases disposed of summarily." The former were for convenience designated " more serious" and the latter " less serious " offences.

In the new classification all " indictable offences " of a kindred character are grouped together irrespective of the particular manner in which they came under the cognizance of the authorities, or of the method of disposal of the charges founded upon them. Thus the more serious crimes properly come under the head indictable offences, and the less serious under non-indictable offences, all of which are disposed of summarily.*

Grouping of offences.

Indictable offences are grouped under the following six classes:—

Class I.—Offences against the person.
Class II.—Offences against property with violence.
Class III.—Offences against property without violence.
Class IV.—Malicious injuries to property.
Class V.—Forgery and offences against the currency.
Class VI.—Other offences not included in the above classes.

The crimes comprised in each class will be found set forth at each margin of the tables.

The offences disposed of summarily are classified under two heads, viz.:—

Section A.—Indictable offences disposed of summarily.
Section B.—Other offences disposed of summarily.

It is to be noted that the crimes under Section A are also included in the group of indictable offences above referred to, and that many of the minor cases, that is non-indictable offences, although classed as " offences," are more of a civil than a criminal character, as I have frequently pointed out in previous reports.

* Three Schedules, showing in detail the alterations in classification here referred to, will be found on pages 33–58 of the Criminal Statistics of 1895.

I.—Introductory Remarks.

Quasi criminal cases.

In addition to the cases last referred to, the proceedings in the Courts of Summary Jurisdiction include a large group of *quasi* criminal cases which are not included in the Tables relating to criminal offences, but are set forth separately in Table 18. The following is a list of the subjects dealt with in the proceedings here referred to:—

Securities.
Maintenance.
Goods stolen (Restoration of).
Employers and Workmen.
Children.
Sanitary Law.
Other Orders.

Comparative Tables.

Comparative tables showing in a summary form the state of crime in Ireland, and how it has been dealt with during each of the twenty years, 1877–96, with quinquennial averages under each head and each item of comparison have been compiled, and will be found on pages 26–35.

These comparisons will be found in Tables A, B, C, and D. Tables A, B, and C, refer respectively to crimes dealt with at Assizes and Quarter Sessions, those dealt with by summary jurisdiction, and offences of an indictable character as reported to the police. Table D gives a summary of Tables A, B, and C under more condensed headings for the quinquennial averages and for the year 1896 only. In Table E, parts I. and II., which follows, is shown the geographical distribution of crime during the last quinquennial period under some of the principal heads selected so as to demonstrate the relative status of crime in each county in Ireland. Part I. gives this information regarding the counties arranged in alphabetical order by provinces, and Part II. shows the counties grouped according to their several degrees of criminality under each of the selected heads.

II.—INCREASE AND DECREASE OF CRIME.

II.—Increase and Decrease of Crime.

Standards by which to measure prevalence of crime.

The number of "Indictable Offences" may be taken as the more correct standard by which to measure the prevalence of crime in relation to the population. In making this remark I must not be taken as denying that many of the non-indictable offences which are disposed of summarily, and constitute a considerable number of the cases dealt with by Magistrates in Petty Sessions and Police Courts, are of a decidedly criminal nature. Many of them are of a sufficiently serious character to indicate a general state of disorder and demoralization in a community amongst which they are numerous; such, for example, as drunkenness, and drunkenness with disorderly conduct, offences which in many cases lead up to crimes of an indictable character.

The main fallacy in taking the number of non-indictable offences of all kinds as an absolute measure of the criminality of a community is that many of the cases partake largely of a civil character; others, again, and these in considerable numbers, consist of cases in which orders are made to maintain certain civil rights, or to secure the discharge of civil duties. Cases distinctly of the latter character are now shown separately under the title of Quasi Criminal Offences (Table 18, p. 93), and in the year 1895 they amounted to about 10,000, and in the year 1896 to about 14,000. Most of such cases were formerly found among "Cases disposed of Summarily," and were included in "Minor Offences" in the reports, under the old system. Another group of the cases "Disposed of Summarily" were proceedings against weekly tenants in towns, which are especially numerous in Dublin. These appeared both in the Civil and the

Criminal statistics in certain places. Such cases are now separated from the Criminal statistics proper. I may here point out that these cases tended to increase the number of apparent crimes committed, and must be allowed for when instituting comparisons with the statistics for years anterior to 1895.

II.—*Increase and Decrease of Crime.*

Comparison of offences in 1896 with those in 1895.

In former annual reports it was the custom each year to compare the numbers of the more serious and the less serious offences, and the total of both classes with the corresponding numbers for the year immediately preceding. This is done in the subjoined statement for the years 1895 and 1896, the grouping of the offences being in accordance with the new system. The figures for cases disposed of summarily show the number of persons proceeded against in such cases; those for cases not disposed of summarily have reference to the number of crimes committed.

—	1895.		1896.		Increase.	
	Number.	Rate per 100,000 of estimated population.	Number.	Rate per 100,000 of estimated population.	Number.	Rate per 100,000 of estimated population.
Indictable offences:—						
Not disposed of summarily,	4,143	91·0	5,461	120·3	1,318	29·3
Disposed of summarily,	3,305	73·3	3,320	73·8	15	0·5
Non-indictable offences disposed of summarily,	180,519	3,966·0	193,834	4,226·5	13,315	280·5
Total,	187,960	4,130·3	201,625	4,431·5	13,645	310·2

Indictable offences per 10,000 of population in 1896 and ten preceding years.

The following summary shows the rate per 10,000 of the estimated population in the middle of each year represented by the number of cases in each class of serious or "Indictable" Offences in Ireland during 1896 and each of the ten years preceding, with the average annual rates for those ten years. It gives a view of the variations which have taken place during the eleven years in the proportional number of more serious offences in Ireland, allowing for the estimated decrease of the population. The rates for nearly all of the classes are in excess of the corresponding rates for the year 1895, but they do not differ very materially from the average rates for the ten years 1886–95.

Nature of Offences.	Number of Indictable Offences in every 10,000 of the Estimated Population.											
	Year										Average for the 10 years preceding.	Year 1896.
	1886.	1887.	1888.	1889.	1890.	1891.	1892.	1893.	1894.	1895.		
1. Against the Person,	2·07	[illegible]	[illegible]	[illegible]	[illegible]	2·16	[illegible]	[illegible]	[illegible]	1·70	[illegible]	[illegible]
2. Against Property with Violence.	1·03	0·78	0·73	[illegible]	[illegible]	[illegible]	0·70	0·44	[illegible]	[illegible]	[illegible]	[illegible]
3. Against Property without Violence.	[illegible]	[illegible]	[illegible]	[illegible]	[illegible]	[illegible]	[illegible]	[illegible]	[illegible]	[illegible]	13·75	[illegible]
4. Malicious, against Property,	1·39	1·42	1·42	1·43	1·38	1·41	1·40	1·45	[illegible]	[illegible]	1·47	1·40
5. Forgery and against Currency.	0·14	0·18	[illegible]	[illegible]	[illegible]	0·10	[illegible]	[illegible]	[illegible]	[illegible]	[illegible]	[illegible]
6. Not included in foregoing,	[illegible]	[illegible]	[illegible]	[illegible]	[illegible]	[illegible]	[illegible]	[illegible]	[illegible]	[illegible]	[illegible]	[illegible]
Total,	21·46	[illegible]	[illegible]	[illegible]	[illegible]	[illegible]	[illegible]	18·67	[illegible]	[illegible]	[illegible]	[illegible]

III.—NATURE OF CRIMES.

III.—*Nature of Crimes.*

As the variations in classification do not alter any of the technical denominations under which crime is classified, the headings under which the different kinds of crime are discussed are the same as in all previous years dealt with.

During the years 1882–5, and 1887–92, the Prevention of Crimes Act, 1882, and the Criminal Law and Procedure Act, 1887, respectively, were in operation in several

III.—*Nature of Crime.*

parts of Ireland, and under these Acts, in addition to cases which might have been disposed of summarily by Magistrates in Petty Sessions, many cases were dealt with which, in ordinary course, would have been returned for trial at Quarter Sessions or Assizes. The circumstances being exceptional, it was decided to exclude all the cases under these Acts in the years 1883–5 and 1887–92 from the ordinary Tables and Summaries in the Reports for those years, and to give them in special Tables only, and they are also omitted from the retrospective Summary Tables in this volume, but the following statement shows the number of persons proceeded against under these Acts during each of the years here referred to:—

Persons proceeded against under Crimes Acts in the years 1883–5 and 1887–92.

Years.	Number of Persons proceeded against.	Years.	Number of Persons proceeded against.
1883, . . .	641	1888, . . .	1,475
1884, . . .	701	1889, . . .	639
1885, . . .	313	1890, . . .	531
		1891, . . .	313
1887, . . .	629	1892, . . .	156

Classification of serious crimes. Table 20, Comparative Table C.

The heads under which the various classes of serious crime are treated are as follows:—

Class I.—Offences against the Person.

Class II.—Offences against Property with Violence.

Class III.—Offences against Property without Violence.

Class IV.—Malicious Injury to Property.

Class V.—Forgery and Offences against the Currency.

Class VI.—Other Offences not included in the above Classes.

In the six classes here mentioned, the figures are taken from the returns of cases reported to the police.

Class I.—Offences against the Person.

Offences against the person.

The cases in this class numbered 867 for the year 1896, as compared with 776 for the preceding year, the number for which year was 834 under that for 1894.

The number of cases of murder was 41, as compared with 43 in the previous year, and an average of 45 for the 5 years 1891–5. Of attempts to murder there were 7 as compared with 19 for the previous year, and with an average of 4·6 for the 5 years ending with 1895. Cases of manslaughter were 67 as compared with 74 for the year 1895, and a quinquennial average of 73·8. Thus the cases of homicide and attempted homicide show a decline as compared with recent standards.

Class II.—Offences against Property with Violence.

Offences against property with violence.

The cases of this nature reported to the police amounted to 456, compared with 362 in the preceding year, and an average of 352·4 for the quinquennial period 1891–5. The principal items in this class are burglary, house and shop breaking, amounting to 363 of the total of 456; these, with robbery, amounting to 73 cases, practically make up the class.

Class III.—Offences against Property without Violence.

Offences against property without violence.

The offences of this class returned in 1896 number 6,285, as compared with 5,987 in 1895, and an average of 5,775 for the five years 1891–5. This class practically means cases of larceny.

Class IV.—Malicious Injuries to Property.

Malicious injuries to property.

The number of offences of this character was practically the same in both of the years 1895 and 1896, viz., 689 in the former and 681 in the latter year. In 1894 the number was 653, with this exception the cases were less numerous in 1896 than in any other year since 1876. The 681 offences in 1896 consisted of 279 cases of arson, 161 of killing and maiming cattle, and 241 tabulated under the head of "other malicious injuries."

Class V.—Forgery and Offences against the Currency.

Forgery and Offences against the currency.

But few offences of this class are committed in Ireland: the number for the year 1896 is 39, and there were only 2 more in the previous year. They showed a general tendency to decrease during the past 20 years.

Class VI.—Other Indictable Offences.

Other indictable offences.

The indictable offences not included in the foregoing classes numbered 463 in the year 1896; they do not appear to call for any special comment.

Offences disposed of Summarily.

Offences disposed of summarily. Table 15.

Under this division there are two classes, denoted (A) and (B) in the tables.

The cases under the head A consist of some indictable offences which have been discussed in the above remarks dealing with the police returns of crimes committed. It may here, however, be noted that of the total number of indictable offences (8,801), no less than 3,320, or 37·7 per cent., were disposed of summarily. The bulk of the 3,320 cases so disposed of were larcenies.

Under Section (B) are included all non-indictable offences disposed of summarily, and although these are exclusive of the cases referred to above as quasi-criminal, they nevertheless comprise a large number of cases, more of a civil than a criminal character, such as some of the offences against the Highway Acts, Police Regulations, Sanitary Laws, Hackney Carriage cases, &c.

Drunkenness and assaults. Tables 16–17.

A very large number of the cases which come under division (B) consist of drunkenness, drunkenness and disorderly conduct, and common assaults. The number of the latter (common assaults) in 1896 was 20,388, or 10 per cent. of all crimes committed. In the case of drunkenness the number is still more remarkable, as it amounts to 90,848, being 44·8 per cent. of all crimes committed, and 48·1 per cent. of all cases disposed of summarily.

The common assault cases disposed of summarily, and the cases of drunkenness (including drunkenness and disorderly conduct), are set out in the following statement, and a comparison instituted with each of the ten years preceding.

—	1886.	1887.	1888.	1889.	1890.	1891.	1892.	1893.	1894.	1895.	Average Annual Number (1886–95).	1896.
Common Assaults, . . .	[illegible]	[illegible]	[illegible]	[illegible]	[illegible]	[illegible]	[illegible]	[illegible]	[illegible]	[illegible]	[illegible]	[illegible]
Drunkenness and Drunk and Disorderly, . . .	[illegible]	[illegible]	[illegible]	[illegible]	[illegible]	[illegible]	[illegible]	[illegible]	[illegible]	[illegible]	[illegible]	[illegible]

Quasi-Criminal Offences.

The offences under this head being more of a civil than a criminal character, scarcely come within the limits of the subject dealt with in the preceding paragraphs. Excluding orders (numbering about 14,000) for the recovery of tenements overheld in towns, the detailed numbers of which are given in the Civil Statistics, applications for orders amounted to about 14,000 in the year 1896. Considerably more than one-third (5,135) of these cases were cases for Orders to enter into security to keep the peace or find bail. About 15 per cent. of the whole, or 2,160, related to children, comprising 946 school attendance orders, 1,196 Industrial school orders, and 18 custody orders under the 1894 Act for the Prevention of Cruelty to Children. The remaining cases do not require special notice.

IV.—GEOGRAPHICAL DISTRIBUTION OF CRIME.

The general distribution of crime throughout the County, City, and Town Districts into which Ireland is divided for criminal jurisdiction and police purposes, is shown in the following statement for the years 1895 and 1896, with the increase or decrease in each district in the latter year.

Counties, Counties of Cities, Towns, Ridings and Dublin Police District.	Population in 1871 in Thousands.	Indictable Offences.					Non-indictable Offences.					Total.				
		[illegible]	[illegible]	Increase.	Decrease.	Rate per 10,000 of Population in [illegible]	[illegible]	[illegible]	Increase.	Decrease.	Rate per 10,000 of Population in [illegible]	[illegible]	[illegible]	Increase.	Decrease.	Rate per 10,000 of Population in [illegible]
Total of Ireland,	[illegible]	[illegible]	[illegible]	[illegible]	[illegible]	[illegible]	[illegible]	[illegible]	[illegible]	[illegible]	[illegible]	[illegible]	[illegible]	[illegible]	[illegible]	[illegible]
Leinster.																
Carlow,	[illegible]	[illegible]	[illegible]	[illegible]	[illegible]	[illegible]	[illegible]	[illegible]	[illegible]	[illegible]	[illegible]	[illegible]	[illegible]	[illegible]	[illegible]	[illegible]
Drogheda Town,	[illegible]	[illegible]	[illegible]	[illegible]	[illegible]	[illegible]	[illegible]	[illegible]	[illegible]	[illegible]	[illegible]	[illegible]	[illegible]	[illegible]	[illegible]	[illegible]
Dublin,	[illegible]	[illegible]	[illegible]	[illegible]	[illegible]	[illegible]	[illegible]	[illegible]	[illegible]	[illegible]	[illegible]	[illegible]	[illegible]	[illegible]	[illegible]	[illegible]
Dublin Metropolitan Police District,	[illegible]	[illegible]	[illegible]	[illegible]	[illegible]	[illegible]	[illegible]	[illegible]	[illegible]	[illegible]	[illegible]	[illegible]	[illegible]	[illegible]	[illegible]	[illegible]
Kildare,	[illegible]	[illegible]	[illegible]	[illegible]	[illegible]	[illegible]	[illegible]	[illegible]	[illegible]	[illegible]	[illegible]	[illegible]	[illegible]	[illegible]	[illegible]	[illegible]
Kilkenny,	[illegible]	[illegible]	[illegible]	[illegible]	[illegible]	[illegible]	[illegible]	[illegible]	[illegible]	[illegible]	[illegible]	[illegible]	[illegible]	[illegible]	[illegible]	[illegible]
King's County,	[illegible]	[illegible]	[illegible]	[illegible]	[illegible]	[illegible]	[illegible]	[illegible]	[illegible]	[illegible]	[illegible]	[illegible]	[illegible]	[illegible]	[illegible]	[illegible]
Longford,	[illegible]	[illegible]	[illegible]	[illegible]	[illegible]	[illegible]	[illegible]	[illegible]	[illegible]	[illegible]	[illegible]	[illegible]	[illegible]	[illegible]	[illegible]	[illegible]
Louth,	[illegible]	[illegible]	[illegible]	[illegible]	[illegible]	[illegible]	[illegible]	[illegible]	[illegible]	[illegible]	[illegible]	[illegible]	[illegible]	[illegible]	[illegible]	[illegible]
Meath,	[illegible]	[illegible]	[illegible]	[illegible]	[illegible]	[illegible]	[illegible]	[illegible]	[illegible]	[illegible]	[illegible]	[illegible]	[illegible]	[illegible]	[illegible]	[illegible]
Queen's County,	[illegible]	[illegible]	[illegible]	[illegible]	[illegible]	[illegible]	[illegible]	[illegible]	[illegible]	[illegible]	[illegible]	[illegible]	[illegible]	[illegible]	[illegible]	[illegible]
Westmeath,	[illegible]	[illegible]	[illegible]	[illegible]	[illegible]	[illegible]	[illegible]	[illegible]	[illegible]	[illegible]	[illegible]	[illegible]	[illegible]	[illegible]	[illegible]	[illegible]
Wexford,	[illegible]	[illegible]	[illegible]	[illegible]	[illegible]	[illegible]	[illegible]	[illegible]	[illegible]	[illegible]	[illegible]	[illegible]	[illegible]	[illegible]	[illegible]	[illegible]
Wicklow,	[illegible]	[illegible]	[illegible]	[illegible]	[illegible]	[illegible]	[illegible]	[illegible]	[illegible]	[illegible]	[illegible]	[illegible]	[illegible]	[illegible]	[illegible]	[illegible]
Total of Leinster,	[illegible]	[illegible]	[illegible]	[illegible]	[illegible]	[illegible]	[illegible]	[illegible]	[illegible]	[illegible]	[illegible]	[illegible]	[illegible]	[illegible]	[illegible]	[illegible]
Munster.																
Clare,	[illegible]	[illegible]	[illegible]	[illegible]	[illegible]	[illegible]	[illegible]	[illegible]	[illegible]	[illegible]	[illegible]	[illegible]	[illegible]	[illegible]	[illegible]	[illegible]
Cork, E.R.,	[illegible]	[illegible]	[illegible]	[illegible]	[illegible]	[illegible]	[illegible]	[illegible]	[illegible]	[illegible]	[illegible]	[illegible]	[illegible]	[illegible]	[illegible]	[illegible]
Cork, W.R.,	[illegible]	[illegible]	[illegible]	[illegible]	[illegible]	[illegible]	[illegible]	[illegible]	[illegible]	[illegible]	[illegible]	[illegible]	[illegible]	[illegible]	[illegible]	[illegible]
Cork City,	[illegible]	[illegible]	[illegible]	[illegible]	[illegible]	[illegible]	[illegible]	[illegible]	[illegible]	[illegible]	[illegible]	[illegible]	[illegible]	[illegible]	[illegible]	[illegible]
Kerry,	[illegible]	[illegible]	[illegible]	[illegible]	[illegible]	[illegible]	[illegible]	[illegible]	[illegible]	[illegible]	[illegible]	[illegible]	[illegible]	[illegible]	[illegible]	[illegible]
Limerick,	[illegible]	[illegible]	[illegible]	[illegible]	[illegible]	[illegible]	[illegible]	[illegible]	[illegible]	[illegible]	[illegible]	[illegible]	[illegible]	[illegible]	[illegible]	[illegible]
Limerick City,	[illegible]	[illegible]	[illegible]	[illegible]	[illegible]	[illegible]	[illegible]	[illegible]	[illegible]	[illegible]	[illegible]	[illegible]	[illegible]	[illegible]	[illegible]	[illegible]
Tipperary, N.R.,	[illegible]	[illegible]	[illegible]	[illegible]	[illegible]	[illegible]	[illegible]	[illegible]	[illegible]	[illegible]	[illegible]	[illegible]	[illegible]	[illegible]	[illegible]	[illegible]
Tipperary, S.R.,	[illegible]	[illegible]	[illegible]	[illegible]	[illegible]	[illegible]	[illegible]	[illegible]	[illegible]	[illegible]	[illegible]	[illegible]	[illegible]	[illegible]	[illegible]	[illegible]
Waterford,	[illegible]	[illegible]	[illegible]	[illegible]	[illegible]	[illegible]	[illegible]	[illegible]	[illegible]	[illegible]	[illegible]	[illegible]	[illegible]	[illegible]	[illegible]	[illegible]
Waterford City,	[illegible]	[illegible]	[illegible]	[illegible]	[illegible]	[illegible]	[illegible]	[illegible]	[illegible]	[illegible]	[illegible]	[illegible]	[illegible]	[illegible]	[illegible]	[illegible]
Total of Munster,	[illegible]	[illegible]	[illegible]	[illegible]	[illegible]	[illegible]	[illegible]	[illegible]	[illegible]	[illegible]	[illegible]	[illegible]	[illegible]	[illegible]	[illegible]	[illegible]
Ulster.																
Antrim,	[illegible]	[illegible]	[illegible]	[illegible]	[illegible]	[illegible]	[illegible]	[illegible]	[illegible]	[illegible]	[illegible]	[illegible]	[illegible]	[illegible]	[illegible]	[illegible]
Armagh,	[illegible]	[illegible]	[illegible]	[illegible]	[illegible]	[illegible]	[illegible]	[illegible]	[illegible]	[illegible]	[illegible]	[illegible]	[illegible]	[illegible]	[illegible]	[illegible]
Belfast City,	[illegible]	[illegible]	[illegible]	[illegible]	[illegible]	[illegible]	[illegible]	[illegible]	[illegible]	[illegible]	[illegible]	[illegible]	[illegible]	[illegible]	[illegible]	[illegible]
Carrickfergus Town,	[illegible]	[illegible]	[illegible]	[illegible]	[illegible]	[illegible]	[illegible]	[illegible]	[illegible]	[illegible]	[illegible]	[illegible]	[illegible]	[illegible]	[illegible]	[illegible]
Cavan,	[illegible]	[illegible]	[illegible]	[illegible]	[illegible]	[illegible]	[illegible]	[illegible]	[illegible]	[illegible]	[illegible]	[illegible]	[illegible]	[illegible]	[illegible]	[illegible]
Donegal,	[illegible]	[illegible]	[illegible]	[illegible]	[illegible]	[illegible]	[illegible]	[illegible]	[illegible]	[illegible]	[illegible]	[illegible]	[illegible]	[illegible]	[illegible]	[illegible]
Down,	[illegible]	[illegible]	[illegible]	[illegible]	[illegible]	[illegible]	[illegible]	[illegible]	[illegible]	[illegible]	[illegible]	[illegible]	[illegible]	[illegible]	[illegible]	[illegible]
Fermanagh,	[illegible]	[illegible]	[illegible]	[illegible]	[illegible]	[illegible]	[illegible]	[illegible]	[illegible]	[illegible]	[illegible]	[illegible]	[illegible]	[illegible]	[illegible]	[illegible]
Londonderry,	[illegible]	[illegible]	[illegible]	[illegible]	[illegible]	[illegible]	[illegible]	[illegible]	[illegible]	[illegible]	[illegible]	[illegible]	[illegible]	[illegible]	[illegible]	[illegible]
Monaghan,	[illegible]	[illegible]	[illegible]	[illegible]	[illegible]	[illegible]	[illegible]	[illegible]	[illegible]	[illegible]	[illegible]	[illegible]	[illegible]	[illegible]	[illegible]	[illegible]
Tyrone,	[illegible]	[illegible]	[illegible]	[illegible]	[illegible]	[illegible]	[illegible]	[illegible]	[illegible]	[illegible]	[illegible]	[illegible]	[illegible]	[illegible]	[illegible]	[illegible]
Total of Ulster,	[illegible]	[illegible]	[illegible]	[illegible]	[illegible]	[illegible]	[illegible]	[illegible]	[illegible]	[illegible]	[illegible]	[illegible]	[illegible]	[illegible]	[illegible]	[illegible]
Connaught.																
Galway, E.R.,	[illegible]	[illegible]	[illegible]	[illegible]	[illegible]	[illegible]	[illegible]	[illegible]	[illegible]	[illegible]	[illegible]	[illegible]	[illegible]	[illegible]	[illegible]	[illegible]
Galway, W.R.,	[illegible]	[illegible]	[illegible]	[illegible]	[illegible]	[illegible]	[illegible]	[illegible]	[illegible]	[illegible]	[illegible]	[illegible]	[illegible]	[illegible]	[illegible]	[illegible]
Galway Town,	[illegible]	[illegible]	[illegible]	[illegible]	[illegible]	[illegible]	[illegible]	[illegible]	[illegible]	[illegible]	[illegible]	[illegible]	[illegible]	[illegible]	[illegible]	[illegible]
Leitrim,	[illegible]	[illegible]	[illegible]	[illegible]	[illegible]	[illegible]	[illegible]	[illegible]	[illegible]	[illegible]	[illegible]	[illegible]	[illegible]	[illegible]	[illegible]	[illegible]
Mayo,	[illegible]	[illegible]	[illegible]	[illegible]	[illegible]	[illegible]	[illegible]	[illegible]	[illegible]	[illegible]	[illegible]	[illegible]	[illegible]	[illegible]	[illegible]	[illegible]
Roscommon,	[illegible]	[illegible]	[illegible]	[illegible]	[illegible]	[illegible]	[illegible]	[illegible]	[illegible]	[illegible]	[illegible]	[illegible]	[illegible]	[illegible]	[illegible]	[illegible]
Sligo,	[illegible]	[illegible]	[illegible]	[illegible]	[illegible]	[illegible]	[illegible]	[illegible]	[illegible]	[illegible]	[illegible]	[illegible]	[illegible]	[illegible]	[illegible]	[illegible]
Total of Connaught,	[illegible]	[illegible]	[illegible]	[illegible]	[illegible]	[illegible]	[illegible]	[illegible]	[illegible]	[illegible]	[illegible]	[illegible]	[illegible]	[illegible]	[illegible]	[illegible]

IV.—Geographical Distribution of Crime in 1895 and 1896.

Offences in each county. Tables 18 and 21.

Taking indictable offences as the more important indication of the prevalence of crime it is shown that there was an increase of these in 22 districts and a decrease in 19 districts, and that in two districts (Cork City and Monaghan County) the numbers were the same in both years. The districts of increase were Drogheda Town, the Dublin Metropolitan Police District, Waterford City, Belfast City, Carrickfergus Town, Galway Town, and the following, King's County, Meath, Queen's, Westmeath, Wicklow, Cork W.R., Tipperary N.R., Armagh, Cavan, Donegal, Down, Fermanagh, Londonderry, Tyrone, Roscommon, and Sligo.

With respect to non-indictable offences there was an increase in 31 districts, and a decrease in 12.

Taking all forms of offences collectively, the numbers also show an increase in 31 districts, and a decrease in 12.

Offences in each county per 100,000 of population.

In the following lists the various districts are arranged from the lowest to the highest ratios per 100,000 inhabitants for each group, and for total of all kinds of crime in the year 1896.

Indictable Offences in the Year, 1896.

Counties &c., arranged in order from lowest rate to highest.

1. Wexford.	16. Roscommon.	31. King's.
2. Mayo.	17. Leitrim.	32. Dublin.
3. Donegal.	18. Down.	33. Westmeath.
4. Galway, W.R.	19. Galway, E.R.	34. Wicklow.
5. Waterford.	20. Londonderry.	35. Galway Town.
6. Sligo.	21. Queen's.	36. Carrickfergus Town.
7. Monaghan.	22. Armagh.	37. Kildare.
8. Cork, W.R.	23. Louth.	38. Drogheda Town.
9. Antrim.	24. Meath.	39. Limerick City.
10. Kilkenny.	25. Tipperary, S.R.	40. Cork City.
11. Carlow.	26. Fermanagh.	41. Waterford City.
12. Cork, E.R.	27. Tipperary, N.R.	42. Dublin Metropolitan Police District.
13. Cavan.	28. Kerry.	43. Belfast City.
14. Tyrone.	29. Longford.	
15. Limerick.	30. Clare.	

Persons tried Summarily for Non-Indictable Offences in the year 1896.

Counties, &c., arranged in order from lowest rate to highest.

1. Carlow.	16. Dublin.	31. Limerick.
2. Down.	17. Cork, W.R.	32. Longford.
3. Wexford.	18. Galway, W.R.	33. Wicklow.
4. Donegal.	19. Meath.	34. Belfast City.
5. Fermanagh.	20. Kilkenny.	35. Queen's.
6. Monaghan.	21. Armagh.	36. Westmeath.
7. Antrim.	22. Kerry.	37. Drogheda Town.
8. Louth.	23. Galway, E.R.	38. Kildare.
9. Carrickfergus Town.	24. Cavan.	39. Cork City.
10. Londonderry.	25. Tipperary, N.R.	40. Dublin Metropolitan Police District.
11. Sligo.	26. Clare.	41. Limerick City.
12. Mayo.	27. Cork, E.R.	42. Waterford City.
13. Roscommon.	28. Tipperary, S.R.	43. Galway Town.
14. Leitrim.	29. Waterford.	
15. Tyrone.	30. King's.	

All Criminal Offences and Charges in the Year 1896.

Counties &c., arranged in order from lowest rate to highest.

1. Carlow.
2. Down.
3. Wexford.
4. Donegal.
5. Fermanagh.
6. Monaghan.
7. Antrim.
8. Louth.
9. Londonderry.
10. Carrickfergus Town.
11. Mayo.
12. Sligo.
13. Roscommon.
14. Leitrim.
15. Tyrone.
16. Dublin.
17. Cork, W.R.
18. Galway, W.R.
19. Kilkenny.
20. Meath.
21. Armagh.
22. Kerry.
23. Galway, E.R.
24. Cavan.
25. Tipperary, N.R.
26. Clare.
27. Cork, E.R.
28. Tipperary, S.R.
29. Waterford.
30. King's.
31. Limerick.
32. Longford.
33. Wicklow.
34. Queen's.
35. Westmeath.
36. Belfast City.
37. Drogheda Town.
38. Kildare.
39. Cork City.
40. Dublin Metropolitan Police District.
41. Limerick City.
42. Galway Town.
43. Waterford City.

It will be observed that the large towns occupy unfavourable positions in all these lists. In connection with this point it is important to consider more in detail the relative proportion of crime in large town districts as compared with the total of crime in Ireland, and in comparison with districts where the populations are either altogether rural or where residents in towns form a comparatively small portion of the community. The following statement illustrates this point by showing the proportion of crime under certain headings in each of the towns having, in 1891, a population of twenty thousand and upwards; in all other districts; and in the total of Ireland.

Table showing for the Year 1896, the Number of (1) Offences of all kinds; (2) Indictable Offences; (3) Non-indictable Offences; (4) Cases of Drunkenness; in each of the Town Districts, which in 1891 had a population of 20,000 or upwards, and in all other parts of Ireland; with the respective rates per 100,000 of the population.

Cities, &c.	Population in 1891 (in thousands)	Offences: Total		All Indictable Offences		All Non-indictable Offences		Drunkenness (included in non-indictable offences)	
		Number	Rate per 100,000 of population	Number	Rate per 100,000 of population	Number	Rate per 100,000 of population	Number	Rate per 100,000 of population
Dublin Metropolitan Police District,	832	53,645	6,157·6	2,439	[illegible]	51,206	7,444·9	7,380	[illegible]
Cork City,	75	5,773	7,700·0	214	285·0	5,559	7,413·0	3,663	[illegible]
Limerick City,	37	3,015	8,148·6	85	229·7	2,930	7,918·9	1,466	3,961·9
Waterford City,	21	2,869	13,709·5	61	290·7	2,808	12,332·8	1,387	6,604·8
Belfast City,	256	16,348	6,385·3	1,954	763·3	14,394	5,622·0	8,033	3,264·1
Londonderry City,	33	2,119	6,421·2	77	233·3	2,042	6,187·9	1,364	4,133·3
Total of above,	774	57,571	7,438·1	4,862	628·2	52,719	6,811·2	20,124	2,600·0
All other places,	3,931	144,081	3,664·6	3,969	100·6	140,115	3,564·4	70,219	1,786·3
Total for Ireland,	4,705	201,652	4,285·6	8,831	187·0	192,834	4,098·5	90,343	1,920·1

IV.—Geographical Distribution of Crime.

Offences in Large Town Districts compared with those in other districts.

It will be observed that of the 201,635 cases of crime of all kinds in Ireland in 1896 there were 57,571 or 28·6 per cent. among the town populations dealt with in the foregoing statement, although the aggregate population of these towns (774,006) constituted only 16·5 per cent. of the population of Ireland in the year 1891. The crime rate per 100,000 amounted to 7,438·1 in the town populations against 3,664·8 in the remainder of the population. In fact the town crime rate is almost double the country rate for non-indictable and more than six times the country rate for indictable offences. As already pointed out when dealing with the nature of crime a very large proportion is made up of assaults and drunkenness. It is a salient point in the above statement that cases of drunkenness constitute 45 per cent. of the total number of offences in Ireland: in the large towns the proportion was 35 per cent. and in other districts 49 per cent. While the proportion of drunkenness to the total number of cases of crime in the large towns is less than in the other districts the ratio of drunkenness to the population is greater, being at the rate of 2,600 per 100,000 in the former as compared with 1,786 in the latter.

Distribution of crime in counties. Comparative Table E, Parts I. and II.

In Comparative Table E, Part II., will be found the geographical distribution by counties (including the towns situated therein) of the principal crimes or groups of crimes during the five years 1892–96. In this Table the counties are arranged in alphabetical order by provinces. In Table E, Part I., the counties are arranged in order for each class of crime from that where there was least to that where there was the greatest prevalence of crime, and in some columns the counties are grouped under certain degrees of criminality. From the first column in this Part, which shows for the five years 1892–6 the average annual number of indictable offences per 100,000 population, it will be observed that the rates range from 56·78 per 100,000 in Donegal to 651·98 in Dublin. In 18 counties and ridings the rate was under 100; in 19 it ranged between 100 and 200; and in 3—Kildare (220·21), Antrim (304·05), and, as above stated, Dublin—it exceeded 200. The rates for "Crimes against Property," "Crimes of Violence," and "Crimes against Morals" and "Suicides" are given in columns 2, 3, 4, and 6 respectively.

Distribution of drunkenness, Comparative Table E.

Column 5 shows the average rates represented by cases of drunkenness, which range from 1,113 per 100,000 of the population in the County of Roscommon to 3,028 (or nearly treble the Roscommon rate) in Waterford.

V.—PROCEDURE FOR THE PUNISHMENT OF CRIME.

V.—Procedure for the Punishment of Crime.

The Police, as is well known, act as public prosecutors in the great majority of cases in Ireland, and in most of the more serious offences, the preliminary proceedings are instituted by them. The offices of Crown and Sessional Crown Solicitor are amalgamated, and the duties of the united offices are performed by a Crown Solicitor in the Counties of Carlow, Cavan, Cork City, Down, Dublin, Galway, Kildare, Limerick County and City, Longford, Mayo, Monaghan, Queen's, Roscommon, Waterford, Westmeath, Wexford, and Wicklow. Elsewhere where no amalgamation of offices has yet taken place, Crown business at Assizes or Quarter Sessions is discharged by Crown or Sessional Crown Solicitors, respectively. Coroners' Courts deal in the first instance with many cases where questions of homicide are concerned, and verdicts of Coroners' Juries are given, implicating or exonerating certain persons. There are not, however, any returns of the proceedings of Coroners' Courts furnished for the purposes of the Statistical Tables appended to this Report.

Districts Proclaimed. Tables 10, 11, and 12.

This is a convenient place to refer to the special feature in the administration of the criminal law in Ireland, by which certain districts are proclaimed under special

Acts of Parliament. The particulars of the proclaimed districts and the Acts of Parliament under which the proclamations were issued, will be found in Tables 10, 11 and 12, p. 74. The districts were the same in 1896 as in the previous year. *V.—Procedure for the Prevention of Crime.*

The particulars of the proceedings in criminal cases at Assizes and Quarter Sessions will be found in Tables 1 to 7. *Assizes and Quarter Sessions.*

The subjoined statement gives in a summary manner, for 1896, and each of the ten years preceding, the number of persons tried by jury at Assizes, at the Dublin Commission Court and at Quarter Sessions and how their cases were disposed of:— *Tables 1 to 7 and Comparative Table A.*

Year.	Tried.	Convicted or Detained as Insane.	Acquitted.	Proportion per cent. of those Tried who were — Convicted or Detained as Insane.	Acquitted.
1886, . . .	2,311	1,633	678	70·7	29·3
1887, . . .	1,891	1,434	457	75·8	24·2
1888, . . .	1,704	1,240	464	72·8	27·2
1889, . . .	1,656	1,243	413	75·1	24·9
1890, . . .	1,647	1,207	440	73·3	26·7
1891, . . .	1,751	1,294	457	73·9	26·1
1892, . . .	1,638	1,209	429	73·8	26·2
1893, . . .	1,913	1,398	515	73·2	26·8
1894, . . .	2,004	1,465	539	73·1	26·9
1895, . . .	1,575	1,113	462	70·6	29·4
1896, . . .	1,746	1,333	413	76·3	23·7

In Comparative Table A will be found a twenty years' retrospect of the number of persons for trial at Assizes and Quarter Sessions with the nature of offences in each year from 1877 to 1896, also quinquennial averages.

In Table 8 will be found the particulars of the cost of criminal proceedings at Assizes and Quarter Sessions for the year ended the 31st March, 1896, the total amount for Assizes being £34,126, and for Quarter Sessions, £7,509, as compared with £38,183, and £8,552 respectively, for the year ended 31st March, 1895. *Cost of Criminal Proceedings. Table 8.*

Court for Crown Cases Reserved.

There were only two cases dealt with in the Court for Crown Cases Reserved: one from the Munster Winter Assizes, the other from the County Down Spring Assizes; in both cases the conviction and sentence were affirmed. For offences see Table 9. In 1895 the number of cases was the same. *Court for Crown Cases Reserved. Table 9.*

Courts of Summary Jurisdiction.

The particulars of criminal proceedings in Courts of Summary Jurisdiction in 1896 will be found in Tables 15 to 17. In the following statement a summary is given of the disposal of these cases for 1896 and each of the preceding ten years. *Courts of Summary Jurisdiction. Tables 15–17.*

Year.	Persons proceeded against.	Convicted.	Discharged.	Proportion per cent. of those proceeded against who were — Convicted.	Discharged.
1886, . . .	212,432	177,756	34,676	83·7	16·3
1887, . . .	216,445	180,831	35,614	83·5	16·5
1888, . . .	227,129	193,467	33,662	85·2	14·8
1889, . . .	230,718	198,211	32,507	85·9	14·1
1890, . . .	233,173	200,808	32,365	86·1	13·9
1891, . . .	230,057	196,569	33,488	85·4	14·6
1892, . . .	223,714	191,418	32,296	85·6	14·4
1893, . . .	216,118	182,438	33,680	84·4	15·6
1894, . . .	216,597	186,251	30,346	86·0	14·0
1895, . . .	183,827	153,776	30,051	83·7	16·3
1896, . . .	196,154	164,749	31,405	84·0	16·0

V.—*Pro-*
dure for the
Punishment
of Crime.

In Comparative Table B will be found a retrospect for the twenty years 1877–96 of the number of persons tried summarily* and the nature of offences for each year during that period, with quinquennial averages. Special attention is directed to the notes prefixed to Tables 15 and 16, explanatory of these Tables and consequently of Comparative Table B. In connection with the subject of Courts of Summary Jurisdiction, attention may be again called to the Table (18) of Quasi Criminal cases dealt with already at page 14.

APPEALS TO QUARTER SESSIONS.

Appeals to
Quarter
Sessions.
Table 19.

The number and character of the appeals to Quarter Sessions from convictions by Magistrates will be found in Table 19. These appeals numbered 425 in 1896, and were disposed of as follows:—Affirmed, 178; reversed, 107; varied, 58; otherwise disposed of, 82.

VI.—CRIMINALS AND OTHERS IN CONFINEMENT AND KNOWN CRIMINALS AT LARGE.

VI.—
Criminals
and others
in confine-
ment and
known
Criminals
at large.

CHARACTER OF PERSONS PROSECUTED.

Character
of persons
prosecuted.
Table 23.

In Table 23 will be found some particulars as to the previous character of persons prosecuted during the year. From this Table it appears that the vast majority of the persons proceeded against come under the head of " previous character good or unknown." Of 2,796 persons not dealt with by summary jurisdiction 2,035, and of 196,215 tried summarily, 183,379, come under this denomination. These numbers are so large, and the description so indefinite, that it is useless to enter into an analysis of the remaining figures which represent but a small portion of the persons prosecuted.

SUSPECTED PERSONS AT LARGE AND HOUSES OF BAD CHARACTER.

Suspected
persons at
large and
houses of
bad
character.
Tables 25
and 27.

In Table 25 will be found the numbers of suspected persons at large on the first Tuesday in April, 1896. The total number is 1,413, comprising 479 thieves, 43 receivers, and 75 persons otherwise habitually engaged in crime, with 816 other suspected persons. Besides these there were 141 persons under the supervision of the police.

There were in all 199 houses of bad character which may be taken to mean the places usually resorted to by the persons above referred to and their confederates.

PERSONS IN CONFINEMENT.

Persons in
confine-
ment.
Admissions
to places of
detention.
Tables 30,
41, 43, 46,
and 51.

The disposal of persons committed in the year 1896 under the various methods of procedure for the punishment or the prevention of crime is shown in the following statement:—

ADMISSIONS TO PLACES OF DETENTION.	Men and Boys.	Women and Girls.	Total.
Total in all Ireland.	26,176	11,987	38,168
Into Prisons, Bridewells, and Reformatories:—			
Into Larger Local Prisons, . . .	20,820	10,719	31,539
Into Bridewells and Lock-ups, . .	876	197	1,073
Into Minor Local Prisons, . . .	1,215	325	1,540
Into Reformatories. . . .	110	9	119
Total, . . .	23,010	11,250	34,280
Into Lunatic Asylums (criminal and dangerous lunatics),	1,474	1,056	2,530
Into Industrial Schools, ...	692	686	1,378

* Exclusive of Persons proceeded against under Crimes Acts in the years 1882–3 and 1887–92.

It will be observed that there were 38,168 persons admitted to places of confinement during the year 1896, and that of these 25,176, or about two-thirds, were males, and 12,992, or about one-third, females. Among these 38,168 were 2,530 lunatics admitted into asylums and 1,378 children admitted to industrial schools, so that 3,908, or a little over 10 per cent. of the total admissions to places of detention, were of persons who cannot be considered as criminals. In addition to these exceptions there are some young people and lunatics included among the admissions to prisons and bridewells who were only temporarily detained prior to admission to schools or lunatic asylums. VI.—*Criminals and others in confinement and known Criminals at large.*

Compared with the respective numbers for the preceding year, the admissions to Reformatories, Lunatic Asylums, and Industrial Schools show no appreciable variation, but the receptions of prisoners rose from 31,380 to 34,141, an increase of 8·8 per cent.

Prisons.

The following statement shows by age periods the number of convicted prisoners (other than those committed for naval and military offences), committed to the larger and minor local prisons during the year 1896 (see Table 35). Prisons. Ages of convicted prisoners committed during 1896. Table 35.

Ages.	Total of both Sexes.	Men and Boys.	Women and Girls.	Proportion per cent.	
				Men and Boys.	Women and Girls.
Total,	27,273	16,970	10,303	100·	100·
Under twelve years,	16	12	4	0·1	0·0
Twelve years and under sixteen,	147	131	16	0·7	0·1
Sixteen years and under twenty-one,	3,021	2,322	699	13·7	6·8
Twenty-one years and under thirty,	9,529	6,627	2,902	39·0	28·2
Thirty years and under forty,	8,134	4,785	3,349	28·2	32·5
Forty years and under fifty,	4,979	3,286	1,693	19·4	16·4
Fifty years and under sixty,	2,372	1,459	913	8·6	8·9
Sixty years and upwards,	1,769	1,211	558	7·1	5·4
Age not ascertained,	7	4	3	–	–

There were only 20 girls under 16 years of age—4 under 12 years, and 16 aged 12 and under 16—among the 10,303 females convicted; the number of boys under 12 years was 12, and that of older boys, aged 12 and under 16, was 131. Thus there were in all only 16 convicted persons under 12 years of age committed to prison during the year 1896. The total number of convicted males committed to these prisons was 16,970, and of females 10,303, or little more than one-half the number of males. The number of prisoners received into each prison will be found in Table 30, and particulars as to the disposal of prisoners in Tables 31A and 31B. Particulars as to the nature of sentences will be found in Table 32, and details regarding the length of these sentences in Table 33.

Habitual criminals, or those who had been previously convicted, constitute a very large proportion of those admitted to prison. Of 27,273 convicted prisoners admitted to the larger and minor local prisons, no less than 20,219 had been previously convicted. Of these, 3,840 had been once previously convicted, 2,255 twice, 1,466 thrice, 1,141 four times, 963 five times, 3,013 six to ten times, 2,821 from eleven to twenty times, and 4,699 above twenty times. It will be observed that a very large proportion are included in the last two periods, the figures showing 7,522 committals of persons who had previously been convicted upwards of ten times. In Table 36 will be found the birthplaces of those committed to prison. Habitual criminals. Table 34.

The state of education of prisoners is shown in the following statement where a comparison is made with the state of education of persons of 12 years and upwards of the general population as ascertained from the Irish Census returns for 1891. For State of education of prisoners, Table 37.

this purpose it is only possible to compare the prisoners with those in the general population, 12 years old and upwards, who can and those who cannot read and write. As there were only 16 prisoners in 1896 under the age of 12 years this insignificant disturbance does not appreciably affect the accuracy of the comparison:—

Degree of Instruction.	Number of Prisoners.			Proportion Per cent.			Corresponding proportion in General Population 12 years old and upwards.		
	Males.	Females.	Total.	Males.	Females.	Total.	Males.	Females.	Total.
Read, or read and write imperfectly,	3,488	1,481	4,969	18·9	14·4	17·3	84·2	82·2	83·2
Read and write well,	9,617	4,563	14,180	50·2	44·3	48·1			
Superior education,	187	6	193	1·0	0·0	0·7			
Total read, or read and write,	13,292	6,050	19,342	70·1	58·7	66·1	84·2	82·2	83·2
Neither read nor write,	5,673	4,251	9,924	29·9	41·3	33·9	15·8	17·8	16·8
Instruction not ascertained,	5	2	7	–	–	–	–	–	–
General Total,	18,970	10,303	29,273	100·0	100·0	100·0	100·0	100·0	100·0

It will be observed from the foregoing tabular statement that while 33·9 per cent. of convicted prisoners committed to prison in 1896 were absolutely illiterate, only 16·8 per cent. of the general population in 1891 were in a similar condition of ignorance, and there is no doubt that the percentage of illiterate among the general population was considerably less in 1896 than in 1891. It is specially noticeable that the disparity is more marked among the female than the male prisoners.

The previous occupations of prisoners are dealt with in Table 38, but as the classification of occupations is different from that employed by the Census Commissioners in their report it is impossible to institute comparisons between the occupations of prisoners and those of the general population in a manner similar to that adopted regarding education. It is interesting, however, to note that of the 29,273 prisoners dealt with, 1,106 belonged to the domestic servant class, 13,680, by far the largest proportion, to the labouring classes, 666 to the class of factory workers, 3,454 to the artizan class, 243 to overseers of labour, 235 to the class of shopmen, shopwomen, and clerks, 2,171 to the class of shopkeepers and dealers, 88 to professional employments, 319 to the class of sailors, marines, and soldiers, and no less than 4,451 (or 43 per cent. of the 10,303 female prisoners) are classified as prostitutes. The remainder of the prisoners either had no occupation or their sphere of life was not ascertained.

Reformatory Schools.

With respect to institutions for the prevention of crime, namely, Reformatory and Industrial Schools, the following statement deals with juvenile criminals under Reformatory control in the year 1896, compared with 1895, and the details for 1896 will be found in Tables 41–4.

Number of Children on the Rolls of Reformatory Schools in Ireland.	End of 1896.			End of 1895.	Increase in 1896.	Decrease in 1896.
	Boys.	Girls.	Total Boys and Girls.	Total.		
In School,	497	46	543	579	–	36
On Licence,	23	8	31	24	7	–
Remained in School, sentence expired,	–	–	–	1	–	1
Absconded, sentence unexpired,	5	–	5	4	1	–
In Prison,	3	–	3	2	1	–
Total,	528	54	582	610	–	28

From this table it appears that there was a decrease of 28 in the number of children on the rolls of Reformatory Schools in Ireland at the end of 1896, as compared with the number at the close of the preceding year, which was 13 below that for 31st December, 1894. There were 35 less in the schools under sentence and 7 more on licence. Five of those on the rolls at the close of 1896 had absconded, with sentences unexpired, being one over the number under this heading in 1895. *VI.—Criminals and others in confinement and Inmates. Criminals at large.*

The total number on the rolls at the close of the year 1896 was 584 (526 boys and only 58 girls). The number committed during the year was 119, showing a decrease of 3 as compared with the committals for the preceding year, which were 13 under the number for the year 1894. The number of boys committed in 1896 was 110, or 2 less than in the year 1895, and the number of girls 9, or one under the number for 1895, and 6 under that for 1894.

The social condition of the young persons committed in 1896 to Reformatories in Ireland is shown in the following table:— *Social condition on admission. Table 42.*

—	Boys.	Girls.	Proportion per cent.	
			Boys.	Girls.
Total committed,	110	9	100·	100·
Illegitimate, deserted, or both parents destitute or criminal,	3	1	2·7	11·1
Both parents alive, not included in foregoing,	64	3	58·2	33·3
One parent dead,	34	4	30·9	44·4
Total orphans,	9	1	8·2	11·1

Only one of the 9 girls, and 3 of the 110 boys come under the head of the illegitimate, the deserted, and those having both parents destitute or criminal. Those having both parents living, and who are not included in the foregoing, formed 58 per cent. of the boys and 33 per cent. of the girls. The orphans (including those having one parent dead) were 39 per cent. of boys and 56 per cent. of girls.

The degree of education (on admission) of children committed to Reformatory Schools is shown in the following summary:— *Degree of education. Table 43.*

—	Boys.	Girls.	Proportion per cent.	
			Boys.	Girls.
Total committed,	110	9	100·	100·
Neither read nor write,	36	7	32·7	77·8
Read, or read and write imperfectly,	62	2	56·4	22·2
Read and write well,	11	–	10·0	–
Superior instruction,	1	–	0·9	–

The want of education is seen from this summary, which shows that only 12 of the 110 boys and none of the 9 girls admitted could read and write well.

Industrial Schools.

Excluding Lunatic Asylums, the institutions in which the largest number of persons were in custody at the end of the year were Industrial Schools. Particulars regarding them are given in Tables 45-7. *Industrial Schools. Tables 45-7.*

The total number of Industrial Schools in 1896 was 72, being 2 over the number in 1895. Of the 72 schools 27 were in Munster, 20 in Leinster, 15 in Connaught, and 10 in Ulster.

VI.—Criminals and others in custody and Juvenile Criminals or boys. — Number on rolls of Industrial Schools. Table 45.

The following summary shows the number of children under warrant of detention in Industrial Schools in Ireland at the end of 1896, as compared with similar statistics for the end of 1895:—

Children on the Rolls of Industrial Schools in Ireland.	End of 1896.			End of 1895.	Increase, 1896.	Decrease, 1896.
	Boys.	Girls.	Total.			
In School,	3,483	4,360	7,843	7,780	63	–
On Licence,	273	380	653	658	–	5
Absconded,	7	–	7	5	2	–
Retained in school, sentence expired,	11	73	84	80	4	–
Total,	3,774	4,813	8,587	8,503	84	–

It appears from this table that the number of children on the rolls of Industrial Schools in Ireland at the end of 1896 (8,587) was 84 over that for the close of the preceding year, which was 80 under the number at the end of 1894. Of the total number, 7,843 were in the schools undergoing their sentence of detention, 84 were retained in school with their own consent although their sentence had expired, 653 were on licence, and 7 (all boys) had absconded.

Ages on admission to Industrial Schools. Table 43.

The following figures show the ages of the children placed in these schools in 1896.—

Ages of Children.	Boys and Girls.	Boys.	Girls.	Percentage of Total	
				Boys.	Girls.
Total,	1,378	692	686	100·	100·
Under 6 years,	71	14	57	2·0	8·3
6 and under 8 years,	414	177	237	25·6	34·6
8 and under 10 years,	373	199	174	28·8	25·4
10 and under 12 years,	331	200	131	28·9	19·1
12 years and upwards,	189	102	87	14·7	12·7

It appears from these figures that 68 per cent. of the girls and 56 per cent. of the boys were brought under careful training in these schools at the early age of under ten years.

In 1895, 728 girls were sent to Industrial Schools, as compared with 609 boys; the respective numbers for 1896 were:—Girls, 686; boys, 692.

Criminal and Dangerous Lunatics.

Criminal and Dangerous Lunatics in confinement. Tables 48–52.

The insane persons who come under the cognisance of the Criminal Law are of two classes, viz.:—One consisting of those persons who have actually committed criminal offences, and would, were they sane persons, be liable to punishment for their crimes, and the other, and by far the more numerous class, consisting of persons who have not committed any criminal act, but who, having shown signs of mental derangement, have become a source of anxiety to their friends and neighbours who apprehend some danger at their hands. The former class are, in the first instance, treated as criminal cases, and proceedings instituted with the view of bringing them to justice for the crimes with which they are charged. These persons are sent for trial, and on being found insane are detained as lunatics and sent to the Criminal Lunatic

Asylum; to these may be added persons who become insane while awaiting trial or during imprisonment. The class of dangerous lunatics are dealt with in a different way. On being suspected as insane they are charged before two Justices of the Peace (or a Metropolitan Police Magistrate) as being dangerous lunatics, and if the charge be proved to the satisfaction of the Justices an order is signed for their committal to a lunatic asylum; in such cases it is not necessary to prove an actual criminal offence. In no sense can these persons be considered as criminals. In fact this method of procedure is usually adopted as the means of placing under restraint ordinary troublesome lunatics belonging to the industrial classes of the community. VI.—Criminals and others in confinement and Insane Criminals at large.

The following summary shows the judgments or orders under which criminal and dangerous lunatics were committed to asylums in Ireland in 1896. Judgments or Orders under which Criminal and Dangerous Lunatics were committed to Asylums in 1896.

Judgments or Orders of Committal.	Number.	Proportion per cent.
Total committed during year, ...	2,210	100·
Committed to asylums by Justices as dangerous, under sect. 30 & 31 Vic., c. 118, s. 10, ...	2,100	95·0
Transmitted from prisons by Lord Lieutenant's warrant:—		
Certified insane after conviction, . . .	73	3·3
Found insane on arraignment, ...	16	0·7
Became insane after committal and before trial, . .	13	0·6
Special verdict of guilty, but insane, . . .	6	0·3
Admitted under Army Act, 1881, sec. 91, . .	15	0·6

It appears that 95·0 per cent. of the lunatics were committed direct to asylums by Justices as dangerous with intent to commit crime, and that only 4·4 per cent. were sent by Lord Lieutenant's warrant; 15, or 0·6 per cent., were committed under the Army Act, 1881.

The Statistics as to criminal lunatics will be found in Tables 48, 49, 50; and those relating to dangerous lunatics in Tables 51 and 52.

VII.—POLICE ESTABLISHMENTS.

The following summary shows the Police Force in Ireland in 1894, compared with the number in 1893, at the periods of the year stated in the tables:— VII.—Police Establishments. Police Establishments. Table 13.

Constabulary and Police.	1893.	1894.	Increase, 1894.	Decrease, 1894.
Royal Irish Constabulary.				
Officers, ...	259	258	-	1
Head-Constables, Constables, &c., . .	11,701	11,642	-	59
Total .	11,960	11,900	-	60
Dublin Metropolitan Police. (Table 14.)				
Superior Officers, ...	54	54	-	-
Sergeants, Constables, &c., ...	1,163	1,163	-	-
Total, .	1,217	1,217	-	-
Grand Total, .	13,177	13,117	-	60

VII.—*Police Establishments.*

Police Establishments. Tables 13 and 14.

A column in table 13 in the Appendix shows the proportion which the number of effective force of Constabulary bears to the population (according to the Census of 1891) in the various counties, and in provincial towns with a separate Police force, in Ireland. In the following counties the proportion of Police to population is the smallest, as will be seen from the table:—

Londonderry,	12 in every 10,000 of the population in 1891.		
Antrim,	13	"	"
Down,	13	"	"
Tyrone,	14	"	"
Armagh,	15	"	"

Proportion of Police to population. Tables 13 and 14.

In the following counties the proportion of Police is the largest:—

Clare,	40 in every 10,000 of the population in 1891.		
Westmeath,	39	"	"
Limerick,	37	"	"
Meath,	36	"	"

The proportion of Police in the principal Cities and Towns is as follows:—

Galway,	84 in every 10,000 of the population in 1891.		
Waterford,	53	"	"
Belfast City Force,	33	"	"
Dublin Metropolitan Police District,	63	"	"
Drogheda,	39	"	"
Kilkenny,	38	"	"
Londonderry,	27	"	"
Cork,	33	"	"
Limerick,	33	"	"

The proportion of Police—excluding County Inspectors and District Inspectors, but including Depot and Reserve Force—to the estimated population of Ireland in 1896 was 28 in every 10,000 of the people.

Detectives.

In the Royal Irish Constabulary the members of the different branches of the Force are selected for special duty when necessary; in the Police of the Dublin Metropolitan Police District an entire division consisting of 39 effective men (10 detective officers, 13 Constables, and 16 Sergeants), 4 Inspectors, and 1 Superintendent, are employed as detectives.

Cost of Establishments. Tables 13 and 14.

The following table shows the total cost (including Appropriations in aid) of the Police Establishments in Ireland for the year ended 31st March, 1896, as compared with that for the preceding year:—

Cost of Police Establishments.	1895.	1896.	Increase, 1896.	Decrease, 1896.
	£	£	£	£
Total of all Ireland,	1,645,458	1,647,345	1,887	—
Royal Irish Constabulary,	1,482,077	1,484,261	2,184	—
Dublin Metropolitan Police,	163,381	163,084	—	297

THOS. W. GRIMSHAW.

12th *August*, 1899.

IRELAND.

COMPARATIVE AND SUMMARY TABLES,
YEARS 1877–96.

TABLE A.—ASSIZES AND QUARTER SESSIONS, ...
" B.—COURTS OF SUMMARY JURISDICTION, ...
" C.—CRIMES COMMITTED, ...
" D.—SUMMARY OF THE FOREGOING TABLES, . . .
" E.—GEOGRAPHICAL DISTRIBUTION OF CRIME, . . .

TABLE A.—ASSIZES AND QUARTER SESSIONS, 1877 to 1896.—Number of

Offences.	1877	[illegible]	[illegible]	[illegible]	[illegible]	Annual Average, 1877-81	[illegible]	[illegible]	[illegible]	[illegible]	[illegible]	Annual Average, [illegible]
CLASS I.—Offences against the Person.												
[illegible]	[illegible]	[illegible]	[illegible]	[illegible]	[illegible]	[illegible]	[illegible]	[illegible]	[illegible]	[illegible]	[illegible]	[illegible]
Total of Class I.	[illegible]	[illegible]	[illegible]	[illegible]	[illegible]	[illegible]	[illegible]	[illegible]	[illegible]	[illegible]	[illegible]	[illegible]
CLASS II.—Offences against Property with Violence.												
[illegible]	[illegible]	[illegible]	[illegible]	[illegible]	[illegible]	[illegible]	[illegible]	[illegible]	[illegible]	[illegible]	[illegible]	[illegible]
Total of Class II.	[illegible]	[illegible]	[illegible]	[illegible]	[illegible]	[illegible]	[illegible]	[illegible]	[illegible]	[illegible]	[illegible]	[illegible]
CLASS III.—Offences against Property without Violence.												
[illegible]	[illegible]	[illegible]	[illegible]	[illegible]	[illegible]	[illegible]	[illegible]	[illegible]	[illegible]	[illegible]	[illegible]	[illegible]
Total of Class III.	[illegible]	[illegible]	[illegible]	[illegible]	[illegible]	[illegible]	[illegible]	[illegible]	[illegible]	[illegible]	[illegible]	[illegible]
CLASS IV.—Malicious Injuries to Property.												
[illegible]	[illegible]	[illegible]	[illegible]	[illegible]	[illegible]	[illegible]	[illegible]	[illegible]	[illegible]	[illegible]	[illegible]	[illegible]
Total of Class IV.	[illegible]	[illegible]	[illegible]	[illegible]	[illegible]	[illegible]	[illegible]	[illegible]	[illegible]	[illegible]	[illegible]	[illegible]
CLASS V.—Forgery and Offences against the Currency.												
[illegible]	[illegible]	[illegible]	[illegible]	[illegible]	[illegible]	[illegible]	[illegible]	[illegible]	[illegible]	[illegible]	[illegible]	[illegible]
Total of Class V.	[illegible]	[illegible]	[illegible]	[illegible]	[illegible]	[illegible]	[illegible]	[illegible]	[illegible]	[illegible]	[illegible]	[illegible]
CLASS VI.—Other offences not included in the above Classes.												
[illegible]	[illegible]	[illegible]	[illegible]	[illegible]	[illegible]	[illegible]	[illegible]	[illegible]	[illegible]	[illegible]	[illegible]	[illegible]
Total of Class VI.	[illegible]	[illegible]	[illegible]	[illegible]	[illegible]	[illegible]	[illegible]	[illegible]	[illegible]	[illegible]	[illegible]	[illegible]
GRAND TOTAL.	[illegible]	[illegible]	[illegible]	[illegible]	[illegible]	[illegible]	[illegible]	[illegible]	[illegible]	[illegible]	[illegible]	[illegible]

NOTE.—If Indictable Offences tried summarily are added, so as to give the total

Offences.	1877	[illegible]	[illegible]	[illegible]	[illegible]	Annual Average, 1877-81	[illegible]	[illegible]	[illegible]	[illegible]	[illegible]	Annual Average, [illegible]
[illegible]	[illegible]	[illegible]	[illegible]	[illegible]	[illegible]	[illegible]	[illegible]	[illegible]	[illegible]	[illegible]	[illegible]	[illegible]
Total of Class III.	[illegible]	[illegible]	[illegible]	[illegible]	[illegible]	[illegible]	[illegible]	[illegible]	[illegible]	[illegible]	[illegible]	[illegible]
GRAND TOTAL.	[illegible]	[illegible]	[illegible]	[illegible]	[illegible]	[illegible]	[illegible]	[illegible]	[illegible]	[illegible]	[illegible]	[illegible]

NOTE.—Owing to changes in classification, &c., some of the

Persons for Trial and Nature of Offences in each year from 1877 to 1886

1877.	1878.	1879.	1880.	1881.	Annual Average, 1877-81.	1882.	1883.	1884.	1885.	1886.	Annual Average, 1882-86.	OFFENCES.
												CLASS I.—Offences against the Person.
[illegible]	[illegible]	[illegible]	[illegible]	[illegible]	[illegible]	[illegible]	[illegible]	[illegible]	[illegible]	[illegible]	[illegible]	Murder. [illegible]
[illegible]	[illegible]	[illegible]	[illegible]	[illegible]	[illegible]	[illegible]	[illegible]	[illegible]	[illegible]	[illegible]	[illegible]	Manslaughter. [illegible]
[illegible]	[illegible]	[illegible]	[illegible]	[illegible]	[illegible]	[illegible]	[illegible]	[illegible]	[illegible]	[illegible]	[illegible]	Total of Class I.
												CLASS II.—Offences against Property with Violence.
[illegible]	[illegible]	[illegible]	[illegible]	[illegible]	[illegible]	[illegible]	[illegible]	[illegible]	[illegible]	[illegible]	[illegible]	Burglary. [illegible]
[illegible]	[illegible]	[illegible]	[illegible]	[illegible]	[illegible]	[illegible]	[illegible]	[illegible]	[illegible]	[illegible]	[illegible]	Total of Class II.
												CLASS III.—Offences against Property without Violence.
[illegible]	[illegible]	[illegible]	[illegible]	[illegible]	[illegible]	[illegible]	[illegible]	[illegible]	[illegible]	[illegible]	[illegible]	Larceny of Horses and Cattle. [illegible]
[illegible]	[illegible]	[illegible]	[illegible]	[illegible]	[illegible]	[illegible]	[illegible]	[illegible]	[illegible]	[illegible]	[illegible]	Total of Class III.
												CLASS IV.—Malicious Injuries to Property.
[illegible]	[illegible]	[illegible]	[illegible]	[illegible]	[illegible]	[illegible]	[illegible]	[illegible]	[illegible]	[illegible]	[illegible]	Arson, &c. [illegible]
[illegible]	[illegible]	[illegible]	[illegible]	[illegible]	[illegible]	[illegible]	[illegible]	[illegible]	[illegible]	[illegible]	[illegible]	Total of Class IV.
												CLASS V.—Forgery and Offences against the Currency.
[illegible]	[illegible]	[illegible]	[illegible]	[illegible]	[illegible]	[illegible]	[illegible]	[illegible]	[illegible]	[illegible]	[illegible]	Forgery. [illegible]
[illegible]	[illegible]	[illegible]	[illegible]	[illegible]	[illegible]	[illegible]	[illegible]	[illegible]	[illegible]	[illegible]	[illegible]	Total of Class V.
												CLASS VI.—Other Offences not included in the above Classes.
[illegible]	[illegible]	[illegible]	[illegible]	[illegible]	[illegible]	[illegible]	[illegible]	[illegible]	[illegible]	[illegible]	[illegible]	Treason, &c. [illegible]
[illegible]	[illegible]	[illegible]	[illegible]	[illegible]	[illegible]	[illegible]	[illegible]	[illegible]	[illegible]	[illegible]	[illegible]	Total of Class VI.
[illegible]	[illegible]	[illegible]	[illegible]	[illegible]	[illegible]	[illegible]	[illegible]	[illegible]	[illegible]	[illegible]	[illegible]	GRAND TOTAL.

of Persons tried for Indictable Offences, the following alterations have to be made:—

[illegible]	[illegible]	[illegible]	[illegible]	[illegible]	[illegible]	[illegible]	[illegible]	[illegible]	[illegible]	[illegible]	[illegible]	Larceny from the Person. [illegible]
[illegible]	[illegible]	[illegible]	[illegible]	[illegible]	[illegible]	[illegible]	[illegible]	[illegible]	[illegible]	[illegible]	[illegible]	Receiving Stolen Goods.
[illegible]	[illegible]	[illegible]	[illegible]	[illegible]	[illegible]	[illegible]	[illegible]	[illegible]	[illegible]	[illegible]	[illegible]	Total of Class III.
[illegible]	[illegible]	[illegible]	[illegible]	[illegible]	[illegible]	[illegible]	[illegible]	[illegible]	[illegible]	[illegible]	[illegible]	GRAND TOTAL.

Averages given in the above Table are for periods less than five years.

TABLE B.—COURTS OF SUMMARY JURISDICTION, 1877 to 1896.—Number

OFFENCES.	1877.	[illegible]	[illegible]	[illegible]	[illegible]	Annual Average, 1877-81.	[illegible]	[illegible]	[illegible]	[illegible]	[illegible]	Annual Average, [illegible]
SECTION A.— Indictable Offences tried Summarily.												
Simple Larceny. Larceny from the Person. Larceny by a Servant. Embezzlement. Receiving Stolen Goods.	[illegible]	[illegible]	[illegible]	[illegible]	[illegible]	[illegible]	[illegible]	[illegible]	[illegible]	[illegible]	[illegible]	[illegible]
[illegible]	.	.	.	.	[illegible]	[illegible]	[illegible]	71	[illegible]	[illegible]	[illegible]	[illegible]
Other Indictable Offences tried Summarily.	4	4	[illegible]	[illegible]	.	[illegible]	.	.	.	.	.	.
Total of Section A.	[illegible]	[illegible]	[illegible]	[illegible]	[illegible]	[illegible]	[illegible]	[illegible]	[illegible]	[illegible]	[illegible]	[illegible]
SECTION B.— Other Offences tried Summarily.												
Adulteration of Food and Drugs.	.	.	.	.	[illegible]	[illegible]	[illegible]	[illegible]	[illegible]	[illegible]	[illegible]	[illegible]
[illegible]	[illegible]	[illegible]	[illegible]	[illegible]	[illegible]	[illegible]	[illegible]	[illegible]	[illegible]	[illegible]	[illegible]	[illegible]

of Persons Tried," and Nature of Offences, in each Year, from 1877 to 1896.

[illegible]	[illegible]	[illegible]	[illegible]	[illegible]	Annual Average, [illegible]	[illegible]	[illegible]	[illegible]	[illegible]	[illegible]	Annual Average, [illegible]	OFFENCES.
												SECTION (A).—
[illegible]	[illegible]	[illegible]	[illegible]	[illegible]	[illegible]	[illegible]	[illegible]	[illegible]	[illegible]	[illegible]	[illegible]	[illegible]
[illegible]	[illegible]	[illegible]	[illegible]	[illegible]	[illegible]	[illegible]	[illegible]	[illegible]	[illegible]	[illegible]	[illegible]	Total of Section A.
												SECTION (B).—
[illegible]	[illegible]	[illegible]	[illegible]	[illegible]	[illegible]	[illegible]	[illegible]	[illegible]	[illegible]	[illegible]	[illegible]	Adulteration of Food and Drugs.
[illegible]	[illegible]	[illegible]	[illegible]	[illegible]	[illegible]	[illegible]	[illegible]	[illegible]	[illegible]	[illegible]	[illegible]	[illegible]
[illegible]	[illegible]	[illegible]	[illegible]	[illegible]	[illegible]	[illegible]	[illegible]	[illegible]	[illegible]	[illegible]	[illegible]	Total of Section (B).
[illegible]	[illegible]	[illegible]	[illegible]	[illegible]	[illegible]	[illegible]	[illegible]	[illegible]	[illegible]	[illegible]	[illegible]	GRAND TOTAL.

TABLE 6.—CRIMES COMMITTED, 1877 to 1886.—Number of Crimes (Indictable

OFFENCES.	1877.	[illegible]	[illegible]	[illegible]	[illegible]	Annual Average, 1877-81.	[illegible]	[illegible]	[illegible]	[illegible]	[illegible]	Annual Average, [illegible]
CLASS I. Offences against the Person.												
[illegible]	[illegible]	[illegible]	[illegible]	[illegible]	[illegible]	[illegible]	[illegible]	[illegible]	[illegible]	[illegible]	[illegible]	[illegible]
Total of Class I.	[illegible]	[illegible]	[illegible]	[illegible]	[illegible]	[illegible]	[illegible]	[illegible]	[illegible]	[illegible]	[illegible]	[illegible]
CLASS II. Offences against Property with Violence.												
[illegible]	[illegible]	[illegible]	[illegible]	[illegible]	[illegible]	[illegible]	[illegible]	[illegible]	[illegible]	[illegible]	[illegible]	[illegible]
Total of Class II.	[illegible]	[illegible]	[illegible]	[illegible]	[illegible]	[illegible]	[illegible]	[illegible]	[illegible]	[illegible]	[illegible]	[illegible]
CLASS III. Offences against Property without Violence.												
[illegible]	[illegible]	[illegible]	[illegible]	[illegible]	[illegible]	[illegible]	[illegible]	[illegible]	[illegible]	[illegible]	[illegible]	[illegible]
Total of Class III.	[illegible]	[illegible]	[illegible]	[illegible]	[illegible]	[illegible]	[illegible]	[illegible]	[illegible]	[illegible]	[illegible]	[illegible]
CLASS IV. Malicious Injuries to Property.												
[illegible]	[illegible]	[illegible]	[illegible]	[illegible]	[illegible]	[illegible]	[illegible]	[illegible]	[illegible]	[illegible]	[illegible]	[illegible]
Total of Class IV.	[illegible]	[illegible]	[illegible]	[illegible]	[illegible]	[illegible]	[illegible]	[illegible]	[illegible]	[illegible]	[illegible]	[illegible]
CLASS V. Forgery and Offences against the Currency.												
[illegible]	[illegible]	[illegible]	[illegible]	[illegible]	[illegible]	[illegible]	[illegible]	[illegible]	[illegible]	[illegible]	[illegible]	[illegible]
Total of Class V.	[illegible]	[illegible]	[illegible]	[illegible]	[illegible]	[illegible]	[illegible]	[illegible]	[illegible]	[illegible]	[illegible]	[illegible]
CLASS VI. Other Offences not included in the above Classes.												
[illegible]	[illegible]	[illegible]	[illegible]	[illegible]	[illegible]	[illegible]	[illegible]	[illegible]	[illegible]	[illegible]	[illegible]	[illegible]
Total of Class VI.	[illegible]	[illegible]	[illegible]	[illegible]	[illegible]	[illegible]	[illegible]	[illegible]	[illegible]	[illegible]	[illegible]	[illegible]
GRAND TOTAL.	[illegible]	[illegible]	[illegible]	[illegible]	[illegible]	[illegible]	[illegible]	[illegible]	[illegible]	[illegible]	[illegible]	[illegible]

Offences) reported to the Police as committed in each Year from 1877 to 1896.*

1877.	1878.	1879.	1880.	1881.	Annual Average, 1877-81.	1882.	1883.	1884.	1885.	1886.	Annual Average, 1882-86.	OFFENCES.
												CLASS I. Offences against the Person.
[illegible]	[illegible]	[illegible]	[illegible]	[illegible]	[illegible]	[illegible]	[illegible]	[illegible]	[illegible]	[illegible]	[illegible]	[illegible]
[illegible]	[illegible]	[illegible]	[illegible]	[illegible]	[illegible]	[illegible]	[illegible]	[illegible]	[illegible]	[illegible]	[illegible]	Total of Class I.
												CLASS II. Offences against Property, with Violence.
[illegible]	[illegible]	[illegible]	[illegible]	[illegible]	[illegible]	[illegible]	[illegible]	[illegible]	[illegible]	[illegible]	[illegible]	[illegible]
[illegible]	[illegible]	[illegible]	[illegible]	[illegible]	[illegible]	[illegible]	[illegible]	[illegible]	[illegible]	[illegible]	[illegible]	Total of Class II.
												CLASS III. Offences against Property, without Violence.
[illegible]	[illegible]	[illegible]	[illegible]	[illegible]	[illegible]	[illegible]	[illegible]	[illegible]	[illegible]	[illegible]	[illegible]	[illegible]
[illegible]	[illegible]	[illegible]	[illegible]	[illegible]	[illegible]	[illegible]	[illegible]	[illegible]	[illegible]	[illegible]	[illegible]	Total of Class III.
												CLASS IV. Malicious Injuries to Property.
[illegible]	[illegible]	[illegible]	[illegible]	[illegible]	[illegible]	[illegible]	[illegible]	[illegible]	[illegible]	[illegible]	[illegible]	[illegible]
[illegible]	[illegible]	[illegible]	[illegible]	[illegible]	[illegible]	[illegible]	[illegible]	[illegible]	[illegible]	[illegible]	[illegible]	Total of Class IV.
												CLASS V. Forgery and Offences against the Currency.
[illegible]	[illegible]	[illegible]	[illegible]	[illegible]	[illegible]	[illegible]	[illegible]	[illegible]	[illegible]	[illegible]	[illegible]	[illegible]
[illegible]	[illegible]	[illegible]	[illegible]	[illegible]	[illegible]	[illegible]	[illegible]	[illegible]	[illegible]	[illegible]	[illegible]	Total of Class V.
												CLASS VI.

TABLE D.—SUMMARY OF THE THREE PRECEDING TABLES with the proportion of Persons Tried and of Crimes to Population.

—	Average Annual Number for each Period of Five Years.				Number for [illegible]	Proportion per [illegible] Population.				
	[illegible]	[illegible]	[illegible]	[illegible]		[illegible]	[illegible]	[illegible]	[illegible]	[illegible]
TABLE A.—ASSIZES AND QUARTER SESSIONS—PERSONS FOR TRIAL.										
Class I.—Offences against the Person.										
Offences of Violence	[illegible]	[illegible]	[illegible]	[illegible]	[illegible]	[illegible]	[illegible]	[illegible]	[illegible]	[illegible]
Offences against Morals	[illegible]	[illegible]	[illegible]	[illegible]	[illegible]	[illegible]	[illegible]	[illegible]	[illegible]	[illegible]
Total of Class I.	[illegible]	[illegible]	[illegible]	[illegible]	[illegible]	[illegible]	[illegible]	[illegible]	[illegible]	[illegible]
Class II.—Crimes against Property with Violence.										
Total of Class II.	[illegible]	[illegible]	[illegible]	[illegible]	[illegible]	[illegible]	[illegible]	[illegible]	[illegible]	[illegible]
* Class III.—Crimes against Property without Violence.										
Larceny	[illegible]	[illegible]	[illegible]	[illegible]	[illegible]	[illegible]	[illegible]	[illegible]	[illegible]	[illegible]
Embezzlement	[illegible]	[illegible]	[illegible]	[illegible]	[illegible]	[illegible]	[illegible]	[illegible]	[illegible]	[illegible]
Frauds	[illegible]	[illegible]	[illegible]	[illegible]	[illegible]	[illegible]	[illegible]	[illegible]	[illegible]	[illegible]
Total of Class III.	[illegible]	[illegible]	[illegible]	[illegible]	[illegible]	[illegible]	[illegible]	[illegible]	[illegible]	[illegible]
Class IV.—Malicious Injuries to Property.										
Total of Class IV.	[illegible]	[illegible]	[illegible]	[illegible]	[illegible]	[illegible]	[illegible]	[illegible]	[illegible]	[illegible]
Class V.—Forgery and Offences against the Currency.										
Forgery	[illegible]	[illegible]	[illegible]	[illegible]	[illegible]	[illegible]	[illegible]	[illegible]	[illegible]	[illegible]
Coining	[illegible]	[illegible]	[illegible]	[illegible]	[illegible]	[illegible]	[illegible]	[illegible]	[illegible]	[illegible]
Total of Class V.	[illegible]	[illegible]	[illegible]	[illegible]	[illegible]	[illegible]	[illegible]	[illegible]	[illegible]	[illegible]
Class VI.—Other Offences not included in the above Classes.										
Total of Class VI.	[illegible]	[illegible]	[illegible]	[illegible]	[illegible]	[illegible]	[illegible]	[illegible]	[illegible]	[illegible]
GRAND TOTAL OF TABLE A.	[illegible]	[illegible]	[illegible]	[illegible]	[illegible]	[illegible]	[illegible]	[illegible]	[illegible]	[illegible]

* If Indictable Offences *Tried Summarily* are added—so as to give the Total of Persons tried for Indictable Offences—the following alterations have to be made:—

Larceny	[illegible]	[illegible]	[illegible]	[illegible]	[illegible]	[illegible]	[illegible]	[illegible]	[illegible]	[illegible]
Embezzlement	[illegible]	[illegible]	[illegible]	[illegible]	[illegible]	[illegible]	[illegible]	[illegible]	[illegible]	[illegible]
Total of Class III.	[illegible]	[illegible]	[illegible]	[illegible]	[illegible]	[illegible]	[illegible]	[illegible]	[illegible]	[illegible]
GRAND TOTAL	[illegible]	[illegible]	[illegible]	[illegible]	[illegible]	[illegible]	[illegible]	[illegible]	[illegible]	[illegible]

TABLE D.—SUMMARY OF THE THREE PRECEDING TABLES with the proportion of Persons Tried and of Crime to Population—*continued*.

—	Average Annual Number for each Period of Five Years.				Number for [illegible]	Proportion per [illegible] Population.				
	[illegible]	[illegible]	[illegible]	[illegible]		[illegible]	[illegible]	[illegible]	[illegible]	[illegible]
TABLE B.—RESULTS OF SUMMARY JURISDICTION—NUMBER OF PERSONS TRIED.										
Indictable Offences tried Summarily	[illegible]	[illegible]	[illegible]	[illegible]	[illegible]	[illegible]	[illegible]	[illegible]	[illegible]	[illegible]
Non-indictable Offences (cases of):—										
Assaults	[illegible]	[illegible]	[illegible]	[illegible]	[illegible]	[illegible]	[illegible]	[illegible]	[illegible]	[illegible]
Stealing and Receiving Animals, Fruit, &c.	[illegible]	[illegible]	[illegible]	[illegible]	[illegible]	[illegible]	[illegible]	[illegible]	[illegible]	[illegible]
Malicious Damage	[illegible]	[illegible]	[illegible]	[illegible]	[illegible]	[illegible]	[illegible]	[illegible]	[illegible]	[illegible]
[illegible] Acts, Offences against	[illegible]	[illegible]	[illegible]	[illegible]	[illegible]	[illegible]	[illegible]	[illegible]	[illegible]	[illegible]
Game Laws, Offences against	[illegible]	[illegible]	[illegible]	[illegible]	[illegible]	[illegible]	[illegible]	[illegible]	[illegible]	[illegible]
Drunkenness	[illegible]	[illegible]	[illegible]	[illegible]	[illegible]	[illegible]	[illegible]	[illegible]	[illegible]	[illegible]
[illegible] Act, Offences [illegible]	-	-	-	[illegible]	[illegible]	-	-	-	[illegible]	[illegible]
TOTAL OF TABLE B.	[illegible]	[illegible]	[illegible]	[illegible]	[illegible]	[illegible]	[illegible]	[illegible]	[illegible]	[illegible]
TABLE C.—CRIMES COMMITTED—NUMBER OF CRIMES REPORTED TO THE POLICE.										
CLASS I.—Offences against the Person.										
Offences of Violence	[illegible]	[illegible]	[illegible]	[illegible]	[illegible]	[illegible]	[illegible]	[illegible]	[illegible]	[illegible]
Crimes against Morals	[illegible]	[illegible]	[illegible]	[illegible]	[illegible]	[illegible]	[illegible]	[illegible]	[illegible]	[illegible]
Total of Class I.	[illegible]	[illegible]	[illegible]	[illegible]	[illegible]	[illegible]	[illegible]	[illegible]	[illegible]	[illegible]
CLASS II.—Crimes against Property with Violence.										
Total of Class II.	[illegible]	[illegible]	[illegible]	[illegible]	[illegible]	[illegible]	[illegible]	[illegible]	[illegible]	[illegible]
CLASS III.—Crimes against Property without Violence.										
Larceny	[illegible]	[illegible]	[illegible]	[illegible]	[illegible]	[illegible]	[illegible]	[illegible]	[illegible]	[illegible]
Receiving	[illegible]	[illegible]	[illegible]	[illegible]	[illegible]	[illegible]	[illegible]	[illegible]	[illegible]	[illegible]
Frauds	[illegible]	[illegible]	[illegible]	[illegible]	[illegible]	[illegible]	[illegible]	[illegible]	[illegible]	[illegible]
Total of Class III.	[illegible]	[illegible]	[illegible]	[illegible]	[illegible]	[illegible]	[illegible]	[illegible]	[illegible]	[illegible]
CLASS IV.—Malicious Injuries to Property.										
Total of Class IV.	[illegible]	[illegible]	[illegible]	[illegible]	[illegible]	[illegible]	[illegible]	[illegible]	[illegible]	[illegible]
CLASS V.—Forgery and Offences against the Currency.										
Forgery	[illegible]	[illegible]	[illegible]	[illegible]	[illegible]	[illegible]	[illegible]	[illegible]	[illegible]	[illegible]
Coining	[illegible]	[illegible]	[illegible]	[illegible]	[illegible]	[illegible]	[illegible]	[illegible]	[illegible]	[illegible]
Total of Class V.	[illegible]	[illegible]	[illegible]	[illegible]	[illegible]	[illegible]	[illegible]	[illegible]	[illegible]	[illegible]
CLASS VI.—Other Offences not included in the above Classes.										
Total of Class VI.	[illegible]	[illegible]	[illegible]	[illegible]	[illegible]	[illegible]	[illegible]	[illegible]	[illegible]	[illegible]
GRAND TOTAL OF TABLE C.	[illegible]	[illegible]	[illegible]	[illegible]	[illegible]	[illegible]	[illegible]	[illegible]	[illegible]	[illegible]

TABLE K.—GEOGRAPHICAL DISTRIBUTION OF CRIME.—Proportion to [illegible] and of Suicides in each [illegible]

(1.) COUNTIES ARRANGED ACCORDING TO PROPORTION [illegible]

(1) All Crimes [illegible]

County.	Annual Average, [illegible] per [illegible] Population.
Donegal	[illegible]
Wexford	[illegible]
Sligo	[illegible]
Mayo	[illegible]
Cork, W.R.	[illegible]
Roscommon	[illegible]
Galway, W.R.	[illegible]
Monaghan	[illegible]
Down	[illegible]
Cavan	[illegible]
Tyrone	[illegible]
Carlow	[illegible]
Londonderry	[illegible]
Fermanagh	[illegible]
Leitrim	[illegible]
Meath	[illegible]
Armagh	[illegible]
Galway, E.R.	[illegible]
Kilkenny	[illegible]
Queen's	[illegible]
Tipperary, N.R.	[illegible]
Louth	[illegible]
Longford	[illegible]
Westmeath	[illegible]
Kerry	[illegible]
King's	[illegible]
Tipperary, S.R.	[illegible]
Wicklow	[illegible]
Limerick	[illegible]
Waterford	[illegible]
Cork, E.R.	[illegible]
Clare	[illegible]
Kildare	[illegible]
Antrim	[illegible]
Dublin	[illegible]

(2) Crimes against Property.

Group	County.	Annual Average, [illegible] per [illegible] Population.
No. 1.—Under [illegible] Crimes per [illegible] Population.	Donegal	[illegible]
	Sligo	[illegible]
	Wexford	[illegible]
No. 2.—[illegible] and under [illegible] Crimes.	Mayo	[illegible]
	Cork, W.R.	[illegible]
	Galway, W.R.	[illegible]
	Roscommon	[illegible]
No. 3.—[illegible] and under [illegible] Crimes.	Cavan	[illegible]
	Leitrim	[illegible]
	Tyrone	[illegible]
	Monaghan	[illegible]
No. 4.—[illegible] and under [illegible] Crimes.	Down	[illegible]
	Londonderry	[illegible]
	Carlow	[illegible]
No. 5.—[illegible] and under [illegible] Crimes.	Longford	[illegible]
	Meath	[illegible]
	Fermanagh	[illegible]
	Galway, E.R.	[illegible]
No. 6.—[illegible] and under [illegible] Crimes.	Armagh	[illegible]
	Kilkenny	[illegible]
	Tipperary, N.R.	[illegible]
	Queen's	[illegible]
	Westmeath	[illegible]
No. 7.—[illegible] and under [illegible] Crimes.	Clare	[illegible]
	Louth	[illegible]
	Kerry	[illegible]
	King's	[illegible]
	Tipperary, S.R.	[illegible]
	Limerick	[illegible]
	Cork, E.R.	[illegible]
	Wicklow	[illegible]
	Waterford	[illegible]
No. 8.—[illegible] and under [illegible] Crimes.	Kildare	[illegible]
No. 9.—Above [illegible] Crimes.	Antrim	[illegible]
	Dublin	[illegible]

Offences against [illegible]

(3) Crimes of Violence.

Group	County.	Annual Average, [illegible] per [illegible] Population.
No. 1.—Under [illegible] Crimes per [illegible] Population.	Wexford	[illegible]
	Galway, E.R.	[illegible]
	Down	[illegible]
	Sligo	[illegible]
	Queen's	[illegible]
	Donegal	[illegible]
No. 2.—[illegible] Crimes and under [illegible]	Fermanagh	[illegible]
	Carlow	[illegible]
	Monaghan	[illegible]
	Cork, W.R.	[illegible]
	Kilkenny	[illegible]
	Mayo	[illegible]
	Kerry	[illegible]
	Kildare	[illegible]
	Roscommon	[illegible]
	Wicklow	[illegible]
	Armagh	[illegible]
	Westmeath	[illegible]
	Antrim	[illegible]
	King's	[illegible]
	Clare	[illegible]
	Meath	[illegible]
No. 3.—[illegible] Crimes and under [illegible]	Londonderry	[illegible]
	Galway, W.R.	[illegible]
	Tipperary, N.R.	[illegible]
	Cavan	[illegible]
	Louth	[illegible]
	[illegible]	[illegible]
	[illegible]	[illegible]
	Tyrone	[illegible]
	Cork, E.R.	[illegible]
	[illegible]	[illegible]
	Tipperary, S.R.	[illegible]
No. 4.—[illegible] Crimes and under [illegible]	Longford	[illegible]
No. 5.—[illegible] Crimes and upwards.	Dublin	[illegible]

Population of Indictable Offences,* of Persons proceeded against for Drunkenness, County of Ireland.

OF CRIMES AND OFFENCES TO POPULATION.

[illegible] Group	County	Annual Average per 100,000 Population
No. 1	Mayo	[illegible]
No. 2	Cavan	[illegible]
	Donegal	[illegible]
	Sligo	[illegible]
	Leitrim	[illegible]
	Kerry	[illegible]
	Roscommon	[illegible]
	Fermanagh	[illegible]
No. 3	Monaghan	[illegible]
	Cork, W.R.	[illegible]
	Tyrone	[illegible]
	Armagh	[illegible]
	Meath	[illegible]
	Louth	[illegible]
	Galway, W.R.	[illegible]
	Queen's	[illegible]
No. 4	Galway, E.R.	[illegible]
	Longford	[illegible]
	[illegible]	[illegible]
	[illegible]	[illegible]
	[illegible]	[illegible]
	[illegible]	[illegible]
	Carlow	[illegible]
	Londonderry	[illegible]
	Cork, E.R.	[illegible]
	Tipperary, N.R.	[illegible]
	Down	[illegible]
No. 5	Tipperary, S.R.	[illegible]
	Kilkenny	[illegible]
	Limerick	[illegible]
	Antrim	[illegible]
	Kildare	[illegible]
	Dublin	[illegible]
	King's	[illegible]
	Wicklow	[illegible]

[illegible] Group	County	Annual Average per 100,000 Population
No. 1	[illegible]	[illegible]
	[illegible]	[illegible]
	Carlow	[illegible]
	Cork, W.R.	[illegible]
	Wexford	[illegible]
	Sligo	[illegible]
	Donegal	[illegible]
No. 2	Leitrim	[illegible]
	Kerry	[illegible]
	Meath	[illegible]
	Galway, W.R.	[illegible]
	[illegible]	[illegible]
	Londonderry	[illegible]
	Tipperary, N.R.	[illegible]
	Fermanagh	[illegible]
	Monaghan	[illegible]
	Galway, E.R.	[illegible]
	Cork, E.R.	[illegible]
	Kilkenny	[illegible]
	Clare	[illegible]
No. 3	Antrim	[illegible]
	Wicklow	[illegible]
	Dublin	[illegible]
	Louth	[illegible]
	Cavan	[illegible]
	Tyrone	[illegible]
	King's	[illegible]
	Westmeath	[illegible]
	Armagh	[illegible]
	Longford	[illegible]
	Tipperary, S.R.	[illegible]
No. 4	Limerick	[illegible]
	Queen's	[illegible]
	Kildare	[illegible]
	Waterford	[illegible]

County	Annual Average per 100,000 Population
Donegal	[illegible]
Kerry	[illegible]
Kilkenny	[illegible]
Roscommon	[illegible]
Mayo	[illegible]
Galway, E.R.	[illegible]
Galway, W.R.	
Sligo	[illegible]
Monaghan	[illegible]
Fermanagh	[illegible]
Tipperary, N.R.	[illegible]
Tipperary, S.R.	
Clare	[illegible]
Tyrone	[illegible]
Westmeath	[illegible]
Meath	[illegible]
Londonderry	[illegible]
[illegible]	[illegible]
[illegible]	[illegible]
Wexford	[illegible]
Queen's	[illegible]
[illegible]	[illegible]
Wicklow	[illegible]
Cork, E.R.	[illegible]
Cork, W.R.	
Carlow	[illegible]
Armagh	[illegible]
Louth	[illegible]
Waterford	[illegible]
Antrim	[illegible]
[illegible]	[illegible]
Down	[illegible]
Dublin	[illegible]
[illegible]	[illegible]
Limerick	[illegible]

* [illegible] on pages [illegible].

TABLE X.—GEOGRAPHICAL DISTRIBUTION OF CRIME.—Annual Average (1892-96), and Proportion to Population of Indictable Offences,* of Persons proceeded against for Drunkenness, and of Suicides in each County in Ireland.

(II.) COUNTIES ARRANGED IN ALPHABETICAL ORDER BY PROVINCES.

County.	All Crimes (Indictable Offences).		Crimes against Property.		Crimes against the Person				Drunkenness.		Suicides.	
					Offences of Violence.		[illegible]					
	Annual Average, 1892-96.	Proportion per 100,000 Population.	Annual Average, 1892-96.	Proportion per 100,000 Population.	Annual Average, 1892-96.	Proportion per 100,000 Population.	Annual Average, 1892-96.	Proportion per 100,000 Population.	Annual Average, 1892-96.	Proportion per 100,000 Population.	Annual Average, 1892-96.	Proportion per 100,000 Population.
LEINSTER:												
Carlow,	[illegible]	[illegible]	[illegible]	[illegible]	[illegible]	[illegible]	[illegible]	[illegible]	[illegible]	[illegible]	[illegible]	[illegible]
Dublin,	[illegible]	[illegible]	[illegible]	[illegible]	[illegible]	[illegible]	[illegible]	[illegible]	[illegible]	[illegible]	[illegible]	[illegible]
Kildare,	[illegible]	[illegible]	[illegible]	[illegible]	[illegible]	[illegible]	[illegible]	[illegible]	[illegible]	[illegible]	[illegible]	[illegible]
Kilkenny,	[illegible]	[illegible]	[illegible]	[illegible]	[illegible]	[illegible]	[illegible]	[illegible]	[illegible]	[illegible]	[illegible]	[illegible]
King's,	[illegible]	[illegible]	[illegible]	[illegible]	[illegible]	[illegible]	[illegible]	[illegible]	[illegible]	[illegible]	[illegible]	[illegible]
Longford,	[illegible]	[illegible]	[illegible]	[illegible]	[illegible]	[illegible]	[illegible]	[illegible]	[illegible]	[illegible]	[illegible]	[illegible]
Louth,	[illegible]	[illegible]	[illegible]	[illegible]	[illegible]	[illegible]	[illegible]	[illegible]	[illegible]	[illegible]	[illegible]	[illegible]
Meath,	[illegible]	[illegible]	[illegible]	[illegible]	[illegible]	[illegible]	[illegible]	[illegible]	[illegible]	[illegible]	[illegible]	[illegible]
Queen's,	[illegible]	[illegible]	[illegible]	[illegible]	[illegible]	[illegible]	[illegible]	[illegible]	[illegible]	[illegible]	[illegible]	[illegible]
Westmeath,	[illegible]	[illegible]	[illegible]	[illegible]	[illegible]	[illegible]	[illegible]	[illegible]	[illegible]	[illegible]	[illegible]	[illegible]
Wexford,	[illegible]	[illegible]	[illegible]	[illegible]	[illegible]	[illegible]	[illegible]	[illegible]	[illegible]	[illegible]	[illegible]	[illegible]
Wicklow,	[illegible]	[illegible]	[illegible]	[illegible]	[illegible]	[illegible]	[illegible]	[illegible]	[illegible]	[illegible]	[illegible]	[illegible]
MUNSTER:												
Clare,	[illegible]	[illegible]	[illegible]	[illegible]	[illegible]	[illegible]	[illegible]	[illegible]	[illegible]	[illegible]	[illegible]	[illegible]
Cork, E.R.,	[illegible]	[illegible]	[illegible]	[illegible]	[illegible]	[illegible]	[illegible]	[illegible]	[illegible]	[illegible]	[illegible]	[illegible]
Cork, W.R.,	[illegible]	[illegible]	[illegible]	[illegible]	[illegible]	[illegible]	[illegible]	[illegible]	[illegible]	[illegible]		
Kerry,	[illegible]	[illegible]	[illegible]	[illegible]	[illegible]	[illegible]	[illegible]	[illegible]	[illegible]	[illegible]	[illegible]	[illegible]
Limerick,	[illegible]	[illegible]	[illegible]	[illegible]	[illegible]	[illegible]	[illegible]	[illegible]	[illegible]	[illegible]	[illegible]	[illegible]
Tipperary, N.R.,	[illegible]	[illegible]	[illegible]	[illegible]	[illegible]	[illegible]	[illegible]	[illegible]	[illegible]	[illegible]	[illegible]	[illegible]
Tipperary, S.R.,	[illegible]	[illegible]	[illegible]	[illegible]	[illegible]	[illegible]	[illegible]	[illegible]	[illegible]	[illegible]		
Waterford,	[illegible]	[illegible]	[illegible]	[illegible]	[illegible]	[illegible]	[illegible]	[illegible]	[illegible]	[illegible]	[illegible]	[illegible]
ULSTER:												
Antrim,	[illegible]	[illegible]	[illegible]	[illegible]	[illegible]	[illegible]	[illegible]	[illegible]	[illegible]	[illegible]	[illegible]	[illegible]
Armagh,	[illegible]	[illegible]	[illegible]	[illegible]	[illegible]	[illegible]	[illegible]	[illegible]	[illegible]	[illegible]	[illegible]	[illegible]
Cavan,	[illegible]	[illegible]	[illegible]	[illegible]	[illegible]	[illegible]	[illegible]	[illegible]	[illegible]	[illegible]	[illegible]	[illegible]
Donegal,	[illegible]	[illegible]	[illegible]	[illegible]	[illegible]	[illegible]	[illegible]	[illegible]	[illegible]	[illegible]	[illegible]	[illegible]
Down,	[illegible]	[illegible]	[illegible]	[illegible]	[illegible]	[illegible]	[illegible]	[illegible]	[illegible]	[illegible]	[illegible]	[illegible]
Fermanagh,	[illegible]	[illegible]	[illegible]	[illegible]	[illegible]	[illegible]	[illegible]	[illegible]	[illegible]	[illegible]	[illegible]	[illegible]
Londonderry,	[illegible]	[illegible]	[illegible]	[illegible]	[illegible]	[illegible]	[illegible]	[illegible]	[illegible]	[illegible]	[illegible]	[illegible]
Monaghan,	[illegible]	[illegible]	[illegible]	[illegible]	[illegible]	[illegible]	[illegible]	[illegible]	[illegible]	[illegible]	[illegible]	[illegible]
Tyrone,	[illegible]	[illegible]	[illegible]	[illegible]	[illegible]	[illegible]	[illegible]	[illegible]	[illegible]	[illegible]	[illegible]	[illegible]
CONNAUGHT:												
Galway, E.R.,	[illegible]	[illegible]	[illegible]	[illegible]	[illegible]	[illegible]	[illegible]	[illegible]	[illegible]	[illegible]		
Galway, W.R.,	[illegible]	[illegible]	[illegible]	[illegible]	[illegible]	[illegible]	[illegible]	[illegible]	[illegible]	[illegible]	[illegible]	[illegible]
Leitrim,	[illegible]	[illegible]	[illegible]	[illegible]	[illegible]	[illegible]	[illegible]	[illegible]	[illegible]	[illegible]	[illegible]	[illegible]
Mayo,	[illegible]	[illegible]	[illegible]	[illegible]	[illegible]	[illegible]	[illegible]	[illegible]	[illegible]	[illegible]	[illegible]	[illegible]
Roscommon,	[illegible]	[illegible]	[illegible]	[illegible]	[illegible]	[illegible]	[illegible]	[illegible]	[illegible]	[illegible]	[illegible]	[illegible]
Sligo,	[illegible]	[illegible]	[illegible]	[illegible]	[illegible]	[illegible]	[illegible]	[illegible]	[illegible]	[illegible]	[illegible]	[illegible]
Total,	[illegible]	[illegible]	[illegible]	[illegible]	[illegible]	[illegible]	[illegible]	[illegible]	[illegible]	[illegible]	[illegible]	[illegible]

ANNUAL STATISTICS FOR THE YEAR 1896.

	Page
TABLES 1 TO 9.—ASSIZES AND QUARTER SESSIONS, . .	41
TABLES 10, 11, 12.—DISTRICTS PROCLAIMED, . . .	73
TABLES 13, 14.—POLICE ESTABLISHMENTS, ...	75
TABLES 15 TO 19.—COURTS OF SUMMARY JURISDICTION AND APPEALS TO QUARTER SESSIONS, ...	81
TABLES 20 TO 29.—POLICE RETURNS OF CRIME, ...	99
TABLES 30 TO 40.—PRISONS, ...	120
TABLES 41 TO 47.—REFORMATORY AND INDUSTRIAL SCHOOLS, .	150
TABLES 48 TO 52.—CRIMINAL AND DANGEROUS LUNATICS, . .	163

Notes to Tables 1, 3, and 5.

(*a.*) The titles of offences (Column 1) are much condensed. The fuller titles, and the offences comprised under each head, are given on page 36 of the Criminal Statistics for the year 1896.

(*b.*) The Tables show the number of persons prosecuted, not the number of offences. Where, therefore, any person is prosecuted at the same Assizes or Sessions for several offences, one offence has to be selected for tabulation; and the rule to be followed is to select that for which the proceedings were carried to the furthest stage—to trial if there were several indictments, to conviction and sentence if prisoner was tried on several charges. If there are several convictions, the offence selected is that for which the heaviest punishment was awarded. If the final result of proceedings on two or more charges is the same, the more serious offence (as measured by the maximum penalty allowed by the law) appears in the Tables.

(*c.*) Where, in addition to the offence thus selected for detailed tabulation, the same person is prosecuted for other offences of a distinct character, and charged in separate indictments, the number of these additional charges is given in columns 22 to 24 of the Tables, column 22 giving the total number of such charges, column 23 the number resulting in convictions, and column 24 the number for which separate sentences (not concurrent with those in columns 11 to 17) are passed. Only distinct offences charged in separate indictments are included in these columns; additional indictments merely varying the form of the charge, and additional charges appearing as counts in the same indictment, are excluded.

(*d.*) Where a person is prosecuted for one offence and convicted for another (e.g. committed for murder and convicted of manslaughter), the case appears only under the offence of which he was convicted.

(*e.*) Columns 2, 3, and 4 ("Numbers for Trial") include only such cases as actually came before the Assizes or Quarter Sessions. Persons who die, escape from prison, abscond while on bail, or are removed to an asylum before trial, are not included.

(*f.*) Column 13 ("Imprisonment") does not include the sentences of imprisonment which sometimes precede sentences of detention in a Reformatory School, nor does it include sentences of imprisonment in default of payment of fine, or in default of finding sureties.

(*g.*) Columns 15 and 16 ("Fine") include all cases where payment of a fine is imposed as the sentence or part of the sentence, whether the fine is actually paid or not.

(*h.*) Columns 17 and 21 ("Recognizances") include cases where recognizances are required, whether with or without sureties, and, if sureties are required, whether they are found or not.

(*i.*) Columns 18 to 21 are for those cases where more than one punishment is imposed for the same offence. Thus, if a person convicted of larceny is sentenced to be imprisoned and whipped, the imprisonment appears in Column 13, the whipping in column 20.

ASSIZES AND QUARTER SESSIONS.

1.—ASSIZES.—Number of Persons for Trial, Nature of Offences, and Results of Proceedings.

2.—ASSIZES.—Length of Sentences.

3.—QUARTER SESSIONS.—Number of Persons for Trial, Nature of Offences, and Results of Proceedings.

4.—QUARTER SESSIONS.—Length of Sentences.

5.—ASSIZES AND QUARTER SESSIONS.—Number of Persons for Trial, Nature of Offences, and Results of Proceedings.

6.—ASSIZES AND QUARTER SESSIONS.—Number of Persons for Trial for each Offence in each County.

7.—ASSIZES AND QUARTER SESSIONS.—Number of Persons for Trial, and Results of Proceedings in each Court.

8.—COSTS OF CRIMINAL PROCEEDINGS.

9.—COURT FOR CROWN CASES RESERVED.

ASSIZES AND

TABLE 1.—ASSIZES.—Numbers of Persons for Trial,

Offences. (1)	Persons for Trial: Total (2)	Males (3)	Females (4)	Not Tried: No Prosecution (5)	No Bill (6)	Found insane on arraignment (7)	Acquitted (8)	Found not guilty on ground of insanity (9)	Convicted and: Total (10)	Death (11)	Penal Servitude (12)	Imprisonment (13)
Class I.—Offences against the Person.												
1. Murder,	[illegible]	[illegible]	[illegible]	[illegible]	.		1	11	[illegible]	[illegible]	[illegible]	-	.
2. Attempts to murder,	[illegible]	[illegible]	[illegible]		.	.	[illegible]	.	[illegible]	.	2	.
3. Conspiracy or Incitement to Murder,	.			.	.	.	.	.	.	.	.	.
4. Manslaughter,	[illegible]	[illegible]	7	[illegible]	7	1	[illegible]	-	[illegible]	.	[illegible]	14
5. Felonious Wounding,	[illegible]	[illegible]	1	[illegible]	.	1	[illegible]	-	[illegible]	.	2	[illegible]
6. Endangering Railway Passengers,	[illegible]	[illegible]	[illegible]	.	.	1	[illegible]	1	.	.	.	.
7. Malicious Wounding (Misdemeanours),	[illegible]	[illegible]	7	[illegible]	1	.	[illegible]	[illegible]	[illegible]	.	.	21
8. Assaults,	[illegible]	[illegible]	[illegible]	[illegible]	1	.	[illegible]	.	[illegible]	.	.	[illegible]
9. Intimidation and Molestation,	1	1	.	.	.	.	1	.	.	.	.	.
10. Cruelty to Children,	[illegible]	1	6	-	.	.	[illegible]	.	6	.	.	6
11. Abandoning Children under two years,	7	2	.	-	.	.	.	-	9	.	.	.
12. Child Stealing,	.		.	.	.	.	.	.	.	.	.	.
13. Procuring Abortion,	.		.	.	.	.	.	.	.	.	.	.
14. Concealment of Birth,	[illegible]	1	[illegible]	1	7	.	[illegible]	.	[illegible]	.	.	1
15. Unnatural Offences,	[illegible]	[illegible]	.	1	.	.	1	.	.	.	.	.
16. Attempts to Commit Unnatural Offences,	1	1	.	.	.	.	.	.	1	.	1	.
17. Indecency with Males,	[illegible]	[illegible]	.	.	.	.	[illegible]	.	[illegible]	.	.	7
18. Rape,	[illegible]	[illegible]	.	[illegible]	[illegible]	.	7	.	1	.	[illegible]	[illegible]
19. Indecent Assaults on Females,	[illegible]	[illegible]	.	[illegible]	[illegible]	.	[illegible]	.	[illegible]	.	[illegible]	[illegible]
20. Defilement of Girls under 13,	[illegible]	[illegible]	.	[illegible]	.	.	[illegible]	.	[illegible]	.	[illegible]	[illegible]
21. Defilement of Girls under 16,	1	1	.	[illegible]	.	.	.	.	.	.	.	.
22. Householder permitting Defilement of Girls,	.	.	.	.	.	.	.	.	.	.	.	.
23. Procuration,	.	.	.	.	.	.	.	.	.	.	.	.
24. Abduction,	1	1	.	.	.	.	.	.	1	.	.	1
25. Bigamy,	[illegible]	[illegible]	1	.	.	.	[illegible]	.	1	.	1	[illegible]
26. Other Offences against the Person,	[illegible]	[illegible]	1	.	[illegible]	.	.	.	[illegible]	.	.	1
Total of Class I.,	[illegible]	[illegible]	74	[illegible]	17	[illegible]	[illegible]	7	[illegible]	3	[illegible]	[illegible]
Class II.—Offences against Property with Violence.												
27. Sacrilege,	.	.	.	.	.	.	.	.	.	.	.	.
28. Burglary,	[illegible]	[illegible]	.	-	.	[illegible]	[illegible]	.	[illegible]	.	[illegible]	[illegible]
29. Housebreaking,	[illegible]	[illegible]	1	.	.	.	[illegible]	1	[illegible]	.	[illegible]	[illegible]
30. Shopbreaking,	[illegible]	[illegible]	.	[illegible]	.	.	.	.	[illegible]	.	1	[illegible]
31. Attempts to break into Houses, Shops, &c.,	1	1	.	.	.	.	.	.	1	.	.	1
32. Entering with intent to Commit Felony,	[illegible]	[illegible]	.	1	.	.	[illegible]	.	7	.	.	[illegible]
33. Possession of Housebreaking Tools, &c.,	.	.	.	.	.	.	.	.	.	.	.	.
34. Robbery,	[illegible]	[illegible]	[illegible]	[illegible]	.	.	[illegible]	.	[illegible]	.	[illegible]	[illegible]
35. Extortion by Threats to Accuse,	.	.	.	.	.	.	.	.	.	.	.	.
36. Extortion by other Threats,	.	.	.	.	.	.	.	.	.	.	.	.
Total of Class II.,	[illegible]	[illegible]	[illegible]	[illegible]	.	[illegible]	[illegible]	1	[illegible]	.	[illegible]	[illegible]
Class III.—Offences against Property without Violence.												
37. Larceny of Horses and Cattle,	[illegible]	[illegible]	1	[illegible]	[illegible]	.	1	.	21	-	[illegible]	[illegible]
38. Larceny from the Person,	[illegible]	[illegible]	[illegible]	[illegible]	[illegible]	.	1	.	[illegible]	.	1	[illegible]
39. Larceny in House,	[illegible]	[illegible]	[illegible]	.	.	.	.	.	[illegible]	.	.	[illegible]
40. Larceny by a Servant,	[illegible]	1	1	.	.	.	1	.	1	-	.	1
41. Embezzlement,	[illegible]	[illegible]	.	.	.	.	1	.	[illegible]	-	.	[illegible]
42. Larceny of Post Letters,	[illegible]	[illegible]	.	.	.	.	.	.	[illegible]	.	.	[illegible]
43. Other Aggravated Larcenies,	.	.	.	.	.	.	.	.	.	.	.	.
44. Simple Larceny and Minor Larcenies,	[illegible]	[illegible]	[illegible]	[illegible]	[illegible]	1	[illegible]	.	[illegible]	.	[illegible]	[illegible]
45. Obtaining by False Pretences,	[illegible]	[illegible]	[illegible]	[illegible]	.	.	[illegible]	.	[illegible]	.	[illegible]	[illegible]
46. Frauds by Bankers, &c.,	.	.	.	.	.	.	.	.	.	.	.	.
47. Falsifying Accounts,	.	.	.	.	.	.	.	.	.	.	.	.
48. Other Frauds,	[illegible]	[illegible]	.	.	.	.	1	.	[illegible]	.	.	[illegible]
49. Receiving Stolen Goods,	[illegible]	[illegible]	[illegible]	.	1	.	1	.	[illegible]	.	.	[illegible]
50. Offences in Bankruptcy,	[illegible]	[illegible]	.	.	.	.	[illegible]	.	[illegible]	.	1	[illegible]
Total of Class III.,	[illegible]	[illegible]	[illegible]	[illegible]	[illegible]	1	[illegible]	.	[illegible]	.	[illegible]	[illegible]

IRELAND.

QUARTER SESSIONS.

Nature of Offences, and Results of Proceedings.

Sentences				Cases where a Sentence Postponed or Ajourned				Acquittals			(25)	(26)	OFFENCES.
(14)	(15)	(16)	(17)	(18)	(19)	(20)	(21)	(22)	(23)	(24)			
													Class I.—Offences against the Person.
.	.	.	.	.	.	.	.	.	.	.	.	5	1. Murder.
.	.	.	.	.	.	.	.	.	.	.	.	.	2. Attempt to Murder.
.	.	.	.	.	.	.	.	.	.	.	.	.	3. Conspiracy or Incitement to Murder.
.	.	.	6	.	.	.	.	5	.	.	.	.	4. Manslaughter.
.	.	.	3	.	.	.	1	.	.	.	.	.	5. Felonious Wounding.
.	.	.	.	.	.	.	.	.	.	.	.	.	6. Endangering Railway Passengers.
.	.	.	4	.	.	.	10	1	.	1	.	.	7. Malicious Wounding (Misdemeanour).
.	1	.	[illegible]	.	1	.	1	[illegible]	.	.	.	.	8. Assault.
.	.	.	.	.	.	.	.	.	.	.	.	.	9. Infanticide and Exposure.
.	.	.	5	.	.	.	.	.	.	.	.	.	10. Cruelty to Children.
.	.	.	1	.	.	.	.	.	.	.	.	.	11. Abandoning Children under two years.
.	.	.	.	.	.	.	.	.	.	.	.	.	12. Child Stealing.
.	.	.	.	.	.	.	.	.	.	.	.	.	13. Procuring Abortion.
.	.	.	17	.	.	.	.	1	.	.	.	.	14. Concealment of Birth.
.	.	.	.	.	.	.	.	.	.	.	.	.	15. Unnatural Offences.
.	.	.	.	.	.	.	.	.	.	.	.	.	16. Attempts to Commit Unnatural Offences.
.	.	.	.	.	.	.	.	.	.	.	.	.	17. Indecency with Males.
.	.	.	.	.	.	.	.	1	.	.	.	.	18. Rape.
.	.	.	3	.	.	.	.	1	1	.	.	.	19. Indecent Assaults on Females.
.	.	.	1	.	.	.	.	2	.	.	.	.	20. Defilement of Girls under 13.
.	.	.	.	.	.	.	.	.	.	.	.	.	21. Defilement of Girls under 16.
.	.	.	.	.	.	.	.	.	.	.	.	.	22. Householder permitting Defilement of Girls.
.	.	.	.	.	.	.	.	.	.	.	.	.	23. Procuration.
.	.	.	.	.	.	.	.	.	.	.	.	.	24. Abduction.
.	.	.	.	.	.	.	.	.	.	.	.	.	25. Bigamy.
.	.	.	2	.	.	.	.	.	.	.	.	.	26. Other Offences against the Person.
.	1	.	[illegible]	.	1	.	13	27	5	1	.	5	Total of Class I.
													Class II.—Offences against Property with Violence.
.	.	.	.	.	.	.	.	.	.	.	.	.	27. Sacrilege.
.	.	.	3	.	.	.	.	15	1	1	.	.	28. Burglary.
.	.	.	.	.	.	.	.	1	.	.	.	.	29. Housebreaking.
.	.	.	1	.	.	.	.	.	.	.	.	.	30. Shopbreaking.
.	.	.	.	.	.	.	.	.	.	.	.	.	31. Attempts to break into Houses, Shops, &c.
.	1	.	1	.	.	.	.	.	.	1	.	.	32. Entering with intent to Commit Felony.
.	.	.	.	.	.	.	.	.	.	.	.	.	33. Possession of Housebreaking Tools, &c.
.	.	.	.	.	.	.	.	2	.	.	.	.	34. Robbery.
.	.	.	.	.	.	.	.	.	.	.	.	.	35. Extortion by Threats to Accuse.
.	.	.	.	.	.	.	.	.	.	.	.	.	36. Extortion by other Threats.

TABLE 1—*continued*—ASSIZES.—Number of Persons for Trial,

OFFENCES.	[illegible]			[illegible]			[illegible]	[illegible]	[illegible]			
	Total.	Males.	Females.	[illegible]	[illegible]	[illegible]	[illegible]	[illegible]	[illegible]	[illegible]	[illegible]	[illegible]
(1)	(2)	(3)	(4)	(5)	(6)	(7)	(8)	(9)	(10)	(11)	(12)	(13)
Class IV.—Malicious Injuries to Property.												
51. Arson,	[illegible]	[illegible]	[illegible]	[illegible]	[illegible]	.	[illegible]	.	[illegible]	.	[illegible]	[illegible]
52. Setting Fire to Crops, &c.,	[illegible]	[illegible]	.	.	.	.	.	.	[illegible]	.	.	[illegible]
53. Killing and Maiming Cattle,	[illegible]	[illegible]	.	[illegible]	.	.	.	.	[illegible]	.	.	[illegible]
54. Malicious Use, &c., of Explosives,	[illegible]	[illegible]	.	.	.	.	.	.	[illegible]	.	.	[illegible]
55. Destroying Ships,	.	.	.	.	.	.	.	.	.	.	.	.
56. Destroying Railways,	.	.	.	.	.	.	.	.	.	.	.	.
57. Destroying Trees and Shrubs,	.	.	.	.	.	.	.	.	.	.	.	.
58. Other Malicious Injuries,	[illegible]	[illegible]	[illegible]	.	[illegible]	.	[illegible]	.	[illegible]	.	.	[illegible]
Total of Class IV.,	[illegible]	[illegible]	[illegible]	[illegible]	[illegible]	.	[illegible]	.	[illegible]	.	1	[illegible]
Class V.—Forgery and Offences against the Currency.												
59. Forgery and Uttering (Felony),	[illegible]	[illegible]	[illegible]	[illegible]	.	.	[illegible]	.	[illegible]	.	.	[illegible]
60. Forgery (Misdemeanour),	[illegible]	[illegible]	.	.	.	.	[illegible]	.	[illegible]	.	.	[illegible]
61. Coining,	.	.	.	.	.	.	.	.	.	.	.	.
62. Uttering Counterfeit Coin,	[illegible]	[illegible]	.	.	[illegible]	.	[illegible]	.	[illegible]	.	.	[illegible]
Total of Class V.,	[illegible]	[illegible]	1	[illegible]	[illegible]	.	[illegible]	.	[illegible]	.	.	[illegible]
Class VI.—Other Offences not included in the above Classes.												
Offences against the Crown and Public Order.												
63. High Treason,	.	.	.	.	.	.	.	.	.	.	.	.
64. Treason Felony,	.	.	.	.	.	.	.	.	.	.	.	.
65. Riot,	[illegible]	[illegible]	.	.	.	.	[illegible]	.	[illegible]	.	.	[illegible]
66. Unlawful Assembly,	[illegible]	[illegible]	.	[illegible]	.	.	[illegible]	.	[illegible]	.	.	[illegible]
67. Intimidation by Threatening Letters, Notices, or otherwise,	[illegible]	[illegible]	.	.	.	.	.	.	[illegible]	.	.	[illegible]
68. Demand or Robbery of Arms,	.	.	.	.	.	.	.	.	.	.	.	.
69. [illegible]	.	.	.	.	.	.	.	.	.	.	.	.
70. Other Offences,	[illegible]	[illegible]	1	[illegible]	.	.	[illegible]	.	[illegible]	.	.	[illegible]
Offences against Public Justice.												
71. Extortion by Officers, &c.,	.	.	.	.	.	.	.	.	.	.	.	.
72. Bribery, &c.,	[illegible]	1	.	.	.	.	.	.	1	.	.	[illegible]
73. Perjury,	[illegible]	[illegible]	[illegible]	[illegible]	[illegible]	.	[illegible]	.	1	.	.	[illegible]
74. Rescue and Escape,	[illegible]	[illegible]	.	[illegible]	.	.	.	.	.	.	.	.
75. Other Offences,	[illegible]	[illegible]	[illegible]	.	.	.	.	.	[illegible]	.	.	.
Offences against Religion.												
76. Blasphemy, &c.,	.	.	.	.	.	.	.	.	.	.	.	.
Offences against Law of Nations.												
77. Piracy,	.	.	.	.	.	.	.	.	.	.	.	.
78. Slave Trade,	.	.	.	.	.	.	.	.	.	.	.	.
79. Libel,	1	[illegible]	.	.	.	.	.	.	[illegible]	.	.	[illegible]
80. [illegible]	.	.	.	.	.	.	.	.	.	.	.	.
81. Indecent Exposure,	[illegible]	[illegible]	.	[illegible]	.	.	.	.	[illegible]	.	.	[illegible]
82. Keeping Disorderly Houses,	.	.	.	.	.	.	.	.	.	.	.	.
83. Other Nuisances,	.	.	.	.	.	.	.	.	.	.	.	.
84. [illegible] (attempting to commit),	[illegible]	[illegible]	[illegible]	[illegible]	[illegible]	[illegible]	.	1	[illegible]	.	.	[illegible]
85. Other Misdemeanours,	[illegible]	[illegible]	1	1	[illegible]	.	.	.	[illegible]	.	.	.
Total of Class VI.,	[illegible]	[illegible]	[illegible]	[illegible]	[illegible]	1	[illegible]	[illegible]	[illegible]	.	.	[illegible]
GRAND TOTAL,	[illegible]	[illegible]	[illegible]	[illegible]	[illegible]	[illegible]	[illegible]	[illegible]	[illegible]	[illegible]	[illegible]	[illegible]

QUARTER SESSIONS.

Nature of Offences, and Results of Proceedings.

[illegible]				[illegible]				[illegible]					OFFENCES.
(14)	(15)	(16)	(17)	(18)	(19)	(20)	(21)	(22)	(23)	(24)	(25)	(26)	
													Class IV.—Malicious Injuries to Property.
.	.	.	[illegible]	.	.	.	1	.	.	.	.	.	51 Arson.
.	.	.	.	.	.	.	.	.	.	.	.	.	52 Setting Fire to Crops, &c.
.	.	.	.	.	.	.	.	1	.	.	.	.	53 Killing and Maiming Cattle.
.	.	.	1	.	.	.	.	.	.	.	.	.	54 Malicious Use, &c., of Explosives.
.	.	.	.	.	.	.	.	.	.	.	.	.	55 Destroying Ships.
.	.	.	.	.	.	.	.	.	.	.	.	.	56 Destroying Railways.
.	.	.	.	.	.	.	.	.	.	.	.	.	57 Destroying Trees and Shrubs.
.	.	.	1	.	.	.	.	[illegible]	.	.	.	.	58 Other Malicious Injuries.
.	.	.	[illegible]	.	.	.	1	[illegible]	.	.	.	.	Total of Class IV.
													Class V.—Forgery and Offences against the Currency.
.	.	.	.	.	.	.	.	[illegible]	[illegible]	.	.	.	59 Forgery and Uttering (Felony).
.	.	.	.	.	.	.	.	1	.	.	.	.	60 Forgery (Misdemeanour).
.	.	.	.	.	.	.	.	.	.	.	.	.	61 Coining.
.	.	.	.	.	.	.	.	.	.	.	.	.	62 Uttering Counterfeit Coin.
.	.	.	.	.	.	.	.	[illegible]	1	.	.	.	Total of Class V.
													Class VI.—Other Offences not included in the above Classes.
													Offences against the State and Public Order.
.	.	.	.	.	.	.	.	.	.	.	.	.	63 High Treason.
.	.	.	.	.	.	.	.	.	.	.	.	.	64 Treason Felony.
.	.	.	[illegible]	.	.	.	.	.	.	.	.	.	65 Riot.
.	.	.	[illegible]	.	.	.	.	1	.	.	.	.	66 Unlawful Assembly.
.	.	.	.	.	.	.	.	.	.	.	.	.	67 Intimidation by Threatening Letters, Notices, or otherwise.
.	.	.	.	.	.	.	.	.	.	.	.	.	68 Demand or Delivery of Arms.
.	.	.	.	.	.	.	.	.	.	.	.	.	69 Assaulting Dwelling Houses (by armed Parties).
.	.	.	.	.	.	.	.	.	.	.	.	.	70 Other Offences.
													Offences against Public Justice.
.	.	.	.	.	.	.	.	.	.	.	.	.	71 Extortion by Officers, &c.
.	.	.	.	.	1	.	.	.	.	.	.	.	72 Bribery, &c.
.	.	.	.	.	.	.	.	.	.	.	.	.	73 Perjury.
.	.	.	.	.	.	.	.	.	.	.	.	.	74 Escape and Rescue.
.	.	.	7	.	.	.	.	.	.	.	.	.	75 Other Offences.
													Offences against Religion.
.	.	.	.	.	.	.	.	.	.	.	.	.	76 Blasphemy, &c.
													Offences against Law of Nations.
.	.	.	.	.	.	.	.	.	.	.	.	.	77 Piracy.
.	.	.	.	.	.	.	.	.	.	.	.	.	78 Slave Trade.
.	.	.	.	.	.	.	.	.	.	.	.	.	79 Libel.
.	.	.	.	.	.	.	.	.	.	.	.	.	80 Poaching.
.	.	.	.	.	.	.	.	.	.	.	.	.	81 Indecent Exposure.
.	.	.	.	.	.	.	.	.	.	.	.	.	82 Keeping Disorderly Houses.
.	.	.	.	.	.	.	.	.	.	.	.	.	83 Other Nuisances.
.	.	.	1	.	.	.	.	.	.	.	.	.	84 Suicide (attempting to commit).
.	.	.	1	.	.	.	.	.	.	.	.	.	85 Other Misdemeanours.
.	.	.	[illegible]	.	1	.	.	1	.	.	.	.	Total of Class VI.
1	1	.	[illegible]	.	[illegible]	.	[illegible]	[illegible]	[illegible]	[illegible]	.	[illegible]	GRAND TOTAL.

TABLE 2.—ASSIZES.—

OFFENCES.	SENTENCES.												
	Penal Servitude.												
Class I.—Offences against the Person.													
1. Murder,	.	.	.	.	.	.	.	.	.	.	.	.	.
2. Attempt to Murder,	[illegible]	.	.	.	.	.	.	.	.	.	.	.	[illegible]
3. Conspiracy or Incitement to Murder,	.	.	.	.	.	.	.	.	.	.	.	.	.
4. Manslaughter,	[illegible]	.	.	.	[illegible]	.	.	[illegible]	.	.	[illegible]	.	[illegible]
5. Felonious wounding,	[illegible]	.	.	.	.	.	.	.	.	.	.	.	.
6. Endangering Railway Passengers,	.	.	.	.	.	.	.	.	.	.	.	.	.
7. Malicious wounding (misdemeanour),	.	.	.	.	.	.	.	.	.	.	.	.	.
8. Assault,	.	.	.	.	.	.	.	.	.	.	.	.	.
9. Intimidation and Molestation,	.	.	.	.	.	.	.	.	.	.	.	.	.
10. Cruelty to Children,	.	.	.	.	.	.	.	.	.	.	.	.	.
11. Abandoning Children under Two Years,	.	.	.	.	.	.	.	.	.	.	.	.	.
12. Child Stealing,	.	.	.	.	.	.	.	.	.	.	.	.	.
13. Procuring Abortion,	.	.	.	.	.	.	.	.	.	.	.	.	.
14. Concealment of Birth,	.	.	.	.	.	.	.	.	.	.	.	.	.
15. Unnatural Offences,	.	.	.	.	.	.	.	.	.	.	.	.	.
16. Attempts to commit Unnatural Offences,	[illegible]	.	.	.	.	.	.	.	.	.	.	.	.
17. Indecency with Males,	.	.	.	.	.	.	.	.	.	.	.	.	.
18. Rape,	[illegible]	.	.	.	.	.	.	.	.	.	.	.	[illegible]
19. Indecent Assaults on Females,	[illegible]	.	.	.	.	[illegible]	.	.	.	.	.	.	.
20. Defilement of Girls under 13,	[illegible]	.	.	.	.	.	.	.	.	.	.	[illegible]	[illegible]
21. Defilement of Girls under 16,	[illegible]	.	.	.	.	.	.	.	.	.	.	.	.
22. Householder permitting Defilement of Girls,	.	.	.	.	.	.	.	.	.	.	.	.	.
23. Procuration,	.	.	.	.	.	.	.	.	.	.	.	.	.
24. Abduction,	.	.	.	.	.	.	.	.	.	.	.	.	.
25. Bigamy,	[illegible]	.	.	.	.	.	.	.	.	.	.	.	[illegible]
26. Other Offences against the Person,	.	.	.	.	.	.	.	.	.	.	.	.	.
Total of Class I.,	[illegible]	.	.	.	[illegible]	[illegible]	.	[illegible]	.	.	[illegible]	.	[illegible]
Class II.—Offences against Property with Violence.													
27. Sacrilege,	.	.	.	.	.	.	.	.	.	.	.	.	.
28. Burglary,	[illegible]	.	.	.	.	.	.	.	.	.	.	.	.
29. Housebreaking,	[illegible]	.	.	.	.	.	.	.	.	.	.	.	[illegible]
30. Shopbreaking,	[illegible]	.	.	.	.	.	.	.	.	.	.	.	[illegible]
31. Attempts to break into Houses, Shops, &c.,	.	.	.	.	.	.	.	.	.	.	.	.	.
32. Entering with intent to commit Felony,	.	.	.	.	.	.	.	.	.	.	.	.	.
33. Possession of Housebreaking Tools,	.	.	.	.	.	.	.	.	.	.	.	.	.
34. Robbery,	[illegible]	.	.	.	.	.	.	[illegible]	.	.	.	.	.
35. Extortion by Threats to Accuse,	.	.	.	.	.	.	.	.	.	.	.	.	.
36. Extortion by other Threats,	.	.	.	.	.	.	.	.	.	.	.	.	.
Total of Class II.,	[illegible]	.	.	.	.	.	.	[illegible]	.	.	.	.	[illegible]
Class III.—Offences against Property without Violence.													
37. Larceny of Horses and Cattle,	[illegible]	.	.	.	.	.	.	.	.	.	.	.	[illegible]
38. Larceny from the Person,	[illegible]	.	.	.	.	.	.	.	.	.	.	.	[illegible]
39. Larceny in House,	.	.	.	.	.	.	.	.	.	.	.	.	.
40. Larceny by a Servant,	.	.	.	.	.	.	.	.	.	.	.	.	.
41. Embezzlement,	.	.	.	.	.	.	.	.	.	.	.	.	.
42. Larceny of Post Letters,	.	.	.	.	.	.	.	.	.	.	.	.	.
43. Other Aggravated Larcenies,	.	.	.	.	.	.	.	.	.	.	.	.	.
44. Simple Larceny and Minor Larcenies,	[illegible]	.	.	.	.	.	.	.	.	.	.	.	[illegible]
45. Obtaining by False Pretences,	[illegible]	.	.	.	.	.	.	.	.	.	.	.	[illegible]
46. Frauds by Bankers, &c.,	.	.	.	.	.	.	.	.	.	.	.	.	.
47. Falsifying Accounts,	.	.	.	.	.	.	.	.	.	.	.	.	.
48. Other Frauds,	.	.	.	.	.	.	.	.	.	.	.	.	.
49. Receiving Stolen Goods,	[illegible]	.	.	.	.	.	.	.	.	.	.	.	[illegible]
50. Offences in Bankruptcy,	.	.	.	.	.	.	.	.	.	.	.	.	.
Total of Class III.,	[illegible]	.	.	.	.	.	.	.	.	.	.	.	[illegible]

QUARTER SESSIONS.

Length of Sentences.

SENTENCES.												OFFENCES.
		IMPRISONMENT.										
[illegible]	[illegible]	Total.	[illegible]	[illegible]	[illegible]	[illegible]	[illegible]	[illegible]	[illegible]	[illegible]	[illegible]	
												Class I.—Offences against the Person.
.	.	.	.	.	.	.	.	.	.	.	.	1. Murder.
.	[illegible]	.	.	.	.	.	.	.	.	.	.	2. Attempt to Murder.
.	.	.	.	.	.	.	.	.	.	.	.	3. Conspiracy or Incitement to Murder.
.	[illegible]	[illegible]	.	.	[illegible]	[illegible]	[illegible]	[illegible]	[illegible]	.	.	4. Manslaughter.
.	[illegible]	[illegible]	.	.	[illegible]	[illegible]	[illegible]	[illegible]	[illegible]	.	1	5. Felonious Wounding.
.	.	.	.	.	.	.	.	.	.	.	.	6. Endangering Railway Passengers.
.	.	[illegible]	.	.	[illegible]	[illegible]	[illegible]	[illegible]	[illegible]	.	[illegible]	7. Malicious Wounding (misdemeanour).
.	.	[illegible]	.	.	[illegible]	[illegible]	[illegible]	[illegible]	[illegible]	[illegible]	[illegible]	8. Assault.
.	.	.	.	.	.	.	.	.	.	.	.	9. Intimidation and Molestation.
.	.	[illegible]	.	.	.	[illegible]	.	.	.	[illegible]	.	10. Cruelty to Children.
.	.	.	.	.	.	.	.	.	.	.	.	11. Abandoning Children under Two Years.
.	.	.	.	.	.	.	.	.	.	.	.	12. Child Stealing.
.	.	.	.	.	.	.	.	.	.	.	.	13. Procuring Abortion.
.	.	[illegible]	.	.	.	.	.	[illegible]	[illegible]	.	1	14. Concealment of Birth.
.	.	.	.	.	.	.	.	.	.	.	.	15. Unnatural Offences.
.	[illegible]	.	.	.	.	.	.	.	.	.	.	16. Attempts to commit Unnatural Offences.
.	.	[illegible]	.	.	.	.	.	.	[illegible]	.	.	17. Indecency with Males.
.	[illegible]	[illegible]	.	.	[illegible]	[illegible]	[illegible]	.	.	.	.	18. Rape.
.	.	[illegible]	.	.	[illegible]	[illegible]	[illegible]	[illegible]	[illegible]	[illegible]	.	19. Indecent Assaults on Females.
.	[illegible]	[illegible]	.	.	[illegible]	[illegible]	.	[illegible]	.	.	.	20. Defilement of Girls under 13.
.	.	.	.	.	.	.	.	.	.	.	.	21. Defilement of Girls under 16.
.	.	.	.	.	.	.	.	.	.	.	.	22. Householder permitting Defilement of Girls.
.	.	.	.	.	.	.	.	.	.	.	.	23. Procuration.
.	.	[illegible]	.	.	.	.	.	.	[illegible]	.	.	24. Abduction.
.	[illegible]	[illegible]	.	.	[illegible]	[illegible]	[illegible]	[illegible]	.	[illegible]	.	25. Bigamy.
.	.	[illegible]	.	.	.	.	.	[illegible]	.	.	.	26. Other Offences against the Person.
.	[illegible]	[illegible]	.	.	[illegible]	[illegible]	[illegible]	[illegible]	[illegible]	[illegible]	[illegible]	Total of Class I.
												Class II.—Offences against Property with Violence.
.	.	.	.	.	.	.	.	.	.	.	.	27. Sacrilege.
.	[illegible]	[illegible]	.	.	[illegible]	[illegible]	.	[illegible]	[illegible]	.	.	28. Burglary.
.	[illegible]	[illegible]	.	.	[illegible]	[illegible]	[illegible]	[illegible]	[illegible]	.	.	29. Housebreaking.
.	.	[illegible]	.	.	.	[illegible]	[illegible]	[illegible]	.	[illegible]	.	30. Shopbreaking.
.	.	[illegible]	.	.	[illegible]	[illegible]	.	.	.	.	.	31. Attempts to break into Houses, Shops, &c.
.	.	[illegible]	.	.	.	[illegible]	[illegible]	[illegible]	.	.	.	32. Entering with intent to commit Felony.
.	.	.	.	.	.	.	.	.	.	.	.	33. Possession of Housebreaking Tools, &c.
.	[illegible]	[illegible]	.	.	.	[illegible]	.	[illegible]	[illegible]	.	.	34. Robbery.
.	.	.	.	.	.	.	.	.	.	.	.	35. Extortion by Threats to Accuse.
.	.	.	.	.	.	.	.	.	.	.	.	36. Extortion by Other Threats.
.	[illegible]	[illegible]	.	.	1	[illegible]	[illegible]	[illegible]	[illegible]	1	.	Total of Class II.
												Class III.—Offences against Property without Violence.
[illegible]	.	[illegible]	.	.	.	[illegible]	[illegible]	[illegible]	[illegible]	[illegible]	.	37. Larceny of Horses and Cattle.
.	.	[illegible]	.	.	.	[illegible]	[illegible]	[illegible]	[illegible]	.	.	38. Larceny from the Person.
.	.	[illegible]	.	.	.	[illegible]	.	[illegible]	[illegible]	.	1	39. Larceny in House.
.	.	[illegible]	.	.	.	.	.	[illegible]	.	.	.	40. Larceny by a Servant.
.	.	[illegible]	.	.	1	.	.	[illegible]	[illegible]	[illegible]	.	41. Embezzlement.
.	.	[illegible]	.	.	.	[illegible]	.	.	[illegible]	.	.	42. Larceny of Post Letters.
.	.	.	.	.	.	.	.	.	.	.	.	43. Other Aggravated Larcenies.
.	[illegible]	[illegible]	.	.	[illegible]	[illegible]	[illegible]	[illegible]	[illegible]	[illegible]	[illegible]	44. Simple Larceny and Minor Larcenies.
.	[illegible]	[illegible]	.	.	[illegible]	[illegible]	[illegible]	[illegible]	[illegible]	[illegible]	[illegible]	45. Obtaining by False Pretences.
.	.	.	.	.	.	.	.	.	.	.	.	46. Frauds by Bailees, &c.
.	.	.	.	.	.	.	.	.	.	.	.	47. Falsifying Accounts.
.	.	[illegible]	.	.	.	.	.	[illegible]	[illegible]	.	.	48. Other Frauds.
.	.	[illegible]	.	.	1	[illegible]	.	[illegible]	[illegible]	[illegible]	1	49. Receiving Stolen Goods.
.	.	[illegible]	.	.	.	.	.	[illegible]	.	.	.	50. Offences in Bankruptcy.
[illegible]	[illegible]	[illegible]	.	.	[illegible]	[illegible]	[illegible]	[illegible]	[illegible]	[illegible]	[illegible]	Total of Class III.

TABLE 3—continued—ASSIZES.—

OFFENCES.	SENTENCES. Penal Servitude.												
	Death.	Life.	[illegible] Years.	[illegible] Years.	[illegible] Years.	[illegible] Years.	[illegible] Years.	[illegible] Years.	[illegible] Years.	[illegible] Years.	[illegible] Years.	[illegible] Years.	[illegible] Years.
Class IV.—Malicious Injuries to Property.													
[illegible]. Arson,	1	.	.	.	.	.	.	.	.	.	.	.	.
[illegible]. Setting Fire to Crops, &c.,	.	.	.	.	.	.	.	.	.	.	.	.	.
[illegible]. Killing and Maiming Cattle,	.	.	.	.	.	.	.	.	.	.	.	.	.
[illegible]. [illegible], &c., of [illegible]	.	.	.	.	.	.	.	.	.	.	.	.	.
[illegible]. Destroying Ships,	.	.	.	.	.	.	.	.	.	.	.	.	.
[illegible]. Destroying Railways,	.	.	.	.	.	.	.	.	.	.	.	.	.
[illegible]. Destroying Trees and Shrubs,	.	.	.	.	.	.	.	.	.	.	.	.	.
[illegible]. Other Malicious Injuries,	.	.	.	.	.	.	.	.	.	.	.	.	.
Total of Class IV.,	1	.	.	.	.	.	.	.	.	.	.	.	.
Class V.—Forgery and Offences against the Currency.													
[illegible]. Forgery and Uttering (Felony),	.	.	.	.	.	.	.	.	.	.	.	.	.
[illegible]. Forgery (Misdemeanour),	.	.	.	.	.	.	.	.	.	.	.	.	.
[illegible]. Coining,	.	.	.	.	.	.	.	.	.	.	.	.	.
[illegible]. Uttering Counterfeit Coin,	.	.	.	.	.	.	.	.	.	.	.	.	.
Total of Class V.,	.	.	.	.	.	.	.	.	.	.	.	.	.
Class VI.—Other Offences not included in the above Classes.													
Offences against the State and Public Order.													
[illegible]. High Treason,	.	.	.	.	.	.	.	.	.	.	.	.	.
[illegible]. Treason-Felony,	.	.	.	.	.	.	.	.	.	.	.	.	.
[illegible]. Riot,	.	.	.	.	.	.	.	.	.	.	.	.	.
[illegible]. Unlawful Assembly,	.	.	.	.	.	.	.	.	.	.	.	.	.
[illegible]. Intimidation by Threatening Letters, Notices, or otherwise,	.	.	.	.	.	.	.	.	.	.	.	.	.
[illegible]. Demand or Robbery of Arms,	.	.	.	.	.	.	.	.	.	.	.	.	.
[illegible]. Assembling [illegible] Dwelling Houses by [illegible] [illegible],	.	.	.	.	.	.	.	.	.	.	.	.	.
[illegible]. Other Offences,	.	.	.	.	.	.	.	.	.	.	.	.	.
Offences against Public Justice.													
[illegible]. [illegible] by Officers, &c.,	.	.	.	.	.	.	.	.	.	.	.	.	.
[illegible]. Bribery, &c.,	.	.	.	.	.	.	.	.	.	.	.	.	.
[illegible]. Perjury,	.	.	.	.	.	.	.	.	.	.	.	.	.
[illegible]. Escape and Rescue,	.	.	.	.	.	.	.	.	.	.	.	.	.
[illegible]. Other Offences,	.	.	.	.	.	.	.	.	.	.	.	.	.
Offences against Religion.													
[illegible]. [illegible], &c.,	.	.	.	.	.	.	.	.	.	.	.	.	.
Offences against Law of Nations.													
[illegible]. Piracy,	.	.	.	.	.	.	.	.	.	.	.	.	.
[illegible]. Slave Trade,	.	.	.	.	.	.	.	.	.	.	.	.	.
[illegible]. Libel,	.	.	.	.	.	.	.	.	.	.	.	.	.
[illegible]. [illegible],	.	.	.	.	.	.	.	.	.	.	.	.	.
[illegible]. Indecent Exposure,	.	.	.	.	.	.	.	.	.	.	.	.	.
[illegible]. Keeping Disorderly Houses,	.	.	.	.	.	.	.	.	.	.	.	.	.
[illegible]. Other Nuisances,	.	.	.	.	.	.	.	.	.	.	.	.	.
[illegible]. [illegible] attempting to [illegible],	.	.	.	.	.	.	.	.	.	.	.	.	.
[illegible]. Other Misdemeanours,	.	.	.	.	.	.	.	.	.	.	.	.	.
Total of Class VI.,	.	.	.	.	.	.	.	.	.	.	.	.	.
GRAND TOTAL,	[illegible]	.	.	.	5	1	.	6	.	.	9	.	[illegible]

QUARTER SESSIONS.

Length of Sentences.

[illegible]												OFFENCES.
		Imprisonment.										
[illegible]	[illegible]	Total	[illegible]	[illegible]	[illegible]	[illegible]	[illegible]	[illegible]	[illegible]	[illegible]	[illegible]	
												Class IV.—Malicious Offences against Property.
.	1	[illegible]	.	.	.	1	.	[illegible]	[illegible]	1	.	61. Arson.
.	.	[illegible]	.	.	.	.	.	[illegible]	.	.	.	62. Setting Fire to Crops, &c.
.	.	[illegible]	.	.	.	.	.	.	1	.	.	63. Killing and Maiming Cattle.
.	.	[illegible]	.	.	.	.	.	.	[illegible]	[illegible]	.	64. Malicious Use, &c., of Explosives.
.	.	.	.	.	.	.	.	.	.	.	.	65. Destroying Ships.
.	.	.	.	.	.	.	.	.	.	.	.	66. Destroying Railways.
.	.	.	.	.	.	.	.	.	.	.	.	67. Destroying Trees and Shrubs.
.	.	[illegible]	.	.	.	1	1	1	[illegible]	1	.	68. Other Malicious Injuries.
.	1	[illegible]	.	.	.	2	4	[illegible]	[illegible]	[illegible]	.	Total of Class IV.
												Class V.—Forgery and Offences against the Currency.
.	.	[illegible]	.	.	.	.	.	[illegible]	[illegible]	1	.	69. Forgery and Uttering (Felony).
.	.	1	.	.	.	.	.	.	1	.	.	70. Forgery (Misdemeanour).
.	.	.	.	.	.	.	.	.	.	.	.	71. Coining.
.	.	[illegible]	.	.	.	.	2	.	.	.	.	72. Uttering Counterfeit Coin.
.	.	[illegible]	.	.	.	.	[illegible]	[illegible]	[illegible]	[illegible]	.	Total of Class V.
												Class VI.—Offences not included in the above Classes.
												Offences against the State and Public Order.
.	.	.	.	.	.	.	.	.	.	.	.	73. High Treason.
.	.	.	.	.	.	.	.	.	.	.	.	74. Treason Felony.
.	.	[illegible]	.	.	.	.	.	[illegible]	[illegible]	[illegible]	.	75. Riot.
.	.	[illegible]	.	.	.	.	1	.	[illegible]	.	.	76. Unlawful Assembly.
.	.	[illegible]	.	.	.	.	.	1	.	.	.	77. Intimidation by Threatening Letters, Notices or otherwise.
.	.	.	.	.	.	.	.	.	.	.	.	78. Seizure or Robbery of Arms.
.	.	.	.	.	.	.	.	.	.	.	.	79. Attacking Dwelling Houses (by firing shots into them).
.	.	[illegible]	.	.	.	.	.	1	.	.	.	80. Other Offences.
												Offences against Public Justice.
.	.	.	.	.	.	.	.	.	.	.	.	81. [illegible], &c.
.	.	1	.	.	.	.	.	.	.	1	.	82. Bribery, &c.
.	.	[illegible]	.	.	.	1	1	[illegible]	.	[illegible]	.	83. Perjury.
.	.	.	.	.	.	.	.	.	.	.	.	84. Escape and Rescue.
.	.	.	.	.	.	.	.	.	.	.	.	85. Other Offences.
												Offences against Religion.
.	.	.	.	.	.	.	.	.	.	.	.	86. Blasphemy, &c.
												Offences against Law of Nations.
.	.	.	.	.	.	.	.	.	.	.	.	87. Piracy.
.	.	.	.	.	.	.	.	.	.	.	.	88. Slave Trade.
.	.	1	.	.	.	.	.	1	.	.	.	89. Libel.
.	.	.	.	.	.	.	.	.	.	.	.	90. Nuisances.
.	.	[illegible]	.	.	.	.	.	2	1	.	.	91. Indecent Exposure.
.	.	.	.	.	.	.	.	.	.	.	.	92. Keeping Disorderly Houses.
.	.	.	.	.	.	.	.	.	.	.	.	93. Other Nuisances.
.	.	[illegible]	.	.	.	.	.	.	.	[illegible]	.	94. Suicide (attempting to commit).
.	.	.	.	.	.	.	.	.	.	.	.	95. Other Misdemeanours.
.	.	[illegible]	.	.	.	1	1	1	[illegible]	[illegible]	.	Total of Class VI.
1	[illegible]	[illegible]	.	.	[illegible]	[illegible]	[illegible]	[illegible]	[illegible]	[illegible]	[illegible]	GRAND TOTAL.

TABLE 2.—QUARTER SESSIONS.—Number of Persons for Trial,

OFFENCES. (1)	Committed for Trial: Total (2)	Males (3)	Females (4)	Not Tried: (5)	(6)	(7)	(8)	(9)	Convicted and: (10)	(11)	(12)
Class I.—Offences against the Person.											
1. Murder,	.	.	.	.	.	.	.	.	.	.	.
2. Attempt to Murder,	[illegible]	[illegible]	[illegible]	[illegible]	.	.	[illegible]	.	.	.	.
3. Conspiracy or Incitement to Murder,	.	.	.	.	.	.	.	.	.	.	.
4. Manslaughter,	[illegible]	[illegible]	.	.	[illegible]	.	[illegible]	.	.	.	.
5. Felonious Wounding,	[illegible]	[illegible]	.	[illegible]	[illegible]	.	[illegible]	.	[illegible]	.	.
6. Endangering Railway Passengers,	[illegible]	[illegible]	.	.	[illegible]	.	.	.	.	.	.
7. Malicious Wounding (Misdemeanour),	[illegible]	[illegible]	[illegible]	[illegible]	[illegible]	.	[illegible]	.	[illegible]	.	[illegible]
8. Assault,	[illegible]	[illegible]	7	[illegible]	[illegible]	.	[illegible]	[illegible]	[illegible]	.	.
9. Intimidation and Molestation,	[illegible]	[illegible]	[illegible]	.	[illegible]	.	.	.	.	.	.
10. Cruelty to Children,	[illegible]	[illegible]	.	.	.	.	.	.	[illegible]	.	.
11. Abandoning Children under two years,	[illegible]	.	[illegible]	[illegible]	.	.	.	.	[illegible]	.	.
12. Child Stealing,	.	.	.	.	.	.	.	.	.	.	.
13. Procuring Abortion,	.	.	.	.	.	.	.	.	.	.	.
14. Concealment of Birth,	[illegible]	.	[illegible]	.	.	.	.	.	[illegible]	.	.
15. Unnatural Offences,	.	.	.	.	.	.	.	.	.	.	.
16. Attempts to Commit Unnatural Offences,	.	.	.	.	.	.	.	.	.	.	.
17. Indecency with Males,	[illegible]	[illegible]	.	.	[illegible]	.	.	.	[illegible]	.	.
18. Rape,	[illegible]	[illegible]	.	.	.	.	[illegible]	.	.	.	.
19. Indecent Assault on Females,	[illegible]	[illegible]	.	[illegible]	[illegible]	.	[illegible]	.	[illegible]	.	.
20. Defilement of Girls under 13,	[illegible]	[illegible]	.	[illegible]	.	.	.	.	[illegible]	.	.
21. Defilement of Girls under 16,	[illegible]	[illegible]	.	.	[illegible]	.	.	.	[illegible]	.	.
22. Householder permitting Defilement of Girls,	.	.	.	.	.	.	.	.	.	.	.
23. Procuration,	.	.	.	.	.	.	.	.	.	.	.
24. Abduction,	[illegible]	.	[illegible]	.	[illegible]	.	.	.	.	.	.
25. Bigamy,	[illegible]	[illegible]	.	.	.	.	.	.	[illegible]	.	.
26. Other Offences against the Person,	[illegible]	[illegible]	.	.	.	.	.	.	[illegible]	.	.
Total of Class I.	[illegible]	[illegible]	[illegible]	[illegible]	[illegible]	.	[illegible]	[illegible]	[illegible]	.	[illegible]
Class II.—Offences against Property with Violence.											
27. Sacrilege,	.	.	.	.	.	.	.	.	.	.	.
28. Burglary,	[illegible]	[illegible]	.	.	[illegible]	.	.	.	[illegible]	.	[illegible]
29. Housebreaking,	[illegible]	[illegible]	[illegible]	[illegible]	[illegible]	.	[illegible]	.	[illegible]	.	[illegible]
30. Shopbreaking,	[illegible]	[illegible]	.	[illegible]	.	.	[illegible]	.	[illegible]	.	.
31. Attempts to break into Houses, Shops, &c.,	.	.	.	.	.	.	.	.	.	.	.
32. Entering with intent to Commit Felony,	[illegible]	[illegible]	[illegible]	[illegible]	.	.	[illegible]	.	[illegible]	.	.
33. Possession of Housebreaking Tools, &c.,	.	.	.	.	.	.	.	.	.	.	.
34. Robbery,	[illegible]	[illegible]	.	.	.	.	[illegible]	.	[illegible]	.	[illegible]
35. Extortion by Threats to Accuse,	.	.	.	.	.	.	.	.	.	.	.
36. Extortion by other Threats,	.	.	.	.	.	.	.	.	.	.	.
Total of Class II.	[illegible]	[illegible]	[illegible]	[illegible]	[illegible]	.	[illegible]	.	[illegible]	.	[illegible]
Class III.—Offences against Property without Violence.											
37. Larceny of Horses and Cattle,	[illegible]	[illegible]	.	[illegible]	7	[illegible]	[illegible]	.	[illegible]	.	[illegible]
38. Larceny from the Person,	[illegible]	[illegible]	[illegible]	[illegible]	[illegible]	.	[illegible]	.	[illegible]	.	[illegible]
39. Larceny in House,	[illegible]	[illegible]	[illegible]	.	.	.	[illegible]	.	[illegible]	.	[illegible]
40. Larceny by a Servant,	[illegible]	[illegible]	[illegible]	.	[illegible]	.	.	.	[illegible]	.	.
41. Embezzlement,	[illegible]	[illegible]	.	[illegible]	[illegible]	.	[illegible]	.	[illegible]	.	.
42. Larceny of Post Letters,	.	.	.	.	.	.	.	.	.	.	.
43. Other Aggravated Larcenies,	[illegible]	[illegible]	.	[illegible]	[illegible]	.	.	.	.	.	.
44. Simple Larceny and Minor Larcenies,	[illegible]	[illegible]	[illegible]	[illegible]	[illegible]	.	[illegible]	.	[illegible]	.	[illegible]
45. Obtaining by False Pretences,	[illegible]	[illegible]	[illegible]	[illegible]	[illegible]	.	[illegible]	.	[illegible]	.	.
46. Frauds by Bankers, &c.,	.	.	.	.	.	.	.	.	.	.	.
47. Falsifying Accounts,	.	.	.	.	.	.	.	.	.	.	.
48. Other Frauds,	[illegible]	[illegible]	.	.	.	.	.	.	[illegible]	.	.
49. Receiving Stolen Goods,	[illegible]	[illegible]	[illegible]	.	.	.	[illegible]	.	[illegible]	.	[illegible]
50. Offences in Bankruptcy,	.	.	.	.	.	.	.	.	.	.	.

QUARTER SESSIONS.

Nature of Offences, and Results of Proceedings.

[illegible]					[illegible]				[illegible]			OFFENCES.
[illegible]	[illegible]	[illegible]	[illegible]	[illegible]	[illegible]	[illegible]	[illegible]	[illegible]	[illegible]	[illegible]	[illegible]	
												Class I.—Offences against the Person.
.	.	.	.	.	.	.	.	.	.	.	.	1. Murder.
.	.	.	.	.	.	.	.	.	.	.	.	2. Attempts to Murder.
.	.	.	.	.	.	.	.	.	.	.	.	3. Conspiracy or Incitement to Murder.
.	.	.	.	.	.	.	.	.	.	.	.	4. Manslaughter.
6	.	.	.	1	.	.	.	.	.	.	.	5. Felonious Wounding.
.	.	.	.	.	.	.	.	.	.	.	.	6. Endangering Railway Passengers.
43	.	1	.	17	.	3	.	[illegible]	6	6	[illegible]	7. Malicious Wounding (Misdemeanour).
38	.	6	.	13	.	.	.	[illegible]	7	[illegible]	[illegible]	8. Assaults.
.	.	.	.	.	.	.	.	.	.	.	.	9. Intimidation and Molestation.
1	.	.	.	.	.	.	.	.	.	.	.	10. Cruelty to Children.
.	.	.	.	1	.	.	.	.	.	.	.	11. Abandoning Children under two years.
.	.	.	.	.	.	[illegible]	.	.	.	.	.	12. Child Stealing.
.	.	.	.	.	.	.	.	.	.	.	.	13. Procuring Abortion.
1	.	.	.	1	.	.	.	.	.	.	.	14. Concealment of Birth.
.	.	.	.	.	.	.	.	.	.	.	.	15. Unnatural Offences.
.	.	.	.	.	.	.	.	.	.	.	.	16. Attempts to Commit Unnatural Offences.
1	.	.	.	.	.	.	.	.	.	.	.	17. Indecency with Males.
.	.	.	.	.	.	.	.	.	.	.	.	18. Rape.
13	.	.	.	3	.	.	.	.	1	.	.	19. Indecent Assaults on Females.
6	.	.	.	.	.	.	.	.	.	.	.	20. Defilement of Girls under 13.
1	.	.	.	.	.	.	.	.	.	.	.	21. Defilement of Girls under 16.
.	.	.	.	.	.	.	.	.	.	.	.	22. Householder permitting Defilement of Girls.
.	.	.	.	.	[illegible]	.	.	.	.	.	.	23. Procuration.
.	.	.	.	.	.	.	.	.	.	.	.	24. Abduction.
[illegible]	.	.	.	.	.	.	.	.	.	.	.	25. Bigamy.
.	.	.	.	1	.	.	.	.	.	.	.	26. Other Offences against the Person.
136	.	6	.	60	.	3	.	4	9	6	4	Total of Class I.
												Class II.—Offences against Property with Violence.
.	.	.	.	.	.	.	.	.	.	.	.	27. Sacrilege.
1	.	.	.	1	.	.	.	.	.	.	.	28. Burglary.
10	.	.	.	2	1	.	.	.	6	1	1	29. Housebreaking.
4	.	.	.	2	3	.	.	.	27	27	9	30. Shopbreaking.
.	.	.	.	.	.	.	.	.	.	.	.	31. Attempts to break into Houses, Shops, &c.
1	.	.	.	1	.	.	.	.	.	.	.	32. Entering with intent to commit Felony.
.	.	.	.	.	.	.	.	.	.	.	.	33. Possession of Housebreaking Tools, &c.
6	.	.	.	.	.	.	.	.	.	.	.	34. Robbery.
.	.	.	.	.	.	.	.	.	.	.	.	35. Extortion by Threats to Accuse.
.	.	.	.	.	.	.	.	.	.	.	.	36. Extortion by other Threats.
25	.	.	.	5	3	.	.	.	40	38	6	Total of Class II.
												Class III.—Offences against Property without Violence.
14	.	.	.	5	.	.	.	.	1	.	.	37. Larceny of Horses and Cattle.
16	.	.	.	1	1	.	.	.	.	.	.	38. Larceny from the Person.
4	1	.	.	.	1	.	.	.	.	.	.	39. Larceny in House.
7	.	.	.	6	.	.	.	.	.	.	.	40. Larceny by a Servant.
1	.	.	.	.	.	.	.	.	6	4	1	41. Embezzlement.
.	.	.	.	.	.	.	.	.	.	.	.	42. Larceny of Post Letters.
.	.	.	.	.	.	.	.	.	1	.	.	43. Other Aggravated Larcenies.
61	.	.	.	17	5	.	.	.	62	11	3	44. Simple Larceny and Minor Larcenies.
30	1	.	1	13	1	.	.	.	11	1	1	45. Obtaining by False Pretences.
.	.	.	.	.	.	.	.	.	.	.	.	46. Frauds by Bankers, &c.
.	.	.	.	.	.	.	.	.	.	.	.	47. Falsifying Accounts.
1	.	.	.	.	.	.	.	.	.	.	.	48. Other Frauds.
10	.	.	.	3	1	.	.	.	1	6	4	49. Receiving Stolen Goods.
.	.	.	.	.	.	.	.	.	.	.	.	50. Offences in Bankruptcy.
156	2	.	.	50	10	.	.	.	84	23	16	Total of Class III.

ASSIZES AND

TABLE 3—*continued*.—QUARTER SESSIONS.—Number of Persons for Trial,

OFFENCES.	Persons sent for Trial: Total.	Males.	Females.	Not Tried: [illegible]	[illegible]	[illegible]	Acquitted.	[illegible]	Convicted and: Total	[illegible]	[illegible]
(1)	(2)	(3)	(4)	(5)	(6)	(7)	(8)	(9)	(10)	(11)	(12)
Class IV.—Malicious Injuries to Property.											
53. Arson,	[illegible]	[illegible]	[illegible]	[illegible]	[illegible]	.	[illegible]	.	[illegible]	.	[illegible]
54. Setting Fire to Crops, &c.,	[illegible]	[illegible]	.	-	-	.	-	.	[illegible]	-	[illegible]
55. Killing and Maiming Cattle,	[illegible]	[illegible]	.	-	[illegible]	.	[illegible]	.	[illegible]	.	-
56. Malicious Use, &c., of Explosives,	.	-	.	-	.	.	.	.	.	-	.
57. Destroying Ships,	-	-	.	-	.	.	.	.	-	.	.
58. Destroying Railways,	-	-	.	-	.	.	.	.	-	.	.
59. Destroying Trees and Shrubs,	-	-	.	.	.	.	.	.	-	-	.
60. Other Malicious Injuries,	[illegible]	[illegible]	.	[illegible]	[illegible]	.	[illegible]	.	[illegible]	.	[illegible]
Total of Class IV.	[illegible]	[illegible]	[illegible]	[illegible]	[illegible]	-	[illegible]	.	[illegible]	.	[illegible]
Class V.—Forgery and Offences against the Currency.											
61. Forgery and Uttering (Felony),	[illegible]	[illegible]	.	.	.	-	.	.	[illegible]	.	.
62. Forgery (Misdemeanour),	[illegible]	[illegible]	.	.	.	.	[illegible]	.	[illegible]	.	.
63. Coining,	[illegible]	[illegible]	.	[illegible]	.	.	-	.	[illegible]	.	[illegible]
64. Uttering Counterfeit Coin,	[illegible]	[illegible]	.	[illegible]	[illegible]	.	.	.	[illegible]	.	.
Total of Class V.	[illegible]	[illegible]	.	[illegible]	[illegible]	.	[illegible]	.	[illegible]	.	[illegible]
Class VI.—Other Offences not included in the above Classes.											
Offences against the State and Public Order.											
65. High Treason,	.	.	.	.	.	.	-	.	.	.	.
66. Treason Felony,	.	.	.	.	-	.	-	.	.	.	.
67. Riot,	[illegible]	[illegible]	.	.	[illegible]	.	-	.	.	.	.
68. Unlawful Assembly,	[illegible]	[illegible]	.	[illegible]	.	.	.	.	[illegible]	.	.
69. Intimidation by Threatening Letters, Notices, or otherwise,	-	.	.	.	.	-	.	.	-	.	.
70. Demand or Robbery of Arms,	.	-	.	-	-	.	-	.	-	-	.
71. Assaulting Dwelling Houses, by firing shots into them,	-	.	.	.	.	.	.	.	.	.	.
72. Other Offences,	[illegible]	[illegible]	.	[illegible]	[illegible]	-	[illegible]	.	-	.	.
Offences against Public Justice.											
71. [illegible] by Officers, &c.,	.	.	.	.	.	.	.	.	-	.	-
72. Bribery, &c.,	.	.	.	.	.	.	.	.	.	.	.
73. Perjury,	-	.	.	.	.	.	.	.	-	.	.
74. Escape and Rescue,	[illegible]	[illegible]	[illegible]	[illegible]	[illegible]	.	[illegible]	.	[illegible]	.	.
75. Other Offences,	[illegible]	[illegible]	[illegible]	.	.	.	-	.	[illegible]	.	.
Offences against Religion.											
76. Blasphemy, &c.,	.	.	.	.	.	.	.	.	.	.	.
Offences against Law of Nations.											
77. Piracy,	.	.	-	.	.	.	.	.	.	.	.
78. Slave Trade,	.	-	.	.	.	.	.	-	.	.	.
79. Libel,	-	-	.	.	.	.	.	.	-	.	.
80. Publishing,	.	.	-	.	.	.	-	.	.	-	.
81. Indecent Exposure,	[illegible]	[illegible]	-	.	.	.	[illegible]	.	[illegible]	-	.
82. Keeping Disorderly Houses,	.	.	.	.	.	.	.	-	.	.	.
83. Other Nuisances,	.	.	.	.	.	.	.	-	.	.	.
84. Suicide (attempting to commit),	[illegible]	[illegible]	[illegible]	.	[illegible]	[illegible]	[illegible]	[illegible]	[illegible]	.	.
85. Other Misdemeanours,	[illegible]	[illegible]	[illegible]	[illegible]	[illegible]	.	[illegible]	.	[illegible]	.	.
Total of Class VI.	[illegible]	[illegible]	[illegible]	[illegible]	[illegible]	[illegible]	[illegible]	[illegible]	[illegible]	.	.
GRAND TOTAL	[illegible]	[illegible]	[illegible]	[illegible]	[illegible]	[illegible]	[illegible]	[illegible]	[illegible]	.	[illegible]

QUARTER SESSIONS.

Nature of Offences, and Results of Proceedings.

[illegible]					[illegible]				[illegible]			OFFENCES.
[illegible]	[illegible]	[illegible]	[illegible]	[illegible]	[illegible]	[illegible]	[illegible]	[illegible]	[illegible]	[illegible]	[illegible]	
												Class IV.—Malicious Injuries to Property.
4	.	.	.	.	.	.	.	.	.	.	.	51. Arson.
.	.	.	.	.	.	.	.	.	.	.	.	52. Setting Fire to Crops, &c.
6	1	.	.	.	.	.	.	.	.	.	.	53. Killing and Maiming Cattle.
.	.	.	.	.	.	.	.	.	.	.	.	54. [illegible] &c., of Machinery.
.	.	.	.	.	.	.	.	.	.	.	.	55. Destroying Ships.
.	.	.	.	.	.	.	.	.	.	.	.	56. Destroying Railways.
.	.	.	.	.	.	.	.	.	.	.	.	57. Destroying Trees and Shrubs.
75	.	.	.	8	.	.	.	.	.	.	.	58. Other Malicious Injuries.
[illegible]	1	.	.	3	.	.	.	.	.	.	.	Total of Class IV.
												Class V.—Forgery and Offences against the Currency.
4	.	.	.	.	.	.	.	.	.	.	.	59. Forging and Uttering (Felony).
9	.	.	.	.	.	.	.	.	.	.	.	60. Forgery (Misdemeanour).
1	.	.	.	.	.	.	.	.	.	.	.	61. Coining.
5	.	.	.	.	.	.	.	.	1	.	.	62. Uttering Counterfeit Coin.
9	.	.	.	.	.	.	.	.	1	.	.	Total of Class V.
												Class VI.—Other Offences not included in the above Classes.
												Offences against the State and Public Order.
.	.	.	.	.	.	.	.	.	.	.	.	63. High Treason.
.	.	.	.	.	.	.	.	.	.	.	.	64. Treason Felony.
.	.	.	.	.	.	.	.	.	.	.	.	65. Riot.
3	.	.	.	4	.	.	.	.	.	.	.	66. Unlawful Assembly.
.	.	.	.	.	.	.	.	.	.	.	.	67. Intimidation by Threatening Letters, Notices, or otherwise.
.	.	.	.	.	.	.	.	.	.	.	.	68. Demand or Robbery of Arms.
.	.	.	.	.	.	.	.	.	.	.	.	69. Attacking Dwelling Houses (by firing shots).
.	.	.	.	.	.	.	.	.	.	.	.	70. Other Offences.
												Offences against Public Justice.
.	.	.	.	.	.	.	.	.	.	.	.	71. Extortion by Officers, &c.
.	.	.	.	.	.	.	.	.	.	.	.	72. Bribery, &c.
.	.	.	.	.	.	.	.	.	.	.	.	73. Perjury.
3	.	.	.	[illegible]	.	.	.	.	1	4	[illegible]	74. Rescue and Escape.
.	.	.	.	3	.	.	.	.	.	.	.	75. Other Offences.
												Offences against Religion.
.	.	.	.	.	.	.	.	.	.	.	.	76. Blasphemy, &c.
												Offences against Law of Nations.
.	.	.	.	.	.	.	.	.	.	.	.	77. Piracy.
.	.	.	.	.	.	.	.	.	.	.	.	78. Slave Trade.
.	.	.	.	.	.	.	.	.	.	.	.	79. Libel.
.	.	.	.	.	.	.	.	.	.	.	.	80. Poaching.
1	.	.	.	.	.	.	.	.	.	.	.	81. Indecent Exposure.
.	.	.	.	.	.	.	.	.	.	.	.	82. Keeping Disorderly Houses.
.	.	.	.	.	.	.	.	.	.	.	.	83. Other Nuisances.
4	.	.	.	8	.	.	.	.	.	.	.	84. [illegible].
7	.	.	.	6	.	.	.	.	.	.	.	85. Other Misdemeanours.
[illegible]	.	.	.	[illegible]	.	.	.	.	4	2	[illegible]	Total of Class VI.
[illegible]	4	4	.	[illegible]	[illegible]	9	.	4	[illegible]	71	[illegible]	GRAND TOTAL.

ASSIZES AND

TABLE 4.—QUARTER

OFFENCES.	[illegible]												
	Penal Servitude.												
	Total	Life	[illegible] Years	[illegible] Years	[illegible] Years	[illegible] Years	[illegible] Years	[illegible] Years	[illegible] Years	[illegible] Years	[illegible] Years	[illegible] Years	[illegible] Years
Class I.—Offences against the Person.													
1. Murder,	.	.	.	.	.	.	.	.	.	.	.	.	.
2. Attempt to Murder,	.	.	.	.	.	.	.	.	.	.	.	.	.
3. Conspiracy or Incitement to Murder,	.	.	.	.	.	.	.	.	.	.	.	.	.
4. Manslaughter,	.	.	.	.	.	.	.	.	.	.	.	.	.
5. Felonious Wounding,	.	.	.	.	.	.	.	.	.	.	.	.	.
6. Endangering Railway Passengers,	.	.	.	.	.	.	.	.	.	.	.	.	.
7. Malicious Wounding (Misdemeanour),	1	.	.	.	.	.	.	.	.	.	.	.	.
8. Assault,	.	.	.	.	.	.	.	.	.	.	.	.	.
9. Intimidation and Molestation,	.	.	.	.	.	.	.	.	.	.	.	.	.
10. Cruelty to Children,	.	.	.	.	.	.	.	.	.	.	.	.	.
11. Abandoning Children under two years,	.	.	.	.	.	.	.	.	.	.	.	.	.
12. Child Stealing,	.	.	.	.	.	.	.	.	.	.	.	.	.
13. Procuring Abortion,	.	.	.	.	.	.	.	.	.	.	.	.	.
14. Concealment of Birth,	.	.	.	.	.	.	.	.	.	.	.	.	.
15. Unnatural Offences,	.	.	.	.	.	.	.	.	.	.	.	.	.
16. Attempts to Commit Unnatural Offences,	.	.	.	.	.	.	.	.	.	.	.	.	.
17. Indecency with Males,	.	.	.	.	.	.	.	.	.	.	.	.	.
18. Rape,	.	.	.	.	.	.	.	.	.	.	.	.	.
19. Indecent Assaults on Females,	.	.	.	.	.	.	.	.	.	.	.	.	.
20. Defilement of Girls under 13,	.	.	.	.	.	.	.	.	.	.	.	.	.
21. Defilement of Girls under 16,	.	.	.	.	.	.	.	.	.	.	.	.	.
22. Householder permitting Defilement of Girls,	.	.	.	.	.	.	.	.	.	.	.	.	.
23. Procuration,	.	.	.	.	.	.	.	.	.	.	.	.	.
24. Abduction,	.	.	.	.	.	.	.	.	.	.	.	.	.
25. Bigamy,	.	.	.	.	.	.	.	.	.	.	.	.	.
26. Other Offences against the Person,	.	.	.	.	.	.	.	.	.	.	.	.	.
Total of Class I.	1	.	.	.	.	.	.	.	.	.	.	.	.
Class II.—Offences against Property with Violence.													
27. Sacrilege,	.	.	.	.	.	.	.	.	.	.	.	.	.
28. Burglary,	1	.	.	.	.	.	.	1	.	.	.	.	.
29. Housebreaking,	1	.	.	.	.	.	.	.	.	.	.	.	.
30. Shopbreaking,	.	.	.	.	.	.	.	.	.	.	.	.	.
31. Attempts to break into Houses, Shops, &c.,	.	.	.	.	.	.	.	.	.	.	.	.	.
32. Entering with intent to commit Felony,	.	.	.	.	.	.	.	.	.	.	.	.	.
33. Possession of House-breaking Tools, &c.,	.	.	.	.	.	.	.	.	.	.	.	.	.
34. Robbery,	1	.	.	.	.	.	.	.	.	.	.	.	1
35. Extortion by Threats to Accuse,	.	.	.	.	.	.	.	.	.	.	.	.	.
36. Extortion by other Threats,	.	.	.	.	.	.	.	.	.	.	.	.	.
Total of Class II.	3	.	.	.	.	.	.	1	.	.	.	.	1
Class III.—Offences against Property without Violence.													
37. Larceny of Horses and Cattle,	1	.	.	.	.	.	.	.	.	.	.	.	1
38. Larceny from the Person,	6	.	.	.	.	.	.	2	.	.	.	.	1
39. Larceny in House,	1	.	.	.	.	.	.	.	.	.	.	.	1
40. Larceny by a Servant,	.	.	.	.	.	.	.	.	.	.	.	.	.
41. Embezzlement,	.	.	.	.	.	.	.	.	.	.	.	.	.
42. Larceny of Post Letters,	.	.	.	.	.	.	.	.	.	.	.	.	.
43. Other Aggravated Larcenies,	.	.	.	.	.	.	.	.	.	.	.	.	.
44. Simple Larceny and Minor Larcenies,	3	.	.	.	.	.	.	.	.	.	.	.	.
45. Obtaining by False Pretences,	.	.	.	.	.	.	.	.	.	.	.	.	.
46. Frauds by Bankers, &c.,	.	.	.	.	.	.	.	.	.	.	.	.	.
47. Falsifying Accounts,	.	.	.	.	.	.	.	.	.	.	.	.	.
48. Other Frauds,	.	.	.	.	.	.	.	.	.	.	.	.	.
49. Receiving Stolen Goods,	1	.	.	.	.	.	.	.	.	.	.	.	1
50. Offences in Bankruptcy,	.	.	.	.	.	.	.	.	.	.	.	.	.
Total of Class III.	12	.	.	.	.	.	.	2	.	.	.	.	4

QUARTER SESSIONS.

SESSIONS.—Length of Sentences.

[illegible]	[illegible]	[illegible]	[illegible]	[illegible]	[illegible]	[illegible]	[illegible]	[illegible]	[illegible]	[illegible]	[illegible]	OFFENCES.
												Class I.—Offences against the Person.
.	.	.	.	.	.	.	.	.	.	.	.	1. Murder.
.	.	.	.	.	.	.	.	.	.	.	.	2. Attempt to Murder.
.	.	.	.	.	.	.	.	.	.	.	.	3. Conspiracy or &c., to Murder.
.	.	.	.	.	.	.	.	.	.	.	.	4. Manslaughter.
.	.	[illegible]	.	.	[illegible]	.	[illegible]	[illegible]	.	[illegible]	.	5. Felonious Wounding.
.	.	.	.	.	.	.	.	.	.	.	.	6. Endangering Railway Passengers.
.	1	[illegible]	.	.	[illegible]	1	[illegible]	[illegible]	[illegible]	[illegible]	.	7. Malicious Wounding (Misdemeanour).
.	.	[illegible]	.	.	.	[illegible]	[illegible]	[illegible]	[illegible]	[illegible]	[illegible]	8. Assaults.
.	.	.	.	.	.	.	.	.	.	.	.	9. Intimidation and Molestation.
.	.	[illegible]	.	.	.	.	.	.	[illegible]	.	.	10. Cruelty to Children.
.	.	.	.	.	.	.	.	.	.	.	.	11. Abandoning Children under two years.
.	.	.	.	.	.	.	.	.	.	.	.	12. Child Stealing.
.	.	.	.	.	.	.	.	.	.	.	.	13. Procuring Abortion.
.	.	1	.	.	.	.	.	.	.	.	1	14. Concealment of Birth.
.	.	.	.	.	.	.	.	.	.	.	.	15. Unnatural Offences.
.	.	.	.	.	.	.	.	.	.	.	.	16. Attempts to Commit Unnatural Offences.
.	.	[illegible]	.	1	.	1	.	[illegible]	.	.	.	17. Indecency with Males.
.	.	.	.	.	.	.	.	.	.	.	.	18. Rape.
.	.	[illegible]	.	[illegible]	1	[illegible]	[illegible]	[illegible]	[illegible]	.	.	19. Indecent Assaults on Females.
.	.	[illegible]	.	1	.	.	[illegible]	[illegible]	.	.	.	20. Defilement of Girls under 13.
.	.	1	.	.	1	.	.	.	.	.	.	21. Defilement of Girls under 16.
.	.	.	.	.	.	.	.	.	.	.	.	22. Householder permitting Defilement of Girls.
.	.	.	.	.	.	.	.	.	.	.	.	23. Procuration.
.	.	.	.	.	.	.	.	.	.	.	.	24. Abduction.
.	.	[illegible]	.	.	.	.	.	[illegible]	1	.	.	25. Bigamy.
.	.	.	.	.	.	.	.	.	.	.	.	26. Other Offences against the Person.
.	1	[illegible]	.	[illegible]	[illegible]	[illegible]	[illegible]	[illegible]	[illegible]	[illegible]	[illegible]	Total of Class I.
												Class II.—Offences against Property with Violence.
.	.	.	.	.	.	.	.	.	.	.	.	27. Sacrilege.
.	.	[illegible]	.	.	.	1	.	1	.	.	.	28. Burglary.
.	1	[illegible]	.	.	.	1	1	[illegible]	[illegible]	[illegible]	.	29. Housebreaking.
.	.	[illegible]	.	.	1	1	[illegible]	[illegible]	1	.	.	30. Shopbreaking.
.	.	.	.	.	.	.	.	.	.	.	.	31. Attempts to break into Houses, Shops, &c.
.	.	1	.	.	.	.	.	.	.	1	.	32. Entering with intent to Commit Felony.
.	.	.	.	.	.	.	.	.	.	.	.	33. Possession of Housebreaking Tools, &c.
.	.	[illegible]	.	.	1	[illegible]	1	[illegible]	.	.	.	34. Robbery.
.	.	.	.	.	.	.	.	.	.	.	.	35. Extortion by Threats to Accuse.
.	.	.	.	.	.	.	.	.	.	.	.	36. Extortion by other Threats.
.	1	[illegible]	.	.	1	[illegible]	[illegible]	[illegible]	[illegible]	[illegible]	.	Total of Class II.
												Class III.—Offences against Property without Violence.
.	.	[illegible]	.	1	.	[illegible]	1	[illegible]	[illegible]	[illegible]	.	37. Larceny of Horses and Cattle.
.	.	[illegible]	.	1	[illegible]	[illegible]	[illegible]	1	[illegible]	[illegible]	.	38. Larceny from the Person.
.	.	[illegible]	.	.	.	[illegible]	1	[illegible]	1	.	.	39. Larceny in House.
.	.	[illegible]	.	.	1	1	1	[illegible]	.	1	.	40. Larceny by a Servant.
.	.	[illegible]	.	.	.	[illegible]	.	[illegible]	[illegible]	.	.	41. Embezzlement.
.	.	.	.	.	.	.	.	.	.	.	.	42. Larceny of Post Letters.
.	.	.	.	.	.	.	.	.	.	.	.	43. Other Aggravated Larcenies.
.	[illegible]	[illegible]	.	.	.	[illegible]	[illegible]	[illegible]	[illegible]	[illegible]	1	44. Simple Larceny and Minor Larcenies.
.	.	[illegible]	.	1	.	[illegible]	1	[illegible]	[illegible]	[illegible]	.	45. Obtaining by False Pretences.
.	.	.	.	.	.	.	.	.	.	.	.	46. Frauds by Bankers, &c.
.	.	.	.	.	.	.	.	.	.	.	.	47. Falsifying Accounts.
.	.	1	.	.	.	.	.	.	1	.	.	48. Other Frauds.
.	.	[illegible]	.	.	.	1	[illegible]	[illegible]	[illegible]	1	1	49. Receiving Stolen Goods.
.	.	.	.	.	.	.	.	.	.	.	.	50. Offences in Bankruptcy.
.	[illegible]	[illegible]	.	[illegible]	[illegible]	[illegible]	[illegible]	[illegible]	[illegible]	[illegible]	[illegible]	Total of Class III.

Class VI.—Other Offences not included in the above Classes.

Offences against the State and Public Order.

High Treason, ...
Treason Felony, ...
Riot, ...
Unlawful Assembly, ...
Intimidation by Threatening Letters, Notices, or otherwise,
Demand or Robbery of Arms, ...
Assaulting Dwelling Houses (by firing shots into them),
Other Offences, ...

Offences against Public Justice.

Extortion by Officers, &c., ...
Bribery, &c., ...
Perjury, ...
Rescue and Escape, ...
Other Offences, ...

Offences against Religion.

Blasphemy, &c., ...

Offences against Law of Nations.

Piracy, ...
Slave Trade, ...

Libel, ...
[illegible], ...
Indecent Exposure, ...
Keeping Disorderly Houses, ...
Other Nuisances, ...
Suicide (attempting to commit), ...
Other Misdemeanours, ...

QUARTER SESSIONS.

SESSIONS.—Length of Sentences.

[illegible] Years	[illegible] Years	[illegible]	[illegible]	[illegible]	[illegible]	[illegible]	[illegible]	[illegible]	[illegible]	[illegible]	[illegible]	OFFENCES.
												Class IV.—Malicious Injuries to Property.
.	.	4	.	.	1	1	.	1	.	1	.	51. Arson.
.	1	.	.	.	.	.	.	.	.	.	.	52. Setting Fire to Crops, &c.
.	.	.	.	.	.	.	.	.	.	.	.	53. Killing and Maiming Cattle.
.	.	1	.	.	.	1	.	.	.	.	.	54. Malicious Use, &c., of Explosives.
.	.	.	.	.	.	.	.	.	.	.	.	55. Destroying Ships.
.	.	.	.	.	.	.	.	.	.	.	.	56. Destroying Railways.
.	.	.	.	.	.	.	.	.	.	.	.	57. Destroying Trees and Shrubs.
.	.	12	.	.	.	1	3	2	8	1	1	58. Other Malicious Injuries.
.	1	17	.	.	1	8	7	4	8	3	8	Total of Class IV.
												Class V.—Forgery and Offences against the Currency.
.	.	4	.	.	.	3	.	8	.	.	.	59. Forgery and Uttering (Felony).
.	.	8	.	.	.	.	.	1	.	.	1	60. Forgery (Misdemeanour).
.	1	1	.	.	.	1	.	.	.	.	.	61. Coining.
.	.	7	.	.	.	.	.	.	1	1	.	62. Uttering Counterfeit Coin.
.	1	9	.	.	.	3	.	4	1	1	1	Total of Class V.
												Class VI.—Other Offences not included in the above Classes.
												Offences against the State and Public Order.
.	.	.	.	.	.	.	.	.	.	.	.	63. High Treason.
.	.	.	.	.	.	.	.	.	.	.	.	64. Treason Felony.
.	.	.	.	.	.	.	.	.	.	.	.	65. Riot.
.	.	3	.	.	.	.	.	.	8	.	.	66. Unlawful Assembly.
.	.	.	.	.	.	.	.	.	.	.	.	67. Intimidation by Threatening Letters, Notices, or otherwise.
.	.	.	.	.	.	.	.	.	.	.	.	68. Demand or Robbery of Arms.
.	.	.	.	.	.	.	.	.	.	.	.	69. Attacking Dwelling Houses (by firing shots into them).
.	.	.	.	.	.	.	.	.	.	.	.	70. Other Offences.
												Offences against Public Justice.
.	.	.	.	.	.	.	.	.	.	.	.	71. Extortion by Officers, &c.
.	.	.	.	.	.	.	.	.	.	.	.	72. Bribery, &c.
.	.	.	.	.	.	.	.	.	.	.	.	73. Perjury.
.	.	3	.	.	.	.	.	1	1	1	.	74. Escape and Rescue.
.	.	.	.	.	.	.	.	.	.	.	.	75. Other Offences.
												Offences against Religion.
.	.	.	.	.	.	.	.	.	.	.	.	76. Blasphemy, &c.
												Offences against Law of Nations.
.	.	.	.	.	.	.	.	.	.	.	.	77. Piracy.
.	.	.	.	.	.	.	.	.	.	.	.	78. Slave Trade.
.	.	.	.	.	.	.	.	.	.	.	.	79. Libel.
.	.	.	.	.	.	.	.	.	.	.	.	80. Nuisances.
.	.	1	.	.	.	.	.	1	.	.	.	81. Indecent Exposure.
.	.	.	.	.	.	.	.	.	.	.	.	82. Keeping Disorderly Houses.
.	.	.	.	.	.	.	.	.	.	.	.	83. Other Nuisances.
.	.	1	.	1	.	.	.	7	.	7	.	84. Suicide (attempting to commit).
.	.	3	.	.	.	.	.	1	7	.	.	85. Other Misdemeanours.
.	.	15	.	1	.	.	.	5	6	5	.	Total of Class VI.
.	10	123	.	4	17	48	37	125	114	41	10	GRAND TOTAL.

TABLE 5.—ASSIZES AND QUARTER SESSIONS.—Numbers of

OFFENCES.	Persons for Trial.			Not Tried.					Convicted, &c.			
	Total.	Males.	Females.	[illegible]	[illegible]	[illegible]	Acquitted.	[illegible]	[illegible]	[illegible]	[illegible]	[illegible]
(1)	(2)	(3)	(4)	(5)	(6)	(7)	(8)	(9)	(10)	(11)	(12)	(13)
Class I.—Offences against the Person.												
Murder	[illegible]	[illegible]	[illegible]	[illegible]	.	1	[illegible]	[illegible]	[illegible]	[illegible]	.	.
Attempt to Murder	[illegible]	[illegible]	[illegible]	[illegible]	.	.	[illegible]	.	[illegible]	.	[illegible]	.
Conspiracy or Incitement to Murder	.	.	.	.	.	.	.	.	.	.	.	.
Manslaughter	[illegible]	[illegible]	[illegible]	[illegible]	[illegible]	1	[illegible]	.	[illegible]	.	[illegible]	[illegible]
Felonious Wounding	[illegible]	[illegible]	[illegible]	[illegible]	[illegible]	1	[illegible]	.	[illegible]	.	[illegible]	[illegible]
Endangering Railway Passengers	[illegible]	[illegible]	[illegible]	.	[illegible]	1	[illegible]	[illegible]	.	.	.	.
Malicious Wounding (Misdemeanour)	[illegible]	[illegible]	[illegible]	[illegible]	[illegible]	.	[illegible]	[illegible]	[illegible]	.	[illegible]	[illegible]
Assault	[illegible]	[illegible]	[illegible]	[illegible]	[illegible]	.	[illegible]	[illegible]	[illegible]	.	.	[illegible]
Intimidation and Molestation	[illegible]	[illegible]	[illegible]	.	[illegible]	.	[illegible]	.	.	.	.	.
Cruelty to Children	[illegible]	[illegible]	[illegible]	.	.	.	[illegible]	.	[illegible]	.	.	[illegible]
Abandoning Children under two years	[illegible]	[illegible]	[illegible]	[illegible]	.	.	.	.	[illegible]	.	.	.
Child Stealing	.	.	.	.	.	.	.	.	.	.	.	.
Procuring Abortion	.	.	.	.	.	.	.	.	.	.	.	.
Concealment of Birth	[illegible]	.	[illegible]	[illegible]	[illegible]	.	[illegible]	.	[illegible]	.	.	[illegible]
Unnatural Offences	[illegible]	[illegible]	.	[illegible]	.	.	[illegible]	.	.	.	.	.
Attempts to commit Unnatural Offences	[illegible]	[illegible]	.	.	.	.	.	.	[illegible]	.	[illegible]	.
Indecency with Males	[illegible]	[illegible]	.	.	[illegible]	.	[illegible]	.	[illegible]	.	.	[illegible]
Rape	[illegible]	[illegible]	.	[illegible]	[illegible]	.	[illegible]	.	[illegible]	.	[illegible]	[illegible]
Indecent Assaults on Females	[illegible]	[illegible]	.	[illegible]	[illegible]	.	[illegible]	.	[illegible]	.	[illegible]	[illegible]
Defilement of Girls under 13	[illegible]	[illegible]	.	[illegible]	.	.	[illegible]	.	[illegible]	.	[illegible]	[illegible]
Defilement of Girls under 16	[illegible]	[illegible]	.	[illegible]	[illegible]	.	.	.	[illegible]	.	.	[illegible]
Householder permitting Defilement of Girls	.	.	.	.	.	.	.	.	.	.	.	.
Procuration	.	.	.	.	.	.	.	.	.	.	.	.
Abduction	[illegible]	[illegible]	[illegible]	.	[illegible]	.	.	.	[illegible]	.	.	[illegible]
Bigamy	[illegible]	[illegible]	[illegible]	.	.	.	[illegible]	.	[illegible]	.	[illegible]	[illegible]
Other Offences against the Person	[illegible]	[illegible]	[illegible]	.	[illegible]	.	.	.	[illegible]	.	.	[illegible]
Total of Class I.	[illegible]	[illegible]	[illegible]	[illegible]	[illegible]	[illegible]	[illegible]	[illegible]	[illegible]	[illegible]	[illegible]	[illegible]
Class II.—Offences against Property with Violence.												
Sacrilege	.	.	.	.	.	.	.	.	.	.	.	.
Burglary	[illegible]	[illegible]	.	.	[illegible]	[illegible]	[illegible]	.	[illegible]	.	[illegible]	[illegible]
Housebreaking	[illegible]	[illegible]	[illegible]	[illegible]	[illegible]	.	[illegible]	[illegible]	[illegible]	.	[illegible]	[illegible]
Shopbreaking	[illegible]	[illegible]	.	[illegible]	.	.	[illegible]	.	[illegible]	.	[illegible]	[illegible]
Attempts to break into Houses, Shops, &c.	[illegible]	[illegible]	.	.	.	.	.	.	[illegible]	.	.	[illegible]
Entering with intent to commit Felony	[illegible]	[illegible]	[illegible]	[illegible]	.	.	[illegible]	.	[illegible]	.	.	[illegible]
Possession of Housebreaking Tools, &c.	.	.	.	.	.	.	.	.	.	.	.	.
Robbery	[illegible]	[illegible]	[illegible]	[illegible]	.	.	[illegible]	.	[illegible]	.	[illegible]	[illegible]
Extortion by Threats to Accuse	.	.	.	.	.	.	.	.	.	.	.	.
Extortion by other Threats	.	.	.	.	.	.	.	.	.	.	.	.
Total of Class II.	[illegible]	[illegible]	[illegible]	[illegible]	[illegible]	[illegible]	[illegible]	[illegible]	[illegible]	.	[illegible]	[illegible]
Class III.—Offences against Property without Violence.												
Larceny of Horses and Cattle	[illegible]	[illegible]	[illegible]	[illegible]	[illegible]	[illegible]	[illegible]	.	[illegible]	.	[illegible]	[illegible]
Larceny from the Person	[illegible]	[illegible]	[illegible]	[illegible]	[illegible]	.	[illegible]	.	[illegible]	.	[illegible]	[illegible]
Larceny in House	[illegible]	[illegible]	[illegible]	.	.	.	[illegible]	.	[illegible]	.	[illegible]	[illegible]
Larceny by a Servant	[illegible]	[illegible]	[illegible]	.	[illegible]	.	[illegible]	.	[illegible]	.	.	[illegible]
Embezzlement	[illegible]	[illegible]	.	[illegible]	[illegible]	.	[illegible]	.	[illegible]	.	.	[illegible]
Larceny of Post Letters	[illegible]	[illegible]	.	.	.	.	.	.	[illegible]	.	.	[illegible]
Other Aggravated Larcenies	[illegible]	[illegible]	.	[illegible]	[illegible]	.	.	.	.	.	.	.
Simple Larceny and Minor Larcenies	[illegible]	[illegible]	[illegible]	[illegible]	[illegible]	[illegible]	[illegible]	.	[illegible]	.	[illegible]	[illegible]
Obtaining by False Pretences	[illegible]	[illegible]	[illegible]	[illegible]	[illegible]	.	[illegible]	.	[illegible]	.	[illegible]	[illegible]
Frauds by Bankers, &c.	.	.	.	.	.	.	.	.	.	.	.	.
Falsifying Accounts	.	.	.	.	.	.	.	.	.	.	.	.
Other Frauds	[illegible]	[illegible]	.	.	.	.	[illegible]	.	[illegible]	.	.	[illegible]
Receiving Stolen Goods	[illegible]	[illegible]	[illegible]	.	[illegible]	.	[illegible]	.	[illegible]	.	[illegible]	[illegible]
Offences in Bankruptcy	[illegible]	[illegible]	.	.	.	.	[illegible]	.	[illegible]	.	.	[illegible]

QUARTER SESSIONS.

Persons for Trial, Nature of Offences, and Results of Proceedings.

[illegible]				[illegible]				[illegible]					OFFENCES.
(16)	(17)	(18)	(19)	(20)	(21)	(22)	(23)	(24)	(25)	(26)	(27)	(28)	
													Class I.—Offences against the Person.
.	.	.	.	.	.	.	.	.	.	.	.	3	1. Murder.
.	.	.	.	.	.	.	.	.	.	.	.	.	2. Attempt to Murder.
.	.	.	.	.	.	.	.	.	.	.	.	.	3. Conspiracy or Incitement to Murder.
.	.	.	6	.	.	.	.	6	.	.	.	.	4. Manslaughter.
.	.	.	6	.	.	.	1	.	.	.	.	.	5. Felonious Wounding.
.	.	.	.	.	.	.	.	.	.	.	.	.	6. Endangering Railway Passengers.
.	1	.	10	.	1	.	11	[illegible]	6	2	.	.	7. Malicious Wounding (Misdemeanour).
.	6	.	[illegible]	.	1	.	1	11	1	7	.	.	8. Assault.
.	.	.	.	.	.	.	.	.	.	.	.	.	9. Intimidation and Molestation.
.	.	.	3	.	.	.	.	.	.	.	.	.	10. Cruelty to Children.
.	.	.	9	.	.	.	.	.	.	.	.	.	11. Abandoning Children under two years.
.	.	.	.	.	.	.	.	.	.	.	.	.	12. Child Stealing.
.	.	.	.	.	.	.	.	.	.	.	.	.	13. Procuring Abortion.
.	.	.	[illegible]	.	.	.	.	1	.	.	.	.	14. Concealment of Birth.
.	.	.	.	.	.	.	.	.	.	.	.	.	15. Unnatural Offences.
.	.	.	.	.	.	.	.	.	.	.	.	.	16. Attempts to commit Unnatural Offences.
.	.	.	.	.	.	.	.	.	.	.	.	.	17. Indecency with Males.
.	.	.	.	.	.	.	.	1	.	.	.	.	18. Rape.
.	.	.	1	.	.	.	.	4	1	.	.	.	19. Indecent Assaults on Females.
.	.	.	1	.	.	.	.	3	.	.	.	.	20. Defilement of Girls under 13.
.	.	.	.	.	.	.	.	.	.	.	.	.	21. Defilement of Girls under 16.
.	.	.	.	.	.	.	.	.	.	.	.	.	22. Householder permitting defilement of Girls.
.	.	.	.	.	.	.	.	.	.	.	.	.	23. Procuration.
.	.	.	.	.	.	.	.	.	.	.	.	.	24. Abduction.
.	.	.	.	.	.	.	.	.	.	.	.	.	25. Bigamy.
.	.	.	3	.	.	.	.	.	.	.	.	.	26. Other Offences against the Person.
.	1	.	[illegible]	.	1	.	[illegible]	[illegible]	6	6	.	3	Total of Class I.
													Class II.—Offences against Property with Violence.
.	.	.	.	.	.	.	.	.	.	.	.	.	27. Sacrilege.
.	.	.	3	.	.	.	.	[illegible]	6	1	.	.	28. Burglary.
.	.	.	3	1	.	.	.	4	1	1	.	.	29. Housebreaking.
.	.	.	6	6	.	.	.	[illegible]	[illegible]	3	.	.	30. Shopbreaking.
.	.	.	.	.	.	.	.	.	.	.	.	.	31. Attempts to break into Houses, Shops, &c.
1	.	.	8	.	.	.	.	.	.	1	.	.	32. Entering with intent to Commit Felony.
.	.	.	.	.	.	.	.	.	.	.	.	.	33. Possession of Housebreaking Tools, &c.
.	.	.	.	.	.	.	.	3	.	.	.	.	34. Robbery.
.	.	.	.	.	.	.	.	.	.	.	.	.	35. Extortion by Threats to Accuse.
.	.	.	.	.	.	.	.	.	.	.	.	.	36. Extortion by other Threats.
1	.	.	[illegible]	6	.	.	.	[illegible]	[illegible]	6	.	.	Total of Class II.
													Class III.—Offences against Property without Violence.
.	.	.	9	.	.	.	.	9	.	.	.	.	37. Larceny of Horses and Cattle.
.	.	.	9	1	.	.	.	.	.	.	.	.	38. Larceny from the Person.
1	.	.	1	1	.	.	.	1	9	.	.	.	39. Larceny in a House.
.	.	.	1	.	.	.	.	.	.	.	.	.	40. Larceny by a Servant.
.	.	.	1	.	.	.	.	[illegible]	11	.	.	.	41. Embezzlement.

TABLE 5—*continued*.—ASSIZES AND QUARTER SESSIONS.—Numbers of

OFFENCES. (1)	Persons for Trial. Total. (2)	Males. (3)	Females. (4)	Not Tried. No Prosecution. (5)	No Bill. (6)	Found Insane on Arraignment. (7)	Acquitted. (8)	Special Verdict of Guilty, but Insane. (9)	Convicted and Total. (10)	Death. (11)	Penal Servitude. (12)	Imprisonment. (13)
Class IV.—Malicious Injuries to Property.												
[illegible]. Arson.	[illegible]	[illegible]	[illegible]	[illegible]	[illegible]		[illegible]	.	[illegible]	.	1	[illegible]
[illegible]. Setting Fire to Crops, &c.	[illegible]	[illegible]	.	.	.	.	.	.	7	.	1	1
[illegible]. Killing and Maiming Cattle	6	5		1	1	.	1	.	[illegible]	.	.	[illegible]
[illegible]. Malicious Injuries, &c., by Explosives	[illegible]	[illegible]			.	.	.	.	[illegible]	.	.	1
[illegible]. Destroying Ships			.	.	.	.	.	.	.	.	.	.
[illegible]. Destroying Railways				.	.	.	.	.	.	.	.	.
[illegible]. Destroying Trees and Shrubs				.	.	.	.	.	.	.	.	.
[illegible]. Other Malicious Injuries	[illegible]	[illegible]	[illegible]	1	[illegible]		[illegible]	.	[illegible]	.	1	[illegible]
Total of Class IV.	[illegible]	[illegible]	[illegible]	[illegible]	[illegible]	.	14	.	[illegible]	.	[illegible]	[illegible]
Class V.—Forgery and Offences against the Currency.												
[illegible]. Forgery and Uttering (Felony)	[illegible]	[illegible]	1	[illegible]	.	.	[illegible]	.	[illegible]	-	.	[illegible]
[illegible]. Forgery (Misdemeanour)	[illegible]	[illegible]	-	.	-	.	[illegible]	-	[illegible]	-	.	[illegible]
[illegible]. Coining	[illegible]	4	-	1			.	-	[illegible]	.	[illegible]	1
[illegible]. Uttering Counterfeit Coin	6	[illegible]	.	1	[illegible]	.	1	.	[illegible]	.	-	[illegible]
Total of Class V.	[illegible]	[illegible]	1	1	[illegible]	.	[illegible]	-	[illegible]	.	[illegible]	[illegible]
Class VI.—Other Offences not included in the above Classes.												
Offences against the State and Public Order.												
[illegible]. High Treason	.	.	.	.	.	.	.	.	.	.	.	.
[illegible]. Treason Felony	.	.	.	.	.	.	.	.	.	.	.	.
[illegible]. Riot	[illegible]	[illegible]	.	.	[illegible]	.	1	.	[illegible]	.	.	[illegible]
[illegible]. Unlawful Assembly	[illegible]	[illegible]	.	[illegible]	.	.	[illegible]	.	[illegible]	.	.	4
[illegible]. Intimidation by Threatening Letters, Notices, or otherwise	1	1	.	.	.	.	.	.	1	.	.	[illegible]
[illegible]. Dispersal or Robbery of Arms	.	.	.	.	.	.	.	.	.	.	.	.
[illegible]. Assaulting Dwelling Houses (by firing into them)	.	.	.	.	.	.	.	.	.	.	.	.
[illegible]. Other Offences	[illegible]	[illegible]	1	[illegible]	[illegible]	.	[illegible]	.	1	.	.	1
Offences against Public Justice.												
[illegible]. Extortion by Officers, &c.	.	.	.	.	.	.	.	.	.	.	.	.
[illegible]. Bribery, &c.	[illegible]	[illegible]	.	.	.	.	.	.	[illegible]	.	.	[illegible]
[illegible]. Perjury	[illegible]	[illegible]	[illegible]	[illegible]	[illegible]	.	[illegible]	.	[illegible]	.	.	[illegible]
[illegible]. Rescues and Escapes	[illegible]	[illegible]	[illegible]	[illegible]	[illegible]	.	[illegible]	.	[illegible]	.	.	3
[illegible]. Other Offences	7	5	[illegible]	[illegible]	.	.	.	.	[illegible]	.	.	.
Offences against Religion.												
[illegible]. Blasphemy, &c.	.	.	.	.	.	.	.	.	.	.	.	.
Offences against Law of Nations.												
[illegible]. Piracy	.	.	.	.	.	.	.	.	.	.	.	.
[illegible]. Slave Trade	.	.	.	.	.	.	.	.	.	.	.	.
[illegible]. Libel	[illegible]	[illegible]	.	.	.	.	.	.	1	.	.	[illegible]
[illegible]. [illegible]	.	.	.	.	.	.	.	.	.	.	.	.
[illegible]. Indecent Exposure	[illegible]	[illegible]	.	1	.	.	1	.	[illegible]	.	.	[illegible]
[illegible]. Keeping Disorderly Houses	.	.	.	.	.	.	.	.	.	.	.	.
[illegible]. Other Nuisances	.	.	.	.	.	.	.	.	.	.	.	.
[illegible]. Suicide (attempting to commit)	[illegible]	17	7	[illegible]	[illegible]	[illegible]	1	3	[illegible]	.	-	[illegible]
[illegible]. Other Misdemeanours	[illegible]	[illegible]	[illegible]	[illegible]	[illegible]	.	[illegible]	.	[illegible]	.	.	[illegible]
Total of Class VI.	[illegible]	[illegible]	[illegible]	[illegible]	[illegible]	[illegible]	[illegible]	[illegible]	[illegible]	.	.	[illegible]
GRAND TOTAL	[illegible]	[illegible]	[illegible]	[illegible]	[illegible]	[illegible]	[illegible]	[illegible]	[illegible]	1	[illegible]	[illegible]

QUARTER SESSIONS.

Persons for Trial, Nature of Offences, and Results of Proceedings.

[illegible]				[illegible]				[illegible]					OFFENCES.
(16)	(17)	(18)	(19)	(20)	(21)	(22)	(23)	(24)	(25)	(26)	(27)	(28)	
													Class IV.—Malicious Injuries to Property.
.	.	.	8	.	.	.	1	.	.	.	.	.	54. Arson.
.	.	.	.	.	.	.	.	.	.	.	.	.	55. Setting Fire to Crops, &c.
1	.	.	.	.	.	.	.	1	.	.	.	.	56. Killing and Maiming Cattle.
.	.	.	1	.	.	.	.	.	.	.	.	.	64. Malicious Use, &c., of Explosives.
.	.	.	.	.	.	.	.	.	.	.	.	.	65. Destroying Ships.
.	.	.	.	.	.	.	.	.	.	.	.	.	66. Destroying Railways.
.	.	.	.	.	.	.	.	.	.	.	.	.	67. Destroying Trees and Shrubs.
.	.	.	4	.	.	.	.	[illegible]	.	.	.	.	68. Other Malicious Injuries.
1	.	.	11	.	.	.	1	5	.	.	.	.	Total of Class IV.
													Class V.—Forgery and Offences against the Currency.
.	.	.	.	.	.	.	.	[illegible]	1	.	.	.	69. Forgery and Uttering (Felony).
.	.	.	.	.	.	.	.	1	.	.	.	.	70. Forgery (Misdemeanour).
.	.	.	.	.	.	.	.	.	.	.	.	.	71. Coining.
.	.	.	.	.	.	.	.	1	.	.	.	.	72. Uttering Counterfeit Coin.
.	.	.	.	.	.	.	.	[illegible]	1	.	.	.	Total of Class V.
													Class VI.—Other Offences not included in the above Classes.
													Offences against the State and Public Order.
.	.	.	.	.	.	.	.	.	.	.	.	.	73. High Treason.
.	.	.	.	.	.	.	.	.	.	.	.	.	74. Treason Felony.
.	.	.	8	.	.	.	.	.	.	.	.	.	75. Riot.
.	.	.	[illegible]	.	.	.	.	1	.	.	.	.	76. Unlawful Assembly.
.	.	.	.	.	.	.	.	.	.	.	.	.	77. Intimidation by Threatening Letters, Notices, or otherwise.
.	.	.	.	.	.	.	.	.	.	.	.	.	78. Possession or Delivery of Arms.
.	.	.	.	.	.	.	.	.	.	.	.	.	79. Assaulting Revenue Officers or [illegible]
.	.	.	.	.	.	.	.	.	.	.	.	.	80. Other Offences.
													Offences against Public Justice.
.	.	.	.	.	.	.	.	.	.	.	.	.	81. Extortion by Officers, &c.
.	.	.	.	.	1	.	.	.	.	.	.	.	82. Bribery, &c.
.	.	.	.	.	.	.	.	.	.	.	.	.	83. Perjury.
.	.	.	[illegible]	.	.	.	.	[illegible]	[illegible]	[illegible]	.	.	84. Rescue and Escape.
.	.	.	4	.	.	.	.	.	.	.	.	.	85. Other Offences.
													Offences against Religion.
.	.	.	.	.	.	.	.	.	.	.	.	.	86. Blasphemy, &c.
													Offences against Law of Nations.
.	.	.	.	.	.	.	.	.	.	.	.	.	87. Piracy.
.	.	.	.	.	.	.	.	.	.	.	.	.	88. Slave Trade.
.	.	.	.	.	.	.	.	.	.	.	.	.	89. Libel.
.	.	.	.	.	.	.	.	.	.	.	.	.	90. Gambling.
.	.	.	.	.	.	.	.	.	.	.	.	.	91. [illegible]
.	.	.	.	.	.	.	.	.	.	.	.	.	92. Keeping Disorderly Houses.
.	.	.	.	.	.	.	.	.	.	.	.	.	93. Other Nuisances.
.	.	.	1	.	.	.	.	.	.	.	.	.	94. Suicide (attempting to commit).
.	.	.	7	.	.	.	.	.	.	.	.	.	95. Other Misdemeanours.
.	.	.	[illegible]	.	1	.	.	4	[illegible]	[illegible]	.	.	Total of Class VI.
[illegible]	[illegible]	.	[illegible]	[illegible]	[illegible]	.	[illegible]	[illegible]	[illegible]	[illegible]	.	[illegible]	GRAND TOTAL.

TABLE 6.—ASSIZES AND QUARTER SESSIONS.—Number

OFFENCES.	[illegible]	[illegible]	[illegible]	[illegible]	[illegible]	[illegible]	[illegible]	[illegible]	[illegible]	[illegible]	[illegible]	[illegible]	[illegible]	[illegible]	[illegible]	[illegible]	[illegible]	[illegible]	[illegible]	[illegible]	[illegible]
Class I.—Offences against the Person.																					
1. Murder,	[illegible]	[illegible]	[illegible]	[illegible]	[illegible]	[illegible]	[illegible]	[illegible]	[illegible]	[illegible]	[illegible]	[illegible]	[illegible]	[illegible]	[illegible]	[illegible]	[illegible]	[illegible]	[illegible]	[illegible]	[illegible]
2. Attempt to Murder,	[illegible]	[illegible]	[illegible]	[illegible]	[illegible]	[illegible]	[illegible]	[illegible]	[illegible]	[illegible]	[illegible]	[illegible]	[illegible]	[illegible]	[illegible]	[illegible]	[illegible]	[illegible]	[illegible]	[illegible]	[illegible]
3. Conspiracy or Incitement to Murder,	[illegible]	[illegible]	[illegible]	[illegible]	[illegible]	[illegible]	[illegible]	[illegible]	[illegible]	[illegible]	[illegible]	[illegible]	[illegible]	[illegible]	[illegible]	[illegible]	[illegible]	[illegible]	[illegible]	[illegible]	[illegible]
4. Manslaughter,	[illegible]	[illegible]	[illegible]	[illegible]	[illegible]	[illegible]	[illegible]	[illegible]	[illegible]	[illegible]	[illegible]	[illegible]	[illegible]	[illegible]	[illegible]	[illegible]	[illegible]	[illegible]	[illegible]	[illegible]	[illegible]
5. Felonious Wounding,	[illegible]	[illegible]	[illegible]	[illegible]	[illegible]	[illegible]	[illegible]	[illegible]	[illegible]	[illegible]	[illegible]	[illegible]	[illegible]	[illegible]	[illegible]	[illegible]	[illegible]	[illegible]	[illegible]	[illegible]	[illegible]
6. Endangering Railway Passengers,	[illegible]	[illegible]	[illegible]	[illegible]	[illegible]	[illegible]	[illegible]	[illegible]	[illegible]	[illegible]	[illegible]	[illegible]	[illegible]	[illegible]	[illegible]	[illegible]	[illegible]	[illegible]	[illegible]	[illegible]	[illegible]
7. Malicious Wounding (Misdemeanour),	[illegible]	[illegible]	[illegible]	[illegible]	[illegible]	[illegible]	[illegible]	[illegible]	[illegible]	[illegible]	[illegible]	[illegible]	[illegible]	[illegible]	[illegible]	[illegible]	[illegible]	[illegible]	[illegible]	[illegible]	[illegible]
8. Assault,	[illegible]	[illegible]	[illegible]	[illegible]	[illegible]	[illegible]	[illegible]	[illegible]	[illegible]	[illegible]	[illegible]	[illegible]	[illegible]	[illegible]	[illegible]	[illegible]	[illegible]	[illegible]	[illegible]	[illegible]	[illegible]
9. Intimidation and Molestation,	[illegible]	[illegible]	[illegible]	[illegible]	[illegible]	[illegible]	[illegible]	[illegible]	[illegible]	[illegible]	[illegible]	[illegible]	[illegible]	[illegible]	[illegible]	[illegible]	[illegible]	[illegible]	[illegible]	[illegible]	[illegible]
10. Cruelty to Children,	[illegible]	[illegible]	[illegible]	[illegible]	[illegible]	[illegible]	[illegible]	[illegible]	[illegible]	[illegible]	[illegible]	[illegible]	[illegible]	[illegible]	[illegible]	[illegible]	[illegible]	[illegible]	[illegible]	[illegible]	[illegible]
11. Abandoning Children under two years,	[illegible]	[illegible]	[illegible]	[illegible]	[illegible]	[illegible]	[illegible]	[illegible]	[illegible]	[illegible]	[illegible]	[illegible]	[illegible]	[illegible]	[illegible]	[illegible]	[illegible]	[illegible]	[illegible]	[illegible]	[illegible]
12. Child Stealing,	[illegible]	[illegible]	[illegible]	[illegible]	[illegible]	[illegible]	[illegible]	[illegible]	[illegible]	[illegible]	[illegible]	[illegible]	[illegible]	[illegible]	[illegible]	[illegible]	[illegible]	[illegible]	[illegible]	[illegible]	[illegible]
13. Procuring Abortion,	[illegible]	[illegible]	[illegible]	[illegible]	[illegible]	[illegible]	[illegible]	[illegible]	[illegible]	[illegible]	[illegible]	[illegible]	[illegible]	[illegible]	[illegible]	[illegible]	[illegible]	[illegible]	[illegible]	[illegible]	[illegible]
14. Concealment of Birth,	[illegible]	[illegible]	[illegible]	[illegible]	[illegible]	[illegible]	[illegible]	[illegible]	[illegible]	[illegible]	[illegible]	[illegible]	[illegible]	[illegible]	[illegible]	[illegible]	[illegible]	[illegible]	[illegible]	[illegible]	[illegible]
15. Unnatural Offences,	[illegible]	[illegible]	[illegible]	[illegible]	[illegible]	[illegible]	[illegible]	[illegible]	[illegible]	[illegible]	[illegible]	[illegible]	[illegible]	[illegible]	[illegible]	[illegible]	[illegible]	[illegible]	[illegible]	[illegible]	[illegible]
16. Attempt to Commit Unnatural Offences,	[illegible]	[illegible]	[illegible]	[illegible]	[illegible]	[illegible]	[illegible]	[illegible]	[illegible]	[illegible]	[illegible]	[illegible]	[illegible]	[illegible]	[illegible]	[illegible]	[illegible]	[illegible]	[illegible]	[illegible]	[illegible]
17. Indecency with Males,	[illegible]	[illegible]	[illegible]	[illegible]	[illegible]	[illegible]	[illegible]	[illegible]	[illegible]	[illegible]	[illegible]	[illegible]	[illegible]	[illegible]	[illegible]	[illegible]	[illegible]	[illegible]	[illegible]	[illegible]	[illegible]
18. Rape,	[illegible]	[illegible]	[illegible]	[illegible]	[illegible]	[illegible]	[illegible]	[illegible]	[illegible]	[illegible]	[illegible]	[illegible]	[illegible]	[illegible]	[illegible]	[illegible]	[illegible]	[illegible]	[illegible]	[illegible]	[illegible]
19. Indecent Assaults on Females,	[illegible]	[illegible]	[illegible]	[illegible]	[illegible]	[illegible]	[illegible]	[illegible]	[illegible]	[illegible]	[illegible]	[illegible]	[illegible]	[illegible]	[illegible]	[illegible]	[illegible]	[illegible]	[illegible]	[illegible]	[illegible]
20. Defilement of Girls under 13,	[illegible]	[illegible]	[illegible]	[illegible]	[illegible]	[illegible]	[illegible]	[illegible]	[illegible]	[illegible]	[illegible]	[illegible]	[illegible]	[illegible]	[illegible]	[illegible]	[illegible]	[illegible]	[illegible]	[illegible]	[illegible]
21. Defilement of Girls under 16,	[illegible]	[illegible]	[illegible]	[illegible]	[illegible]	[illegible]	[illegible]	[illegible]	[illegible]	[illegible]	[illegible]	[illegible]	[illegible]	[illegible]	[illegible]	[illegible]	[illegible]	[illegible]	[illegible]	[illegible]	[illegible]
22. Householder permitting Defilement of Girls,	[illegible]	[illegible]	[illegible]	[illegible]	[illegible]	[illegible]	[illegible]	[illegible]	[illegible]	[illegible]	[illegible]	[illegible]	[illegible]	[illegible]	[illegible]	[illegible]	[illegible]	[illegible]	[illegible]	[illegible]	[illegible]
23. Procuration,	[illegible]	[illegible]	[illegible]	[illegible]	[illegible]	[illegible]	[illegible]	[illegible]	[illegible]	[illegible]	[illegible]	[illegible]	[illegible]	[illegible]	[illegible]	[illegible]	[illegible]	[illegible]	[illegible]	[illegible]	[illegible]
24. Abduction,	[illegible]	[illegible]	[illegible]	[illegible]	[illegible]	[illegible]	[illegible]	[illegible]	[illegible]	[illegible]	[illegible]	[illegible]	[illegible]	[illegible]	[illegible]	[illegible]	[illegible]	[illegible]	[illegible]	[illegible]	[illegible]
25. Bigamy,	[illegible]	[illegible]	[illegible]	[illegible]	[illegible]	[illegible]	[illegible]	[illegible]	[illegible]	[illegible]	[illegible]	[illegible]	[illegible]	[illegible]	[illegible]	[illegible]	[illegible]	[illegible]	[illegible]	[illegible]	[illegible]
26. Other Offences against the Person,	[illegible]	[illegible]	[illegible]	[illegible]	[illegible]	[illegible]	[illegible]	[illegible]	[illegible]	[illegible]	[illegible]	[illegible]	[illegible]	[illegible]	[illegible]	[illegible]	[illegible]	[illegible]	[illegible]	[illegible]	[illegible]
Total of Class I.,	[illegible]	[illegible]	[illegible]	[illegible]	[illegible]	[illegible]	[illegible]	[illegible]	[illegible]	[illegible]	[illegible]	[illegible]	[illegible]	[illegible]	[illegible]	[illegible]	[illegible]	[illegible]	[illegible]	[illegible]	[illegible]
Class II.—Offences against Property with Violence.																					
27. Sacrilege,	[illegible]	[illegible]	[illegible]	[illegible]	[illegible]	[illegible]	[illegible]	[illegible]	[illegible]	[illegible]	[illegible]	[illegible]	[illegible]	[illegible]	[illegible]	[illegible]	[illegible]	[illegible]	[illegible]	[illegible]	[illegible]
28. Burglary,	[illegible]	[illegible]	[illegible]	[illegible]	[illegible]	[illegible]	[illegible]	[illegible]	[illegible]	[illegible]	[illegible]	[illegible]	[illegible]	[illegible]	[illegible]	[illegible]	[illegible]	[illegible]	[illegible]	[illegible]	[illegible]
29. Housebreaking,	[illegible]	[illegible]	[illegible]	[illegible]	[illegible]	[illegible]	[illegible]	[illegible]	[illegible]	[illegible]	[illegible]	[illegible]	[illegible]	[illegible]	[illegible]	[illegible]	[illegible]	[illegible]	[illegible]	[illegible]	[illegible]
30. Shopbreaking,	[illegible]	[illegible]	[illegible]	[illegible]	[illegible]	[illegible]	[illegible]	[illegible]	[illegible]	[illegible]	[illegible]	[illegible]	[illegible]	[illegible]	[illegible]	[illegible]	[illegible]	[illegible]	[illegible]	[illegible]	[illegible]
31. Attempts to break into Houses, Shops, &c.,	[illegible]	[illegible]	[illegible]	[illegible]	[illegible]	[illegible]	[illegible]	[illegible]	[illegible]	[illegible]	[illegible]	[illegible]	[illegible]	[illegible]	[illegible]	[illegible]	[illegible]	[illegible]	[illegible]	[illegible]	[illegible]
32. Entering with intent to Commit Felony,	[illegible]	[illegible]	[illegible]	[illegible]	[illegible]	[illegible]	[illegible]	[illegible]	[illegible]	[illegible]	[illegible]	[illegible]	[illegible]	[illegible]	[illegible]	[illegible]	[illegible]	[illegible]	[illegible]	[illegible]	[illegible]
33. Possession of Housebreaking Tools, &c.,	[illegible]	[illegible]	[illegible]	[illegible]	[illegible]	[illegible]	[illegible]	[illegible]	[illegible]	[illegible]	[illegible]	[illegible]	[illegible]	[illegible]	[illegible]	[illegible]	[illegible]	[illegible]	[illegible]	[illegible]	[illegible]
34. Robbery,	[illegible]	[illegible]	[illegible]	[illegible]	[illegible]	[illegible]	[illegible]	[illegible]	[illegible]	[illegible]	[illegible]	[illegible]	[illegible]	[illegible]	[illegible]	[illegible]	[illegible]	[illegible]	[illegible]	[illegible]	[illegible]
35. Extortion by Threats to Accuse,	[illegible]	[illegible]	[illegible]	[illegible]	[illegible]	[illegible]	[illegible]	[illegible]	[illegible]	[illegible]	[illegible]	[illegible]	[illegible]	[illegible]	[illegible]	[illegible]	[illegible]	[illegible]	[illegible]	[illegible]	[illegible]
36. Extortion by other Threats,	[illegible]	[illegible]	[illegible]	[illegible]	[illegible]	[illegible]	[illegible]	[illegible]	[illegible]	[illegible]	[illegible]	[illegible]	[illegible]	[illegible]	[illegible]	[illegible]	[illegible]	[illegible]	[illegible]	[illegible]	[illegible]
Total of Class II.,	[illegible]	[illegible]	[illegible]	[illegible]	[illegible]	[illegible]	[illegible]	[illegible]	[illegible]	[illegible]	[illegible]	[illegible]	[illegible]	[illegible]	[illegible]	[illegible]	[illegible]	[illegible]	[illegible]	[illegible]	[illegible]
Class III.—Offences against Property without Violence.																					
37. Larceny of Horses and Cattle,	[illegible]	[illegible]	[illegible]	[illegible]	[illegible]	[illegible]	[illegible]	[illegible]	[illegible]	[illegible]	[illegible]	[illegible]	[illegible]	[illegible]	[illegible]	[illegible]	[illegible]	[illegible]	[illegible]	[illegible]	[illegible]
38. Larceny from the Person,	[illegible]	[illegible]	[illegible]	[illegible]	[illegible]	[illegible]	[illegible]	[illegible]	[illegible]	[illegible]	[illegible]	[illegible]	[illegible]	[illegible]	[illegible]	[illegible]	[illegible]	[illegible]	[illegible]	[illegible]	[illegible]
39. Larceny by Servants,	[illegible]	[illegible]	[illegible]	[illegible]	[illegible]	[illegible]	[illegible]	[illegible]	[illegible]	[illegible]	[illegible]	[illegible]	[illegible]	[illegible]	[illegible]	[illegible]	[illegible]	[illegible]	[illegible]	[illegible]	[illegible]
40. Larceny in a Dwelling,	[illegible]	[illegible]	[illegible]	[illegible]	[illegible]	[illegible]	[illegible]	[illegible]	[illegible]	[illegible]	[illegible]	[illegible]	[illegible]	[illegible]	[illegible]	[illegible]	[illegible]	[illegible]	[illegible]	[illegible]	[illegible]
41. Embezzlement,	[illegible]	[illegible]	[illegible]	[illegible]	[illegible]	[illegible]	[illegible]	[illegible]	[illegible]	[illegible]	[illegible]	[illegible]	[illegible]	[illegible]	[illegible]	[illegible]	[illegible]	[illegible]	[illegible]	[illegible]	[illegible]
42. Larceny of Post Letters,	[illegible]	[illegible]	[illegible]	[illegible]	[illegible]	[illegible]	[illegible]	[illegible]	[illegible]	[illegible]	[illegible]	[illegible]	[illegible]	[illegible]	[illegible]	[illegible]	[illegible]	[illegible]	[illegible]	[illegible]	[illegible]
43. Other Aggravated Larcenies,	[illegible]	[illegible]	[illegible]	[illegible]	[illegible]	[illegible]	[illegible]	[illegible]	[illegible]	[illegible]	[illegible]	[illegible]	[illegible]	[illegible]	[illegible]	[illegible]	[illegible]	[illegible]	[illegible]	[illegible]	[illegible]
44. Simple Larceny and Minor Larcenies,	[illegible]	[illegible]	[illegible]	[illegible]	[illegible]	[illegible]	[illegible]	[illegible]	[illegible]	[illegible]	[illegible]	[illegible]	[illegible]	[illegible]	[illegible]	[illegible]	[illegible]	[illegible]	[illegible]	[illegible]	[illegible]
45. Obtaining by False Pretences,	[illegible]	[illegible]	[illegible]	[illegible]	[illegible]	[illegible]	[illegible]	[illegible]	[illegible]	[illegible]	[illegible]	[illegible]	[illegible]	[illegible]	[illegible]	[illegible]	[illegible]	[illegible]	[illegible]	[illegible]	[illegible]
46. Frauds by Bankers, &c.,	[illegible]	[illegible]	[illegible]	[illegible]	[illegible]	[illegible]	[illegible]	[illegible]	[illegible]	[illegible]	[illegible]	[illegible]	[illegible]	[illegible]	[illegible]	[illegible]	[illegible]	[illegible]	[illegible]	[illegible]	[illegible]
47. Falsifying Accounts,	[illegible]	[illegible]	[illegible]	[illegible]	[illegible]	[illegible]	[illegible]	[illegible]	[illegible]	[illegible]	[illegible]	[illegible]	[illegible]	[illegible]	[illegible]	[illegible]	[illegible]	[illegible]	[illegible]	[illegible]	[illegible]
48. Other Frauds,	[illegible]	[illegible]	[illegible]	[illegible]	[illegible]	[illegible]	[illegible]	[illegible]	[illegible]	[illegible]	[illegible]	[illegible]	[illegible]	[illegible]	[illegible]	[illegible]	[illegible]	[illegible]	[illegible]	[illegible]	[illegible]
49. Receiving Stolen Goods,	[illegible]	[illegible]	[illegible]	[illegible]	[illegible]	[illegible]	[illegible]	[illegible]	[illegible]	[illegible]	[illegible]	[illegible]	[illegible]	[illegible]	[illegible]	[illegible]	[illegible]	[illegible]	[illegible]	[illegible]	[illegible]
50. Offences in Bankruptcy,	[illegible]	[illegible]	[illegible]	[illegible]	[illegible]	[illegible]	[illegible]	[illegible]	[illegible]	[illegible]	[illegible]	[illegible]	[illegible]	[illegible]	[illegible]	[illegible]	[illegible]	[illegible]	[illegible]	[illegible]	[illegible]
Total of Class III.,	[illegible]	[illegible]	[illegible]	[illegible]	[illegible]	[illegible]	[illegible]	[illegible]	[illegible]	[illegible]	[illegible]	[illegible]	[illegible]	[illegible]	[illegible]	[illegible]	[illegible]	[illegible]	[illegible]	[illegible]	[illegible]

QUARTER SESSIONS.

... of Persons for Trial for each Offence in each County.

Counties	OFFENCES
	Class I.—Offences against the Person.
[illegible]	1 Murder.
[illegible]	2 Attempt to Murder.
[illegible]	3 Conspiracy or Incitement to Murder.
[illegible]	4 Manslaughter.
[illegible]	5 Felonious Wounding.
[illegible]	6 Endangering Railway Passengers.
[illegible]	7 Malicious Wounding (Misdemeanour).
[illegible]	8 Assault.
[illegible]	9 Intimidation and Menaces.
[illegible]	10 Cruelty to Children.
[illegible]	11 Abandoning Children under two years.
[illegible]	12 Child Stealing.
[illegible]	13 Procuring Abortion.
[illegible]	14 Concealment of Birth.
[illegible]	15 Unnatural Offences.
[illegible]	16 Attempts to Commit Unnatural Offences.
[illegible]	17 Indecency with Males.
[illegible]	18 Rape.
[illegible]	19 Indecent Assaults on Females.
[illegible]	20 Defilement of Girls under 13.
[illegible]	21 Defilement of Girls under 16.
[illegible]	22 Householders permitting Defilement of Girls.
[illegible]	23 Procuration.
[illegible]	24 Abduction.
[illegible]	25 Bigamy.
[illegible]	26 Other Offences against the Person.
[illegible]	Total of Class I.
	Class II.—Offences against Property with Violence.
[illegible]	27 Sacrilege.
[illegible]	28 Burglary.
[illegible]	29 Housebreaking.
[illegible]	30 Shopbreaking.
[illegible]	31 Attempts to break into Houses, Shops, &c.
[illegible]	32 Entering with intent to Commit Felony.
[illegible]	33 Possession of Housebreaking Tools, &c.
[illegible]	34 Robbery.
[illegible]	35 Extortion by Threats to Accuse.
[illegible]	36 Extortion by other Threats.
[illegible]	Total of Class II.
	Class III.—Offences against Property without Violence.
[illegible]	37 Larceny of Horses and Cattle.
[illegible]	38 Larceny from the Person.
[illegible]	39 Larceny in House.
[illegible]	40 Larceny by a Servant.
[illegible]	41 Embezzlement.
[illegible]	42 Larceny of Post Letters.
[illegible]	43 Other Aggravated Larcenies.
[illegible]	44 Simple Larceny and Minor Larcenies.
[illegible]	45 Obtaining by False Pretences.
[illegible]	46 Frauds by Bankers, &c.
[illegible]	47 Falsifying Accounts.
[illegible]	48 Other Frauds.
[illegible]	49 Receiving Stolen Goods.
[illegible]	50 Offences in Bankruptcy.
[illegible]	Total of Class III.

TABLE 6—continued—ASSIZES AND QUARTER SESSIONS.—Number

Offences.	
Class IV.—Malicious Injuries to Property.	
61. Arson,	[illegible]
62. Setting Fire to Crops, &c.	[illegible]
63. Killing and Maiming Cattle,	[illegible]
64. Malicious Injuries, &c., of Buildings, &c.	[illegible]
65. Destroying Ships,	[illegible]
66. Destroying Railways,	[illegible]
67. Destroying Trees and Shrubs,	[illegible]
68. Other Malicious Injuries,	[illegible]
Total of Class IV.,	[illegible]
Class V.—Forgery and offences against the Currency.	
69. Forgery and Uttering (Felony),	[illegible]
60. Forgery (Misdemeanour),	[illegible]
61. Coining,	[illegible]
62. Uttering Counterfeit Coin,	[illegible]
Total of Class V.,	[illegible]
Class VI.—Other offences not included in the above Classes.	
Offences against the State and Public Order.	
63. High Treason,	[illegible]
64. Treason Felony,	[illegible]
65. Riot,	[illegible]
66. Unlawful Assembly,	[illegible]
67. Intimidation by Threatening Letters, Notices, or otherwise,	[illegible]
68. Demand or Robbery of Arms,	[illegible]
69. Assaulting Dwelling Houses (by being disguised),	[illegible]
70. Other Offences,	[illegible]
Offences against Public Justice.	
71. Rescued by Officers, &c.,	[illegible]
72. Bribery, &c.,	[illegible]
73. Perjury,	[illegible]
74. Escape and Rescue,	[illegible]
75. Other Offences,	[illegible]
Offences against Religion.	
76. Blasphemy, &c.,	[illegible]
Offences against Laws of Nations.	
77. Piracy,	[illegible]
78. Slave Trade,	[illegible]
79. Libel,	[illegible]
80. Nuisances,	[illegible]
81. Indecent Exposure,	[illegible]
82. Keeping Disorderly Houses,	[illegible]
83. Other Nuisances,	[illegible]
84. Attempts to commit offences,	[illegible]
85. Other Misdemeanours,	[illegible]

QUARTER SESSIONS.

of Persons for Trial for each Offence in each County.

Class IV.—Malicious Injuries to Property.

[illegible]

Total of Class IV.

Class V.—Forgery and Offences against the Currency.

[illegible]

Total of Class V.

Class VI.—Other Offences not included in the above Classes.

[illegible]

Total of Class VI.

GRAND TOTAL.

TABLE 7.—ASSIZES AND QUARTER SESSIONS.—Number of Persons for Trial, and Results of Proceedings in each Court.

County.	Court.	No. of Persons for Trial.	Not Tried: No Prosecution.	Not Tried: No Bill.	Not Tried: Bound Over or Otherwise.	Acquitted.	Special Verdict of Guilty but Insane.	Total Convicted.	Death.	Penal Servitude.	Imprisonment.	Other Punishments.	Population.*
(1)	(2)	(3)	(4)	(5)	(6)	(7)	(8)	(9)	(10)	(11)	(12)	(13)	(14)
ANTRIM,	Assizes,	[illegible]	[illegible]		[illegible]	[illegible]	[illegible]	[illegible]	.	[illegible]	[illegible]	[illegible]	[illegible]
	Quarter Sessions,	[illegible]	.	[illegible]	[illegible]	[illegible]	.	[illegible]	.	.	[illegible]	[illegible]	[illegible]
	Belfast Quarter Sessions,	[illegible]	[illegible]	[illegible]	.	[illegible]	.	[illegible]	.	.	[illegible]	[illegible]	[illegible]
	Total,	[illegible]	[illegible]	[illegible]	[illegible]	[illegible]	[illegible]	[illegible]	.	[illegible]	[illegible]	[illegible]	[illegible]
ARMAGH,	Assizes,	[illegible]	.	.	.	[illegible]	.	[illegible]	[illegible]	[illegible]	[illegible]	[illegible]	[illegible]
	Quarter Sessions,	[illegible]	[illegible]	[illegible]	.	[illegible]	.	[illegible]	.	.	[illegible]	[illegible]	[illegible]
	Total,	[illegible]	[illegible]	[illegible]	.	[illegible]	.	[illegible]	[illegible]	[illegible]	[illegible]	[illegible]	[illegible]
CARLOW,	Assizes,	[illegible]	[illegible]	.	.	[illegible]	.	[illegible]	.	.	[illegible]	[illegible]	[illegible]
	Quarter Sessions,	[illegible]	[illegible]	.	.	[illegible]	.	[illegible]	.	.	.	[illegible]	[illegible]
	Total,	[illegible]	[illegible]	.	.	[illegible]	.	[illegible]	.	.	[illegible]	[illegible]	[illegible]
CARRICKFERGUS,	Assizes,	[illegible]	.	.	.	.	.	[illegible]	.	.	[illegible]	.	[illegible]
	Quarter Sessions,	[illegible]	.	.	.	.	.	[illegible]	.	.	[illegible]	.	[illegible]
	Total,	[illegible]	.	.	.	.	.	[illegible]	.	.	[illegible]	.	[illegible]
CAVAN,	Assizes,	[illegible]	[illegible]	.	.	[illegible]	.	[illegible]	.	.	[illegible]	[illegible]	[illegible]
	Quarter Sessions,	[illegible]	[illegible]	[illegible]	.	[illegible]	.	[illegible]	.	.	[illegible]	[illegible]	[illegible]
	Total,	[illegible]	[illegible]	[illegible]	.	[illegible]	.	[illegible]	.	.	[illegible]	[illegible]	[illegible]
CLARE,	Assizes,	[illegible]	[illegible]	[illegible]	[illegible]	[illegible]	.	[illegible]	.	.	[illegible]	[illegible]	[illegible]
	Quarter Sessions,	[illegible]	[illegible]	[illegible]	.	[illegible]	.	[illegible]	.	.	[illegible]	.	[illegible]
	Total,	[illegible]	[illegible]	[illegible]	[illegible]	[illegible]	.	[illegible]	.	.	[illegible]	[illegible]	[illegible]
CORK,	Assizes,	[illegible]	[illegible]	.	[illegible]	[illegible]	[illegible]	[illegible]	[illegible]	[illegible]	[illegible]	[illegible]	[illegible]
	Quarter Sessions,	[illegible]	[illegible]	[illegible]	.	[illegible]	.	[illegible]	.	.	[illegible]	[illegible]	[illegible]
	Total,	[illegible]	[illegible]	[illegible]	[illegible]	[illegible]	[illegible]	[illegible]	[illegible]	[illegible]	[illegible]	[illegible]	[illegible]
[illegible] CORK,	Assizes,	[illegible]	[illegible]	[illegible]	.	[illegible]	.	[illegible]	.	.	[illegible]	.	[illegible]
	Quarter Sessions,	[illegible]	[illegible]	[illegible]	.	.	.	[illegible]	.	[illegible]	[illegible]	[illegible]	[illegible]
	Total,	[illegible]	[illegible]	[illegible]	.	[illegible]	.	[illegible]	.	[illegible]	[illegible]	[illegible]	[illegible]
DONEGAL,	Assizes,	[illegible]	[illegible]	.	.	[illegible]	.	[illegible]	.	[illegible]	[illegible]	[illegible]	[illegible]
	Quarter Sessions,	[illegible]	[illegible]	[illegible]	.	[illegible]	.	[illegible]	.	.	[illegible]	[illegible]	[illegible]
	Total,	[illegible]	[illegible]	[illegible]	.	[illegible]	.	[illegible]	.	[illegible]	[illegible]	[illegible]	[illegible]
DOWN,	Assizes,	[illegible]	[illegible]	[illegible]	.	[illegible]	[illegible]	[illegible]	.	[illegible]	[illegible]	[illegible]	[illegible]
	Quarter Sessions,	[illegible]	.	[illegible]	.	[illegible]	.	[illegible]	.	.	[illegible]	[illegible]	[illegible]
	Total,	[illegible]	[illegible]	[illegible]	.	[illegible]	[illegible]	[illegible]	.	[illegible]	[illegible]	[illegible]	[illegible]
DROGHEDA,	Assizes,	[illegible]	.	.	.	.	.	[illegible]	.	.	[illegible]	.	[illegible]
	Quarter Sessions,	[illegible]	.	.	.	.	[illegible]	[illegible]	.	[illegible]	[illegible]	[illegible]	[illegible]
	Total,	[illegible]	.	.	.	.	[illegible]	[illegible]	.	[illegible]	[illegible]	[illegible]	[illegible]

* Population under the jurisdiction of each Court, the total population in [illegible], given under the [illegible].
[illegible]
[illegible]

[illegible]	[illegible]	[illegible]	[illegible]	[illegible]	[illegible]	[illegible]	[illegible]	[illegible]	[illegible]
[illegible]	[illegible]	[illegible]		[illegible]	.	[illegible]	.	[illegible]	[illegible]
[illegible]	[illegible]	.	.	[illegible]	[illegible]	[illegible]	.	.	[illegible]
[illegible]	[illegible]	[illegible]	.	[illegible]	[illegible]	[illegible]	.	[illegible]	[illegible]
[illegible]	[illegible]	[illegible]	[illegible]	[illegible]	[illegible]	[illegible]	.	[illegible]	[illegible]
17 b	[illegible]	[illegible]	.	[illegible]	.	[illegible]	.	[illegible]	[illegible]
[illegible]	[illegible]	[illegible]	[illegible]	[illegible]	[illegible]	[illegible]	.	[illegible]	[illegible]
[illegible]	[illegible]	.	.	[illegible]	.	[illegible]	.	.	[illegible]
[illegible]	[illegible]	[illegible]	.	[illegible]	.	[illegible]	.	.	[illegible]
[illegible]	[illegible]	[illegible]	.	[illegible]	.	[illegible]	.	.	[illegible]
[illegible]	[illegible]	[illegible]	.	[illegible]	.	[illegible]	.	[illegible]	[illegible]
[illegible]	.	.	.	[illegible]	.	[illegible]	.	.	[illegible]
[illegible]	[illegible]	[illegible]	.	[illegible]	.	[illegible]	.	[illegible]	[illegible]
[illegible]	.	.	.	.	.	[illegible]	.	.	[illegible]
[illegible]	.	[illegible]	.	.	.	.	.	.	.
[illegible]	.	[illegible]	.	.	.	[illegible]	.	.	[illegible]
[illegible]	[illegible]	.	.	[illegible]	[illegible]	[illegible]	.	[illegible]	[illegible]
[illegible]	[illegible]	[illegible]	.	[illegible]	.	[illegible]	.	.	[illegible]
[illegible]	[illegible]	[illegible]	.	[illegible]	[illegible]	[illegible]	.	[illegible]	[illegible]
[illegible]	[illegible]	.	.	[illegible]	.	[illegible]	.	.	[illegible]
[illegible]	[illegible]	[illegible]	.	[illegible]	.	[illegible]	.	.	[illegible]
[illegible]	[illegible]	[illegible]	.	[illegible]	.	[illegible]	.	.	[illegible]
[illegible]	[illegible]	[illegible]	.	[illegible]	.	[illegible]	.	[illegible]	[illegible]
[illegible]	[illegible]	[illegible]	.	[illegible]	.	[illegible]	.	.	[illegible]
[illegible]	[illegible]	[illegible]	.	[illegible]	.	[illegible]	.	[illegible]	[illegible]
.	.	.	.	.	.	.	.	.	.
[illegible]	.	[illegible]	.	.	.	[illegible]	.	.	[illegible]
[illegible]	.	[illegible]	.	.	.	[illegible]	.	.	[illegible]
[illegible]	.	.	.	[illegible]	.	[illegible]	.	.	[illegible]
[illegible]	.	[illegible]	.	[illegible]	.	[illegible]	.	[illegible]	[illegible]
[illegible]	.	[illegible]	.	[illegible]	.	[illegible]	.	[illegible]	[illegible]
[illegible]	[illegible]	[illegible]	.	[illegible]	.	[illegible]	.	[illegible]	[illegible]
[illegible]	[illegible]	[illegible]	.	[illegible]	.	[illegible]	.	.	[illegible]
[illegible]	[illegible]	[illegible]	.	[illegible]	.	[illegible]	.	[illegible]	[illegible]

ASSIZES AND QUARTER SESSIONS.

TABLE 7—continued.—ASSIZES AND QUARTER SESSIONS.—Number of Persons for Trial, and Results of Proceedings in each Court.

County.	Court.	No. of Persons for Trial.	Not Tried: No Prosecution.	Not Tried: No Bill.	Not Tried: Found Insane on Arraignment.	Acquitted.	Special Verdict of Guilty but Insane.	Total Convicted.	Death.	Penal Servitude.	Imprisonment.	Other Punishments.	Population.*
(1)	(2)	(3)	(4)	(5)	(6)	(7)	(8)	(9)	(10)	(11)	(12)	(13)	(14)
Limerick,	Assizes,	[illegible]	[illegible]	[illegible]	[illegible]	[illegible]	.	[illegible]	.	[illegible]	[illegible]	[illegible]	[illegible]
	Quarter Sessions,	[illegible]	[illegible]	[illegible]	.	[illegible]	.	[illegible]	.	.	[illegible]	[illegible]	[illegible]
	Total,	[illegible]	[illegible]	[illegible]	[illegible]	[illegible]	.	[illegible]	.	[illegible]	[illegible]	[illegible]	[illegible]
Limerick City,	Assizes,	[illegible]	[illegible]	.	.	[illegible]	.	[illegible]	.	[illegible]	[illegible]	[illegible]	[illegible]
	Quarter Sessions,	[illegible]	.	.	.	.	.	[illegible]	.	.	[illegible]	.	[illegible]
	Total,	[illegible]	[illegible]	.	.	[illegible]	.	[illegible]	.	[illegible]	[illegible]	[illegible]	[illegible]
Londonderry Co. & City,	Assizes,	[illegible]	[illegible]	[illegible]	.	[illegible]	.	[illegible]	.	[illegible]	[illegible]	[illegible]	[illegible]
	Quarter Sessions,	[illegible]	.	[illegible]	.	[illegible]	[illegible]	[illegible]	.	.	[illegible]	.	[illegible]
	Recorder's Court,	[illegible]	.	.	.	.	.	[illegible]	.	.	[illegible]	.	[illegible]
	Total,	[illegible]	[illegible]	[illegible]	.	[illegible]	[illegible]	[illegible]	.	[illegible]	[illegible]	[illegible]	[illegible]
Longford,	Assizes,	[illegible]	.	[illegible]	.	[illegible]	.	[illegible]	.	[illegible]	[illegible]	[illegible]	[illegible]
	Quarter Sessions,	[illegible]	[illegible]	.	.	[illegible]	.	[illegible]	.	.	[illegible]	[illegible]	[illegible]
	Total,	[illegible]	[illegible]	[illegible]	.	[illegible]	.	[illegible]	.	[illegible]	[illegible]	[illegible]	[illegible]
Louth,	Assizes,	[illegible]	[illegible]	.	.	[illegible]	.	[illegible]	.	.	[illegible]	.	[illegible]
	Quarter Sessions,	[illegible]	[illegible]	[illegible]	.	[illegible]	.	[illegible]	.	.	[illegible]	[illegible]	[illegible]
	Total,	[illegible]	[illegible]	[illegible]	.	[illegible]	.	[illegible]	.	.	[illegible]	[illegible]	[illegible]
Mayo,	Assizes,	[illegible]	[illegible]	.	[illegible]	[illegible]	[illegible]	[illegible]	.	[illegible]	[illegible]	[illegible]	[illegible]
	Quarter Sessions,	[illegible]	[illegible]	[illegible]	.	[illegible]	.	[illegible]	.	.	[illegible]	[illegible]	[illegible]
	Total,	[illegible]	[illegible]	[illegible]	[illegible]	[illegible]	[illegible]	[illegible]	.	[illegible]	[illegible]	[illegible]	[illegible]
Meath,	Assizes,	[illegible]	[illegible]	[illegible]	.	[illegible]	.	[illegible]	.	[illegible]	[illegible]	[illegible]	[illegible]
	Quarter Sessions,	[illegible]	[illegible]	[illegible]	.	[illegible]	.	[illegible]	.	.	[illegible]	[illegible]	[illegible]
	Total,	[illegible]	[illegible]	[illegible]	.	[illegible]	.	[illegible]	.	[illegible]	[illegible]	[illegible]	[illegible]
Monaghan,	Assizes,	[illegible]	.	[illegible]	.	[illegible]	.	[illegible]	.	.	[illegible]	[illegible]	[illegible]
	Quarter Sessions,	[illegible]	[illegible]	.	.	[illegible]	.	[illegible]	.	[illegible]	[illegible]	[illegible]	[illegible]
	Total,	[illegible]	[illegible]	[illegible]	.	[illegible]	.	[illegible]	.	[illegible]	[illegible]	[illegible]	[illegible]
Queen's Co.,	Assizes,	[illegible]	.	.	.	.	.	[illegible]	.	.	[illegible]	[illegible]	[illegible]
	Quarter Sessions,	[illegible]	.	[illegible]	.	[illegible]	.	[illegible]	.	.	[illegible]	.	[illegible]
	Total,	[illegible]	.	[illegible]	.	[illegible]	.	[illegible]	.	.	[illegible]	[illegible]	[illegible]
Roscommon,	Assizes,	[illegible]	[illegible]	[illegible]	.	[illegible]	[illegible]	[illegible]	.	.	[illegible]	[illegible]	[illegible]
	Quarter Sessions,	[illegible]	.	[illegible]	.	[illegible]	.	[illegible]	.	[illegible]	[illegible]	.	[illegible]
	Total,	[illegible]	[illegible]	[illegible]	.	[illegible]	[illegible]	[illegible]	.	[illegible]	[illegible]	[illegible]	[illegible]
Sligo,	Assizes,	[illegible]	[illegible]	.	.	[illegible]	.	[illegible]	.	[illegible]	[illegible]	[illegible]	[illegible]
	Quarter Sessions,	[illegible]	.	.	.	[illegible]	.	[illegible]	.	.	[illegible]	[illegible]	[illegible]
	Total,	[illegible]	[illegible]	.	.	[illegible]	.	[illegible]	.	[illegible]	[illegible]	[illegible]	[illegible]

* Persons under the jurisdiction of each Court, the total population in Counties, given also for each county.
(1) [illegible]
(2) [illegible]

ASSIZES AND QUARTER SESSIONS.

TABLE 7.—*continued*—ASSIZES AND QUARTER SESSIONS.—Number of Persons for Trial, and Results of Proceedings in each Court.

County	Court	No. of Persons for Trial	No True Bill: No Prosecution	No True Bill: No Bill	Found Insane on arraignment	Acquitted	Special Verdict of Guilty but Insane	Persons Convicted: Total Number	Sentenced: Death	Sentenced: Penal Servitude	Sentenced: Imprisonment	Sentenced: Other Punishments	Population*
(1)	(2)	(3)	(4)	(5)	(6)	(7)	(8)	(9)	(10)	(11)	(12)	(13)	(14)
Tipperary, N.R.	Assizes,	[illegible]	[illegible]	.	.	[illegible]	.	[illegible]	.	.	[illegible]	[illegible]	[illegible]
	Quarter Sessions,	[illegible]	.	[illegible]	.	[illegible]	.	[illegible]	.	[illegible]	[illegible]	.	[illegible]
	Total,	[illegible]	[illegible]	[illegible]	.	[illegible]	.	[illegible]	.	[illegible]	[illegible]	[illegible]	[illegible]
Tipperary, S.R.	Assizes,	[illegible]	[illegible]	[illegible]	.	[illegible]	.	[illegible]	.	.	[illegible]	[illegible]	[illegible]
	Quarter Sessions,	[illegible]	.	[illegible]	.	.	.	[illegible]	.	.	[illegible]	.	[illegible]
	Total,	[illegible]	[illegible]	[illegible]	.	[illegible]	.	[illegible]	.	.	[illegible]	[illegible]	[illegible]
Tyrone,	Assizes,	[illegible]	[illegible]	.	.	[illegible]	.	[illegible]	.	[illegible]	[illegible]	[illegible]	[illegible]
	Quarter Sessions,	[illegible]	[illegible]	[illegible]	.	[illegible]	.	[illegible]	.	[illegible]	[illegible]	[illegible]	[illegible]
	Total,	[illegible]	[illegible]	[illegible]	.	[illegible]	.	[illegible]	.	[illegible]	[illegible]	[illegible]	[illegible]
Waterford,	Assizes,	[illegible]	[illegible]	[illegible]	.	[illegible]	.	[illegible]	.	.	[illegible]	[illegible]	[illegible]
	Quarter Sessions,	[illegible]	.	[illegible]	.	[illegible]	.	[illegible]	.	.	[illegible]	.	[illegible]
	Total,	[illegible]	[illegible]	[illegible]	.	[illegible]	.	[illegible]	.	.	[illegible]	[illegible]	[illegible]
Waterford City.	Assizes,	[illegible]	[illegible]	.	.	[illegible]	.	[illegible]	.	.	[illegible]	.	[illegible]
	Quarter Sessions,	[illegible]	.	.	.	[illegible]	.	[illegible]	.	.	[illegible]	[illegible]	[illegible]
	Total,	[illegible]	[illegible]	.	.	[illegible]	.	[illegible]	.	.	[illegible]	[illegible]	[illegible]
Westmeath,	Assizes,	[illegible]	.	.	.	[illegible]	.	[illegible]	.	.	[illegible]	[illegible]	[illegible]
	Quarter Sessions,	[illegible]	[illegible]	[illegible]	.	[illegible]	[illegible]	[illegible]	.	.	[illegible]	[illegible]	[illegible]
	Total,	[illegible]	[illegible]	[illegible]	.	[illegible]	[illegible]	[illegible]	.	.	[illegible]	[illegible]	[illegible]
Wexford,	Assizes,	[illegible]	[illegible]	.	[illegible]	.	.	[illegible]	.	[illegible]	[illegible]	.	[illegible]
	Quarter Sessions,	[illegible]	[illegible]	[illegible]	.	[illegible]	.	[illegible]	.	.	[illegible]	[illegible]	[illegible]
	Total,	[illegible]	[illegible]	[illegible]	[illegible]	[illegible]	.	[illegible]	.	[illegible]	[illegible]	[illegible]	[illegible]
Wicklow,	Assizes,	[illegible]	.	.	.	[illegible]	.	[illegible]	.	[illegible]	[illegible]	[illegible]	[illegible]
	Quarter Sessions,	[illegible]	.	[illegible]	.	[illegible]	.	[illegible]	.	.	[illegible]	[illegible]	[illegible]
	Total,	[illegible]	.	[illegible]	.	[illegible]	.	[illegible]	.	[illegible]	[illegible]	[illegible]	[illegible]
	Grand Total,	[illegible]	[illegible]	[illegible]	[illegible]	[illegible]	[illegible]	[illegible]	[illegible]	[illegible]	[illegible]	[illegible]	[illegible]

* Population under the jurisdiction of each Court, the total population is, therefore, given below for each county.
† [illegible]

TABLE 8.—CRIMINAL PROCEEDINGS.—COSTS.—ACCOUNT for the year ended [illegible] Prosecutions at Assizes, the Dublin Commission Court, and Quarter Sessions, Number of Prosecutions and Amount of Costs under each Head, from [illegible]

COUNTIES, AND COUNTIES OF CITIES AND OF TOWNS.	[illegible]								
	At Assizes and Commission Court [illegible]			At Quarter Sessions			At Petty Sessions [illegible]		
	[illegible]	[illegible]	[illegible]	[illegible]	[illegible]	[illegible]	[illegible]	[illegible]	[illegible]
	£ s. d.		£ s. d.	£ s. d.		£ s. d.			£ s. d.
Antrim, including County of Town of Carrickfergus.	[illegible]	[illegible]	[illegible]	[illegible]	[illegible]	[illegible]	[illegible]	[illegible]	[illegible]
Armagh,	[illegible]	[illegible]	[illegible]	[illegible]	–	—	[illegible]	[illegible]	
Carlow,	[illegible]	[illegible]	[illegible]	—	[illegible]	[illegible]	—	—	
Cavan,	[illegible]	[illegible]	[illegible]	—	[illegible]	[illegible]	[illegible]	[illegible]	
Clare,	[illegible]	[illegible]	[illegible]	[illegible]	–	–	[illegible]	[illegible]	
Cork County,	[illegible]	[illegible]	[illegible]	[illegible]	[illegible]	[illegible]	[illegible]	[illegible]	
Cork City,		[illegible]	[illegible]	—	[illegible]	[illegible]	[illegible]	[illegible]	
Donegal,	[illegible]	[illegible]	[illegible]	[illegible]	[illegible]	[illegible]	[illegible]	[illegible]	
Down,	[illegible]	[illegible]	[illegible]	—	–	—	[illegible]	[illegible]	
Drogheda Town,	[illegible]	[illegible]	[illegible]	—	–	—	–	—	
Dublin County,	[illegible]	[illegible]	[illegible]	—	[illegible]	[illegible]	[illegible]	[illegible]	
Dublin City,		[illegible]	[illegible]	—	[illegible]	[illegible]	[illegible]	[illegible]	
Fermanagh,	[illegible]	[illegible]	[illegible]	[illegible]	[illegible]	[illegible]	[illegible]	[illegible]	
Galway County,	[illegible]	[illegible]	[illegible]	—	[illegible]	[illegible]	[illegible]	[illegible]	
Galway Town,		[illegible]	[illegible]	—	[illegible]	[illegible]	[illegible]	[illegible]	
Kerry,	[illegible]	[illegible]	[illegible]	[illegible]	[illegible]	[illegible]	[illegible]	[illegible]	
Kildare,	[illegible]	[illegible]	[illegible]	—	[illegible]	[illegible]	[illegible]	[illegible]	
Kilkenny County,	[illegible]	[illegible]	[illegible]	[illegible]	[illegible]	[illegible]	[illegible]	[illegible]	
Kilkenny City,		[illegible]	[illegible]	—	[illegible]	[illegible]	[illegible]	[illegible]	
King's County,	[illegible]	[illegible]	[illegible]	[illegible]	–	..	[illegible]	[illegible]	
Leitrim,	[illegible]	[illegible]	[illegible]	[illegible]	[illegible]	[illegible]	[illegible]	[illegible]	
Limerick County,	[illegible]	[illegible]	[illegible]	—	[illegible]	[illegible]	[illegible]	[illegible]	
Limerick City,		[illegible]	[illegible]	—	[illegible]	[illegible]	[illegible]	[illegible]	
Londonderry,	[illegible]	[illegible]	[illegible]	[illegible]	[illegible]	[illegible]	[illegible]	[illegible]	
Longford,	[illegible]	[illegible]	[illegible]	—	[illegible]	[illegible]	[illegible]	[illegible]	
Louth,	[illegible]	[illegible]	[illegible]	[illegible]	[illegible]	[illegible]	[illegible]	[illegible]	
Mayo,	[illegible]	[illegible]	[illegible]	—	[illegible]	[illegible]	[illegible]	[illegible]	
Meath,	[illegible]	[illegible]	[illegible]	[illegible]	.	—	[illegible]	[illegible]	
Monaghan,	[illegible]	[illegible]	[illegible]	—	[illegible]	[illegible]	[illegible]	[illegible]	
Queen's County,	[illegible]	[illegible]	[illegible]	—	[illegible]	[illegible]	[illegible]	[illegible]	
Roscommon,	[illegible]	[illegible]	[illegible]	—	[illegible]	[illegible]	[illegible]	[illegible]	
Sligo,	[illegible]	[illegible]	[illegible]	[illegible]	[illegible]	[illegible]	[illegible]	[illegible]	
Tipperary, North Riding,	[illegible]	[illegible]	[illegible]	[illegible]	[illegible]	[illegible]	[illegible]	[illegible]	
Tipperary, South Riding,									
Tyrone,	[illegible]	[illegible]	[illegible]	[illegible]	[illegible]	[illegible]	[illegible]	[illegible]	
Waterford County,	[illegible]	[illegible]	[illegible]	—	[illegible]	[illegible]	[illegible]	[illegible]	
Waterford City,									
Westmeath,	[illegible]	[illegible]	[illegible]	—	[illegible]	[illegible]	[illegible]	[illegible]	
Wexford,	[illegible]	[illegible]	[illegible]	[illegible]	–	—	[illegible]	[illegible]	
Wicklow,	[illegible]	[illegible]	[illegible]	[illegible]	[illegible]	[illegible]	[illegible]	[illegible]	
Total,	[illegible]	[illegible]	[illegible]	[illegible]	[illegible]	[illegible]	[illegible]	[illegible]	

31st of March, [illegible], of the Sums paid by Her Majesty's Treasury for Criminal and for Proceedings at Petty Sessions, Inquests, and Police Courts, with the Returns made by Crown Solicitors and County and City Financial Officers.

[illegible]								Total.	Counties and Counties of Cities and Towns.
At Assizes.		At Quarter Sessions.		At Petty Sessions and Police Courts.		Under Criminal Justice Act [illegible]			
Number of Prosecutors and Witnesses Paid.	Amount Paid.	Number of Prosecutors and Witnesses Paid.	Amount Paid.	Number of Prosecutors and Witnesses Paid.	Amount Paid.	Number of Prosecutors and Witnesses Paid.	Amount Paid.		
	£ s. d.		£ s. d.		£ s. d.		£ s. d.	£ s. d.	
[illegible]	[illegible]	[illegible]	[illegible]	[illegible]	[illegible]	-	—	[illegible]	Antrim, including County of Town of Carrickfergus.
[illegible]	[illegible]	[illegible]	[illegible]	[illegible]	[illegible]	-	—	[illegible]	Armagh.
[illegible]	[illegible]	[illegible]	[illegible]	[illegible]	[illegible]	-	—	[illegible]	Carlow.
[illegible]	[illegible]	[illegible]	[illegible]	[illegible]	[illegible]	-	—	[illegible]	Cavan.
[illegible]	[illegible]	[illegible]	[illegible]	[illegible]	[illegible]	-	—	[illegible]	Clare.
[illegible]	[illegible]	[illegible]	[illegible]	[illegible]	[illegible]	-	—	[illegible]	Cork County.
[illegible]	[illegible]	[illegible]	[illegible]	[illegible]	[illegible]				Cork City.
[illegible]	[illegible]	[illegible]	[illegible]	-	—	-	—	[illegible]	Donegal.
[illegible]	[illegible]	[illegible]	[illegible]	[illegible]	[illegible]	-	—	[illegible]	Down.
[illegible]	[illegible]	[illegible]	[illegible]	[illegible]	[illegible]	-	—	[illegible]	Drogheda Town.
[illegible]	[illegible]	[illegible]	[illegible]	[illegible]	[illegible]	-	—	[illegible]	Dublin County.
[illegible]	[illegible]	[illegible]	[illegible]	[illegible]	[illegible]				Dublin City.
[illegible]	[illegible]	[illegible]	[illegible]	[illegible]	[illegible]	-	—	[illegible]	Fermanagh.
[illegible]	[illegible]	[illegible]	[illegible]	-	—	-	—	[illegible]	Galway County.
[illegible]	[illegible]	[illegible]	[illegible]	[illegible]	[illegible]				Galway Town.
[illegible]	[illegible]	[illegible]	[illegible]	-	—	-	—	[illegible]	Kerry.
[illegible]	[illegible]	[illegible]	[illegible]	[illegible]	[illegible]	-	—	[illegible]	Kildare.
[illegible]	[illegible]	[illegible]	[illegible]	[illegible]	[illegible]	-	—	[illegible]	Kilkenny County.
[illegible]	[illegible]	[illegible]	[illegible]	[illegible]	[illegible]				Kilkenny City.
[illegible]	[illegible]	[illegible]	[illegible]	[illegible]	[illegible]	-	—	[illegible]	King's County.
[illegible]	[illegible]	[illegible]	[illegible]	[illegible]	[illegible]	-	—	[illegible]	Leitrim.
[illegible]	[illegible]	[illegible]	[illegible]	[illegible]	[illegible]	-	—	[illegible]	Limerick County.
[illegible]	[illegible]	[illegible]	[illegible]	[illegible]	[illegible]				Limerick City.
[illegible]	[illegible]	[illegible]	[illegible]	[illegible]	[illegible]	-	—	[illegible]	Londonderry.
[illegible]	[illegible]	[illegible]	[illegible]	-	—	-	—	[illegible]	Longford.
[illegible]	[illegible]	[illegible]	[illegible]	[illegible]	[illegible]	-	—	[illegible]	Louth.
[illegible]	[illegible]	[illegible]	[illegible]	-	—	-	—	[illegible]	Mayo.
[illegible]	[illegible]	[illegible]	[illegible]	[illegible]	[illegible]	-	—	[illegible]	Meath.
[illegible]	[illegible]	[illegible]	[illegible]	[illegible]	[illegible]	-	—	[illegible]	Monaghan.
[illegible]	[illegible]	[illegible]	[illegible]	[illegible]	[illegible]	-	—	[illegible]	Queen's County.
[illegible]	[illegible]	[illegible]	[illegible]	[illegible]	[illegible]	-	—	[illegible]	Roscommon.
[illegible]	[illegible]	[illegible]	[illegible]	-	—	-	—	[illegible]	Sligo.
[illegible]	[illegible]	[illegible]	[illegible]	[illegible]	[illegible]	-	—	[illegible]	Tipperary, North Riding.
									Tipperary, South Riding.
[illegible]	[illegible]	[illegible]	[illegible]	[illegible]	[illegible]	-	—	[illegible]	Tyrone.
[illegible]	[illegible]	[illegible]	[illegible]	[illegible]	[illegible]	-	—	[illegible]	Waterford County.
[illegible]	[illegible]	[illegible]	[illegible]	[illegible]	[illegible]				Waterford City.
[illegible]	[illegible]	[illegible]	[illegible]	[illegible]	[illegible]	-	—	[illegible]	Westmeath.
[illegible]	[illegible]	[illegible]	[illegible]	[illegible]	[illegible]	-	—	[illegible]	Wexford.
[illegible]	[illegible]	[illegible]	[illegible]	[illegible]	[illegible]	-	—	[illegible]	Wicklow.
[illegible]	[illegible]	[illegible]	[illegible]	[illegible]	[illegible]	-	—	[illegible]	Total.

TABLE 9.—SUPREME COURTS OF APPEAL.—COURT FOR CROWN CASES RESERVED.—Return showing the cases reserved for the consideration of the Court, in the Year 1886. By the Master of the Crown Office, Queen's Bench Division.

Court.	Name of Case.	Offence.	Result of Cases for Crown Cases Reserved.			
			[illegible]	[illegible]	[illegible]	[illegible]
(1)	(2)	(3)	(4)	(5)	(6)	(7)
Munster Winter Assizes, County of Cork, 3rd December, 1885.	Reg. v. O'Brien.	[illegible]	1	-	-	-
County Down Spring Assizes, 1886.	Reg. v. Walker.	Assault [illegible]	1	-	-	-
Total, . .	2 Cases.	2	2	-	-	-

DISTRICTS PROCLAIMED.

10.—Districts subject to Proclamations in Council under 6 William IV., cap. 13, sec. 12.

11.—Districts subject to Proclamations in Council prohibiting the Carrying or Having of Arms under the Peace Preservation (Ireland) Act, 1881.

12.—Districts subject to Proclamations in Council prohibiting the Carrying of Arms under the Peace Preservation (Ireland) Act, 1881.

TABLES SHOWING DISTRICTS PROCLAIMED.

TABLE 10.—RETURN showing the several Districts which were subject to Proclamations in Council under 6 Wm. IV., Cap. 13, Sec. 13, on the 31st December, 1896.

Counties.	Proclaimed Districts.	Date of Proclamation.
Clare,	The County,	[illegible] January, 18[illegible]
Cork (a)	"	[illegible] April,
Galway,	"	[illegible] October, 18[illegible]
Kerry,	"	[illegible] October,
Limerick,	"	[illegible]

(a) [illegible]

THE PEACE PRESERVATION (IRELAND) ACT, 1881, as continued and amended by THE PEACE PRESERVATION (IRELAND) CONTINUANCE ACT, 1886, the CRIMINAL LAW AND PROCEDURE (IRELAND) ACT, 1887, and the EXPIRING LAWS CONTINUANCE ACTS.

TABLE 11.—RETURN No. 1, showing the several Districts which were under the operation of Proclamations in Council under the above Act, prohibiting the Carrying or Having of Arms, &c., on the 31st December, 1896.

County, &c.	Proclaimed Districts.	Date of Proclamation.
Armagh,	The Parishes of Ballymyre, [illegible], Creggan, [illegible], and [illegible].	[illegible] March, 18[illegible]
Belfast,	The Borough,	[illegible] July, 18[illegible]
Carlow,	The County,	[illegible] December, 18[illegible]
Clare,	"	[illegible] April, "
Cork,	"	" "
Cork City,	The County of the City	" "
Donegal,	The Baronies of [illegible], [illegible], and [illegible] and the Parishes of [illegible] in the Barony of [illegible].	
Drogheda,	The County of the Town,	[illegible] November, "
Dublin,	The County,	" "
Dublin City,	The Metropolitan Police District (a),	" "
Galway,	The County,	[illegible] April, "
Galway Town,	The County of the Town,	" "
Kerry,	The County,	" "
Kildare,	"	[illegible] December, "
Kilkenny,	" (b)	[illegible] May, "
King's,	"	[illegible] June, "
Leitrim,	"	[illegible] April, "
Limerick,	"	" "
Limerick City,	The County of the City,	" "
Londonderry City,	The Borough,	[illegible] July, 18[illegible]
Longford,	The County,	[illegible] April, 18[illegible]
Mayo,	"	" "
Meath,	"	[illegible] December, "
Monaghan,	The Baronies of Farney and Cremorne, and Parish of [illegible],	[illegible] August, 18[illegible]
Queen's,	The County,	[illegible] April, 18[illegible]
Roscommon,	"	" "
Sligo,	"	" "
Tipperary,	" (c)	[illegible] December, "
Waterford,	"	" "
Waterford City,	The County of the City	" "
Westmeath,	The County,	[illegible] April, "
Wexford,	"	[illegible] December, "

(a) [illegible]
(b) [illegible]
(c) [illegible]

TABLE 12.—RETURN No. 2, showing the several Districts which were under the operation of Proclamation in Council under the above Act, prohibiting the Carrying of Arms, &c., on the 31st December, 1896.

County, &c.	Proclaimed Districts.	Date of Proclamation.
Armagh,	That part of the Parish of Newry in which is situate that portion of the town of Newry which is in the County Armagh, and also that part of the Barony of Lower Orior which is contiguous to the aforesaid part of the Parish of Newry.	[illegible] November, 18[illegible]
Cavan,	The County,	[illegible] April, 18[illegible]
Down,	The Barony or Lordship of Newry,	[illegible] November, 18[illegible]
Fermanagh,	The County,	[illegible]
Monaghan,	The County (a),	[illegible] April, 18[illegible]
Tyrone,	The Baronies of Dungannon Upper and Middle,	[illegible] May,
	The Baronies of Omagh East, Omagh West, and Clogher,	[illegible] December, 18[illegible]

(a) The Baronies of Farney and Cremorne and the Parish of [illegible] were prohibited for having or carrying Arms, &c., on [illegible] August, 18[illegible].

POLICE ESTABLISHMENTS.

13.—Royal Irish Constabulary.

14.—Dublin Metropolitan Police.

TABLE 12.—ESTABLISHMENTS (1).—ROYAL IRISH CONSTABULARY.—Return of Cities and Counties of Towns, at Census of 1891, and Cost under the different Counties and Districts specially charged, in the year ended

Royal Irish Constabulary.	Part I.—Establishment on 30th September, 189[illegible]						
	Inspector-General	[illegible]	District Inspectors	Clerks	[illegible]	Messengers	Total.
Head Office, Dublin Castle,	1	[illegible]	[illegible]	[illegible]	[illegible]	[illegible]	[illegible]

Part II.—Establishment (including Depot) on 30th September, 189[illegible]

[illegible]	[illegible]	[illegible]	[illegible]	[illegible]	[illegible]	[illegible]	Head Constables	[illegible]	Acting Sergeants	Constables	[illegible]	[illegible]	Total.
[illegible]	[illegible]	[illegible]	[illegible]	[illegible]	[illegible]	[illegible]	[illegible]	[illegible]	[illegible]	[illegible]	[illegible]	[illegible]	[illegible]

a [illegible] included in Part II. b Employed as Clerks at Head Office [illegible]
c In years [illegible]

Part III.—Effective Strength of the Force in Counties, and in

Counties, and Counties of Cities and of Towns, with Ridings or Districts.	County and Town Inspectors.	District Inspectors.	Head Constables.	Sergeants, Acting Sergeants, and Constables.	Total Strength [illegible]	Population [illegible] Census of 1891.	Number of [illegible] per 1,000 of Population.
Antrim,	1	[illegible]	[illegible]	[illegible]	[illegible]	[illegible]	[illegible]
Armagh,	1	[illegible]	[illegible]	[illegible]	[illegible]	[illegible]	[illegible]
Carlow,	1	[illegible]	[illegible]	[illegible]	[illegible]	[illegible]	[illegible]
Cavan,	1	[illegible]	[illegible]	[illegible]	[illegible]	[illegible]	[illegible]
Clare,	1	7	[illegible]	[illegible]	[illegible]	[illegible]	[illegible]
Cork, East Riding,	1	11	[illegible]	[illegible]	[illegible]	[illegible]	[illegible]
Cork, West Riding,	1	[illegible]	[illegible]	[illegible]	[illegible]	[illegible]	[illegible]
Donegal,	1	[illegible]	[illegible]	[illegible]	[illegible]	[illegible]	[illegible]
Down,	1	[illegible]	[illegible]	[illegible]	[illegible]	[illegible]	[illegible]
Dublin,	1	[illegible]	[illegible]	[illegible]	[illegible]	[illegible]	[illegible]
Fermanagh,	1	[illegible]	[illegible]	[illegible]	[illegible]	[illegible]	[illegible]
Galway, East Riding,	1	[illegible]	[illegible]	[illegible]	[illegible]	[illegible]	[illegible]
Galway, West Riding,	1	[illegible]	[illegible]	[illegible]	[illegible]		
Kerry,	1	[illegible]	[illegible]	[illegible]	[illegible]	[illegible]	[illegible]
Kildare,	1	[illegible]	[illegible]	[illegible]	[illegible]	[illegible]	[illegible]
Kilkenny,	1	[illegible]	[illegible]	[illegible]	[illegible]	[illegible]	[illegible]
King's,	1	[illegible]	[illegible]	[illegible]	[illegible]	[illegible]	[illegible]
Leitrim,	1	[illegible]	[illegible]	[illegible]	[illegible]	[illegible]	[illegible]
Limerick,	1	7	[illegible]	[illegible]	[illegible]	[illegible]	[illegible]
Londonderry,	1	[illegible]	[illegible]	[illegible]	[illegible]	[illegible]	[illegible]
Longford,	1	3	[illegible]	[illegible]	[illegible]	[illegible]	[illegible]
Louth,	1	[illegible]	[illegible]	[illegible]	[illegible]	[illegible]	[illegible]
Mayo,	1	[illegible]	[illegible]	[illegible]	[illegible]	[illegible]	[illegible]
Meath,	1	[illegible]	[illegible]	[illegible]	[illegible]	[illegible]	[illegible]
Monaghan,	1	[illegible]	[illegible]	[illegible]	[illegible]	[illegible]	[illegible]

(a) In the printed abstract of Census returns the population of Dublin County and City is given as [illegible]. By deducting the population [illegible] outside the Metropolitan Police District, [illegible]
(b) Exclusive of [illegible]

of Establishment on 30th September, 1896, with Population of Counties, and Counties [illegible] Heads of Service, with the proportion paid by Her Majesty's Treasury, and also by 31st March, 1896, made by the Inspector-General.

Cost of Establishment.									
[illegible]	[illegible]	[illegible]	[illegible]	[illegible]	[illegible]	[illegible]	[illegible]	[illegible]	[illegible]
£ s. d.	£ s. d.	£ s. d.	£ s. d.	£ s. d.	£ s. d.	£ s. d.	£ s. d.	£ s. d.	£ s. d.
[illegible]	[illegible]	[illegible]	[illegible]	[illegible]	[illegible]	[illegible]	[illegible]	[illegible]	[illegible]

[illegible]

Counties of Cities and of Towns, on the 30th day of September, 189[illegible].

[illegible]	County and Town Inspectors.	District Inspectors.	Head Constables.	[illegible]	[illegible]	Population according to Census of 1891.	[illegible]
Queen's,	1	[illegible]	[illegible]	[illegible]	[illegible]	[illegible]	[illegible]
Roscommon,	1	[illegible]	[illegible]	[illegible]	[illegible]	[illegible]	[illegible]
Sligo,	1	[illegible]	[illegible]	[illegible]	[illegible]	[illegible]	[illegible]
Tipperary, North Riding,	1	[illegible]	[illegible]	[illegible]	[illegible]	[illegible]	[illegible]
Tipperary, South Riding,	1	7	7	[illegible]	[illegible]	[illegible]	[illegible]
Tyrone,	1	[illegible]	[illegible]	[illegible]	[illegible]	[illegible]	[illegible]
Waterford,	1	[illegible]	[illegible]	[illegible]	[illegible]	[illegible]	[illegible]
Westmeath,	1	[illegible]	[illegible]	[illegible]	[illegible]	[illegible]	[illegible]
Wexford,	1	[illegible]	[illegible]	[illegible]	[illegible]	[illegible]	[illegible]
Wicklow,	1	[illegible]	[illegible]	[illegible]	[illegible]	[illegible]	[illegible]
Cities and Towns.							
Carrickfergus,	-	-	-	[illegible]	[illegible]	[illegible]	[illegible]
Cork,	-	[illegible]	[illegible]	[illegible]	[illegible]	[illegible]	[illegible]
Drogheda,	-	1	1	[illegible]	[illegible]	[illegible]	[illegible]
Galway,	-	1	1	[illegible]	[illegible]	[illegible]	[illegible]
Kilkenny,	-	[illegible]	[illegible]	[illegible]	[illegible]	[illegible]	[illegible]
Limerick,	-	1	1	[illegible]	[illegible]	[illegible]	[illegible]
Londonderry,	-	1	1	[illegible]	[illegible]	[illegible]	[illegible]
Waterford,	-	1	1	[illegible]	[illegible]	[illegible]	[illegible]
Total,	[illegible]	[illegible]	[illegible]	[illegible]	[illegible]	[illegible]	-
Belfast City Force,	1	[illegible]	[illegible]	[illegible]	[illegible]	[illegible]	[illegible]
Reserve Force,	-	[illegible]	[illegible]	[illegible]	(1) [illegible]	-	
Depot,	-	[illegible]	[illegible]	[illegible]	[illegible]	-	-
Total,	[illegible]	[illegible]	[illegible]	[illegible]	[illegible]	[illegible]	[illegible]

[illegible]

PART IV.—AMOUNT CHARGED to COUNTIES and COUNTIES of CITIES and of TOWNS for EXTRA FORCE in the Year ended 30th September, 1896.

Greatest Number of Extra Men chargeable in the Year [illegible], in the month of March, 189[illegible] . . . . . . 1[illegible]	Least Number of Extra Men chargeable in the Year [illegible], in the month of September, 189[illegible] . . . . . . 1[illegible]	Monthly average of Extra Men during the Year . . . . [illegible]

PART V.—A STATEMENT of the COST of the ROYAL IRISH CONSTABULARY FORCE, including all Items of Expenditure which have a direct bearing and reference to the Charge proper for Constabulary purposes, in the Year ended 31st March, 1896.

	£ s. d.
Superintending Officers' Salaries and Allowances . . .	[illegible]
Pay, Rate Pay, and Allowances	[illegible]
Clothing	[illegible]
Arms, Ammunition, Accoutrements, and Saddlery . . .	[illegible] 11
Horses and Forage	[illegible]
Rent of Barracks, Barrack Furniture, Fuel, and Light . . .	[illegible]
Pensions and Gratuities	[illegible]
Miscellaneous	[illegible]
Total	[illegible]

* [illegible] the "Pay" sub-head of the Constabulary Vote, [illegible] "Rent of Barracks."

TABLE 14.—ESTABLISHMENTS (3).—DUBLIN METROPOLITAN POLICE.—Return of Establishment, with Population of Divisions, and Costs under the different Heads of Service, with the Proportion paid by Her Majesty's Treasury, in the Year ended 31st March, 1896, made by the Commissioner of Police.

PART I.	Establishment	Salaries and Pay.	Allowances and Contingent Expenses.	Clothing and Accoutrements.	[illegible]	Horses, Forage, &c.	[illegible] Charges.	Other Miscellaneous Charges.	Total Cost.	Proportion paid by H.M. Treasury.
		£ s. d.	£ s. d.	£ s. d.	£ s. d.	£ s. d.	£ s. d.	£ s. d.	£ s. d.	£ s. d.
Office of Commissioner of Police	[illegible]									
PART II.—ESTABLISHMENT OF DUBLIN METROPOLITAN FORCE.	[illegible]	[illegible]	[illegible]	[illegible]	[illegible]	[illegible]	[illegible]	[illegible]	[illegible]	[illegible]

Part III.—Dublin Police Courts.

Part III.	Number of Courts.	Establishment.				Cost of Establishment.						
		Magistrates.	Clerks.	Police (Officers and Constables).	Total.	Salaries and Pay. (1).	Fuel and Light. (2).	Rents, Taxes, [illegible] (3).	[illegible] (4).	Other [illegible] Charges. (5).	Total Cost. (6).	Proportion paid by [illegible] (7).
						£ s. d.	£ s. d.	£ s. d.	£ s. d.	£ s. d.	£ s. d.	£ s. d.
Police Courts . .	1	4	13	13	30	[illegible]	[illegible]	[illegible]	[illegible]	177 16 1	11,047 [illegible]	[illegible]

Part IV.—Effective Strength of the Force, in Divisions, on 31st March, 189[illegible].

Divisions.	Superintendents.	Inspectors.	Sergeants.	Constables.	Detective Officers.	Total Effective Superintendents, Inspectors, Sergeants, Constables, and Detective Officers.	Population according to Census of 1891.	Number of Persons [illegible] per [illegible] of Population.
1. A, City, S.W. . . .	1	6	[illegible]	[illegible]	–	[illegible]	[illegible]	[illegible]
2. B, ,, S.E. . . .	1	[illegible]	[illegible]	[illegible]	–	[illegible]	[illegible]	[illegible]
3. C, ,, N.E. . . .	[illegible]	[illegible]	[illegible]	[illegible]	–	[illegible]	[illegible]	[illegible]
4. D, ,, N.W., and Rural* .	1	[illegible]	[illegible]	[illegible]	–	[illegible]	[illegible]	[illegible]
5. E, ,, S., and Rural† .	1	[illegible]	[illegible]	[illegible]	–	[illegible]	[illegible]	[illegible]
6. F, Rural‡ . . .	1	[illegible]	[illegible]	[illegible]	–	[illegible]	[illegible]	[illegible]
7. G§	1	6	[illegible]	[illegible]	[illegible]	[illegible]	–	–
Total	7	(a) [illegible]	[illegible]	[illegible]	[illegible]	(a) 1,1[illegible]	[illegible],377	[illegible]

* D, Rural part—[illegible] to [illegible].
† E, Rural part—[illegible] to [illegible].
‡ F, Rural—[illegible].
§ The Officers and Constables of the G Division are employed as "Detectives."
(a) Exclusive of 1 Inspector, [illegible] Sergeants, and [illegible] Constables, employed in Government Departments and on [illegible] service with Public Bodies.

Notes to Tables 15, 16, 17.

(a.) These Tables include only offences tried summarily. All indictable offences where the Court does not actually assume the power to determine the case summarily are excluded. Further, these Tables include only cases where the proceedings are criminal—that is, lead if successful to a conviction. There are a large number of cases which are quasi-criminal in character, but where the procedure is by complaint, leading, not to a conviction, but to the making of an order. These are provided for in a separate Table—No. 18.

(b.) The Tables show the number of persons prosecuted, not the number of offences. Where therefore any person is prosecuted at the same time for several offences, one offence has to be selected for tabulation, and the rules followed are the same as in Table 1 to 5 (see note (b) page 50).

(c.) The offences included under each of the titles of offences in Column 1 are stated on page 46 of the Criminal Statistics for the year 1894.

Notes to Table 18.

(d.) Table 18 corresponds to Tables 1, 3, and 6, and (as regards length of sentences) to Tables 2 and 4.

(e.) Column 4, "Committed to Industrial Schools," includes only those committals to Industrial Schools where an offence is charged—i.e., committals under Section 13 of the Industrial Schools (Ireland) Act, 1868. Other committals to Industrial Schools where the proceedings are not criminal appear in Table 18, and also in Tables 46 to 47.

(f.) Columns 7 to 13, "Imprisonment," do not include the preliminary imprisonment in Reformatory School cases, nor terms of imprisonment in default of paying fine or of finding sureties.

(g.) Column 14, "Reformatory School," contains all cases of persons sentenced to Reformatory School detention, whether they are actually admitted to a reformatory or not. Details as to cases actually received in reformatories are given in Table 41.

(h.) Columns 16 and 19, "Fine," include all cases where a fine is imposed whether the fine is paid or not. The number of persons committed to prison in default of paying fines is given in Tables 33 and 53.

(i.) Columns 17, 17a, and 20, "Recognizances," include all cases where the defendant is ordered to find sureties, whether the sureties are found or not. It must be remembered, however, that the Table applies only to convictions, and thus it does not include cases where a person is required to find sureties upon complaint. These cases are included in Table 18.

Note to Table 19.

(k.) This Table corresponds to Table 8, and the list of Counties is the same.

COURTS OF SUMMARY JURISDICTION.

15.—COURTS OF SUMMARY JURISDICTION.—Number of Persons Tried, Nature of Offences, Results of Proceedings and Length of Sentences.

16.—COURTS OF SUMMARY JURISDICTION.—Number of Persons Tried for each Offence in each County.

17.—COURTS OF SUMMARY JURISDICTION.—Age and Sex of Persons Convicted.

18.—COURTS OF SUMMARY JURISDICTION.—Proceedings in Quasi Criminal Matters.

19.—COURTS OF SUMMARY JURISDICTION.—Appeals to Quarter Sessions.

TABLE 15.—COURTS OF SUMMARY JURISDICTION.—Number of Persons [illegible] and Length [illegible]

OFFENCES. (1)	(2)	(3)	(4)	(5)	(6)	(7)	(8)	(9)	(10)	(11)
Section (A).—Indictable Offences tried Summarily.										
Simple Larceny,	[illegible]	[illegible]	[illegible]	[illegible]	[illegible]	[illegible]	[illegible]	[illegible]	[illegible]	[illegible]
Offences punishable as Simple Larceny,	[illegible]	.	[illegible]	.	[illegible]	[illegible]	.	[illegible]	[illegible]	[illegible]
Larceny from the Person,	[illegible]	[illegible]	[illegible]	.	[illegible]	[illegible]	.	[illegible]	[illegible]	[illegible]
Larceny by a Servant,	[illegible]	[illegible]	[illegible]	[illegible]	[illegible]	[illegible]	.	[illegible]	[illegible]	[illegible]
Embezzlement,	[illegible]	[illegible]	[illegible]	.	[illegible]	[illegible]	.	[illegible]	[illegible]	[illegible]
Receiving Stolen Goods,	[illegible]	[illegible]	[illegible]	.	[illegible]	[illegible]	.	.	[illegible]	.
Endangering Railway Passengers,	[illegible]	.	[illegible]	.	[illegible]	[illegible]	.	.	.	.
Destroying Railways,	.	.	.	.	.	.	.	.	.	.
Offences under the Post Office Laws,	[illegible]	.	.	.	[illegible]	[illegible]	.	.	.	[illegible]
Suicide, Attempting to Commit (in Dublin),	[illegible]	.	[illegible]	.	[illegible]	[illegible]	.	.	[illegible]	[illegible]
Other Indictable Offences committed by Children under 12,	[illegible]	.	.	.	[illegible]	.	.	.	.	.
TOTAL OF SECTION (A),	[illegible]	[illegible]	[illegible]	[illegible]	[illegible]	[illegible]	[illegible]	[illegible]	[illegible]	[illegible]
		[illegible]								
Section (B).—Other Offences tried Summarily.										
Adulteration of Food and Drugs,	[illegible]	[illegible]	[illegible]	.	[illegible]	.	.	.	.	.
Assaults:—										
Aggravated,	[illegible]	[illegible]	[illegible]	[illegible]	[illegible]	[illegible]	.	[illegible]	[illegible]	[illegible]
On Constables,	[illegible]	[illegible]	[illegible]	.	[illegible]	[illegible]	[illegible]	[illegible]	[illegible]	[illegible]
Common,	[illegible]	[illegible]	[illegible]	.	[illegible]	[illegible]	[illegible]	[illegible]	[illegible]	[illegible]
Betting and Gaming,	[illegible]	[illegible]	[illegible]	.	[illegible]	.	.	.	.	.
Brothel Keeping,	[illegible]	.	[illegible]	.	[illegible]	.	.	.	.	.
Cruelty to Animals,	[illegible]	[illegible]	[illegible]	.	[illegible]	[illegible]	.	.	.	[illegible]
Cruelty to Children,	[illegible]	[illegible]	[illegible]	.	[illegible]	[illegible]	.	[illegible]	[illegible]	[illegible]
Diseases of Animals Act, Offences against,	[illegible]	.	[illegible]	.	[illegible]	[illegible]	.	[illegible]	.	.
Dogs, Offences in relation to,	[illegible]	[illegible]	[illegible]	.	[illegible]	.	.	.	.	.
Elementary Education Act, Offences against,	[illegible]	[illegible]	[illegible]	.	[illegible]	.	.	.	.	.
Explosives, Offences in relation to,	[illegible]	.	.	.	[illegible]	.	.	.	.	.
Fishery Laws, Offences against,	[illegible]	[illegible]	[illegible]	.	[illegible]	[illegible]	.	.	[illegible]	.
Game Laws, Offences against:—										
Night Poaching,	[illegible]	[illegible]	[illegible]	.	[illegible]	[illegible]	.	.	[illegible]	[illegible]
Day Poaching,	[illegible]	[illegible]	[illegible]	.	[illegible]	[illegible]	.	.	[illegible]	[illegible]
Unlawful Possession of Game, &c.,	[illegible]	.	[illegible]	.	[illegible]	.	.	.	.	.
Illegal Buying and Selling of Game,	.	.	.	.	.	.	.	.	.	.
Other Offences,	[illegible]	[illegible]	[illegible]	.	[illegible]	[illegible]	.	.	.	.
Highway Acts, Offences against:—										
Offences by Owners and Drivers of Carts,	[illegible]	[illegible]	[illegible]	.	[illegible]	.	.	.	.	.
Obstructions and Nuisances,	[illegible]	[illegible]	[illegible]	.	[illegible]	.	.	.	.	.
Locomotives,	[illegible]	.	[illegible]	.	[illegible]	.	.	.	.	.
[illegible] Act, Offences against,	.	.	.	.	.	.	.	.	.	.
Indecent Advertisements,	[illegible]	.	.	.	[illegible]	.	.	.	.	.
Indecent Exposure,	[illegible]	.	[illegible]	.	[illegible]	[illegible]	.	[illegible]	[illegible]	[illegible]
Intoxicating Liquor Laws, Offences against:—										
Drunkenness,	[illegible]	[illegible]	[illegible]	.	[illegible]	[illegible]	[illegible]	.	[illegible]	[illegible]
Permitting Drunkenness on Licensed Premises,	[illegible]	.	[illegible]	.	[illegible]	.	.	.	.	.
Other Offences against Public Order,	[illegible]	[illegible]	[illegible]	.	[illegible]	[illegible]	.	.	.	.
Illegal Sale of Drink,	[illegible]	[illegible]	[illegible]	.	[illegible]	[illegible]	.	.	.	[illegible]
Offences against Closing Regulations,	[illegible]	[illegible]	[illegible]	.	[illegible]	[illegible]	.	.	.	.
Other Offences,	[illegible]	[illegible]	[illegible]	.	[illegible]	[illegible]	.	.	.	.
Labour Laws, Offences against:—										
Intimidation,	[illegible]	[illegible]	[illegible]	.	[illegible]	.	.	.	.	.
Breach of Contract,	[illegible]	[illegible]	[illegible]	.	[illegible]	[illegible]	.	.	.	.
Offences under Special Trade Acts,	.	.	.	.	.	.	.	.	.	.
Offences under Truck Acts,	.	.	.	.	.	.	.	.	.	.
Mines Acts,	.	.	.	.	.	.	.	.	.	.
Factory Acts,	[illegible]	[illegible]	[illegible]	.	[illegible]	.	.	.	.	.
Shop Hours Acts,	[illegible]	.	[illegible]	.	[illegible]	.	.	.	.	.
Other Acts for Protection of Labour,	[illegible]	.	[illegible]	.	[illegible]	[illegible]	.	.	.	.

Tried during the year 1896, Nature of Offences, Results of Proceedings, of Sentences.

[illegible]	[illegible]	[illegible]	Whipped.	Fine.	[illegible]	[illegible]	Whipped.	Fine.	[illegible]	[illegible]	OFFENCES.
											Section (A).—Indictable Offences tried Summarily.
[illegible]	[illegible]	[illegible]	9	[illegible]	[illegible]	19	.	.	1	.	Simple Larceny.
.	1	.	.	.	.	.	.	.	1	.	Offences punishable as Simple Larceny.
[illegible]	[illegible]	4	.	1	[illegible]	4	.	.	.	.	Larceny from the Person.
[illegible]	[illegible]	8	.	.	[illegible]	.	.	.	.	.	Larceny by a Servant.
8	8	1	.	.	8	.	.	.	.	.	Embezzlement.
1	1	.	.	4	5	.	.	.	.	.	Receiving Stolen Goods.
.	1	.	.	8	.	.	.	.	.	.	[illegible] Railway Passengers.
.	.	.	.	.	.	.	.	.	.	.	[illegible]
.	.	.	.	1	.	.	.	.	.	.	Offences under the Post Office Laws.
8	3	.	.	.	.	.	.	.	6	1	[illegible]
.	.	.	.	.	1	.	.	.	.	.	Other Indictable Offences [illegible] by Children under 12.
[illegible]	[illegible]	[illegible]	6	[illegible]	[illegible]	19	.	.	7	8	TOTAL OF SECTION (A).
					[illegible]						
											Section (B).—Other Offences tried Summarily.
.	.	.	.	[illegible]	.	.	.	.	.	.	Adulteration of Food and Drugs.
											Assaults:—
[illegible]	[illegible]	.	.	[illegible]	1	4	.	.	[illegible]	.	Aggravated.
[illegible]	[illegible]	1	.	[illegible]	6	4	.	.	[illegible]	.	On Constables.
[illegible]	[illegible]	5	.	[illegible]	[illegible]	[illegible]	.	8	[illegible]	.	Common.
.	.	.	.	[illegible]	.	.	.	.	.	.	Betting and Gaming.
.	.	.	.	4	.	1	.	.	.	.	Brothel Keeping.
5	8	.	.	[illegible]	.	.	.	.	.	.	Cruelty to Animals.
[illegible]	[illegible]	.	.	[illegible]	4	1	.	.	[illegible]	.	Cruelty to Children.
.	.	.	.	[illegible]	.	.	.	.	.	.	Diseases of Animals Act, Offences against.
.	.	.	.	[illegible]	.	.	.	.	.	.	Dogs, Offences in relation to.
.	.	.	.	[illegible]	.	.	.	.	.	.	Elementary Education Act, Offences against.
.	.	.	.	4	.	.	.	.	.	.	Explosives, Offences in relation to.
1	.	.	.	[illegible]	9	.	.	.	.	.	Fishery Laws, Offences against.
											Game Laws, Offences against:—
9	9	.	.	[illegible]	.	.	.	.	4	.	Night Poaching.
9	6	.	.	[illegible]	.	.	.	.	.	.	Day Trespass.
.	.	.	.	[illegible]	.	.	.	.	.	.	Unlawful Possession of Game, &c.
.	.	.	.	.	.	.	.	.	.	.	Illegal Buying and Selling of Game.
1	.	.	.	[illegible]	.	.	.	.	.	.	Other Offences.
											Highway Acts, Offences against:—
.	.	.	.	[illegible]	.	.	.	.	.	.	Offences by Owners and Drivers of Carts.
.	.	.	.	[illegible]	.	.	.	.	.	.	Obstructions and Nuisances.
.	.	.	.	[illegible]	.	.	.	.	.	.	Locomotives.
.	.	.	.	.	.	.	.	.	.	.	[illegible] Act, Offences against.
.	.	.	.	1	.	.	.	.	.	.	Indecent Advertisements.
6	8	.	.	[illegible]	1	1	.	.	8	.	Indecent Exposure.
											Intoxicating Liquor Laws, Offences against:—
[illegible]	[illegible]	.	.	[illegible]	4	.	.	6	.	[illegible]	Drunkenness.
.	.	.	.	[illegible]	.	.	.	.	.	.	Permitting Drunkenness on Licensed Premises.
[illegible]	[illegible]	.	.	[illegible]	.	.	.	.	.	.	Other Offences against Public Order.
8	1	.	.	[illegible]	.	.	.	.	.	.	Illegal Sale of Drink.
1	.	.	.	[illegible]	.	.	.	.	.	.	Offences against Closing Regulations.
.	1	.	.	[illegible]	.	.	.	.	.	.	Other Offences.
											Labour Laws, Offences against:—
.	.	.	.	8	.	.	.	.	.	.	Intimidation.
.	7	.	.	[illegible]	.	.	.	.	.	.	Breach of Contract.
.	.	.	.	.	.	.	.	.	.	.	Offences under Special Trade Acts.
.	.	.	.	.	.	.	.	.	.	.	Offences under Truck Acts.
.	.	.	.	.	.	.	.	.	.	.	Mines Acts.
.	.	.	.	[illegible]	.	.	.	.	.	.	Factory Acts.
.	.	.	.	[illegible]	.	.	.	.	.	.	Shop Hours Acts.
.	1	.	.	[illegible]	.	.	.	.	.	.	Other Acts for Protection of Labour.

TABLE 15—*continued*.—COURTS OF SUMMARY JURISDICTION.—Number of Pers[illegible] and Lan[illegible]

OFFENCES. (1)	(2)	(3)	(4)	(5)	(6)	(7)	(8)	(9)	(10)
Summary (B).—Other Offences tried Summarily—*continued*.									
Malicious Damage:—									
To Animals	[illegible]	[illegible]	[illegible]	.	[illegible]	[illegible]	.	.	.
To Fences, &c.	[illegible]	[illegible]	[illegible]	.	[illegible]	[illegible]	.	.	[illegible]
To Trees, Shrubs, &c.	[illegible]	[illegible]	[illegible]	.	[illegible]	[illegible]	.	.	.
To Fruit, &c.	[illegible]	[illegible]	[illegible]	.	[illegible]	.	.	.	.
Other Offences	[illegible]	[illegible]	[illegible]	[illegible]	[illegible]	[illegible]	[illegible]	.	.
Merchant Shipping Act, Offences against	[illegible]	[illegible]	[illegible]	.	[illegible]	[illegible]	.	.	.
Military and Naval Law, Offences against:—									
Army	[illegible]	[illegible]	[illegible]	.	[illegible]	[illegible]	.	[illegible]	[illegible]
Navy	[illegible]	.	.	.	[illegible]	[illegible]	.	.	[illegible]
Volunteers	.	.	.	.	.	.	.	.	.
Parks, Commons, and Open Spaces, Offences in relation to	[illegible]	.	[illegible]	.	[illegible]	.	.	.	.
Pawnbrokers' Acts, Offences under:—									
Offences by Pawnbrokers	[illegible]	[illegible]	[illegible]	.	[illegible]	.	.	.	.
Unlawful Pledging	[illegible]	[illegible]	[illegible]	.	[illegible]	[illegible]	.	.	.
Other Offences	.	.	.	.	.	.	.	.	.
[illegible] Act, Offences against	[illegible]	[illegible]	[illegible]	.	[illegible]	[illegible]	.	.	.
Police Regulations, Offences against:—									
Unlawful Possession	[illegible]	[illegible]	[illegible]	.	[illegible]	[illegible]	.	[illegible]	[illegible]
Dublin Metropolitan Police Act	[illegible]	[illegible]	[illegible]	.	[illegible]	[illegible]	.	.	.
Town Police Clauses Acts	[illegible]	[illegible]	[illegible]	.	[illegible]	[illegible]	.	.	.
Towns Improvement (Ireland) Act, 1854	[illegible]	[illegible]	[illegible]	.	[illegible]	[illegible]	.	.	[illegible]
Summary Jurisdiction (Ireland) Act, 1851	[illegible]	[illegible]	[illegible]	.	[illegible]	[illegible]	.	.	.
Borough Bye-laws	[illegible]	[illegible]	[illegible]	.	[illegible]	[illegible]	.	.	.
Local Acts and Bye-laws	[illegible]	[illegible]	[illegible]	.	[illegible]	[illegible]	.	.	.
Poor Law, Offences against:—									
Neglecting to maintain Family, &c.	[illegible]	[illegible]	[illegible]	.	[illegible]	[illegible]	.	.	[illegible]
Misbehaviour by Paupers	[illegible]	[illegible]	[illegible]	[illegible]	[illegible]	[illegible]	.	[illegible]	[illegible]
Stealing or Destroying Workhouse Clothes	[illegible]	[illegible]	[illegible]	.	[illegible]	[illegible]	.	.	.
Other Offences	[illegible]	[illegible]	[illegible]	.	[illegible]	[illegible]	.	.	.
Prevention of Crimes Acts:—									
Offences by Licence Holders	[illegible]	.	[illegible]	.	[illegible]	[illegible]	[illegible]	[illegible]	[illegible]
Offences by Supervisees	[illegible]	[illegible]	[illegible]	.	[illegible]	[illegible]	.	.	.
Special Offences by [illegible] Persons	.	.	.	.	.	.	.	.	.
Prostitution	[illegible]	[illegible]	[illegible]	.	[illegible]	[illegible]	.	.	[illegible]
Railways, Offences in Relation to	[illegible]	.	[illegible]	.	[illegible]	[illegible]	.	.	.
Revenue Laws, Offences against	[illegible]	[illegible]	[illegible]	.	[illegible]	[illegible]	.	[illegible]	[illegible]
Sanitary Law, Offences against:—									
Public Health Acts	[illegible]	[illegible]	[illegible]	.	[illegible]	[illegible]	.	.	.
Infectious Diseases Acts	[illegible]	.	.	.	[illegible]	.	.	.	.

Tried during the year 1896, Nature of Offences, Results of Proceedings, of Sentences.

Summarily: Imprisonment [illegible] (17)	Imprisonment [illegible] (18)	Reformatory School (19)	Whipping (20)	Fine (21)	Recognizances, &c. [illegible] (22)	[illegible] (23)	Cases where a Sentence Punishment is added: Whipping (24)	Fine (25)	[illegible] (26)	Otherwise disposed of (27)	OFFENCES. (28)
											Section (2):—Other Offences tried Summarily—continued.
											Malicious Damage:—
7	.	.	.	[illegible]	.	.	.	.	.	.	To Animals.
.	[illegible]	.	.	[illegible]	.	.	.	.	.	.	To Persons, &c.
.	[illegible]	.	.	[illegible]	.	.	.	.	.	.	To Trees, Shrubs, &c.
.	.	.	.	7	[illegible]	.	.	.	.	.	To Property, &c.
[illegible]	[illegible]	[illegible]	.	[illegible]	.	[illegible]	.	.	[illegible]	.	Other Offences.
[illegible]	[illegible]	.	.	[illegible]	.	.	.	.	.	[illegible]	Merchant Shipping Act, Offences against.
											Military and Naval Law, Offences against:—
[illegible]	[illegible]	.	.	[illegible]	.	.	.	.	.	[illegible]	Army.
[illegible]	.	.	.	.	.	.	.	.	.	[illegible]	Navy.
.	.	.	.	.	.	.	.	.	.	.	Volunteers.
.	.	.	.	[illegible]	.	.	.	.	.	.	Parks, Commons, and Open Spaces, Offences in relation to.
											Pawnbrokers' Acts, Offences against:—
.	.	.	.	[illegible]	.	.	.	.	.	.	Offences by Pawnbrokers.
[illegible]	[illegible]	.	.	[illegible]	.	.	.	.	.	.	Unlawful Pledging.
.	.	.	.	.	.	.	.	.	.	.	Other Offences.
[illegible]	.	.	.	[illegible]	.	.	.	.	.	.	Peace Preservation Act, Offences against.
											Police Regulations, Offences against:—
[illegible]	[illegible]	[illegible]	.	[illegible]	.	[illegible]	.	.	[illegible]	.	Unlawful Possession.
[illegible]	[illegible]	.	.	[illegible]	.	[illegible]	.	.	[illegible]	.	Dublin Metropolitan Police Act.
[illegible]	[illegible]	.	.	[illegible]	.	.	.	.	.	.	Town Police Clauses Act.
[illegible]	[illegible]	[illegible]	.	[illegible]	.	.	.	.	.	.	Towns Improvement (Ireland) Act, [illegible].
[illegible]	[illegible]	.	.	[illegible]	.	[illegible]	.	.	.	.	Summary Jurisdiction (Ireland) Act, [illegible].
[illegible]	[illegible]	.	.	[illegible]	.	.	.	.	[illegible]	.	Borough Bye-laws.
[illegible]	[illegible]	.	.	[illegible]	.	.	.	.	.	.	Local Acts and Bye-laws.
											Poor Law, Offences against:—
[illegible]	[illegible]	.	.	[illegible]	.	.	.	.	.	.	Neglecting to maintain Family, &c.
[illegible]	[illegible]	[illegible]	.	[illegible]	[illegible]	.	.	.	.	.	Misbehaviour by Paupers.
[illegible]	.	[illegible]	.	[illegible]	[illegible]	.	.	.	.	.	Stealing or Destroying Workhouse Clothes.
[illegible]	[illegible]	[illegible]	.	[illegible]	.	.	.	.	.	.	Other Offences.
											Prevention of Crimes Acts:—
[illegible]	[illegible]	.	.	.	.	.	.	.	.	[illegible]	Offences by Licence Holders.
[illegible]	[illegible]	.	.	.	.	.	.	.	.	.	Offences by Supervisees.
.	.	.	.	.	.	.	.	.	.	.	Special Offences by twice-convicted Persons.
[illegible]	[illegible]	.	.	[illegible]	.	.	.	.	.	.	Prostitution.
.	[illegible]	.	.	[illegible]	.	.	.	.	.	.	Railways, Offences in relation to.
.	.	.	.	[illegible]	.	.	.	.	.	.	Revenue Laws, Offences against.
											Sanitary Law, Offences against:—
[illegible]	.	.	.	[illegible]	.	.	.	.	.	.	Public Health Acts.
.	.	.	.	[illegible]	.	.	.	.	.	.	Infectious Diseases Acts.
.	[illegible]	.	.	[illegible]	.	.	.	.	.	.	Local Acts and Bye-laws.
.	.	.	.	[illegible]	.	.	.	.	.	[illegible]	Stage and Hackney Carriage Regulations, Offences against.
											Stealing:—
.	[illegible]	.	.	[illegible]	.	.	.	.	.	.	Animals (not the subject of Larceny at Common Law).
.	[illegible]	.	.	[illegible]	[illegible]	.	.	.	.	.	Fences, Stiles, Gates, &c.
[illegible]	[illegible]	.	.	[illegible]	[illegible]	.	.	.	.	.	Trees, Shrubs, &c., to the value of 1s.
[illegible]	[illegible]	.	[illegible]	[illegible]	[illegible]	.	.	.	.	.	Growing Fruit, Plants, Vegetables, &c.
[illegible]	[illegible]	.	.	[illegible]	.	.	.	.	.	.	Receiving or possessing Stolen Animals, Trees, Fruit, &c.
.	.	.	.	[illegible]	.	.	.	.	.	.	Streets and Buildings.
.	.	.	.	[illegible]	.	.	.	.	.	.	Sunday Trading, &c.
.	.	.	.	[illegible]	.	.	.	.	.	.	Vaccination Acts, Offences against.
											Vagrancy Acts, Offences against:—
[illegible]	[illegible]	[illegible]	.	[illegible]	[illegible]	[illegible]	.	.	.	.	Begging.
[illegible]	[illegible]	.	.	[illegible]	.	.	.	.	.	.	Sleeping out.
[illegible]	[illegible]	.	.	[illegible]	.	[illegible]	.	.	.	.	Gaming, &c.
.	.	.	.	.	.	.	.	.	.	.	Possessing Picklocks and other Implements.
[illegible]	[illegible]	.	.	.	[illegible]	[illegible]	.	.	[illegible]	.	Found in Enclosed Premises.
[illegible]	[illegible]	[illegible]	.	[illegible]	.	[illegible]	.	.	.	.	Frequenting.
[illegible]	[illegible]	.	.	[illegible]	.	.	.	.	.	.	Other Offences.
.	.	.	.	[illegible]	.	.	.	.	.	.	Weights and Measures Acts, Offences against.
.	.	.	.	.	.	.	.	.	.	.	Wild Birds Protection Acts, Offences against.
.	[illegible]	[illegible]	.	[illegible]	.	.	.	.	.	[illegible]	Other Offences.
[illegible]	[illegible]	[illegible]	[illegible]	[illegible]	[illegible]	[illegible]	–	[illegible]	[illegible]	[illegible]	TOTAL OF SECTION (2).
					[illegible]		[illegible]				
[illegible]	[illegible]	[illegible]	7	[illegible]	[illegible]	[illegible]	.	[illegible]	[illegible]	[illegible]	GRAND TOTAL.
					[illegible]		[illegible]				

IRELAND.

TABLE 16.—COURTS OF SUMMARY JURISDICTION.—Number of Persons

OFFENCES	Total of Persons	[illegible]													
		[illegible]	[illegible]	[illegible]	[illegible]	[illegible]	[illegible]	[illegible]	[illegible]	[illegible]	[illegible]	[illegible]	[illegible]	[illegible]	[illegible]
Section (A).—Indictable Offences tried Summarily.															
Simple Larceny	[illegible]	[illegible]	[illegible]	[illegible]	[illegible]	[illegible]	[illegible]	[illegible]	[illegible]	[illegible]	[illegible]	[illegible]	[illegible]	[illegible]	[illegible]
Offences punishable as Simple Larceny	[illegible]	[illegible]	[illegible]	[illegible]	[illegible]	[illegible]	[illegible]	[illegible]	[illegible]	[illegible]	[illegible]	[illegible]	[illegible]	[illegible]	[illegible]
Larceny from the Person	[illegible]	[illegible]	[illegible]	[illegible]	[illegible]	[illegible]	[illegible]	[illegible]	[illegible]	[illegible]	[illegible]	[illegible]	[illegible]	[illegible]	[illegible]
Larceny by a Servant	[illegible]	[illegible]	[illegible]	[illegible]	[illegible]	[illegible]	[illegible]	[illegible]	[illegible]	[illegible]	[illegible]	[illegible]	[illegible]	[illegible]	[illegible]
Embezzlement	[illegible]	[illegible]	[illegible]	[illegible]	[illegible]	[illegible]	[illegible]	[illegible]	[illegible]	[illegible]	[illegible]	[illegible]	[illegible]	[illegible]	[illegible]
Receiving Stolen Goods	[illegible]	[illegible]	[illegible]	[illegible]	[illegible]	[illegible]	[illegible]	[illegible]	[illegible]	[illegible]	[illegible]	[illegible]	[illegible]	[illegible]	[illegible]
Endangering Railway Passengers	[illegible]	[illegible]	[illegible]	[illegible]	[illegible]	[illegible]	[illegible]	[illegible]	[illegible]	[illegible]	[illegible]	[illegible]	[illegible]	[illegible]	[illegible]
Obstructing Railways	[illegible]	[illegible]	[illegible]	[illegible]	[illegible]	[illegible]	[illegible]	[illegible]	[illegible]	[illegible]	[illegible]	[illegible]	[illegible]	[illegible]	[illegible]
Offences under the Post Office Laws	[illegible]	[illegible]	[illegible]	[illegible]	[illegible]	[illegible]	[illegible]	[illegible]	[illegible]	[illegible]	[illegible]	[illegible]	[illegible]	[illegible]	[illegible]
Suicide, Attempting to Commit (in Dublin)	[illegible]	[illegible]	[illegible]	[illegible]	[illegible]	[illegible]	[illegible]	[illegible]	[illegible]	[illegible]	[illegible]	[illegible]	[illegible]	[illegible]	[illegible]
Other Indictable Offences (committed by Children under 12)	[illegible]	[illegible]	[illegible]	[illegible]	[illegible]	[illegible]	[illegible]	[illegible]	[illegible]	[illegible]	[illegible]	[illegible]	[illegible]	[illegible]	[illegible]
TOTAL OF SECTION (A)	[illegible]	[illegible]	[illegible]	[illegible]	[illegible]	[illegible]	[illegible]	[illegible]	[illegible]	[illegible]	[illegible]	[illegible]	[illegible]	[illegible]	[illegible]
Section (B).—Other Offences tried Summarily.															
Adulteration of Food and Drugs	[illegible]	[illegible]	[illegible]	[illegible]	[illegible]	[illegible]	[illegible]	[illegible]	[illegible]	[illegible]	[illegible]	[illegible]	[illegible]	[illegible]	[illegible]
Assaults:—															
Aggravated	[illegible]	[illegible]	[illegible]	[illegible]	[illegible]	[illegible]	[illegible]	[illegible]	[illegible]	[illegible]	[illegible]	[illegible]	[illegible]	[illegible]	[illegible]
On Constables	[illegible]	[illegible]	[illegible]	[illegible]	[illegible]	[illegible]	[illegible]	[illegible]	[illegible]	[illegible]	[illegible]	[illegible]	[illegible]	[illegible]	[illegible]
Common	[illegible]	[illegible]	[illegible]	[illegible]	[illegible]	[illegible]	[illegible]	[illegible]	[illegible]	[illegible]	[illegible]	[illegible]	[illegible]	[illegible]	[illegible]
Betting and Gaming	[illegible]	[illegible]	[illegible]	[illegible]	[illegible]	[illegible]	[illegible]	[illegible]	[illegible]	[illegible]	[illegible]	[illegible]	[illegible]	[illegible]	[illegible]
[illegible]	[illegible]	[illegible]	[illegible]	[illegible]	[illegible]	[illegible]	[illegible]	[illegible]	[illegible]	[illegible]	[illegible]	[illegible]	[illegible]	[illegible]	[illegible]
Cruelty to Animals	[illegible]	[illegible]	[illegible]	[illegible]	[illegible]	[illegible]	[illegible]	[illegible]	[illegible]	[illegible]	[illegible]	[illegible]	[illegible]	[illegible]	[illegible]
Cruelty to Children	[illegible]	[illegible]	[illegible]	[illegible]	[illegible]	[illegible]	[illegible]	[illegible]	[illegible]	[illegible]	[illegible]	[illegible]	[illegible]	[illegible]	[illegible]
[illegible] of Animals Act, Offences against	[illegible]	[illegible]	[illegible]	[illegible]	[illegible]	[illegible]	[illegible]	[illegible]	[illegible]	[illegible]	[illegible]	[illegible]	[illegible]	[illegible]	[illegible]
[illegible], Offences in relation to	[illegible]	[illegible]	[illegible]	[illegible]	[illegible]	[illegible]	[illegible]	[illegible]	[illegible]	[illegible]	[illegible]	[illegible]	[illegible]	[illegible]	[illegible]
Elementary Education Act, Offences against	[illegible]	[illegible]	[illegible]	[illegible]	[illegible]	[illegible]	[illegible]	[illegible]	[illegible]	[illegible]	[illegible]	[illegible]	[illegible]	[illegible]	[illegible]
Explosives, Offences in relation to	[illegible]	[illegible]	[illegible]	[illegible]	[illegible]	[illegible]	[illegible]	[illegible]	[illegible]	[illegible]	[illegible]	[illegible]	[illegible]	[illegible]	[illegible]
Factory Acts, Offences against	[illegible]	[illegible]	[illegible]	[illegible]	[illegible]	[illegible]	[illegible]	[illegible]	[illegible]	[illegible]	[illegible]	[illegible]	[illegible]	[illegible]	[illegible]
Game Laws, Offences against:—															
Night Poaching	[illegible]	[illegible]	[illegible]	[illegible]	[illegible]	[illegible]	[illegible]	[illegible]	[illegible]	[illegible]	[illegible]	[illegible]	[illegible]	[illegible]	[illegible]
Day Poaching	[illegible]	[illegible]	[illegible]	[illegible]	[illegible]	[illegible]	[illegible]	[illegible]	[illegible]	[illegible]	[illegible]	[illegible]	[illegible]	[illegible]	[illegible]
Unlawful Possession of Game, &c.	[illegible]	[illegible]	[illegible]	[illegible]	[illegible]	[illegible]	[illegible]	[illegible]	[illegible]	[illegible]	[illegible]	[illegible]	[illegible]	[illegible]	[illegible]
Illegal Buying and Selling of Game	[illegible]	[illegible]	[illegible]	[illegible]	[illegible]	[illegible]	[illegible]	[illegible]	[illegible]	[illegible]	[illegible]	[illegible]	[illegible]	[illegible]	[illegible]
Other Offences	[illegible]	[illegible]	[illegible]	[illegible]	[illegible]	[illegible]	[illegible]	[illegible]	[illegible]	[illegible]	[illegible]	[illegible]	[illegible]	[illegible]	[illegible]
Highway Acts, Offences against:—															
Offences by Owners and Drivers of Cars	[illegible]	[illegible]	[illegible]	[illegible]	[illegible]	[illegible]	[illegible]	[illegible]	[illegible]	[illegible]	[illegible]	[illegible]	[illegible]	[illegible]	[illegible]
Obstructions and Nuisances	[illegible]	[illegible]	[illegible]	[illegible]	[illegible]	[illegible]	[illegible]	[illegible]	[illegible]	[illegible]	[illegible]	[illegible]	[illegible]	[illegible]	[illegible]
[illegible]	[illegible]	[illegible]	[illegible]	[illegible]	[illegible]	[illegible]	[illegible]	[illegible]	[illegible]	[illegible]	[illegible]	[illegible]	[illegible]	[illegible]	[illegible]
Housing of the Working Classes Act, Offences against	[illegible]	[illegible]	[illegible]	[illegible]	[illegible]	[illegible]	[illegible]	[illegible]	[illegible]	[illegible]	[illegible]	[illegible]	[illegible]	[illegible]	[illegible]
Indecent Advertisements	[illegible]	[illegible]	[illegible]	[illegible]	[illegible]	[illegible]	[illegible]	[illegible]	[illegible]	[illegible]	[illegible]	[illegible]	[illegible]	[illegible]	[illegible]
Indecent Exposure	[illegible]	[illegible]	[illegible]	[illegible]	[illegible]	[illegible]	[illegible]	[illegible]	[illegible]	[illegible]	[illegible]	[illegible]	[illegible]	[illegible]	[illegible]
Intoxicating Liquor Laws, Offences against:—															
Drunkenness	[illegible]	[illegible]	[illegible]	[illegible]	[illegible]	[illegible]	[illegible]	[illegible]	[illegible]	[illegible]	[illegible]	[illegible]	[illegible]	[illegible]	[illegible]
Permitting Drunkenness on Licensed Premises	[illegible]	[illegible]	[illegible]	[illegible]	[illegible]	[illegible]	[illegible]	[illegible]	[illegible]	[illegible]	[illegible]	[illegible]	[illegible]	[illegible]	[illegible]
Other Offences against Public Order	[illegible]	[illegible]	[illegible]	[illegible]	[illegible]	[illegible]	[illegible]	[illegible]	[illegible]	[illegible]	[illegible]	[illegible]	[illegible]	[illegible]	[illegible]
Illegal Sale of Drink	[illegible]	[illegible]	[illegible]	[illegible]	[illegible]	[illegible]	[illegible]	[illegible]	[illegible]	[illegible]	[illegible]	[illegible]	[illegible]	[illegible]	[illegible]
Offences against Closing Regulations	[illegible]	[illegible]	[illegible]	[illegible]	[illegible]	[illegible]	[illegible]	[illegible]	[illegible]	[illegible]	[illegible]	[illegible]	[illegible]	[illegible]	[illegible]
Other Offences	[illegible]	[illegible]	[illegible]	[illegible]	[illegible]	[illegible]	[illegible]	[illegible]	[illegible]	[illegible]	[illegible]	[illegible]	[illegible]	[illegible]	[illegible]
Labour Laws, Offences against:—															
[illegible]	[illegible]	[illegible]	[illegible]	[illegible]	[illegible]	[illegible]	[illegible]	[illegible]	[illegible]	[illegible]	[illegible]	[illegible]	[illegible]	[illegible]	[illegible]
Breach of Contract	[illegible]	[illegible]	[illegible]	[illegible]	[illegible]	[illegible]	[illegible]	[illegible]	[illegible]	[illegible]	[illegible]	[illegible]	[illegible]	[illegible]	[illegible]
Offences under Special Trade Acts	[illegible]	[illegible]	[illegible]	[illegible]	[illegible]	[illegible]	[illegible]	[illegible]	[illegible]	[illegible]	[illegible]	[illegible]	[illegible]	[illegible]	[illegible]
Offences under Truck Acts	[illegible]	[illegible]	[illegible]	[illegible]	[illegible]	[illegible]	[illegible]	[illegible]	[illegible]	[illegible]	[illegible]	[illegible]	[illegible]	[illegible]	[illegible]
Mines Acts	[illegible]	[illegible]	[illegible]	[illegible]	[illegible]	[illegible]	[illegible]	[illegible]	[illegible]	[illegible]	[illegible]	[illegible]	[illegible]	[illegible]	[illegible]
[illegible] Acts	[illegible]	[illegible]	[illegible]	[illegible]	[illegible]	[illegible]	[illegible]	[illegible]	[illegible]	[illegible]	[illegible]	[illegible]	[illegible]	[illegible]	[illegible]

[illegible]	[illegible]	[illegible]	[illegible]	[illegible]	..	[illegible]
						Assaults:—
[illegible]	[illegible]	[illegible]	[illegible]	9	..	Aggravated.
[illegible]	[illegible]	[illegible]	[illegible]	[illegible]	17	On Constables.
[illegible]	[illegible]	[illegible]	[illegible]	[illegible]	[illegible]	Common.
..	[illegible]	..	..	..	..	Betting and Gaming.
..	..	..	..	..	..	Brothel Keeping.
[illegible]	[illegible]	[illegible]	[illegible]	[illegible]	[illegible]	Cruelty to Animals.
[illegible]	[illegible]	[illegible]	[illegible]	[illegible]	[illegible]	Cruelty to Children.
[illegible]	..	..	..	[illegible]	..	Diseases of Animals Act, Offences against.
[illegible]	[illegible]	[illegible]	[illegible]	[illegible]	[illegible]	Dogs, Offences in relation to.
..	..	..	..	..	..	Elementary Education Act, Offences against.
..	..	..	..	..	..	Explosives, Offences in relation to.
[illegible]	[illegible]	[illegible]	[illegible]	[illegible]	1	Fishery Laws, Offences against.
						Game Laws, Offences against:—
[illegible]	..	[illegible]	..	[illegible]	..	Night Poaching.
[illegible]	..	[illegible]	[illegible]	[illegible]	..	Day Poaching.
[illegible]	..	[illegible]	..	..	..	Unlawful Possession of Game, &c.
..	..	..	..	..	..	Illegal buying and Selling of Game.
..	..	[illegible]	..	1	..	Other Offences.
						Highway Acts, Offences against:—
[illegible]	[illegible]	[illegible]	[illegible]	[illegible]	[illegible]	Offences by Owners and Drivers of Cars.
[illegible]	[illegible]	[illegible]	[illegible]	[illegible]	[illegible]	Obstructions and Nuisances.
..	..	[illegible]	..	..	..	[illegible]
..	..	..	..	..	..	Housing of the Working Classes Act, Offences [illegible]
..	..	..	..	..	..	Indecent Advertisements.
[illegible]	[illegible]	..	[illegible]	..	[illegible]	Indecent Exposure.
						Intoxicating Liquor Laws, Offences against:—
[illegible]	[illegible]	[illegible]	[illegible]	[illegible]	[illegible]	Drunkenness.
[illegible]	..	[illegible]	[illegible]	[illegible]	[illegible]	Permitting Drunkenness on Licensed Premises.
[illegible]	[illegible]	[illegible]	[illegible]	[illegible]	[illegible]	Other Offences against Public Order.
[illegible]	[illegible]	[illegible]	[illegible]	[illegible]	[illegible]	Illegal Sale of Drink.
[illegible]	[illegible]	[illegible]	[illegible]	[illegible]	[illegible]	Offences against Closing Regulations.
[illegible]	[illegible]	[illegible]	[illegible]	[illegible]	[illegible]	Other Offences.
						Labour Laws, Offences against:—
[illegible]	..	..	..	..	..	Intimidation.
[illegible]	..	..	..	..	..	Breach of Contract.
..	..	..	..	..	..	Offences under Special Trade Acts.
..	..	..	..	..	..	Offences under Truck Acts.
..	..	..	..	..	..	Other Acts.

TABLE 10—*continued*.—COURTS OF SUMMARY JURISDICTION.—Number of Persons

Section III.—Other Offences tried Summarily—continued.

Malicious Damage:—
To Animals.
To Fences, &c.
To Trees, Shrubs, &c.
To Fruit, &c.
Other Offences.
Merchant Shipping Act, Offences against.

Military and Naval Laws, Offences against:—
Army.
Navy.
Volunteers.
Parks, Commons, and Open Spaces, Offences in relation to.

Pawnbrokers Acts, Offences against:—
Offences by Pawnbrokers.
Unlawful Pledging.
Other Offences.
[illegible] Act, Offences against.

Police Regulations, Offences against:—
[illegible]
[illegible] Metropolitan Police Act.
Town Police Clauses Act.
[illegible] Act, [illegible]
[illegible] Act, [illegible]
Borough Bye-laws.
Local Acts and Bye-laws.

Poor Laws, Offences against:—
Neglecting to maintain Family, &c.
Misbehaviour by Paupers.
[illegible]
Other Offences.

Prevention of Crimes Acts:—
Offences by Licence Holders.
Offences by Supervisees.
Special Offences by [illegible] Persons.
[illegible]
Railways, Offences in relation to.
Revenue Laws, Offences against.

Sanitary Laws, Offences against:—
Public Health Acts.
[illegible] Acts.
Local Acts and Bye-laws.
[illegible] Offences against.

Stealing:—
Animals.
Fences, Wood, Gates, &c.
Trees, Shrubs, &c., to the value of 1s.
Growing Fruit, Trees, Vegetables, &c.
[illegible]
[illegible]
Sunday Trading, &c.
[illegible] Acts, Offences against.

Vagrancy Acts, Offences against:—
Begging.
Sleeping out.
Gaming, &c.
Possessing Picklocks and other Implements.
Found in Enclosed Premises.
Fortune-telling.
Other Offences.
Weights and Measures Acts, Offences against.
Wild Birds Protection Acts, Offences against.
Other Offences.

TABLE 16—continued—COURTS OF SUMMARY JURISDICTION.—Number of Persons

OFFENCES.	[illegible]	[illegible]	[illegible]	[illegible]	[illegible]	[illegible]	[illegible]	[illegible]	[illegible]	[illegible]
Section (A).—Indictable Offences tried Summarily.										
Simple Larceny,	[illegible]	[illegible]	[illegible]	[illegible]	[illegible]	[illegible]	[illegible]	[illegible]	[illegible]	[illegible]
Offences punishable as Simple Larceny,	[illegible]	[illegible]	[illegible]	[illegible]	[illegible]	[illegible]	[illegible]	[illegible]	[illegible]	[illegible]
Larceny from the Person,	[illegible]	[illegible]	[illegible]	[illegible]	[illegible]	[illegible]	[illegible]	[illegible]	[illegible]	[illegible]
Larceny by a Servant,	[illegible]	[illegible]	[illegible]	[illegible]	[illegible]	[illegible]	[illegible]	[illegible]	[illegible]	[illegible]
Embezzlement,	[illegible]	[illegible]	[illegible]	[illegible]	[illegible]	[illegible]	[illegible]	[illegible]	[illegible]	[illegible]
Receiving Stolen Goods,	[illegible]	[illegible]	[illegible]	[illegible]	[illegible]	[illegible]	[illegible]	[illegible]	[illegible]	[illegible]
Endangering Railway Passengers,	[illegible]	[illegible]	[illegible]	[illegible]	[illegible]	[illegible]	[illegible]	[illegible]	[illegible]	[illegible]
Damaging Railways,	[illegible]	[illegible]	[illegible]	[illegible]	[illegible]	[illegible]	[illegible]	[illegible]	[illegible]	[illegible]
Offences under the Post Office Laws,	[illegible]	[illegible]	[illegible]	[illegible]	[illegible]	[illegible]	[illegible]	[illegible]	[illegible]	[illegible]
Suicide, Attempting to Commit [illegible]	[illegible]	[illegible]	[illegible]	[illegible]	[illegible]	[illegible]	[illegible]	[illegible]	[illegible]	[illegible]
Other indictable Offences [illegible]	[illegible]	[illegible]	[illegible]	[illegible]	[illegible]	[illegible]	[illegible]	[illegible]	[illegible]	[illegible]
Total of Section (A).	[illegible]	[illegible]	[illegible]	[illegible]	[illegible]	[illegible]	[illegible]	[illegible]	[illegible]	[illegible]
Section (B).—Other Offences tried Summarily.										
Adulteration of Food and Drugs,	[illegible]	[illegible]	[illegible]	[illegible]	[illegible]	[illegible]	[illegible]	[illegible]	[illegible]	[illegible]
Assaults:—										
Aggravated,	[illegible]	[illegible]	[illegible]	[illegible]	[illegible]	[illegible]	[illegible]	[illegible]	[illegible]	[illegible]
On Constables,	[illegible]	[illegible]	[illegible]	[illegible]	[illegible]	[illegible]	[illegible]	[illegible]	[illegible]	[illegible]
Common,	[illegible]	[illegible]	[illegible]	[illegible]	[illegible]	[illegible]	[illegible]	[illegible]	[illegible]	[illegible]
Betting and Gaming,	[illegible]	[illegible]	[illegible]	[illegible]	[illegible]	[illegible]	[illegible]	[illegible]	[illegible]	[illegible]
Brothel Keeping,	[illegible]	[illegible]	[illegible]	[illegible]	[illegible]	[illegible]	[illegible]	[illegible]	[illegible]	[illegible]
Cruelty to Animals,	[illegible]	[illegible]	[illegible]	[illegible]	[illegible]	[illegible]	[illegible]	[illegible]	[illegible]	[illegible]
Cruelty to Children,	[illegible]	[illegible]	[illegible]	[illegible]	[illegible]	[illegible]	[illegible]	[illegible]	[illegible]	[illegible]
Diseases of Animals Act, Offences against,	[illegible]	[illegible]	[illegible]	[illegible]	[illegible]	[illegible]	[illegible]	[illegible]	[illegible]	[illegible]
Dogs, Offences in relation to,	[illegible]	[illegible]	[illegible]	[illegible]	[illegible]	[illegible]	[illegible]	[illegible]	[illegible]	[illegible]
Elementary Education Act, Offences against,	[illegible]	[illegible]	[illegible]	[illegible]	[illegible]	[illegible]	[illegible]	[illegible]	[illegible]	[illegible]
Explosives, Offences in relation to,	[illegible]	[illegible]	[illegible]	[illegible]	[illegible]	[illegible]	[illegible]	[illegible]	[illegible]	[illegible]
Fishery Laws, Offences against,	[illegible]	[illegible]	[illegible]	[illegible]	[illegible]	[illegible]	[illegible]	[illegible]	[illegible]	[illegible]
Game Laws, Offences against:—										
Night Poaching,	[illegible]	[illegible]	[illegible]	[illegible]	[illegible]	[illegible]	[illegible]	[illegible]	[illegible]	[illegible]
Day Poaching,	[illegible]	[illegible]	[illegible]	[illegible]	[illegible]	[illegible]	[illegible]	[illegible]	[illegible]	[illegible]
Unlawful Possession of Game, &c.,	[illegible]	[illegible]	[illegible]	[illegible]	[illegible]	[illegible]	[illegible]	[illegible]	[illegible]	[illegible]
Illegal Buying and Selling of Game,	[illegible]	[illegible]	[illegible]	[illegible]	[illegible]	[illegible]	[illegible]	[illegible]	[illegible]	[illegible]
Other Offences,	[illegible]	[illegible]	[illegible]	[illegible]	[illegible]	[illegible]	[illegible]	[illegible]	[illegible]	[illegible]
Highway Acts, Offences against:—										
Offences by Owners and Drivers of Carts,	[illegible]	[illegible]	[illegible]	[illegible]	[illegible]	[illegible]	[illegible]	[illegible]	[illegible]	[illegible]
Obstructions and Nuisances,	[illegible]	[illegible]	[illegible]	[illegible]	[illegible]	[illegible]	[illegible]	[illegible]	[illegible]	[illegible]
Locomotives,	[illegible]	[illegible]	[illegible]	[illegible]	[illegible]	[illegible]	[illegible]	[illegible]	[illegible]	[illegible]
Housing of the Working Classes Act, Offences against,	[illegible]	[illegible]	[illegible]	[illegible]	[illegible]	[illegible]	[illegible]	[illegible]	[illegible]	[illegible]
Indecent Advertisements,	[illegible]	[illegible]	[illegible]	[illegible]	[illegible]	[illegible]	[illegible]	[illegible]	[illegible]	[illegible]
Indecent Exposure,	[illegible]	[illegible]	[illegible]	[illegible]	[illegible]	[illegible]	[illegible]	[illegible]	[illegible]	[illegible]
Intoxicating Liquor Laws, Offences against:—										
Drunkenness,	[illegible]	[illegible]	[illegible]	[illegible]	[illegible]	[illegible]	[illegible]	[illegible]	[illegible]	[illegible]
Permitting Drunkenness on Licensed Premises,	[illegible]	[illegible]	[illegible]	[illegible]	[illegible]	[illegible]	[illegible]	[illegible]	[illegible]	[illegible]
Other Offences against Public Order,	[illegible]	[illegible]	[illegible]	[illegible]	[illegible]	[illegible]	[illegible]	[illegible]	[illegible]	[illegible]
Illegal Sale of Drink,	[illegible]	[illegible]	[illegible]	[illegible]	[illegible]	[illegible]	[illegible]	[illegible]	[illegible]	[illegible]
Offences against Closing Regulations,	[illegible]	[illegible]	[illegible]	[illegible]	[illegible]	[illegible]	[illegible]	[illegible]	[illegible]	[illegible]
Other Offences,	[illegible]	[illegible]	[illegible]	[illegible]	[illegible]	[illegible]	[illegible]	[illegible]	[illegible]	[illegible]
Labour Laws, Offences against:—										
Intimidation,	[illegible]	[illegible]	[illegible]	[illegible]	[illegible]	[illegible]	[illegible]	[illegible]	[illegible]	[illegible]
Breach of Contract,	[illegible]	[illegible]	[illegible]	[illegible]	[illegible]	[illegible]	[illegible]	[illegible]	[illegible]	[illegible]
Offences under Special Trade Acts,	[illegible]	[illegible]	[illegible]	[illegible]	[illegible]	[illegible]	[illegible]	[illegible]	[illegible]	[illegible]
Offences under Truck Acts,	[illegible]	[illegible]	[illegible]	[illegible]	[illegible]	[illegible]	[illegible]	[illegible]	[illegible]	[illegible]
Mines Acts,	[illegible]	[illegible]	[illegible]	[illegible]	[illegible]	[illegible]	[illegible]	[illegible]	[illegible]	[illegible]
Factory Acts,	[illegible]	[illegible]	[illegible]	[illegible]	[illegible]	[illegible]	[illegible]	[illegible]	[illegible]	[illegible]
Shop Hours Acts,	[illegible]	[illegible]	[illegible]	[illegible]	[illegible]	[illegible]	[illegible]	[illegible]	[illegible]	[illegible]
Other Acts for Protection of Labour,	[illegible]	[illegible]	[illegible]	[illegible]	[illegible]	[illegible]	[illegible]	[illegible]	[illegible]	[illegible]

Tried for each Offence in each County, and County of City, or of Town.

			Counties.								OFFENCES.
[illegible]	[illegible]	[illegible]	[illegible]	[illegible]	[illegible]	[illegible]	[illegible]	[illegible]	[illegible]	[illegible]	
											Section (A).—Indictable Offences tried Summarily.
[illegible]	[illegible]	[illegible]	[illegible]	[illegible]	[illegible]	[illegible]	[illegible]	[illegible]	[illegible]	[illegible]	Simple Larceny.
.	.	.	.	.	.	.	.	.	.	.	Offences punishable as Simple Larceny.
[illegible]	[illegible]	[illegible]	[illegible]	[illegible]	[illegible]	[illegible]	[illegible]	.	[illegible]	[illegible]	Larceny from the Person.
.	.	[illegible]	[illegible]	.	[illegible]	[illegible]	.	.	.	[illegible]	Larceny by a Servant.
.	.	.	[illegible]	.	.	[illegible]	.	.	.	.	Embezzlement.
.	.	.	[illegible]	.	[illegible]	.	.	.	[illegible]	.	Receiving Stolen Goods.
.	.	[illegible]	.	.	.	.	.	.	.	.	Endangering Railway Passengers.
.	.	.	.	.	.	.	.	.	.	.	Obstructing Railways.
.	.	.	.	.	.	.	.	.	.	.	Offences against the Post Office Laws.
.	.	.	.	.	.	.	.	.	.	.	Suicide, Attempting to Commit.
.	.	.	.	.	.	.	.	.	.	.	Other indictable Offences [illegible]
[illegible]	[illegible]	[illegible]	[illegible]	[illegible]	[illegible]	[illegible]	[illegible]	[illegible]	[illegible]	[illegible]	Total of Section (A).
											Section (B).—Other Offences tried Summarily.
[illegible]	.	[illegible]	[illegible]	[illegible]	[illegible]	[illegible]	[illegible]	[illegible]	[illegible]	[illegible]	Adulteration of Food and Drugs.
											Assaults:—
[illegible]	.	[illegible]	[illegible]	[illegible]	[illegible]	.	[illegible]	[illegible]	[illegible]	[illegible]	Aggravated.
[illegible]	[illegible]	[illegible]	[illegible]	[illegible]	[illegible]	[illegible]	[illegible]	[illegible]	[illegible]	[illegible]	On Constables.
[illegible]	[illegible]	[illegible]	[illegible]	[illegible]	[illegible]	[illegible]	[illegible]	[illegible]	[illegible]	[illegible]	Common.
.	.	.	.	.	.	.	.	.	.	.	Betting and Gaming.
.	.	[illegible]	.	.	.	.	.	.	.	.	Brothel Keeping.
[illegible]	[illegible]	[illegible]	[illegible]	[illegible]	[illegible]	[illegible]	[illegible]	[illegible]	[illegible]	[illegible]	Cruelty to Animals.
[illegible]	[illegible]	[illegible]	[illegible]	[illegible]	[illegible]	[illegible]	[illegible]	[illegible]	[illegible]	[illegible]	Cruelty to Children.
.	[illegible]	.	[illegible]	[illegible]	.	.	[illegible]	[illegible]	[illegible]	.	Diseases of Animals Act, Offences against.
[illegible]	[illegible]	[illegible]	[illegible]	[illegible]	[illegible]	[illegible]	[illegible]	[illegible]	[illegible]	[illegible]	Dogs, Offences in relation to.
[illegible]	.	[illegible]	.	.	.	.	.	.	.	.	Elementary Education Act, Offences against.
.	.	.	.	.	.	.	.	.	.	.	Explosives, Offences in relation to.
.	.	[illegible]	[illegible]	[illegible]	[illegible]	[illegible]	[illegible]	[illegible]	[illegible]	[illegible]	Fishery Laws, Offences against.
											Game Laws, Offences against:—
.	[illegible]	[illegible]	[illegible]	[illegible]	[illegible]	.	.	[illegible]	[illegible]	[illegible]	Night Poaching.
.	[illegible]	[illegible]	[illegible]	[illegible]	[illegible]	[illegible]	[illegible]	[illegible]	[illegible]	[illegible]	Day Poaching.
.	.	.	.	.	.	.	.	.	.	.	Unlawful Possession of Game, &c.
.	.	.	.	.	.	.	.	.	.	.	Illegal Buying and Selling of Game.
.	.	[illegible]	[illegible]	[illegible]	.	.	.	[illegible]	.	.	Other Offences.
											Highway Acts, Offences against:—
[illegible]	[illegible]	[illegible]	[illegible]	[illegible]	[illegible]	[illegible]	[illegible]	[illegible]	[illegible]	[illegible]	Offences by Owners and Drivers of Carts.
.	[illegible]	[illegible]	[illegible]	[illegible]	[illegible]	[illegible]	[illegible]	[illegible]	[illegible]	[illegible]	Obstructions and Nuisances.
.	.	.	.	.	.	.	.	.	.	.	Locomotives.
.	.	.	.	.	.	.	.	.	.	.	Housing of the Working Classes Act, Offences against.
.	.	.	.	.	.	.	.	.	.	.	Indecent Advertisements.
.	[illegible]	.	[illegible]	.	.	.	[illegible]	[illegible]	[illegible]	.	Indecent Exposure.
											Intoxicating Liquor Laws, Offences against:—
[illegible]	[illegible]	[illegible]	[illegible]	[illegible]	[illegible]	[illegible]	[illegible]	[illegible]	[illegible]	[illegible]	Drunkenness.
.	.	[illegible]	[illegible]	[illegible]	[illegible]	[illegible]	[illegible]	[illegible]	[illegible]	.	Permitting Drunkenness on Licensed Premises.
.	[illegible]	[illegible]	[illegible]	[illegible]	[illegible]	[illegible]	[illegible]	[illegible]	[illegible]	.	Other Offences against [illegible]
.	[illegible]	[illegible]	[illegible]	[illegible]	[illegible]	[illegible]	[illegible]	[illegible]	[illegible]	[illegible]	Illegal Sale of Drink.
[illegible]	[illegible]	[illegible]	[illegible]	[illegible]	[illegible]	[illegible]	[illegible]	[illegible]	[illegible]	[illegible]	Offences against [illegible]
[illegible]	[illegible]	[illegible]	[illegible]	[illegible]	[illegible]	[illegible]	[illegible]	[illegible]	[illegible]	[illegible]	Other Offences.
											Labour Laws, Offences relating to:—
.	.	.	.	.	.	.	.	.	.	.	Intimidation.
[illegible]	[illegible]	[illegible]	[illegible]	.	.	.	.	[illegible]	[illegible]	.	Breach of Contract.
.	.	.	.	.	.	.	.	.	.	.	Offences under Special Trade Acts.
.	.	.	.	.	.	.	.	.	.	.	Offences under Truck Acts.
.	.	.	.	.	.	.	.	.	.	.	Mines Acts.
[illegible]	.	.	[illegible]	.	.	[illegible]	.	.	.	.	Factory Acts.
.	.	[illegible]	.	.	.	.	.	.	.	.	Shop Hours Acts.
[illegible]	.	.	.	.	.	.	.	.	.	.	Other Acts for Protection of Labour.

TABLE 16—*continued.*—COURTS OF SUMMARY JURISDICTION.—Number of Persons

OFFENCES.	Counties (column headings illegible)
Section (B).—Minor Offences (continued)— continued.	
Malicious Damage—	
To Animals,	[illegible]
To Fences, &c.,	[illegible]
To Trees, Shrubs, &c.,	[illegible]
To Trees, &c.,	[illegible]
Other Offences,	[illegible]
[illegible] Act, Offences against,	[illegible]
Military and Naval Law, Offences against—	
Army,	[illegible]
Navy,	[illegible]
Volunteers,	[illegible]
Parks, Commons, and Open Spaces, Offences in relation to,	[illegible]
Pawnbrokers' Acts, Offences under—	
Offences by Pawnbrokers,	[illegible]
[illegible]	[illegible]
Other Offences,	[illegible]
Peace Preservation Act, Offences against,	[illegible]
Police Regulations, Offences against—	
Unlawful Possession,	[illegible]
Dublin Metropolitan Police Act,	[illegible]
Town Police Clauses Acts,	[illegible]
Towns Improvement (Ireland) Act, 1854,	[illegible]
Summary Jurisdiction (Ireland) Act, 1851,	[illegible]
Borough Bye-laws,	[illegible]
Local Acts and Bye-laws,	[illegible]
Poor Law, Offences against—	
[illegible]	[illegible]
[illegible] by Persons,	[illegible]
[illegible]	[illegible]
Other Offences,	[illegible]
Prevention of Crimes Acts—	
[illegible]	[illegible]
[illegible]	[illegible]
[illegible]	[illegible]
Prostitution,	[illegible]
Railways, Offences in relation to,	[illegible]
Revenue Laws, Offences against,	[illegible]
Sanitary Laws, Offences under—	
Public Health Acts,	[illegible]
[illegible] Acts,	[illegible]
Local Acts and Bye-laws,	[illegible]
[illegible]	[illegible]
Stealing—	
Animals,	[illegible]
Fences, [illegible] &c.,	[illegible]
Trees, Shrubs, &c., [illegible]	[illegible]
Growing Fruit, [illegible]	[illegible]
[illegible]	[illegible]
Street [illegible]	[illegible]
Sunday Trading, &c.,	[illegible]
Vaccination Acts, Offences against,	[illegible]
Vagrancy Acts, Offences against—	
Begging,	[illegible]
Sleeping out,	[illegible]
Gaming, &c.,	[illegible]
[illegible]	[illegible]
[illegible]	[illegible]
[illegible]	[illegible]
Other Offences,	[illegible]
Weights and Measures Acts, Offences against,	[illegible]
Wild Birds Protection Acts, Offences against,	[illegible]
Other Offences,	[illegible]
TOTAL OF SECTION (B),	[illegible]
GRAND TOTAL,	[illegible]

[illegible]	[illegible]	[illegible]	[illegible]	[illegible]	
					[illegible]—Other Offences [illegible] continued.
					Malicious Damage:—
[illegible]	[illegible]	[illegible]	[illegible]	[illegible]	To Animals.
[illegible]	[illegible]	[illegible]	[illegible]	[illegible]	To Persons, &c.
[illegible]	[illegible]	[illegible]	[illegible]	[illegible]	To Trees, Shrubs, &c.
[illegible]	[illegible]	[illegible]	[illegible]	[illegible]	To Fruit, &c.
[illegible]	[illegible]	[illegible]	[illegible]	[illegible]	Other Offences.
[illegible]	[illegible]	[illegible]	[illegible]	[illegible]	Merchant Shipping Act, Offences against.
					Military and Naval Law, Offences against:—
[illegible]	[illegible]	[illegible]	[illegible]	[illegible]	Army.
[illegible]	[illegible]	[illegible]	[illegible]	[illegible]	Navy.
[illegible]	[illegible]	[illegible]	[illegible]	[illegible]	Volunteers.
[illegible]	[illegible]	[illegible]	[illegible]	[illegible]	Parks, Commons, and Open Spaces, Offences in relation to.
					Pawnbrokers' Acts, Offences against:—
[illegible]	[illegible]	[illegible]	[illegible]	[illegible]	Offences by Pawnbrokers.
[illegible]	[illegible]	[illegible]	[illegible]	[illegible]	Unlawful Pledging.
[illegible]	[illegible]	[illegible]	[illegible]	[illegible]	Other Offences.
[illegible]	[illegible]	[illegible]	[illegible]	[illegible]	[illegible] Act, Offences against.
					Police Regulations, Offences against:—
[illegible]	[illegible]	[illegible]	[illegible]	[illegible]	[illegible]
[illegible]	[illegible]	[illegible]	[illegible]	[illegible]	[illegible] Police Act.
[illegible]	[illegible]	[illegible]	[illegible]	[illegible]	Town Police Clauses Act.
[illegible]	[illegible]	[illegible]	[illegible]	[illegible]	[illegible] Act, [illegible]
[illegible]	[illegible]	[illegible]	[illegible]	[illegible]	Summary Jurisdiction [illegible] Act, [illegible]
[illegible]	[illegible]	[illegible]	[illegible]	[illegible]	[illegible] By-laws.
[illegible]	[illegible]	[illegible]	[illegible]	[illegible]	Local Acts and By-Laws.
					Poor Law, Offences against:—
[illegible]	[illegible]	[illegible]	[illegible]	[illegible]	[illegible] Family, &c.
[illegible]	[illegible]	[illegible]	[illegible]	[illegible]	Misbehaviour by Paupers.
[illegible]	[illegible]	[illegible]	[illegible]	[illegible]	Stealing or [illegible] Workhouse Clothes.
[illegible]	[illegible]	[illegible]	[illegible]	[illegible]	Other Offences.
					Prevention of Crimes Act:—
[illegible]	[illegible]	[illegible]	[illegible]	[illegible]	Offences by License Holders.
[illegible]	[illegible]	[illegible]	[illegible]	[illegible]	Offences by Supervisees.
[illegible]	[illegible]	[illegible]	[illegible]	[illegible]	Special Offences by [illegible] Persons.
[illegible]	[illegible]	[illegible]	[illegible]	[illegible]	Prostitution.
[illegible]	[illegible]	[illegible]	[illegible]	[illegible]	Railways, Offences in Relation to.
[illegible]	[illegible]	[illegible]	[illegible]	[illegible]	Revenue Laws, Offences against.
					Sanitary Law, Offences against:—
[illegible]	[illegible]	[illegible]	[illegible]	[illegible]	Public Health Acts.
[illegible]	[illegible]	[illegible]	[illegible]	[illegible]	[illegible] Acts.
[illegible]	[illegible]	[illegible]	[illegible]	[illegible]	Local Acts and By-laws.
[illegible]	[illegible]	[illegible]	[illegible]	[illegible]	[illegible], Offences against.
					Stealing:—
[illegible]	[illegible]	[illegible]	[illegible]	[illegible]	[illegible]
[illegible]	[illegible]	[illegible]	[illegible]	[illegible]	[illegible] Gates, &c.
[illegible]	[illegible]	[illegible]	[illegible]	[illegible]	Trees, Shrubs, &c., to the value of 1s.
[illegible]	[illegible]	[illegible]	[illegible]	[illegible]	[illegible], Fruit, Vegetables, &c.
[illegible]	[illegible]	[illegible]	[illegible]	[illegible]	[illegible] Animals, Trees, Fruit, &c.
[illegible]	[illegible]	[illegible]	[illegible]	[illegible]	Streets and Buildings.
[illegible]	[illegible]	[illegible]	[illegible]	[illegible]	Sunday Trading, &c.
[illegible]	[illegible]	[illegible]	[illegible]	[illegible]	[illegible] Acts, Offences against.
					Vagrancy Acts, Offences against:—
[illegible]	[illegible]	[illegible]	[illegible]	[illegible]	Begging.
[illegible]	[illegible]	[illegible]	[illegible]	[illegible]	Sleeping out.
[illegible]	[illegible]	[illegible]	[illegible]	[illegible]	Gambling, &c.
[illegible]	[illegible]	[illegible]	[illegible]	[illegible]	Possessing [illegible] and other [illegible]
[illegible]	[illegible]	[illegible]	[illegible]	[illegible]	Found in Enclosed Premises.
[illegible]	[illegible]	[illegible]	[illegible]	[illegible]	Frequenting.
[illegible]	[illegible]	[illegible]	[illegible]	[illegible]	Other Offences.
[illegible]	[illegible]	[illegible]	[illegible]	[illegible]	Weights and Measures Acts, Offences against.
[illegible]	[illegible]	[illegible]	[illegible]	[illegible]	Wild Birds Protection Acts, Offences against.
[illegible]	[illegible]	[illegible]	[illegible]	[illegible]	Other Offences.

TABLE 17.—COURTS OF SUMMARY JURISDICTION.—Age and Sex of Persons Convicted.

Offences. (1)	Total (2)	Sex of Persons Convicted (3): Males	Females	Age of Persons Convicted
[illegible]	[illegible]	[illegible]	[illegible]	[illegible]
Total of Offences (A)	[illegible]	[illegible]	[illegible]	[illegible]
[illegible]	[illegible]	[illegible]	[illegible]	[illegible]

TABLE 17—continued.—COURTS OF SUMMARY JURISDICTION.—Age and Sex of Persons Convicted.

Offences. (1)	Total (2)	Sex of Persons Convicted (3) Males	Females	Under 12 years (4) M.	F.	(5) M.	F.	(6) M.	F.	(7) M.	F.	(8) M.	F.	(9) M.	F.	(10) M.	F.	(11) M.	F.
[illegible]	[illegible]	[illegible]	[illegible]	[illegible]	[illegible]	[illegible]	[illegible]	[illegible]	[illegible]	[illegible]	[illegible]	[illegible]	[illegible]	[illegible]	[illegible]	[illegible]	[illegible]	[illegible]	[illegible]
Total [illegible]	[illegible]	[illegible]	[illegible]	[illegible]	[illegible]	[illegible]	[illegible]	[illegible]	[illegible]	[illegible]	[illegible]	[illegible]	[illegible]	[illegible]	[illegible]	[illegible]	[illegible]	[illegible]	[illegible]

TABLE 18.—COURTS OF SUMMARY JURISDICTION.—Proceedings in Quasi-Criminal Matters.

Subject of Proceedings. (1)	Number of Applications (2)	Number of Orders made (3)	Total (4)	(5)	(6)	(7)	(8)	(9)	(10)
[illegible]	[illegible]	[illegible]	[illegible]	[illegible]	[illegible]	[illegible]	[illegible]	[illegible]	[illegible]
Total	[illegible]	[illegible]	[illegible]	[illegible]	[illegible]	[illegible]	[illegible]	[illegible]	[illegible]
MAINTENANCE.									
[illegible]	[illegible]	[illegible]	[illegible]	[illegible]	[illegible]	[illegible]	[illegible]	[illegible]	[illegible]
Total	[illegible]	[illegible]	[illegible]	[illegible]	[illegible]	[illegible]	[illegible]	[illegible]	[illegible]

Subject of Proceedings. (1)	Number of Applications (2)	Number of Orders made (3)
GOODS STOLEN, &c.		
[illegible]	[illegible]	[illegible]
Total	[illegible]	[illegible]
EMPLOYERS AND WORKMEN.		
[illegible]	[illegible]	[illegible]
Total	[illegible]	[illegible]
CHILDREN.		
[illegible]	[illegible]	[illegible]
Total	[illegible]	[illegible]

Subject of Proceedings. (1)	Number of Applications (2)	Number of Orders made (3)
SANITARY LAW.		
[illegible]	[illegible]	[illegible]
Total	[illegible]	[illegible]
OTHER ORDERS.		
[illegible]	[illegible]	[illegible]

* [illegible]

TABLE 19.—COURTS OF SUMMARY JURISDICTION.—Appeals to Quarter Sessions from Convictions by Magistrates in the Year 1896.

Section (A.)—Nature of Convictions appealed against and Results of Appeals.

Nature of Convictions Appealed Against	Number of Appeals	Affirmed.	Reversed.	Varied.	Otherwise disposed of
Adulteration of Food and Drugs Acts,	[illegible]	[illegible]	[illegible]	[illegible]	[illegible]
Assaults,	[illegible]	[illegible]	[illegible]	[illegible]	[illegible]
Cruelty to Animals,	[illegible]	[illegible]	[illegible]	.	.
Cruelty to Children,	[illegible]	.	[illegible]	.	.
Dogs, Offences in relation to,	[illegible]	[illegible]	.	.	.
Fishery Laws, Offences against,	[illegible]	[illegible]	[illegible]	[illegible]	[illegible]
Gaming Laws, Offences against,	[illegible]	[illegible]	[illegible]	[illegible]	[illegible]
Highways Acts, Offences against,	[illegible]	[illegible]	.	.	.
Indecent Exposure,	[illegible]	.	[illegible]	[illegible]	.
Intoxicating Liquor Laws, Offences against,	[illegible]	[illegible]	[illegible]	[illegible]	[illegible]
Labour Laws, Offences against,	[illegible]	[illegible]	.	.	.
Malicious Damage,	[illegible]	[illegible]	[illegible]	[illegible]	[illegible]
Railways, Offences in relation to,	[illegible]	[illegible]	.	[illegible]	.
Revenue Acts, Offences against,	[illegible]	[illegible]	[illegible]	.	[illegible]
Sanitary Laws, Offences against,	[illegible]	[illegible]	[illegible]	[illegible]	[illegible]
Stage and Hackney Carriages Regulations, Offences against,	[illegible]	.	.	[illegible]	.
Stealing,	[illegible]	.	[illegible]	.	[illegible]
Streets and Buildings, Offences in relation to,	[illegible]	[illegible]	.	.	.
Summary Jurisdiction Act, Offences against,	[illegible]	[illegible]	.	.	[illegible]
Other Offences,	[illegible]	[illegible]	[illegible]	[illegible]	.
Total,	[illegible]	[illegible]	[illegible]	[illegible]	[illegible]

TABLE 19.—COURTS OF SUMMARY JURISDICTION.—Appeals to Quarter Sessions from Convictions by Magistrates.

Section (B.)—Number of Appeals from Convictions in each County in 1896.

County.	Number of Appeals	Affirmed.	Reversed.	Varied.	Otherwise disposed of
Antrim,	[illegible]	[illegible]	[illegible]	.	[illegible]
Armagh,	[illegible]	[illegible]	.	[illegible]	[illegible]
Belfast,	[illegible]	[illegible]	[illegible]	[illegible]	[illegible]
Carlow,	[illegible]	[illegible]	.	.	[illegible]
Cavan,	[illegible]	[illegible]	[illegible]	.	.
Clare,	[illegible]	[illegible]	[illegible]	[illegible]	.
Cork, E.R.,	[illegible]	[illegible]	[illegible]	.	[illegible]
Cork, W.R.,	[illegible]	[illegible]	.	[illegible]	[illegible]
Cork City,	[illegible]	[illegible]	.	.	.
Donegal,	[illegible]	[illegible]	[illegible]	.	[illegible]
Down,	[illegible]	[illegible]	[illegible]	[illegible]	[illegible]
Dublin,	[illegible]	[illegible]		[illegible]	[illegible]
Dublin City,	[illegible]	[illegible]	[illegible]	[illegible]	[illegible]
Fermanagh,	[illegible]	[illegible]	[illegible]	[illegible]	[illegible]
Galway,	[illegible]	[illegible]	[illegible]	[illegible]	[illegible]
Galway Town,	[illegible]	.	.	.	[illegible]
Kerry,	[illegible]	[illegible]	[illegible]	[illegible]	[illegible]
Kildare,	[illegible]	[illegible]	[illegible]	[illegible]	.
Kilkenny,	[illegible]	[illegible]	[illegible]	.	[illegible]
Kilkenny City,	.	.	.	.	.
King's County,	[illegible]	[illegible]	[illegible]	[illegible]	[illegible]
Leitrim,	[illegible]	[illegible]	[illegible]	.	.
Limerick,	[illegible]	[illegible]	[illegible]	[illegible]	[illegible]
Limerick City,	[illegible]	[illegible]	[illegible]	.	[illegible]
Londonderry,	[illegible]	[illegible]	[illegible]	[illegible]	[illegible]
Londonderry City,	[illegible]	[illegible]	[illegible]	[illegible]	.
Longford,	[illegible]	[illegible]	[illegible]	[illegible]	[illegible]
Louth,	[illegible]	[illegible]	.	[illegible]	[illegible]
Mayo,	[illegible]	[illegible]	[illegible]		[illegible]
Meath,	.		.		.
Monaghan,	[illegible]	[illegible]	.	.	[illegible]
Queen's County,	[illegible]	[illegible]	[illegible]	[illegible]	.
Roscommon,	[illegible]	[illegible]	[illegible]	[illegible]	.
Sligo,	[illegible]	[illegible]	[illegible]	[illegible]	[illegible]
Tipperary,	[illegible]	[illegible]	[illegible]	[illegible]	[illegible]
Tyrone,	[illegible]	[illegible]	[illegible]	[illegible]	.
Waterford,	[illegible]	[illegible]	[illegible]	.	[illegible]
Waterford City,	[illegible]	.	[illegible]	.	[illegible]
Westmeath,	.	.	.	.	.
Wexford,	[illegible]	[illegible]	[illegible]	[illegible]	[illegible]
Wicklow,	[illegible]	[illegible]	.	.	.
Total,	[illegible]	[illegible]	[illegible]	[illegible]	[illegible]

POLICE RETURNS.

Notes to Table 20.

(a.) Column 1, "Offences."—The titles of the offences are the same as in Tables 1 to 3.

(b.) Column 2, "Number of Crimes committed"—This column includes all crimes reported to the police within the year whether committed by the same or different persons, and whether any apprehension takes place within the year or not.

(c.) If there is a committal or conviction within the year, the Table shows the nature of the crime as judicially determined. Failing this, the charge which is named in the summons or warrant on which the prisoner is arrested is taken as determining the crime. If there are no proceedings and no apprehension, the character of the crime is judged by the facts so far as known to the police.

(d.) In columns 6 to 21 the number of persons proceeded against is given, not the number of crimes or charges. A person charged at the same time with several offences appears as one person only. In selecting the offence for tabulation the same principle is followed as in Tables 1 to 3—the charge resulting in conviction or committal for trial has preference to the others; and subject to this the more serious offence is selected. If there are two or more convictions at the same time, that for which the heavier sentence is inflicted is regarded as the more serious. These columns include only cases disposed of within the year. Cases pending at the end of the year are reserved for inclusion in the following year's tables.

(e.) Columns 7, 8, 15, and 16, "Discharged," contain cases where the Magistrate does not assume power to try the case summarily, but discharges the accused under Section 13 of the Petty Sessions (Ireland) Act, 1851, or Section 25 of the Indictable Offences (Ireland) Act, 1849.

(f.) Columns 9 and 17, "Tried Summarily and Discharged," contain cases where, after the Magistrate has decided to deal summarily with the case, the charge is dismissed or withdrawn.

(g.) Columns 10 and 18, "Tried Summarily and Convicted," include cases dealt with under the Probation of First Offenders' Act, 1887.

(h.) Columns 11 and 19, "Committed for Trial and sent to Prison," include all persons committed to prison to await trial, whether they are subsequently released on bail or not.

Notes to Table 21.

(i.) The titles of the offences are the same as in Table 15 (b), and, as in that Table, only criminal proceedings are included.

(j.) Notes (a.) and (d.) above apply to this Table.

(k.) Columns 7 and 11, "Convicted," include cases dealt with under the Probation of First Offenders' Act 1887.

POLICE RETURNS.

20.—INDICTABLE OFFENCES.—Crimes committed, Apprehensions, and Prosecutions.

21.—NON-INDICTABLE OFFENCES.—Apprehensions and Prosecutions.

RETURNS FROM THE SEVERAL COUNTIES—

22.—Indictable Offences.—Crimes, Apprehensions, and Prosecutions in each County.

23.—Non-Indictable Offences.—Apprehensions and Prosecutions in each County.

24.—Indictable Offences.—Nature of Crimes committed in each County.

25.—Character of Persons Prosecuted.

26.—Numbers of Suspected Persons at Large.

27.—Numbers of Houses of Bad Character.

28.—CRIMES (INDICTABLE OFFENCES) COMMITTED, AND APPREHENSIONS IN EACH MONTH OF THE YEAR.

29.—CONVICTIONS FOR DRUNKENNESS THREE TIMES AND UPWARDS IN YEAR.

TABLE 30.—POLICE RETURNS.—INDICTABLE OFFENCES.—

OFFENCES.	CRIMES. Number of Crimes committed.	APPREHENSIONS. Persons Apprehended. Total Number.			Apprehended.			Disposal of Persons. Discharged.		Tried Summarily and	
		Total.	Males.	Females.	[illegible]	[illegible]	[illegible]	[illegible]	[illegible]	[illegible]	[illegible]
(1)	(2)		(3)		(4)	(5)	(6)	(7)	(8)	(9)	(10)
Class I.—Offences against the Person.											
1 Murder (of persons aged above One Year).	[illegible]	[illegible]	[illegible]	[illegible]	[illegible]	[illegible]	[illegible]	[illegible]	[illegible]	[illegible]	[illegible]
Do. (of Infants aged one Year and under).	[illegible]	[illegible]	[illegible]	[illegible]	[illegible]	[illegible]	[illegible]	[illegible]	[illegible]	[illegible]	[illegible]
2 Attempt to Murder.	[illegible]	[illegible]	[illegible]	[illegible]	[illegible]	[illegible]	[illegible]	[illegible]	[illegible]	[illegible]	[illegible]
3 Conspiracy or threats to Murder.	[illegible]	[illegible]	[illegible]	[illegible]	[illegible]	[illegible]	[illegible]	[illegible]	[illegible]	[illegible]	[illegible]
4 Manslaughter.	[illegible]	[illegible]	[illegible]	[illegible]	[illegible]	[illegible]	[illegible]	[illegible]	[illegible]	[illegible]	[illegible]
5 Felonious Wounding.	[illegible]	[illegible]	[illegible]	[illegible]	[illegible]	[illegible]	[illegible]	[illegible]	[illegible]	[illegible]	[illegible]
6 Endangering Railway Passengers.	[illegible]	[illegible]	[illegible]	[illegible]	[illegible]	[illegible]	[illegible]	[illegible]	[illegible]	[illegible]	[illegible]
7 Malicious Wounding (misdemeanour).	[illegible]	[illegible]	[illegible]	[illegible]	[illegible]	[illegible]	[illegible]	[illegible]	[illegible]	[illegible]	[illegible]
8 Assault.	[illegible]	[illegible]	[illegible]	[illegible]	[illegible]	[illegible]	[illegible]	[illegible]	[illegible]	[illegible]	[illegible]
9 [illegible]	[illegible]	[illegible]	[illegible]	[illegible]	[illegible]	[illegible]	[illegible]	[illegible]	[illegible]	[illegible]	[illegible]
10 Cruelty to or neglect of Children.	[illegible]	[illegible]	[illegible]	[illegible]	[illegible]	[illegible]	[illegible]	[illegible]	[illegible]	[illegible]	[illegible]
11 Abandoning Children under two years.	[illegible]	[illegible]	[illegible]	[illegible]	[illegible]	[illegible]	[illegible]	[illegible]	[illegible]	[illegible]	[illegible]
12 Child stealing.	[illegible]	[illegible]	[illegible]	[illegible]	[illegible]	[illegible]	[illegible]	[illegible]	[illegible]	[illegible]	[illegible]
13 Procuring abortion.	[illegible]	[illegible]	[illegible]	[illegible]	[illegible]	[illegible]	[illegible]	[illegible]	[illegible]	[illegible]	[illegible]
14 Concealment of birth.	[illegible]	[illegible]	[illegible]	[illegible]	[illegible]	[illegible]	[illegible]	[illegible]	[illegible]	[illegible]	[illegible]
15 Unnatural offences.	[illegible]	[illegible]	[illegible]	[illegible]	[illegible]	[illegible]	[illegible]	[illegible]	[illegible]	[illegible]	[illegible]
16 Attempts to commit unnatural offences.	[illegible]	[illegible]	[illegible]	[illegible]	[illegible]	[illegible]	[illegible]	[illegible]	[illegible]	[illegible]	[illegible]
17 Indecency with Males.	[illegible]	[illegible]	[illegible]	[illegible]	[illegible]	[illegible]	[illegible]	[illegible]	[illegible]	[illegible]	[illegible]
18 Rape.	[illegible]	[illegible]	[illegible]	[illegible]	[illegible]	[illegible]	[illegible]	[illegible]	[illegible]	[illegible]	[illegible]
19 Indecent assaults on Females.	[illegible]	[illegible]	[illegible]	[illegible]	[illegible]	[illegible]	[illegible]	[illegible]	[illegible]	[illegible]	[illegible]
20 Defilement of Girls under 13.	[illegible]	[illegible]	[illegible]	[illegible]	[illegible]	[illegible]	[illegible]	[illegible]	[illegible]	[illegible]	[illegible]
21 Defilement of Girls under 16.	[illegible]	[illegible]	[illegible]	[illegible]	[illegible]	[illegible]	[illegible]	[illegible]	[illegible]	[illegible]	[illegible]
22 Householder permitting defilement of Girls.	[illegible]	[illegible]	[illegible]	[illegible]	[illegible]	[illegible]	[illegible]	[illegible]	[illegible]	[illegible]	[illegible]
23 Procuration.	[illegible]	[illegible]	[illegible]	[illegible]	[illegible]	[illegible]	[illegible]	[illegible]	[illegible]	[illegible]	[illegible]
24 Abduction.	[illegible]	[illegible]	[illegible]	[illegible]	[illegible]	[illegible]	[illegible]	[illegible]	[illegible]	[illegible]	[illegible]
25 Bigamy.	[illegible]	[illegible]	[illegible]	[illegible]	[illegible]	[illegible]	[illegible]	[illegible]	[illegible]	[illegible]	[illegible]
26 Other offences against the Person.	[illegible]	[illegible]	[illegible]	[illegible]	[illegible]	[illegible]	[illegible]	[illegible]	[illegible]	[illegible]	[illegible]
Total of Class I.	[illegible]	[illegible]	[illegible]	[illegible]	[illegible]	[illegible]	[illegible]	[illegible]	[illegible]	[illegible]	[illegible]
Class II.—Offences against Property with Violence.											
27 Sacrilege.	[illegible]	[illegible]	[illegible]	[illegible]	[illegible]	[illegible]	[illegible]	[illegible]	[illegible]	[illegible]	[illegible]
28 Burglary.	[illegible]	[illegible]	[illegible]	[illegible]	[illegible]	[illegible]	[illegible]	[illegible]	[illegible]	[illegible]	[illegible]
29 Housebreaking.	[illegible]	[illegible]	[illegible]	[illegible]	[illegible]	[illegible]	[illegible]	[illegible]	[illegible]	[illegible]	[illegible]
30 Breaking into Shops, Warehouses, &c.	[illegible]	[illegible]	[illegible]	[illegible]	[illegible]	[illegible]	[illegible]	[illegible]	[illegible]	[illegible]	[illegible]
31 Attempts to break into Houses, Shops, &c.	[illegible]	[illegible]	[illegible]	[illegible]	[illegible]	[illegible]	[illegible]	[illegible]	[illegible]	[illegible]	[illegible]
32 Entering with intent to commit Felony.	[illegible]	[illegible]	[illegible]	[illegible]	[illegible]	[illegible]	[illegible]	[illegible]	[illegible]	[illegible]	[illegible]
33 Possession of Housebreaking Tools, &c.	[illegible]	[illegible]	[illegible]	[illegible]	[illegible]	[illegible]	[illegible]	[illegible]	[illegible]	[illegible]	[illegible]
34 Robbery and Assaults with intent to rob.	[illegible]	[illegible]	[illegible]	[illegible]	[illegible]	[illegible]	[illegible]	[illegible]	[illegible]	[illegible]	[illegible]
35 Extortion by threats [illegible]	[illegible]	[illegible]	[illegible]	[illegible]	[illegible]	[illegible]	[illegible]	[illegible]	[illegible]	[illegible]	[illegible]
36 Extortion by other threats.	[illegible]	[illegible]	[illegible]	[illegible]	[illegible]	[illegible]	[illegible]	[illegible]	[illegible]	[illegible]	[illegible]
Total of Class II.	[illegible]	[illegible]	[illegible]	[illegible]	[illegible]	[illegible]	[illegible]	[illegible]	[illegible]	[illegible]	[illegible]
Class III.—Offences against Property without Violence.											
37 Larceny of Horses, Cattle, and Sheep.	[illegible]	[illegible]	[illegible]	[illegible]	[illegible]	[illegible]	[illegible]	[illegible]	[illegible]	[illegible]	[illegible]
38 Larceny from the Person.	[illegible]	[illegible]	[illegible]	[illegible]	[illegible]	[illegible]	[illegible]	[illegible]	[illegible]	[illegible]	[illegible]
39 Larceny in House.	[illegible]	[illegible]	[illegible]	[illegible]	[illegible]	[illegible]	[illegible]	[illegible]	[illegible]	[illegible]	[illegible]
40 Larceny by a Servant.	[illegible]	[illegible]	[illegible]	[illegible]	[illegible]	[illegible]	[illegible]	[illegible]	[illegible]	[illegible]	[illegible]
41 Embezzlement.	[illegible]	[illegible]	[illegible]	[illegible]	[illegible]	[illegible]	[illegible]	[illegible]	[illegible]	[illegible]	[illegible]
42 Larceny of Post Letters.	[illegible]	[illegible]	[illegible]	[illegible]	[illegible]	[illegible]	[illegible]	[illegible]	[illegible]	[illegible]	[illegible]
43 Other aggravated larcenies.	[illegible]	[illegible]	[illegible]	[illegible]	[illegible]	[illegible]	[illegible]	[illegible]	[illegible]	[illegible]	[illegible]
44 *Simple larceny and minor larcenies.	[illegible]	[illegible]	[illegible]	[illegible]	[illegible]	[illegible]	[illegible]	[illegible]	[illegible]	[illegible]	[illegible]
45 Obtaining goods, &c., by false pretences.	[illegible]	[illegible]	[illegible]	[illegible]	[illegible]	[illegible]	[illegible]	[illegible]	[illegible]	[illegible]	[illegible]
46 Frauds by Bankers, Agents, Directors, &c.	[illegible]	[illegible]	[illegible]	[illegible]	[illegible]	[illegible]	[illegible]	[illegible]	[illegible]	[illegible]	[illegible]
47 [illegible]	[illegible]	[illegible]	[illegible]	[illegible]	[illegible]	[illegible]	[illegible]	[illegible]	[illegible]	[illegible]	[illegible]
48 Other Frauds.	[illegible]	[illegible]	[illegible]	[illegible]	[illegible]	[illegible]	[illegible]	[illegible]	[illegible]	[illegible]	[illegible]
49 Receiving Stolen Goods.	[illegible]	[illegible]	[illegible]	[illegible]	[illegible]	[illegible]	[illegible]	[illegible]	[illegible]	[illegible]	[illegible]
50 Offences in connection with Bankruptcy.	[illegible]	[illegible]	[illegible]	[illegible]	[illegible]	[illegible]	[illegible]	[illegible]	[illegible]	[illegible]	[illegible]
Total of Class III.	[illegible]	[illegible]	[illegible]	[illegible]	[illegible]	[illegible]	[illegible]	[illegible]	[illegible]	[illegible]	[illegible]

* The number of Larcenies, &c., committed as stated above, is exclusive of [illegible] cases where the property stolen was of less value than [illegible] [illegible]

Crimes Committed, Apprehensions, and Prosecutions.

APPREHENSIONS. Apprehended. Committed for Trial and — Sent to Prison.	Bailed.	Otherwise disposed of.	PROCEEDINGS BY SUMMONS. Persons proceeded against by Summons. Total.	Males.	Females.	Results of Persons proceeded against by Summons. Discharged. Charge withdrawn.	Charge dismissed.	Tried summarily and — Discharged.	Convicted.	Committed for Trial and — Sent to Prison.	Bailed.	Otherwise disposed of.	OFFENCES.
													Class I.—Offences against the Person.
[illegible]	[illegible]	[illegible]	[illegible]	[illegible]	[illegible]	[illegible]	[illegible]	[illegible]	[illegible]	[illegible]	[illegible]	[illegible]	1. Murder (of persons aged above one Year).
[illegible]	[illegible]	[illegible]	[illegible]	[illegible]	[illegible]	[illegible]	[illegible]	[illegible]	[illegible]	[illegible]	[illegible]	[illegible]	Ditto (of Infants aged one Year and under).
[illegible]	[illegible]	[illegible]	[illegible]	[illegible]	[illegible]	[illegible]	[illegible]	[illegible]	[illegible]	[illegible]	[illegible]	[illegible]	2. Attempt to Murder.
[illegible]	[illegible]	[illegible]	[illegible]	[illegible]	[illegible]	[illegible]	[illegible]	[illegible]	[illegible]	[illegible]	[illegible]	[illegible]	3. Conspiracy or threats to Murder.
[illegible]	[illegible]	[illegible]	[illegible]	[illegible]	[illegible]	[illegible]	[illegible]	[illegible]	[illegible]	[illegible]	[illegible]	[illegible]	4. Manslaughter.
[illegible]	[illegible]	[illegible]	[illegible]	[illegible]	[illegible]	[illegible]	[illegible]	[illegible]	[illegible]	[illegible]	[illegible]	[illegible]	5. Felonious Wounding.
[illegible]	[illegible]	[illegible]	[illegible]	[illegible]	[illegible]	[illegible]	[illegible]	[illegible]	[illegible]	[illegible]	[illegible]	[illegible]	6. Endangering Railway Passengers.
[illegible]	[illegible]	[illegible]	[illegible]	[illegible]	[illegible]	[illegible]	[illegible]	[illegible]	[illegible]	[illegible]	[illegible]	[illegible]	7. Malicious Wounding (misdemeanour).
[illegible]	[illegible]	[illegible]	[illegible]	[illegible]	[illegible]	[illegible]	[illegible]	[illegible]	[illegible]	[illegible]	[illegible]	[illegible]	8. Assaults.
[illegible]	[illegible]	[illegible]	[illegible]	[illegible]	[illegible]	[illegible]	[illegible]	[illegible]	[illegible]	[illegible]	[illegible]	[illegible]	9. Intimidation and Molestation.
[illegible]	[illegible]	[illegible]	[illegible]	[illegible]	[illegible]	[illegible]	[illegible]	[illegible]	[illegible]	[illegible]	[illegible]	[illegible]	10. Cruelty to or neglect of Children.
[illegible]	[illegible]	[illegible]	[illegible]	[illegible]	[illegible]	[illegible]	[illegible]	[illegible]	[illegible]	[illegible]	[illegible]	[illegible]	11. Abandoning Children under two years.
[illegible]	[illegible]	[illegible]	[illegible]	[illegible]	[illegible]	[illegible]	[illegible]	[illegible]	[illegible]	[illegible]	[illegible]	[illegible]	12. Child stealing.
[illegible]	[illegible]	[illegible]	[illegible]	[illegible]	[illegible]	[illegible]	[illegible]	[illegible]	[illegible]	[illegible]	[illegible]	[illegible]	13. Procuring abortion.
[illegible]	[illegible]	[illegible]	[illegible]	[illegible]	[illegible]	[illegible]	[illegible]	[illegible]	[illegible]	[illegible]	[illegible]	[illegible]	14. Concealment of Birth.
[illegible]	[illegible]	[illegible]	[illegible]	[illegible]	[illegible]	[illegible]	[illegible]	[illegible]	[illegible]	[illegible]	[illegible]	[illegible]	15. Unnatural offences.
[illegible]	[illegible]	[illegible]	[illegible]	[illegible]	[illegible]	[illegible]	[illegible]	[illegible]	[illegible]	[illegible]	[illegible]	[illegible]	16. Attempts to commit unnatural offences.
[illegible]	[illegible]	[illegible]	[illegible]	[illegible]	[illegible]	[illegible]	[illegible]	[illegible]	[illegible]	[illegible]	[illegible]	[illegible]	17. Indecency with Males.
[illegible]	[illegible]	[illegible]	[illegible]	[illegible]	[illegible]	[illegible]	[illegible]	[illegible]	[illegible]	[illegible]	[illegible]	[illegible]	18. Rape.
[illegible]	[illegible]	[illegible]	[illegible]	[illegible]	[illegible]	[illegible]	[illegible]	[illegible]	[illegible]	[illegible]	[illegible]	[illegible]	19. Indecent assaults on Females.
[illegible]	[illegible]	[illegible]	[illegible]	[illegible]	[illegible]	[illegible]	[illegible]	[illegible]	[illegible]	[illegible]	[illegible]	[illegible]	20. Defilement of Girls under 13.
[illegible]	[illegible]	[illegible]	[illegible]	[illegible]	[illegible]	[illegible]	[illegible]	[illegible]	[illegible]	[illegible]	[illegible]	[illegible]	21. Defilement of Girls under 16.
[illegible]	[illegible]	[illegible]	[illegible]	[illegible]	[illegible]	[illegible]	[illegible]	[illegible]	[illegible]	[illegible]	[illegible]	[illegible]	22. Householder permitting defilement of Girls.
[illegible]	[illegible]	[illegible]	[illegible]	[illegible]	[illegible]	[illegible]	[illegible]	[illegible]	[illegible]	[illegible]	[illegible]	[illegible]	23. Procuration.
[illegible]	[illegible]	[illegible]	[illegible]	[illegible]	[illegible]	[illegible]	[illegible]	[illegible]	[illegible]	[illegible]	[illegible]	[illegible]	24. Abduction.
[illegible]	[illegible]	[illegible]	[illegible]	[illegible]	[illegible]	[illegible]	[illegible]	[illegible]	[illegible]	[illegible]	[illegible]	[illegible]	25. Bigamy.
[illegible]	[illegible]	[illegible]	[illegible]	[illegible]	[illegible]	[illegible]	[illegible]	[illegible]	[illegible]	[illegible]	[illegible]	[illegible]	26. Other offences against the Person.
[illegible]	[illegible]	[illegible]	[illegible]	[illegible]	[illegible]	[illegible]	[illegible]	[illegible]	[illegible]	[illegible]	[illegible]	[illegible]	Total of Class I.
													Class II.—Offences against Property with Violence.
[illegible]	[illegible]	[illegible]	[illegible]	[illegible]	[illegible]	[illegible]	[illegible]	[illegible]	[illegible]	[illegible]	[illegible]	[illegible]	27. Sacrilege.
[illegible]	[illegible]	[illegible]	[illegible]	[illegible]	[illegible]	[illegible]	[illegible]	[illegible]	[illegible]	[illegible]	[illegible]	[illegible]	28. Burglary.
[illegible]	[illegible]	[illegible]	[illegible]	[illegible]	[illegible]	[illegible]	[illegible]	[illegible]	[illegible]	[illegible]	[illegible]	[illegible]	29. Housebreaking.
[illegible]	[illegible]	[illegible]	[illegible]	[illegible]	[illegible]	[illegible]	[illegible]	[illegible]	[illegible]	[illegible]	[illegible]	[illegible]	30. Breaking into Shops, Warehouses, &c.
[illegible]	[illegible]	[illegible]	[illegible]	[illegible]	[illegible]	[illegible]	[illegible]	[illegible]	[illegible]	[illegible]	[illegible]	[illegible]	31. Attempts to break into Houses, Shops, &c.
[illegible]	[illegible]	[illegible]	[illegible]	[illegible]	[illegible]	[illegible]	[illegible]	[illegible]	[illegible]	[illegible]	[illegible]	[illegible]	32. Entering with intent to commit Felony.
[illegible]	[illegible]	[illegible]	[illegible]	[illegible]	[illegible]	[illegible]	[illegible]	[illegible]	[illegible]	[illegible]	[illegible]	[illegible]	33. Possession of Housebreaking Tools, &c.
[illegible]	[illegible]	[illegible]	[illegible]	[illegible]	[illegible]	[illegible]	[illegible]	[illegible]	[illegible]	[illegible]	[illegible]	[illegible]	34. Robbery and Assaults with intent to rob.
[illegible]	[illegible]	[illegible]	[illegible]	[illegible]	[illegible]	[illegible]	[illegible]	[illegible]	[illegible]	[illegible]	[illegible]	[illegible]	35. Extortion by threats to accuse of crimes.
[illegible]	[illegible]	[illegible]	[illegible]	[illegible]	[illegible]	[illegible]	[illegible]	[illegible]	[illegible]	[illegible]	[illegible]	[illegible]	36. Extortion by other threats.
[illegible]	[illegible]	[illegible]	[illegible]	[illegible]	[illegible]	[illegible]	[illegible]	[illegible]	[illegible]	[illegible]	[illegible]	[illegible]	Total of Class II.
													Class III.—Offences against Property without Violence.
[illegible]	[illegible]	[illegible]	[illegible]	[illegible]	[illegible]	[illegible]	[illegible]	[illegible]	[illegible]	[illegible]	[illegible]	[illegible]	37. Larceny of Horses, Cattle, and Sheep.
[illegible]	[illegible]	[illegible]	[illegible]	[illegible]	[illegible]	[illegible]	[illegible]	[illegible]	[illegible]	[illegible]	[illegible]	[illegible]	38. Larceny from the Person.
[illegible]	[illegible]	[illegible]	[illegible]	[illegible]	[illegible]	[illegible]	[illegible]	[illegible]	[illegible]	[illegible]	[illegible]	[illegible]	39. Larceny in House.
[illegible]	[illegible]	[illegible]	[illegible]	[illegible]	[illegible]	[illegible]	[illegible]	[illegible]	[illegible]	[illegible]	[illegible]	[illegible]	40. Larceny by a Servant.
[illegible]	[illegible]	[illegible]	[illegible]	[illegible]	[illegible]	[illegible]	[illegible]	[illegible]	[illegible]	[illegible]	[illegible]	[illegible]	41. Embezzlement.
[illegible]	[illegible]	[illegible]	[illegible]	[illegible]	[illegible]	[illegible]	[illegible]	[illegible]	[illegible]	[illegible]	[illegible]	[illegible]	42. Larceny of Post Letters.
[illegible]	[illegible]	[illegible]	[illegible]	[illegible]	[illegible]	[illegible]	[illegible]	[illegible]	[illegible]	[illegible]	[illegible]	[illegible]	43. Other aggravated larcenies.
[illegible]	[illegible]	[illegible]	[illegible]	[illegible]	[illegible]	[illegible]	[illegible]	[illegible]	[illegible]	[illegible]	[illegible]	[illegible]	44. Simple larceny and minor larcenies.
[illegible]	[illegible]	[illegible]	[illegible]	[illegible]	[illegible]	[illegible]	[illegible]	[illegible]	[illegible]	[illegible]	[illegible]	[illegible]	45. Obtaining goods, &c., by false pretences.
[illegible]	[illegible]	[illegible]	[illegible]	[illegible]	[illegible]	[illegible]	[illegible]	[illegible]	[illegible]	[illegible]	[illegible]	[illegible]	46. Frauds by Bankers, Agents, Trustees, &c.
[illegible]	[illegible]	[illegible]	[illegible]	[illegible]	[illegible]	[illegible]	[illegible]	[illegible]	[illegible]	[illegible]	[illegible]	[illegible]	47. Falsifying accounts.
[illegible]	[illegible]	[illegible]	[illegible]	[illegible]	[illegible]	[illegible]	[illegible]	[illegible]	[illegible]	[illegible]	[illegible]	[illegible]	48. Other Frauds.
[illegible]	[illegible]	[illegible]	[illegible]	[illegible]	[illegible]	[illegible]	[illegible]	[illegible]	[illegible]	[illegible]	[illegible]	[illegible]	49. Receiving Stolen Goods.
[illegible]	[illegible]	[illegible]	[illegible]	[illegible]	[illegible]	[illegible]	[illegible]	[illegible]	[illegible]	[illegible]	[illegible]	[illegible]	50. Offences in connection with Bankruptcy.
[illegible]	[illegible]	[illegible]	[illegible]	[illegible]	[illegible]	[illegible]	[illegible]	[illegible]	[illegible]	[illegible]	[illegible]	[illegible]	Total of Class III.

All cases included in columns [illegible] and [illegible] are [illegible] Indictable Offences.

TABLE 20—*continued*—POLICE RETURNS.—INDICTABLE OFFENCES.—

OFFENCES. (1)	Number of Crimes Committed.	Persons Apprehended — Total Number (2): Total.	Males.	Females.	Apprehended: Without Warrant. (7)	On Warrant issued by Police Magistrates (8)	On Warrant issued to Defendants to appear in Court (9)	Discharged: Charge [illegible] (7)	Charge [illegible] (8)	Tried summarily and: Discharged (for [illegible]) (9)	Committed. (10)
Class IV.—Malicious Injuries to Property.											
58. Arson,	[illegible]	[illegible]	[illegible]	[illegible]	[illegible]	[illegible]	-	6	[illegible]	-	-
59. Setting fire to Crops, Plantations, &c.,	[illegible]	[illegible]	[illegible]	-	[illegible]	[illegible]	-	[illegible]	[illegible]	-	-
60. Killing and Maiming Cattle,	[illegible]	[illegible]	[illegible]	-	[illegible]	[illegible]	-	[illegible]	[illegible]	-	-
61. Malicious use, &c., of Explosives,	[illegible]	[illegible]	[illegible]	-	[illegible]	-	-	1	-	-	-
62. Destroying Ships,	[illegible]	-	-	-	-	-	-	-	-	-	-
63. Destroying Railways,	[illegible]	-	-	-	-	-	-	-	-	-	-
64. Destroying Trees and Shrubs,	[illegible]	-	-	-	-	-	-	-	-	-	-
65. Other malicious injuries,	[illegible]	[illegible]	[illegible]	1	[illegible]	-	-	-	[illegible]	-	-
Total of Class IV.,	[illegible]	[illegible]	[illegible]	[illegible]	[illegible]	[illegible]	-	[illegible]	[illegible]	-	-
Class V.—Forgery and Offences against the Currency.											
66. Forgery and Uttering (felony),	[illegible]	[illegible]	[illegible]	1	[illegible]	6	-	-	-	-	-
67. Forgery (misdemeanour),	[illegible]	[illegible]	[illegible]	-	[illegible]	[illegible]	-	1	-	-	-
68. Coining,	[illegible]	[illegible]	[illegible]	-	[illegible]	-	-	-	-	-	-
69. Uttering or Possessing Counterfeit Coin,	[illegible]	[illegible]	[illegible]	-	[illegible]	-	-	[illegible]	[illegible]	-	-
Total of Class V.,	[illegible]	[illegible]	[illegible]	1	[illegible]	[illegible]	-	[illegible]	[illegible]	-	-
Class VI.—Other Offences not included in the above Classes.											
Offences against the State and Public Order: 61. High Treason,	-	-	-	-	-	-	-	-	-	-	-
62. Treason Felony,	-	-	-	-	-	-	-	-	-	-	-
63. Riot,	[illegible]	6	[illegible]	-	[illegible]	[illegible]	-	-	1	-	-
64. Unlawful Assembly,	[illegible]	[illegible]	[illegible]	-	4	-	-	-	[illegible]	-	-
67. Intimidation by Threatening Letters, Notices, or otherwise,	[illegible]	4	[illegible]	[illegible]	[illegible]	[illegible]	-	[illegible]	-	-	-
68. Unlawful or Robbery of Arms,	4	[illegible]	[illegible]	-	[illegible]	-	-	7	[illegible]	-	-
69. Assembling Drilling-[illegible] (by [illegible]),	[illegible]	6	4	-	6	-	-	-	[illegible]	-	-
70. Other offences,	[illegible]	[illegible]	4	[illegible]	[illegible]	6	[illegible]	[illegible]	-	-	-
Offences against Public Justice: 71. Extortion by Officers, &c.,	-	-	-	-	-	-	-	-	-	-	-
72. Bribery, &c.,	7	1	[illegible]	-	[illegible]	-	-	-	[illegible]	-	-
73. Perjury,	[illegible]	[illegible]	[illegible]	[illegible]	[illegible]	[illegible]	-	-	-	-	-
74. Escape and Rescue,	[illegible]	[illegible]	[illegible]	[illegible]	[illegible]	[illegible]	[illegible]	-	[illegible]	-	-
75. Other offences,	4	[illegible]	[illegible]	-	[illegible]	-	-	-	-	-	-
Offences against Religion: 76. Blasphemy, &c.,	-	-	-	-	-	-	-	-	-	-	-
Offences against Law of Nations: 77. Piracy,	-	-	-	-	-	-	-	-	-	-	-
78. Slave Trade,	-	-	-	-	-	-	-	-	-	-	-
79. Libel,	1	[illegible]	[illegible]	-	-	1	-	-	-	-	-
80. Punishable [illegible],	-	-	-	-	-	-	-	-	-	-	-
81. Indecent Exposure,	[illegible]	[illegible]	[illegible]	-	[illegible]	-	-	-	-	-	-
82. Keeping Disorderly Houses,	-	-	-	-	-	-	-	-	-	-	-
83. Other Nuisances,	[illegible]	-	-	-	-	-	-	-	-	-	-
84. Suicide (attempting to commit),	[illegible]	[illegible]	[illegible]	[illegible]	[illegible]	[illegible]	-	6	[illegible]	[illegible]	[illegible]
85. Other misdemeanours,	[illegible]	[illegible]	[illegible]	-	[illegible]	-	-	-	[illegible]	-	-
Total of Class VI.,	[illegible]	[illegible]	[illegible]	[illegible]	[illegible]	[illegible]	[illegible]	[illegible]	[illegible]	[illegible]	[illegible]
GRAND TOTAL,	[illegible]	[illegible]	[illegible]	[illegible]	[illegible]	[illegible]	[illegible]	[illegible]	[illegible]	[illegible]	[illegible]
								[illegible]		[illegible]	
GRAND TOTAL OF PERSONS APPREHENDED AND APPEARING TO SUMMONS.	-	[illegible]	[illegible]	[illegible]	-	-	-	[illegible]	[illegible]	[illegible]	[illegible]
								[illegible]		[illegible]	

Crimes Committed, Apprehensions, and Prosecutions.

Apprehensions: Committed for Trial and Sent to Prison (11)	Bailed (12)	Otherwise dealt with (13)	Proceedings by Summons: Persons dealt with on Summons (14) Total	Males	Females	Charge withdrawn (15)	Charge dismissed (16)	Discharged (17)	Convicted (18)	Sent to Prison (19)	Released on Bail (20)	(21)	OFFENCES.
													Class IV.—Malicious Injuries to Property.
[illegible]	[illegible]	.	[illegible]	[illegible]	.	.	1	.	.	.	1	.	Arson.
[illegible]	.	.	.	.	.	.	.	.	.	.	.	.	Setting fire to Crops, Plantations, &c.
[illegible]	1	.	[illegible]	[illegible]	.	.	[illegible]	.	.	.	1	.	Killing and Maiming Cattle.
.	.	.	.	.	.	.	.	.	.	.	.	.	Malicious [illegible], &c., of Explosives.
.	.	.	.	.	.	.	.	.	.	.	.	.	Destroying Ships.
.	.	.	.	.	.	.	.	.	.	.	.	.	Damaging Railways.
.	.	.	.	.	.	.	.	.	.	.	.	.	Destroying Trees and Shrubs.
[illegible]	[illegible]	.	[illegible]	[illegible]	.	1	[illegible]	.	1	.	.	.	Other malicious injuries.
[illegible]	[illegible]	.	[illegible]	[illegible]	.	1	[illegible]	.	1	.	[illegible]	.	Total of Class IV.
													Class V.—Forgery and Offences against the Currency.
[illegible]	[illegible]	.	1	1	.	.	.	.	.	.	1	.	Forgery and uttering (felony).
.	1	.	1	1	.	.	.	.	.	.	1	.	Forgery (misdemeanour).
[illegible]	.	.	.	.	.	.	.	.	.	.	.	.	Coining.
3	[illegible]	.	.	.	.	.	.	.	.	.	.	.	Uttering or Possessing Counterfeit Coin.
[illegible]	[illegible]	.	[illegible]	[illegible]	.	.	.	.	.	.	[illegible]	.	Total of Class V.
													Class VI.—Other Offences not included in the above Classes.
.	.	.	.	.	.	.	.	.	.	.	.	.	High Treason. (Offences against the State and Public Order)
.	.	.	.	.	.	.	.	.	.	.	.	.	Treason Felony.
[illegible]	.	.	[illegible]	[illegible]	.	.	[illegible]	.	.	.	[illegible]	.	Riot.
.	[illegible]	.	.	.	.	.	.	.	.	.	.	.	Unlawful Assembly.
[illegible]	.	.	1	1	.	.	.	.	.	.	1	.	Intimidation by Threatening Letters, Notices, or otherwise.
[illegible]	.	.	.	.	.	.	.	.	.	.	.	.	Unlawful [illegible] of Arms.
.	1	.	.	.	.	.	.	.	.	.	.	.	Assaulting Dwelling-houses (by firing shots into them).
[illegible]	[illegible]	.	[illegible]	[illegible]	[illegible]	[illegible]	[illegible]	.	.	.	[illegible]	.	Other offences.
.	.	.	.	.	.	.	.	.	.	.	.	.	Extortion by Officers, &c. (Offences against Public Justice)
.	.	.	[illegible]	[illegible]	.	.	.	.	.	.	[illegible]	.	Bribery, &c.
[illegible]	1	.	[illegible]	[illegible]	.	.	.	.	.	.	[illegible]	.	Perjury.
[illegible]	[illegible]	.	[illegible]	[illegible]	[illegible]	[illegible]	[illegible]	.	.	.	[illegible]	.	Rescue and Escape.
.	1	.	[illegible]	[illegible]	.	.	.	.	.	.	[illegible]	.	Other offences.
.	.	.	.	.	.	.	.	.	.	.	.	.	Blasphemy, &c. (Offences against Religion)
.	.	.	.	.	.	.	.	.	.	.	.	.	Piracy. (Offences against the Law of Nations)
.	.	.	.	.	.	.	.	.	.	.	.	.	Slave Trade.
1	.	.	.	.	.	.	.	.	.	.	.	.	Libel.
.	.	.	.	.	.	.	.	.	.	.	.	.	Pensions.
[illegible]	1	.	[illegible]	[illegible]	.	.	[illegible]	.	.	.	.	.	Indecent Exposure.
.	.	.	.	.	.	.	.	.	.	.	.	.	Keeping Disorderly Houses.
.	.	.	[illegible]	[illegible]	1	.	.	.	.	.	[illegible]	.	Other Nuisances.
[illegible]	[illegible]	.	.	.	.	.	.	.	.	.	.	.	Suicide (attempting to commit).
.	.	.	.	.	.	.	.	.	.	.	.	.	Other misdemeanours.
[illegible]	[illegible]	.	[illegible]	[illegible]	[illegible]	[illegible]	[illegible]	.	.	.	[illegible]		Total of Class VI.
[illegible]	[illegible]	[illegible]	[illegible]	[illegible]	[illegible]	[illegible]	[illegible]	[illegible]	[illegible]	[illegible]	[illegible]	1	GRAND TOTAL.
[illegible]						[illegible]		[illegible]		[illegible]			
[illegible]	[illegible]	[illegible]	.	.	.	.	.	.	.	.	.	.	GRAND TOTAL OF PERSONS APPREHENDED AND APPEARING TO SUMMONS.
[illegible]													

the charges against them were disposed of by the Justices. These [illegible] persons are not included in Columns [illegible] to [illegible].

TABLE 21.—POLICE RETURNS.—NON-INDICTABLE

OFFENCES. (1)	APPREHENSIONS. Persons Apprehended. Total Number. (2) Total	Males	Females	Apprehended. Without Warrant. (3)	On Warrant issued in First Instance. (4)	On Warrant issued on Failure to appear to Summons. (5)	Results of Persons Apprehended. Discharged. (6)	Convicted. (7)	Otherwise Disposed of. (8)
Adulteration of Food and Drugs,	.	.	.	.	.	.	.	.	.
Assaults:—									
Aggravated,	[illegible]	[illegible]	[illegible]	[illegible]	[illegible]	1	[illegible]	[illegible]	1
On Constables,	[illegible]	[illegible]	[illegible]	[illegible]	[illegible]	1	[illegible]	[illegible]	.
Common,	[illegible]	[illegible]	[illegible]	[illegible]	[illegible]	[illegible]	[illegible]	[illegible]	.
Betting and Gaming,	[illegible]	[illegible]	.	[illegible]	[illegible]	.	[illegible]	[illegible]	.
Brothel Keeping,	.	.	.	.	.	.	.	.	.
Cruelty to Animals,	[illegible]	[illegible]	.	[illegible]	[illegible]	.	[illegible]	[illegible]	.
Cruelty to Children,	[illegible]	[illegible]	[illegible]	[illegible]	[illegible]	[illegible]	71	[illegible]	.
Diseases of Animals Acts, Offences against,	.	.	.	.	.	.	.	.	.
Dogs, Offences in relation to,	.	.	.	.	.	.	.	.	.
Elementary Education Acts, Offences against,	.	.	.	.	.	.	.	.	.
Explosives, Offences in relation to,	.	.	.	.	.	.	.	.	.
Fishery Laws, Offences against,	.	.	.	.	.	.	.	.	.
Game Laws, Offences against:—									
Night Poaching,	.	.	.	.	.	.	.	.	.
Day Poaching,	.	.	.	.	.	.	.	.	.
Unlawful Possession of Game, &c.	.	.	.	.	.	.	.	.	.
Illegal Buying and Selling of Game,	.	.	.	.	.	.	.	.	.
Other Offences,	.	.	.	.	.	.	.	.	.
Highway Acts, Offences against:—									
Offences by Owners and Drivers of Carts,	[illegible]	[illegible]	.	[illegible]	.	.	[illegible]	[illegible]	.
Obstructions and Nuisances,	[illegible]	[illegible]	76	[illegible]	.	[illegible]	[illegible]	[illegible]	.
Locomotives,	.	.	.	.	.	.	.	.	.
Housing of the Working Classes Act, Offences against,	.	.	.	.	.	.	.	.	.
Indecent Advertisements,	1	1	.	1	.	.	.	1	.
[illegible]	[illegible]	[illegible]	.	[illegible]	1	.	7	[illegible]	.
Intoxicating Liquor Laws, Offences against:—									
Drunkenness,	[illegible]	[illegible]	7,[illegible]	[illegible]	1	[illegible]	[illegible]	[illegible]	.
Permitting Drunkenness on Licensed Premises,	.	.	.	.	.	.	.	.	.
Other Offences against Public Order,	[illegible]	[illegible]	[illegible]	[illegible]	.	.	[illegible]	[illegible]	.
Illegal Sale of Drink,	[illegible]	4	6	1	.	[illegible]	1	[illegible]	.
Offences against Closing Regulations,	.	.	.	.	.	.	.	.	.
Other Offences,	6	6	.	6	.	.	.	5	.
Labour Laws, Offences against:—									
Intimidation,	1	1	.	.	1	.	1	.	.
Breach of Contract,	.	.	.	.	.	.	.	.	.
Offences under Special Trade Acts,	.	.	.	.	.	.	.	.	.
Offences under Truck Acts,	.	.	.	.	.	.	.	.	.
Mines Acts,	.	.	.	.	.	.	.	.	.
Factory Acts,	.	.	.	.	.	.	.	.	.
Shop Hours Acts,	.	.	.	.	.	.	.	.	.
Other Acts for the Protection of Labour,	1	1	.	.	1	.	.	1	.
Malicious Damage:—									
To Animals,	1	1	.	.	1	.	1	.	.
To Fences, &c.,	4	[illegible]	[illegible]	[illegible]	1	.	.	4	.
To Trees, Shrubs, &c.,	.	.	.	.	.	.	.	.	.
To Fruit, &c.	3	[illegible]	.	[illegible]	.	.	[illegible]	1	.
Other Offences,	[illegible]	[illegible]	[illegible]	[illegible]	[illegible]	1	[illegible]	[illegible]	1
Merchant Shipping Act, Offences against,	[illegible]	[illegible]	.	[illegible]	[illegible]	.	1	[illegible]	3
Military and Naval Law, Offences against:—									
Army,	[illegible]	[illegible]	1	[illegible]	[illegible]	.	[illegible]	[illegible]	[illegible]
Navy,	[illegible]	[illegible]	.	[illegible]	[illegible]	.	.	.	[illegible]
Volunteers,	.	.	.	.	.	.	.	.	.
Parks, Commons and Open Spaces, Offences in relation to,	.	.	.	.	.	.	.	.	.

	Assaults:—
8	Aggravated.
111	On Constables.
1,[illegible]	Common.
—	Betting and Gaming.
—	Brothel Keeping.
137	Cruelty to Animals.
57	Cruelty to Children.
25	Diseases of Animals Act, Offences against.
1,077	Dogs, Offences in relation to.
314	Elementary Education Act, Offences against.
—	Explosives, Offences in relation to.
69	Fishery Laws, Offences against.
	Game Laws, Offences against:—
10	Night Poaching.
20	Day Poaching.
1	Unlawful Possession of Game, &c.
—	Illegal Buying and Selling of Game.
7	Other Offences.
	Highway Acts, Offences against:—
400	Offences by Owners and Drivers of Carts.
1,321	Obstructions and Nuisances.
8	Locomotives.
—	Housing of the Working Classes Act, Offences against.
—	Indecent Advertisements.
17	Indecent Exposure.
	Intoxicating Liquor Laws, Offences against:—
2,[illegible]	Drunkenness.
7	Permitting Drunkenness on Licensed Premises.
61	Other Offences against Public Order.
35	Illegal Sale of Drink.
62	Offences against Closing Regulations.
208	Other Offences.
	Labour Laws, Offences against:—
—	Intimidation.
7	Breach of Contracts.
—	Offences under Special Trade Acts.
—	Offences under Truck Acts.
—	Mines Acts.
—	Factory Acts.
9	Shop Hours Acts.
—	Other Acts for the Protection of Labour.
	Malicious Damage:—
6	To Animals.
17	To Fences, &c.
25	To Trees, Shrubs, &c.

TABLE XI.—continued.—POLICE RETURNS.—NON-INDICTABLE

Offences. (1)	Apprehended: Persons Apprehended: Total Number (2): Total	Males	Females	Apprehended: Without Warrant (3)	On Warrant issued in First Instance (4)	On Warrant issued on Failure to Appear to Summons (5)	[illegible] (6)	[illegible] (7)	[illegible] (8)
[illegible] Acts, Offences against:—									
Offences by [illegible],	.	.	.	.	.	.	.	.	.
[illegible]	[illegible]	[illegible]	[illegible]	[illegible]	.	.	[illegible]	[illegible]	.
Other Offences,	.	.	.	.	.	.	.	.	.
[illegible] Act, Offences against,	[illegible]	[illegible]	.	[illegible]	.	.	[illegible]	[illegible]	.
[illegible] Regulations, Offences against:—									
[illegible]	[illegible]	[illegible]	[illegible]	[illegible]	.	.	[illegible]	[illegible]	.
Dublin Metropolitan Police Act,	[illegible]	[illegible]	[illegible]	[illegible]	.	[illegible]	[illegible]	[illegible]	.
Town Police Clauses Acts,	[illegible]	[illegible]	[illegible]	[illegible]	.	.	[illegible]	[illegible]	.
Towns Improvement (Ireland) Act, 1854,	[illegible]	[illegible]	[illegible]	[illegible]	.	.	[illegible]	[illegible]	.
[illegible] (Ireland) Act, [illegible],	7	6	1	[illegible]	1	.	1	[illegible]	.
[illegible]	[illegible]	[illegible]	[illegible]	[illegible]	.	.	[illegible]	[illegible]	.
Local Acts and Bye-laws,	[illegible]	[illegible]	[illegible]	[illegible]	.	.	[illegible]	[illegible]	.
Poor Law, Offences against:—									
[illegible] Family, &c.,	[illegible]	[illegible]	[illegible]	[illegible]	[illegible]	[illegible]	[illegible]	[illegible]	.
[illegible] by Paupers,	[illegible]	[illegible]	[illegible]	[illegible]	[illegible]	.	[illegible]	[illegible]	.
[illegible] Workhouse Clothes,	[illegible]	[illegible]	.	[illegible]	[illegible]	.	[illegible]	[illegible]	.
Other Offences,	[illegible]	[illegible]	[illegible]	[illegible]	[illegible]	.	[illegible]	[illegible]	.
Prevention of Crimes Acts:—									
Offences by Licence Holders,	[illegible]	[illegible]	[illegible]	[illegible]	[illegible]	.	[illegible]	[illegible]	.
Offences by Supervisees,	[illegible]	[illegible]	[illegible]	[illegible]	.	.	[illegible]	[illegible]	.
Second Offences by twice-convicted Persons,	.	.	.	.	.	.	.	.	.
[illegible],	[illegible]	.	[illegible]	[illegible]	.	.	[illegible]	[illegible]	.
Railways, Offences in Relation to,	[illegible]	[illegible]	.	[illegible]	.	.	[illegible]	[illegible]	.
Revenue Laws, Offences against,	[illegible]	[illegible]	[illegible]	[illegible]	[illegible]	.	[illegible]	[illegible]	.
Sanitary Laws, Offences against:—									
Public Health Acts,	[illegible]	[illegible]	.	[illegible]	.	.	[illegible]	.	.
[illegible] Acts,	.	.	.	.	.	.	.	.	.
Local Acts and Bye-laws,	.	.	.	.	.	.	.	.	.
Stage and Hackney Carriage Regulations, Offences against,	[illegible]	[illegible]	.	[illegible]	.	.	[illegible]	[illegible]	.
Stealing:—									
Animals,	[illegible]	[illegible]	[illegible]	[illegible]	[illegible]	.	[illegible]	[illegible]	.
Fences, Stiles, Gates, &c.,	[illegible]	[illegible]	[illegible]	[illegible]	[illegible]	.	[illegible]	[illegible]	.
Trees, Shrubs, &c., to the value of 1s.,	[illegible]	[illegible]	[illegible]	[illegible]	[illegible]	.	[illegible]	[illegible]	.
Growing Fruit, Plants, Vegetables, &c.,	[illegible]	[illegible]	.	[illegible]	[illegible]	.	[illegible]	[illegible]	.
[illegible] Animals, Trees, Fruit, &c.,	[illegible]	[illegible]	.	[illegible]	[illegible]	.	[illegible]	[illegible]	.
[illegible]	.	.	.	.	.	.	.	.	.
Sunday Trading, &c.,	.	.	.	.	.	.	.	.	.
Vaccination Acts, Offences against,	.	.	.	.	.	.	.	.	.
Vagrancy Laws, Offences against:—									
Begging,	[illegible]	[illegible]	[illegible]	[illegible]	[illegible]	.	[illegible]	[illegible]	[illegible]
Sleeping out,	[illegible]	[illegible]	[illegible]	[illegible]	.	.	[illegible]	[illegible]	[illegible]
Gaming, &c.,	[illegible]	[illegible]	.	[illegible]	.	.	[illegible]	[illegible]	.
Possessing Picklocks and other Implements,	.	.	.	.	.	.	.	.	.
Found in Enclosed Premises,	[illegible]	[illegible]	[illegible]	[illegible]	[illegible]	.	[illegible]	[illegible]	.
[illegible]	[illegible]	[illegible]	[illegible]	[illegible]	.	.	[illegible]	[illegible]	[illegible]
Other Offences,	[illegible]	[illegible]	[illegible]	[illegible]	[illegible]	.	[illegible]	[illegible]	.
Weights and Measures Acts, Offences against,	.	.	.	.	.	.	.	.	.
Wild Birds Protection Act, Offences against,	.	.	.	.	.	.	.	.	.
Other Offences,*	[illegible]	[illegible]	[illegible]	[illegible]	.	.	[illegible]	[illegible]	[illegible]
TOTAL,	[illegible]	[illegible]	[illegible]	[illegible]	[illegible]	[illegible]	[illegible]	[illegible]	[illegible]
GRAND TOTAL OF PERSONS APPREHENDED AND DEALT WITH ON SUMMONS,	[illegible]	[illegible]	[illegible]	-	.	.	[illegible]	[illegible]	[illegible]

* [illegible]

OFFENCES.—Apprehensions and Prosecutions.

PERSONS PROCEEDED AGAINST BY SUMMONS.						[illegible]	OFFENCES.
[illegible]			[illegible]				
Total.	Males.	Females.	Discharged.	Convicted.	Otherwise disposed of.		
			(18)	(19)	(20)	(23)	
							Pawnbrokers' Acts, Offences against:—
[illegible]	7	[illegible]	[illegible]	[illegible]	.	1	Offences by Pawnbrokers.
[illegible]	[illegible]	.	[illegible]	.	.		Unlawful Pledging.
.	.	.	.	.	.	.	Other Offences.
[illegible]	[illegible]	.	4	[illegible]	.	.	[illegible] Act, Offences against.
							Police Regulations, Offences against:—
[illegible]	[illegible]	.	[illegible]	[illegible]	.	.	Unlawful Possession.
[illegible]	[illegible]	[illegible]	[illegible]	[illegible]	.	.	Dublin Metropolitan Police Act.
[illegible]	[illegible]	[illegible]	[illegible]	[illegible]	.	[illegible]	Towns Police Clauses Act.
[illegible]	[illegible]	[illegible]	[illegible]	[illegible]	.	[illegible]	Towns Improvement (Ireland) Act, [illegible].
[illegible]	[illegible]	[illegible]	[illegible]	[illegible]	.	[illegible]	[illegible] (Ireland) Act, [illegible].
[illegible]	[illegible]	[illegible]	[illegible]	[illegible]	.	[illegible]	Borough Bye-Laws.
[illegible]	[illegible]	[illegible]	[illegible]	[illegible]	.	[illegible]	Local Acts and Bye-Laws.
							Poor Law, Offences against:—
[illegible]	[illegible]	[illegible]	[illegible]	[illegible]	.	4	Neglecting to maintain Family, &c.
[illegible]	[illegible]	[illegible]	[illegible]	[illegible]	1	[illegible]	Misbehaviour by Paupers.
[illegible]	[illegible]	[illegible]	[illegible]	3	.	[illegible]	[illegible] Workhouse [illegible].
[illegible]	[illegible]	[illegible]	[illegible]	[illegible]	.	[illegible]	Other Offences.
							Prevention of Crimes Act:—
.	.	.	.	.	.	.	Offences by Licence Holders.
.	.	.	.	.	.	.	Offences by [illegible].
.	.	.	.	.	.	.	Special Offences by twice-convicted Persons.
[illegible]	.	[illegible]	7	[illegible]	.	[illegible]	Prostitution.
[illegible]	[illegible]	[illegible]	[illegible]	[illegible]	.	[illegible]	Railways, Offences in Relation to.
[illegible]	[illegible]	[illegible]	[illegible]	[illegible]	.	[illegible]	Revenue Laws, Offences against.
							Sanitary Law, Offences against:—
[illegible]	[illegible]	[illegible]	[illegible]	[illegible]	.	[illegible]	Public Health Acts.
[illegible]	[illegible]	[illegible]	.	[illegible]	.	.	[illegible] Diseases Acts.
[illegible]	[illegible]	[illegible]	[illegible]	[illegible]	.	[illegible]	Local Acts and Bye-Laws.
[illegible]	[illegible]	[illegible]	[illegible]	[illegible]	.	[illegible]	Sheep and Cattle Diseases Regulations, Offences against.
							Stealing:—
[illegible]	[illegible]	1	[illegible]	[illegible]	.	[illegible]	Animals.
[illegible]	[illegible]	[illegible]	[illegible]	[illegible]	.	[illegible]	Flowers, [illegible], &c.
[illegible]	[illegible]	[illegible]	[illegible]	[illegible]	.	[illegible]	Trees, Shrubs, &c., to the value of 1s.
[illegible]	[illegible]	[illegible]	[illegible]	[illegible]	[illegible]	[illegible]	Growing Fruit, Plants, Vegetables, &c.
[illegible]	[illegible]	[illegible]	[illegible]	[illegible]	.	.	[illegible]
[illegible]	[illegible]	.	.	[illegible]	.	.	[illegible]
[illegible]	[illegible]	.	.	[illegible]	.	[illegible]	Street Trading, &c.
[illegible]	[illegible]	[illegible]	[illegible]	[illegible]	.	[illegible]	Vagrancy Acts, Offences against.
							[illegible] Act, Offences against:—
[illegible]	[illegible]	[illegible]	[illegible]	[illegible]	[illegible]	[illegible]	[illegible]
[illegible]	[illegible]	[illegible]	[illegible]	[illegible]	[illegible]	[illegible]	Sleeping out.
[illegible]	[illegible]	.	.	[illegible]	.	.	Gambling, &c.
.	.	.	.	.	.	.	Possessing Picklocks and other Implements.
[illegible]	[illegible]	.	3	[illegible]	.	[illegible]	Found in Enclosed Premises.
.	.	.	.	.	.	.	Frequenting.
[illegible]	[illegible]	[illegible]	[illegible]	[illegible]	.	.	Other Offences.
[illegible]	[illegible]	[illegible]	[illegible]	[illegible]	.	[illegible]	Weights and Measures Acts, Offences against.
[illegible]	[illegible]	.	[illegible]	.	.	.	Wild Birds Protection Acts, Offences against.
[illegible]	[illegible]	[illegible]	[illegible]	[illegible]	.	[illegible]	Other Offences.
[illegible]	[illegible]	[illegible]	[illegible]	[illegible]	[illegible]	[illegible]	TOTAL.
.			.	.		.	GRAND TOTAL OF PERSONS APPREHENDED AND DEALT WITH ON SUMMONS.

[illegible]

[illegible]

TABLE 22.—INDICTABLE OFFENCES.—Crimes, Apprehensions,
TABLE 23.—NON-INDICTABLE OFFENCES. — Apprehensions

(A) INDICTABLE OFFENCES.

[illegible]	[illegible]	[illegible]	[illegible]	[illegible]	[illegible]	[illegible]	[illegible]	[illegible]	[illegible]	[illegible]	[illegible]
LEINSTER.											
[illegible]	[illegible]	[illegible]	[illegible]	[illegible]	[illegible]	[illegible]	[illegible]	[illegible]	[illegible]	[illegible]	[illegible]
[illegible]	[illegible]	[illegible]	[illegible]	[illegible]	[illegible]	[illegible]	[illegible]	[illegible]	[illegible]	[illegible]	[illegible]
[illegible]	[illegible]	[illegible]	[illegible]	[illegible]	[illegible]	[illegible]	[illegible]	[illegible]	[illegible]	[illegible]	[illegible]
[illegible]	[illegible]	[illegible]	[illegible]	[illegible]	[illegible]	[illegible]	[illegible]	[illegible]	[illegible]	[illegible]	[illegible]
[illegible]	[illegible]	[illegible]	[illegible]	[illegible]	[illegible]	[illegible]	[illegible]	[illegible]	[illegible]	[illegible]	[illegible]
[illegible]	[illegible]	[illegible]	[illegible]	[illegible]	[illegible]	[illegible]	[illegible]	[illegible]	[illegible]	[illegible]	[illegible]
[illegible]	[illegible]	[illegible]	[illegible]	[illegible]	[illegible]	[illegible]	[illegible]	[illegible]	[illegible]	[illegible]	[illegible]
[illegible]	[illegible]	[illegible]	[illegible]	[illegible]	[illegible]	[illegible]	[illegible]	[illegible]	[illegible]	[illegible]	[illegible]
[illegible]	[illegible]	[illegible]	[illegible]	[illegible]	[illegible]	[illegible]	[illegible]	[illegible]	[illegible]	[illegible]	[illegible]
[illegible]	[illegible]	[illegible]	[illegible]	[illegible]	[illegible]	[illegible]	[illegible]	[illegible]	[illegible]	[illegible]	[illegible]
[illegible]	[illegible]	[illegible]	[illegible]	[illegible]	[illegible]	[illegible]	[illegible]	[illegible]	[illegible]	[illegible]	[illegible]
[illegible]	[illegible]	[illegible]	[illegible]	[illegible]	[illegible]	[illegible]	[illegible]	[illegible]	[illegible]	[illegible]	[illegible]
[illegible]	[illegible]	[illegible]	[illegible]	[illegible]	[illegible]	[illegible]	[illegible]	[illegible]	[illegible]	[illegible]	[illegible]
[illegible]	[illegible]	[illegible]	[illegible]	[illegible]	[illegible]	[illegible]	[illegible]	[illegible]	[illegible]	[illegible]	[illegible]
[illegible]	[illegible]	[illegible]	[illegible]	[illegible]	[illegible]	[illegible]	[illegible]	[illegible]	[illegible]	[illegible]	[illegible]
TOTAL OF PROVINCE,	[illegible]	[illegible]	[illegible]	[illegible]	[illegible]	[illegible]	[illegible]	[illegible]	[illegible]	[illegible]	[illegible]
MUNSTER.											
[illegible]	[illegible]	[illegible]	[illegible]	[illegible]	[illegible]	[illegible]	[illegible]	[illegible]	[illegible]	[illegible]	[illegible]
[illegible]	[illegible]	[illegible]	[illegible]	[illegible]	[illegible]	[illegible]	[illegible]	[illegible]	[illegible]	[illegible]	[illegible]
[illegible]	[illegible]	[illegible]	[illegible]	[illegible]	[illegible]	[illegible]	[illegible]	[illegible]	[illegible]	[illegible]	[illegible]
[illegible]	[illegible]	[illegible]	[illegible]	[illegible]	[illegible]	[illegible]	[illegible]	[illegible]	[illegible]	[illegible]	[illegible]
[illegible]	[illegible]	[illegible]	[illegible]	[illegible]	[illegible]	[illegible]	[illegible]	[illegible]	[illegible]	[illegible]	[illegible]
[illegible]	[illegible]	[illegible]	[illegible]	[illegible]	[illegible]	[illegible]	[illegible]	[illegible]	[illegible]	[illegible]	[illegible]
[illegible]	[illegible]	[illegible]	[illegible]	[illegible]	[illegible]	[illegible]	[illegible]	[illegible]	[illegible]	[illegible]	[illegible]
[illegible]	[illegible]	[illegible]	[illegible]	[illegible]	[illegible]	[illegible]	[illegible]	[illegible]	[illegible]	[illegible]	[illegible]
[illegible]	[illegible]	[illegible]	[illegible]	[illegible]	[illegible]	[illegible]	[illegible]	[illegible]	[illegible]	[illegible]	[illegible]
[illegible]	[illegible]	[illegible]	[illegible]	[illegible]	[illegible]	[illegible]	[illegible]	[illegible]	[illegible]	[illegible]	[illegible]
[illegible]	[illegible]	[illegible]	[illegible]	[illegible]	[illegible]	[illegible]	[illegible]	[illegible]	[illegible]	[illegible]	[illegible]
TOTAL OF PROVINCE,	[illegible]	[illegible]	[illegible]	[illegible]	[illegible]	[illegible]	[illegible]	[illegible]	[illegible]	[illegible]	[illegible]
ULSTER.											
[illegible]	[illegible]	[illegible]	[illegible]	[illegible]	[illegible]	[illegible]	[illegible]	[illegible]	[illegible]	[illegible]	[illegible]
[illegible]	[illegible]	[illegible]	[illegible]	[illegible]	[illegible]	[illegible]	[illegible]	[illegible]	[illegible]	[illegible]	[illegible]
[illegible]	[illegible]	[illegible]	[illegible]	[illegible]	[illegible]	[illegible]	[illegible]	[illegible]	[illegible]	[illegible]	[illegible]
[illegible]	[illegible]	[illegible]	[illegible]	[illegible]	[illegible]	[illegible]	[illegible]	[illegible]	[illegible]	[illegible]	[illegible]
[illegible]	[illegible]	[illegible]	[illegible]	[illegible]	[illegible]	[illegible]	[illegible]	[illegible]	[illegible]	[illegible]	[illegible]
[illegible]	[illegible]	[illegible]	[illegible]	[illegible]	[illegible]	[illegible]	[illegible]	[illegible]	[illegible]	[illegible]	[illegible]
[illegible]	[illegible]	[illegible]	[illegible]	[illegible]	[illegible]	[illegible]	[illegible]	[illegible]	[illegible]	[illegible]	[illegible]
[illegible]	[illegible]	[illegible]	[illegible]	[illegible]	[illegible]	[illegible]	[illegible]	[illegible]	[illegible]	[illegible]	[illegible]
[illegible]	[illegible]	[illegible]	[illegible]	[illegible]	[illegible]	[illegible]	[illegible]	[illegible]	[illegible]	[illegible]	[illegible]
[illegible]	[illegible]	[illegible]	[illegible]	[illegible]	[illegible]	[illegible]	[illegible]	[illegible]	[illegible]	[illegible]	[illegible]
[illegible]	[illegible]	[illegible]	[illegible]	[illegible]	[illegible]	[illegible]	[illegible]	[illegible]	[illegible]	[illegible]	[illegible]
[illegible]	[illegible]	[illegible]	[illegible]	[illegible]	[illegible]	[illegible]	[illegible]	[illegible]	[illegible]	[illegible]	[illegible]
TOTAL OF PROVINCE,	[illegible]	[illegible]	[illegible]	[illegible]	[illegible]	[illegible]	[illegible]	[illegible]	[illegible]	[illegible]	[illegible]
CONNAUGHT.											
[illegible]	[illegible]	[illegible]	[illegible]	[illegible]	[illegible]	[illegible]	[illegible]	[illegible]	[illegible]	[illegible]	[illegible]
[illegible]	[illegible]	[illegible]	[illegible]	[illegible]	[illegible]	[illegible]	[illegible]	[illegible]	[illegible]	[illegible]	[illegible]
[illegible]	[illegible]	[illegible]	[illegible]	[illegible]	[illegible]	[illegible]	[illegible]	[illegible]	[illegible]	[illegible]	[illegible]
[illegible]	[illegible]	[illegible]	[illegible]	[illegible]	[illegible]	[illegible]	[illegible]	[illegible]	[illegible]	[illegible]	[illegible]
[illegible]	[illegible]	[illegible]	[illegible]	[illegible]	[illegible]	[illegible]	[illegible]	[illegible]	[illegible]	[illegible]	[illegible]
[illegible]	[illegible]	[illegible]	[illegible]	[illegible]	[illegible]	[illegible]	[illegible]	[illegible]	[illegible]	[illegible]	[illegible]
[illegible]	[illegible]	[illegible]	[illegible]	[illegible]	[illegible]	[illegible]	[illegible]	[illegible]	[illegible]	[illegible]	[illegible]
TOTAL OF PROVINCE,	[illegible]	[illegible]	[illegible]	[illegible]	[illegible]	[illegible]	[illegible]	[illegible]	[illegible]	[illegible]	[illegible]

LEINSTER.

Carlow.
Drogheda Town.
Dublin County.
Dublin Metropolitan Police District.
Kildare.
Kilkenny County.
Kilkenny City.
King's County.
Longford.
Louth.
Meath.
Queen's County.
Westmeath.
Wexford.
Wicklow.

TOTAL OF PROVINCE.

MUNSTER.

TABLE 24.—RETURNS FROM THE SEVERAL COUNTIES—
each County, and County

OFFENCES.	Total of Ireland.	Leinster.													
		Total.	Carlow.	Drogheda Town.	Dublin.	Dublin Metropolitan Police District.	Kildare.	Kilkenny.	Kilkenny City.	King's County.	Longford.	Louth.	Meath.	Queen's County.	Westmeath.
Class I.—Offences against the Person.															
1. Murder (of persons aged above one Year)	[illegible]	[illegible]	[illegible]	[illegible]	[illegible]	[illegible]	[illegible]	[illegible]	[illegible]	[illegible]	[illegible]	[illegible]	[illegible]	[illegible]	[illegible]
Ditto (of Infants aged one Year and under)	[illegible]	[illegible]	[illegible]	[illegible]	[illegible]	[illegible]	[illegible]	[illegible]	[illegible]	[illegible]	[illegible]	[illegible]	[illegible]	[illegible]	[illegible]
2. Attempts to Murder,	[illegible]	[illegible]	[illegible]	[illegible]	[illegible]	[illegible]	[illegible]	[illegible]	[illegible]	[illegible]	[illegible]	[illegible]	[illegible]	[illegible]	[illegible]
3. Conspiracy or soliciting to Murder,	[illegible]	[illegible]	[illegible]	[illegible]	[illegible]	[illegible]	[illegible]	[illegible]	[illegible]	[illegible]	[illegible]	[illegible]	[illegible]	[illegible]	[illegible]
4. Manslaughter,	[illegible]	[illegible]	[illegible]	[illegible]	[illegible]	[illegible]	[illegible]	[illegible]	[illegible]	[illegible]	[illegible]	[illegible]	[illegible]	[illegible]	[illegible]
5. Felonious Wounding,	[illegible]	[illegible]	[illegible]	[illegible]	[illegible]	[illegible]	[illegible]	[illegible]	[illegible]	[illegible]	[illegible]	[illegible]	[illegible]	[illegible]	[illegible]
6. Endangering Railway Passengers,	[illegible]	[illegible]	[illegible]	[illegible]	[illegible]	[illegible]	[illegible]	[illegible]	[illegible]	[illegible]	[illegible]	[illegible]	[illegible]	[illegible]	[illegible]
7. Malicious Wounding (misdemeanours),	[illegible]	[illegible]	[illegible]	[illegible]	[illegible]	[illegible]	[illegible]	[illegible]	[illegible]	[illegible]	[illegible]	[illegible]	[illegible]	[illegible]	[illegible]
8. Assaults,	[illegible]	[illegible]	[illegible]	[illegible]	[illegible]	[illegible]	[illegible]	[illegible]	[illegible]	[illegible]	[illegible]	[illegible]	[illegible]	[illegible]	[illegible]
9. Intimidation and Molestation,	[illegible]	[illegible]	[illegible]	[illegible]	[illegible]	[illegible]	[illegible]	[illegible]	[illegible]	[illegible]	[illegible]	[illegible]	[illegible]	[illegible]	[illegible]
10. Cruelty to or neglect of Children,	[illegible]	[illegible]	[illegible]	[illegible]	[illegible]	[illegible]	[illegible]	[illegible]	[illegible]	[illegible]	[illegible]	[illegible]	[illegible]	[illegible]	[illegible]
11. Abandoning Children under two Years,	[illegible]	[illegible]	[illegible]	[illegible]	[illegible]	[illegible]	[illegible]	[illegible]	[illegible]	[illegible]	[illegible]	[illegible]	[illegible]	[illegible]	[illegible]
12. Child stealing,	[illegible]	[illegible]	[illegible]	[illegible]	[illegible]	[illegible]	[illegible]	[illegible]	[illegible]	[illegible]	[illegible]	[illegible]	[illegible]	[illegible]	[illegible]
13. Procuring abortion,	[illegible]	[illegible]	[illegible]	[illegible]	[illegible]	[illegible]	[illegible]	[illegible]	[illegible]	[illegible]	[illegible]	[illegible]	[illegible]	[illegible]	[illegible]
14. Concealment of birth,	[illegible]	[illegible]	[illegible]	[illegible]	[illegible]	[illegible]	[illegible]	[illegible]	[illegible]	[illegible]	[illegible]	[illegible]	[illegible]	[illegible]	[illegible]
15. Unnatural offences,	[illegible]	[illegible]	[illegible]	[illegible]	[illegible]	[illegible]	[illegible]	[illegible]	[illegible]	[illegible]	[illegible]	[illegible]	[illegible]	[illegible]	[illegible]
16. Attempts to commit unnatural offences,	[illegible]	[illegible]	[illegible]	[illegible]	[illegible]	[illegible]	[illegible]	[illegible]	[illegible]	[illegible]	[illegible]	[illegible]	[illegible]	[illegible]	[illegible]
17. Indecency with Males,	[illegible]	[illegible]	[illegible]	[illegible]	[illegible]	[illegible]	[illegible]	[illegible]	[illegible]	[illegible]	[illegible]	[illegible]	[illegible]	[illegible]	[illegible]
18. Rape,	[illegible]	[illegible]	[illegible]	[illegible]	[illegible]	[illegible]	[illegible]	[illegible]	[illegible]	[illegible]	[illegible]	[illegible]	[illegible]	[illegible]	[illegible]
19. Indecent assaults on Females,	[illegible]	[illegible]	[illegible]	[illegible]	[illegible]	[illegible]	[illegible]	[illegible]	[illegible]	[illegible]	[illegible]	[illegible]	[illegible]	[illegible]	[illegible]
20. Defilement of Girls under 13,	[illegible]	[illegible]	[illegible]	[illegible]	[illegible]	[illegible]	[illegible]	[illegible]	[illegible]	[illegible]	[illegible]	[illegible]	[illegible]	[illegible]	[illegible]
21. Defilement of Girls under 16,	[illegible]	[illegible]	[illegible]	[illegible]	[illegible]	[illegible]	[illegible]	[illegible]	[illegible]	[illegible]	[illegible]	[illegible]	[illegible]	[illegible]	[illegible]
22. Householder permitting defilement of Girls,	[illegible]	[illegible]	[illegible]	[illegible]	[illegible]	[illegible]	[illegible]	[illegible]	[illegible]	[illegible]	[illegible]	[illegible]	[illegible]	[illegible]	[illegible]
23. Procuration,	[illegible]	[illegible]	[illegible]	[illegible]	[illegible]	[illegible]	[illegible]	[illegible]	[illegible]	[illegible]	[illegible]	[illegible]	[illegible]	[illegible]	[illegible]
24. Abduction,	[illegible]	[illegible]	[illegible]	[illegible]	[illegible]	[illegible]	[illegible]	[illegible]	[illegible]	[illegible]	[illegible]	[illegible]	[illegible]	[illegible]	[illegible]
25. Bigamy,	[illegible]	[illegible]	[illegible]	[illegible]	[illegible]	[illegible]	[illegible]	[illegible]	[illegible]	[illegible]	[illegible]	[illegible]	[illegible]	[illegible]	[illegible]
26. Other Offences against the Person,	[illegible]	[illegible]	[illegible]	[illegible]	[illegible]	[illegible]	[illegible]	[illegible]	[illegible]	[illegible]	[illegible]	[illegible]	[illegible]	[illegible]	[illegible]
Class II.—Offences against Property with Violence.															
27. Sacrilege,	[illegible]	[illegible]	[illegible]	[illegible]	[illegible]	[illegible]	[illegible]	[illegible]	[illegible]	[illegible]	[illegible]	[illegible]	[illegible]	[illegible]	[illegible]
28. Burglary,	[illegible]	[illegible]	[illegible]	[illegible]	[illegible]	[illegible]	[illegible]	[illegible]	[illegible]	[illegible]	[illegible]	[illegible]	[illegible]	[illegible]	[illegible]
29. Housebreaking,	[illegible]	[illegible]	[illegible]	[illegible]	[illegible]	[illegible]	[illegible]	[illegible]	[illegible]	[illegible]	[illegible]	[illegible]	[illegible]	[illegible]	[illegible]
30. Breaking into Shops, Warehouses, &c.,	[illegible]	[illegible]	[illegible]	[illegible]	[illegible]	[illegible]	[illegible]	[illegible]	[illegible]	[illegible]	[illegible]	[illegible]	[illegible]	[illegible]	[illegible]
31. Attempts to break into Houses, Shops, &c.,	[illegible]	[illegible]	[illegible]	[illegible]	[illegible]	[illegible]	[illegible]	[illegible]	[illegible]	[illegible]	[illegible]	[illegible]	[illegible]	[illegible]	[illegible]
32. Entering with intent to commit Felony,	[illegible]	[illegible]	[illegible]	[illegible]	[illegible]	[illegible]	[illegible]	[illegible]	[illegible]	[illegible]	[illegible]	[illegible]	[illegible]	[illegible]	[illegible]
33. Possession of Housebreaking Tools, &c.,	[illegible]	[illegible]	[illegible]	[illegible]	[illegible]	[illegible]	[illegible]	[illegible]	[illegible]	[illegible]	[illegible]	[illegible]	[illegible]	[illegible]	[illegible]
34. Robbery and Assaults with intent to rob,	[illegible]	[illegible]	[illegible]	[illegible]	[illegible]	[illegible]	[illegible]	[illegible]	[illegible]	[illegible]	[illegible]	[illegible]	[illegible]	[illegible]	[illegible]
35. Extortion by threats to accuse of crime,	[illegible]	[illegible]	[illegible]	[illegible]	[illegible]	[illegible]	[illegible]	[illegible]	[illegible]	[illegible]	[illegible]	[illegible]	[illegible]	[illegible]	[illegible]
36. Extortion by other threats,	[illegible]	[illegible]	[illegible]	[illegible]	[illegible]	[illegible]	[illegible]	[illegible]	[illegible]	[illegible]	[illegible]	[illegible]	[illegible]	[illegible]	[illegible]
Class III.—Offences against Property without Violence.															
37. Larceny of Horses, Cattle, and Sheep,	[illegible]	[illegible]	[illegible]	[illegible]	[illegible]	[illegible]	[illegible]	[illegible]	[illegible]	[illegible]	[illegible]	[illegible]	[illegible]	[illegible]	[illegible]
38. Larceny from the Person,	[illegible]	[illegible]	[illegible]	[illegible]	[illegible]	[illegible]	[illegible]	[illegible]	[illegible]	[illegible]	[illegible]	[illegible]	[illegible]	[illegible]	[illegible]
39. Larceny in House,	[illegible]	[illegible]	[illegible]	[illegible]	[illegible]	[illegible]	[illegible]	[illegible]	[illegible]	[illegible]	[illegible]	[illegible]	[illegible]	[illegible]	[illegible]
40. Larceny by a Servant,	[illegible]	[illegible]	[illegible]	[illegible]	[illegible]	[illegible]	[illegible]	[illegible]	[illegible]	[illegible]	[illegible]	[illegible]	[illegible]	[illegible]	[illegible]
41. Embezzlement,	[illegible]	[illegible]	[illegible]	[illegible]	[illegible]	[illegible]	[illegible]	[illegible]	[illegible]	[illegible]	[illegible]	[illegible]	[illegible]	[illegible]	[illegible]
42. Larceny of Post Letters,	[illegible]	[illegible]	[illegible]	[illegible]	[illegible]	[illegible]	[illegible]	[illegible]	[illegible]	[illegible]	[illegible]	[illegible]	[illegible]	[illegible]	[illegible]
43. Other aggravated Larcenies,	[illegible]	[illegible]	[illegible]	[illegible]	[illegible]	[illegible]	[illegible]	[illegible]	[illegible]	[illegible]	[illegible]	[illegible]	[illegible]	[illegible]	[illegible]
44. Simple larceny and minor larcenies,	[illegible]	[illegible]	[illegible]	[illegible]	[illegible]	[illegible]	[illegible]	[illegible]	[illegible]	[illegible]	[illegible]	[illegible]	[illegible]	[illegible]	[illegible]
45. Obtaining goods, &c., by false pretences,	[illegible]	[illegible]	[illegible]	[illegible]	[illegible]	[illegible]	[illegible]	[illegible]	[illegible]	[illegible]	[illegible]	[illegible]	[illegible]	[illegible]	[illegible]
46. Frauds by Bankers, Agents, Directors, &c.,	[illegible]	[illegible]	[illegible]	[illegible]	[illegible]	[illegible]	[illegible]	[illegible]	[illegible]	[illegible]	[illegible]	[illegible]	[illegible]	[illegible]	[illegible]
47. Falsifying accounts,	[illegible]	[illegible]	[illegible]	[illegible]	[illegible]	[illegible]	[illegible]	[illegible]	[illegible]	[illegible]	[illegible]	[illegible]	[illegible]	[illegible]	[illegible]
48. Other Frauds,	[illegible]	[illegible]	[illegible]	[illegible]	[illegible]	[illegible]	[illegible]	[illegible]	[illegible]	[illegible]	[illegible]	[illegible]	[illegible]	[illegible]	[illegible]
49. Receiving Stolen Goods,	[illegible]	[illegible]	[illegible]	[illegible]	[illegible]	[illegible]	[illegible]	[illegible]	[illegible]	[illegible]	[illegible]	[illegible]	[illegible]	[illegible]	[illegible]
50. Offences in connection with Bankruptcy,	[illegible]	[illegible]	[illegible]	[illegible]	[illegible]	[illegible]	[illegible]	[illegible]	[illegible]	[illegible]	[illegible]	[illegible]	[illegible]	[illegible]	[illegible]

INDICTABLE OFFENCES.—Nature of Crimes Committed in ... of City or of Town.

Offences.	Westmeath.	Wicklow.	Munster. [illegible]	[illegible]	Cork, E.R.	Cork, W.R.	Cork City.	Kerry.	Limerick.	Limerick City.	Tipperary, N.R.	Tipperary, S.R.	Waterford.	Waterford City.
Class I.—Offences against the Person.														
1. Murder (of persons aged above one Year).	[illegible]	[illegible]	[illegible]	[illegible]	[illegible]	[illegible]	[illegible]	[illegible]	[illegible]	[illegible]	[illegible]	[illegible]	[illegible]	[illegible]
Murder (of infants aged one Year and under).	[illegible]	[illegible]	[illegible]	[illegible]	[illegible]	[illegible]	[illegible]	[illegible]	[illegible]	[illegible]	[illegible]	[illegible]	[illegible]	[illegible]
2. Attempt to Murder.	[illegible]	[illegible]	[illegible]	[illegible]	[illegible]	[illegible]	[illegible]	[illegible]	[illegible]	[illegible]	[illegible]	[illegible]	[illegible]	[illegible]
3. Conspiracy or soliciting to Murder.	[illegible]	[illegible]	[illegible]	[illegible]	[illegible]	[illegible]	[illegible]	[illegible]	[illegible]	[illegible]	[illegible]	[illegible]	[illegible]	[illegible]
4. Manslaughter.	[illegible]	[illegible]	[illegible]	[illegible]	[illegible]	[illegible]	[illegible]	[illegible]	[illegible]	[illegible]	[illegible]	[illegible]	[illegible]	[illegible]
5. Felonious Wounding.	[illegible]	[illegible]	[illegible]	[illegible]	[illegible]	[illegible]	[illegible]	[illegible]	[illegible]	[illegible]	[illegible]	[illegible]	[illegible]	[illegible]
6. Endangering Railway Passengers.	[illegible]	[illegible]	[illegible]	[illegible]	[illegible]	[illegible]	[illegible]	[illegible]	[illegible]	[illegible]	[illegible]	[illegible]	[illegible]	[illegible]
7. Malicious Wounding (misdemeanour).	[illegible]	[illegible]	[illegible]	[illegible]	[illegible]	[illegible]	[illegible]	[illegible]	[illegible]	[illegible]	[illegible]	[illegible]	[illegible]	[illegible]
8. Assault.	[illegible]	[illegible]	[illegible]	[illegible]	[illegible]	[illegible]	[illegible]	[illegible]	[illegible]	[illegible]	[illegible]	[illegible]	[illegible]	[illegible]
9. Intimidation and Molestation.	[illegible]	[illegible]	[illegible]	[illegible]	[illegible]	[illegible]	[illegible]	[illegible]	[illegible]	[illegible]	[illegible]	[illegible]	[illegible]	[illegible]
10. Cruelty to or neglect of Children.	[illegible]	[illegible]	[illegible]	[illegible]	[illegible]	[illegible]	[illegible]	[illegible]	[illegible]	[illegible]	[illegible]	[illegible]	[illegible]	[illegible]
11. Abandoning Children under two Years.	[illegible]	[illegible]	[illegible]	[illegible]	[illegible]	[illegible]	[illegible]	[illegible]	[illegible]	[illegible]	[illegible]	[illegible]	[illegible]	[illegible]
12. Child stealing.	[illegible]	[illegible]	[illegible]	[illegible]	[illegible]	[illegible]	[illegible]	[illegible]	[illegible]	[illegible]	[illegible]	[illegible]	[illegible]	[illegible]
13. Procuring abortion.	[illegible]	[illegible]	[illegible]	[illegible]	[illegible]	[illegible]	[illegible]	[illegible]	[illegible]	[illegible]	[illegible]	[illegible]	[illegible]	[illegible]
14. Concealment of birth.	[illegible]	[illegible]	[illegible]	[illegible]	[illegible]	[illegible]	[illegible]	[illegible]	[illegible]	[illegible]	[illegible]	[illegible]	[illegible]	[illegible]
15. Unnatural offences.	[illegible]	[illegible]	[illegible]	[illegible]	[illegible]	[illegible]	[illegible]	[illegible]	[illegible]	[illegible]	[illegible]	[illegible]	[illegible]	[illegible]
16. Attempts to commit unnatural offences.	[illegible]	[illegible]	[illegible]	[illegible]	[illegible]	[illegible]	[illegible]	[illegible]	[illegible]	[illegible]	[illegible]	[illegible]	[illegible]	[illegible]
17. Indecency with Males.	[illegible]	[illegible]	[illegible]	[illegible]	[illegible]	[illegible]	[illegible]	[illegible]	[illegible]	[illegible]	[illegible]	[illegible]	[illegible]	[illegible]
18. Rape.	[illegible]	[illegible]	[illegible]	[illegible]	[illegible]	[illegible]	[illegible]	[illegible]	[illegible]	[illegible]	[illegible]	[illegible]	[illegible]	[illegible]
19. Indecent assaults on Females.	[illegible]	[illegible]	[illegible]	[illegible]	[illegible]	[illegible]	[illegible]	[illegible]	[illegible]	[illegible]	[illegible]	[illegible]	[illegible]	[illegible]
20. Defilement of Girls under 13.	[illegible]	[illegible]	[illegible]	[illegible]	[illegible]	[illegible]	[illegible]	[illegible]	[illegible]	[illegible]	[illegible]	[illegible]	[illegible]	[illegible]
21. Defilement of Girls under 16.	[illegible]	[illegible]	[illegible]	[illegible]	[illegible]	[illegible]	[illegible]	[illegible]	[illegible]	[illegible]	[illegible]	[illegible]	[illegible]	[illegible]
22. Householder permitting defilement of Girls.	[illegible]	[illegible]	[illegible]	[illegible]	[illegible]	[illegible]	[illegible]	[illegible]	[illegible]	[illegible]	[illegible]	[illegible]	[illegible]	[illegible]
23. Procuration.	[illegible]	[illegible]	[illegible]	[illegible]	[illegible]	[illegible]	[illegible]	[illegible]	[illegible]	[illegible]	[illegible]	[illegible]	[illegible]	[illegible]
24. Abduction.	[illegible]	[illegible]	[illegible]	[illegible]	[illegible]	[illegible]	[illegible]	[illegible]	[illegible]	[illegible]	[illegible]	[illegible]	[illegible]	[illegible]
25. Bigamy.	[illegible]	[illegible]	[illegible]	[illegible]	[illegible]	[illegible]	[illegible]	[illegible]	[illegible]	[illegible]	[illegible]	[illegible]	[illegible]	[illegible]
26. Other Offences against the Person.	[illegible]	[illegible]	[illegible]	[illegible]	[illegible]	[illegible]	[illegible]	[illegible]	[illegible]	[illegible]	[illegible]	[illegible]	[illegible]	[illegible]
Class II.—Offences against Property with Violence.														
27. Sacrilege.	[illegible]	[illegible]	[illegible]	[illegible]	[illegible]	[illegible]	[illegible]	[illegible]	[illegible]	[illegible]	[illegible]	[illegible]	[illegible]	[illegible]
28. Burglary.	[illegible]	[illegible]	[illegible]	[illegible]	[illegible]	[illegible]	[illegible]	[illegible]	[illegible]	[illegible]	[illegible]	[illegible]	[illegible]	[illegible]
29. Housebreaking.	[illegible]	[illegible]	[illegible]	[illegible]	[illegible]	[illegible]	[illegible]	[illegible]	[illegible]	[illegible]	[illegible]	[illegible]	[illegible]	[illegible]
30. Breaking into Shops, Warehouses, &c.	[illegible]	[illegible]	[illegible]	[illegible]	[illegible]	[illegible]	[illegible]	[illegible]	[illegible]	[illegible]	[illegible]	[illegible]	[illegible]	[illegible]
31. Attempts to break into Houses, Shops, &c.	[illegible]	[illegible]	[illegible]	[illegible]	[illegible]	[illegible]	[illegible]	[illegible]	[illegible]	[illegible]	[illegible]	[illegible]	[illegible]	[illegible]
32. Entering with intent to commit felony.	[illegible]	[illegible]	[illegible]	[illegible]	[illegible]	[illegible]	[illegible]	[illegible]	[illegible]	[illegible]	[illegible]	[illegible]	[illegible]	[illegible]
33. Possession of Housebreaking Tools, &c.	[illegible]	[illegible]	[illegible]	[illegible]	[illegible]	[illegible]	[illegible]	[illegible]	[illegible]	[illegible]	[illegible]	[illegible]	[illegible]	[illegible]
34. Robbery and Assaults with intent to rob.	[illegible]	[illegible]	[illegible]	[illegible]	[illegible]	[illegible]	[illegible]	[illegible]	[illegible]	[illegible]	[illegible]	[illegible]	[illegible]	[illegible]
35. Extortion by threats to accuse of crimes.	[illegible]	[illegible]	[illegible]	[illegible]	[illegible]	[illegible]	[illegible]	[illegible]	[illegible]	[illegible]	[illegible]	[illegible]	[illegible]	[illegible]
36. Extortion by other threats.	[illegible]	[illegible]	[illegible]	[illegible]	[illegible]	[illegible]	[illegible]	[illegible]	[illegible]	[illegible]	[illegible]	[illegible]	[illegible]	[illegible]
Class III.—Offences against Property without Violence.														
37. Larceny of Horses, Cattle, and Sheep.	[illegible]	[illegible]	[illegible]	[illegible]	[illegible]	[illegible]	[illegible]	[illegible]	[illegible]	[illegible]	[illegible]	[illegible]	[illegible]	[illegible]
38. Larceny from the Person.	[illegible]	[illegible]	[illegible]	[illegible]	[illegible]	[illegible]	[illegible]	[illegible]	[illegible]	[illegible]	[illegible]	[illegible]	[illegible]	[illegible]
39. Larceny in House.	[illegible]	[illegible]	[illegible]	[illegible]	[illegible]	[illegible]	[illegible]	[illegible]	[illegible]	[illegible]	[illegible]	[illegible]	[illegible]	[illegible]
40. Larceny by a Servant.	[illegible]	[illegible]	[illegible]	[illegible]	[illegible]	[illegible]	[illegible]	[illegible]	[illegible]	[illegible]	[illegible]	[illegible]	[illegible]	[illegible]
41. Embezzlement.	[illegible]	[illegible]	[illegible]	[illegible]	[illegible]	[illegible]	[illegible]	[illegible]	[illegible]	[illegible]	[illegible]	[illegible]	[illegible]	[illegible]
42. Larceny of Post Letters.	[illegible]	[illegible]	[illegible]	[illegible]	[illegible]	[illegible]	[illegible]	[illegible]	[illegible]	[illegible]	[illegible]	[illegible]	[illegible]	[illegible]
43. Other aggravated Larcenies.	[illegible]	[illegible]	[illegible]	[illegible]	[illegible]	[illegible]	[illegible]	[illegible]	[illegible]	[illegible]	[illegible]	[illegible]	[illegible]	[illegible]
44. Simple larceny and minor larcenies.	[illegible]	[illegible]	[illegible]	[illegible]	[illegible]	[illegible]	[illegible]	[illegible]	[illegible]	[illegible]	[illegible]	[illegible]	[illegible]	[illegible]
45. Obtaining goods, &c., by false pretences.	[illegible]	[illegible]	[illegible]	[illegible]	[illegible]	[illegible]	[illegible]	[illegible]	[illegible]	[illegible]	[illegible]	[illegible]	[illegible]	[illegible]
46. Frauds by Bankers, Agents, Directors, &c.	[illegible]	[illegible]	[illegible]	[illegible]	[illegible]	[illegible]	[illegible]	[illegible]	[illegible]	[illegible]	[illegible]	[illegible]	[illegible]	[illegible]
47. Falsifying accounts.	[illegible]	[illegible]	[illegible]	[illegible]	[illegible]	[illegible]	[illegible]	[illegible]	[illegible]	[illegible]	[illegible]	[illegible]	[illegible]	[illegible]
48. Other Frauds.	[illegible]	[illegible]	[illegible]	[illegible]	[illegible]	[illegible]	[illegible]	[illegible]	[illegible]	[illegible]	[illegible]	[illegible]	[illegible]	[illegible]
49. Receiving Stolen Goods.	[illegible]	[illegible]	[illegible]	[illegible]	[illegible]	[illegible]	[illegible]	[illegible]	[illegible]	[illegible]	[illegible]	[illegible]	[illegible]	[illegible]
50. Offences in connection with Bankruptcy.	[illegible]	[illegible]	[illegible]	[illegible]	[illegible]	[illegible]	[illegible]	[illegible]	[illegible]	[illegible]	[illegible]	[illegible]	[illegible]	[illegible]

TABLE 24—*continued.*—RETURNS FROM THE SEVERAL COUNTIES.—each County, and County

OFFENCES.	Total of Ireland.	Leinster: Total.	[illegible]	[illegible]	[illegible]	[illegible]	[illegible]	[illegible]	[illegible]	[illegible]	[illegible]	[illegible]	[illegible]	[illegible]	[illegible]	[illegible]
Class IV.—Malicious Injuries to Property.																
55. Arson.	[illegible]	[illegible]	[illegible]	[illegible]	[illegible]	[illegible]	[illegible]	[illegible]	[illegible]	[illegible]	[illegible]	[illegible]	[illegible]	[illegible]	[illegible]	[illegible]
56. Setting Fire to Crops, Plantations, &c.	[illegible]	[illegible]	[illegible]	[illegible]	[illegible]	[illegible]	[illegible]	[illegible]	[illegible]	[illegible]	[illegible]	[illegible]	[illegible]	[illegible]	[illegible]	[illegible]
57. Killing and Maiming Cattle.	[illegible]	[illegible]	[illegible]	[illegible]	[illegible]	[illegible]	[illegible]	[illegible]	[illegible]	[illegible]	[illegible]	[illegible]	[illegible]	[illegible]	[illegible]	[illegible]
58. Malicious ... &c. of Explosives.	[illegible]	[illegible]	[illegible]	[illegible]	[illegible]	[illegible]	[illegible]	[illegible]	[illegible]	[illegible]	[illegible]	[illegible]	[illegible]	[illegible]	[illegible]	[illegible]
59. Destroying Ships.	[illegible]	[illegible]	[illegible]	[illegible]	[illegible]	[illegible]	[illegible]	[illegible]	[illegible]	[illegible]	[illegible]	[illegible]	[illegible]	[illegible]	[illegible]	[illegible]
60. Destroying Railways.	[illegible]	[illegible]	[illegible]	[illegible]	[illegible]	[illegible]	[illegible]	[illegible]	[illegible]	[illegible]	[illegible]	[illegible]	[illegible]	[illegible]	[illegible]	[illegible]
61. Destroying Trees and Shrubs.	[illegible]	[illegible]	[illegible]	[illegible]	[illegible]	[illegible]	[illegible]	[illegible]	[illegible]	[illegible]	[illegible]	[illegible]	[illegible]	[illegible]	[illegible]	[illegible]
62. Other Malicious Injuries.	[illegible]	[illegible]	[illegible]	[illegible]	[illegible]	[illegible]	[illegible]	[illegible]	[illegible]	[illegible]	[illegible]	[illegible]	[illegible]	[illegible]	[illegible]	[illegible]
Class V.—Forgery and Offences against the Currency.																
63. Forgery and Uttering (felony).	[illegible]	[illegible]	[illegible]	[illegible]	[illegible]	[illegible]	[illegible]	[illegible]	[illegible]	[illegible]	[illegible]	[illegible]	[illegible]	[illegible]	[illegible]	[illegible]
64. Forgery (misdemeanour).	[illegible]	[illegible]	[illegible]	[illegible]	[illegible]	[illegible]	[illegible]	[illegible]	[illegible]	[illegible]	[illegible]	[illegible]	[illegible]	[illegible]	[illegible]	[illegible]
65. Coining.	[illegible]	[illegible]	[illegible]	[illegible]	[illegible]	[illegible]	[illegible]	[illegible]	[illegible]	[illegible]	[illegible]	[illegible]	[illegible]	[illegible]	[illegible]	[illegible]
66. Uttering or Possessing Counterfeit Coin.	[illegible]	[illegible]	[illegible]	[illegible]	[illegible]	[illegible]	[illegible]	[illegible]	[illegible]	[illegible]	[illegible]	[illegible]	[illegible]	[illegible]	[illegible]	[illegible]
Class VI.—Other Offences not included in the above Classes.																
Offences against the Crown and Public Order: 67. High Treason.	[illegible]	[illegible]	[illegible]	[illegible]	[illegible]	[illegible]	[illegible]	[illegible]	[illegible]	[illegible]	[illegible]	[illegible]	[illegible]	[illegible]	[illegible]	[illegible]
68. Treason Felony.	[illegible]	[illegible]	[illegible]	[illegible]	[illegible]	[illegible]	[illegible]	[illegible]	[illegible]	[illegible]	[illegible]	[illegible]	[illegible]	[illegible]	[illegible]	[illegible]
69. Riot.	[illegible]	[illegible]	[illegible]	[illegible]	[illegible]	[illegible]	[illegible]	[illegible]	[illegible]	[illegible]	[illegible]	[illegible]	[illegible]	[illegible]	[illegible]	[illegible]
70. Unlawful Assembly.	[illegible]	[illegible]	[illegible]	[illegible]	[illegible]	[illegible]	[illegible]	[illegible]	[illegible]	[illegible]	[illegible]	[illegible]	[illegible]	[illegible]	[illegible]	[illegible]
71. Intimidation by Threatening Letters, Notices, or otherwise.	[illegible]	[illegible]	[illegible]	[illegible]	[illegible]	[illegible]	[illegible]	[illegible]	[illegible]	[illegible]	[illegible]	[illegible]	[illegible]	[illegible]	[illegible]	[illegible]
72. Demand or Robbery of Arms.	[illegible]	[illegible]	[illegible]	[illegible]	[illegible]	[illegible]	[illegible]	[illegible]	[illegible]	[illegible]	[illegible]	[illegible]	[illegible]	[illegible]	[illegible]	[illegible]
73. Assaulting Dwelling-houses (by firing shots into them).	[illegible]	[illegible]	[illegible]	[illegible]	[illegible]	[illegible]	[illegible]	[illegible]	[illegible]	[illegible]	[illegible]	[illegible]	[illegible]	[illegible]	[illegible]	[illegible]
74. Other Offences.	[illegible]	[illegible]	[illegible]	[illegible]	[illegible]	[illegible]	[illegible]	[illegible]	[illegible]	[illegible]	[illegible]	[illegible]	[illegible]	[illegible]	[illegible]	[illegible]
Offences against Public Justice: 75. Extortion by Officers, &c.	[illegible]	[illegible]	[illegible]	[illegible]	[illegible]	[illegible]	[illegible]	[illegible]	[illegible]	[illegible]	[illegible]	[illegible]	[illegible]	[illegible]	[illegible]	[illegible]
76. Bribery, &c.	[illegible]	[illegible]	[illegible]	[illegible]	[illegible]	[illegible]	[illegible]	[illegible]	[illegible]	[illegible]	[illegible]	[illegible]	[illegible]	[illegible]	[illegible]	[illegible]
77. Perjury.	[illegible]	[illegible]	[illegible]	[illegible]	[illegible]	[illegible]	[illegible]	[illegible]	[illegible]	[illegible]	[illegible]	[illegible]	[illegible]	[illegible]	[illegible]	[illegible]
78. Escape and Rescue.	[illegible]	[illegible]	[illegible]	[illegible]	[illegible]	[illegible]	[illegible]	[illegible]	[illegible]	[illegible]	[illegible]	[illegible]	[illegible]	[illegible]	[illegible]	[illegible]
79. Other Offences.	[illegible]	[illegible]	[illegible]	[illegible]	[illegible]	[illegible]	[illegible]	[illegible]	[illegible]	[illegible]	[illegible]	[illegible]	[illegible]	[illegible]	[illegible]	[illegible]
Offences against Religion: 80. Blasphemy, &c.	[illegible]	[illegible]	[illegible]	[illegible]	[illegible]	[illegible]	[illegible]	[illegible]	[illegible]	[illegible]	[illegible]	[illegible]	[illegible]	[illegible]	[illegible]	[illegible]
Offences against Law of Nations: 81. Piracy.	[illegible]	[illegible]	[illegible]	[illegible]	[illegible]	[illegible]	[illegible]	[illegible]	[illegible]	[illegible]	[illegible]	[illegible]	[illegible]	[illegible]	[illegible]	[illegible]
82. Slave Trade.	[illegible]	[illegible]	[illegible]	[illegible]	[illegible]	[illegible]	[illegible]	[illegible]	[illegible]	[illegible]	[illegible]	[illegible]	[illegible]	[illegible]	[illegible]	[illegible]
83. Libel.	[illegible]	[illegible]	[illegible]	[illegible]	[illegible]	[illegible]	[illegible]	[illegible]	[illegible]	[illegible]	[illegible]	[illegible]	[illegible]	[illegible]	[illegible]	[illegible]
84. [illegible]	[illegible]	[illegible]	[illegible]	[illegible]	[illegible]	[illegible]	[illegible]	[illegible]	[illegible]	[illegible]	[illegible]	[illegible]	[illegible]	[illegible]	[illegible]	[illegible]
85. Indecent Exposure.	[illegible]	[illegible]	[illegible]	[illegible]	[illegible]	[illegible]	[illegible]	[illegible]	[illegible]	[illegible]	[illegible]	[illegible]	[illegible]	[illegible]	[illegible]	[illegible]
86. Keeping Disorderly Houses.	[illegible]	[illegible]	[illegible]	[illegible]	[illegible]	[illegible]	[illegible]	[illegible]	[illegible]	[illegible]	[illegible]	[illegible]	[illegible]	[illegible]	[illegible]	[illegible]
87. Other Nuisances.	[illegible]	[illegible]	[illegible]	[illegible]	[illegible]	[illegible]	[illegible]	[illegible]	[illegible]	[illegible]	[illegible]	[illegible]	[illegible]	[illegible]	[illegible]	[illegible]
88. Suicide (attempting to commit).	[illegible]	[illegible]	[illegible]	[illegible]	[illegible]	[illegible]	[illegible]	[illegible]	[illegible]	[illegible]	[illegible]	[illegible]	[illegible]	[illegible]	[illegible]	[illegible]
89. Other Misdemeanours.	[illegible]	[illegible]	[illegible]	[illegible]	[illegible]	[illegible]	[illegible]	[illegible]	[illegible]	[illegible]	[illegible]	[illegible]	[illegible]	[illegible]	[illegible]	[illegible]
TOTAL	[illegible]	[illegible]	[illegible]	[illegible]	[illegible]	[illegible]	[illegible]	[illegible]	[illegible]	[illegible]	[illegible]	[illegible]	[illegible]	[illegible]	[illegible]	[illegible]

INDICTABLE OFFENCES.—Nature of Crimes Committed in each of City or of Town.

Wexford.	Wicklow.	Munster: Total.	Clare.	Cork, E.R.	Cork, W.R.	Cork City.	Kerry.	Limerick.	Limerick City.	Tipperary N.R.	Tipperary S.R.	Waterford.	Waterford City.	OFFENCES.
														Class IV.—Malicious Injuries to Property.
[illegible]	[illegible]	[illegible]	[illegible]	[illegible]	[illegible]	.	[illegible]	[illegible]	[illegible]	[illegible]	[illegible]	[illegible]	[illegible]	51. Arson.
.	[illegible]	[illegible]	[illegible]	[illegible]	[illegible]	.	[illegible]	.	.	[illegible]	[illegible]	.	.	52. Setting Fire to Crops, Plantations, &c.
.	[illegible]	[illegible]	[illegible]	[illegible]	[illegible]	.	[illegible]	[illegible]	.	[illegible]	[illegible]	[illegible]	.	53. Killing and Maiming Cattle.
.	.	.	.	.	.	.	.	.	.	.	.	.	.	54. Malicious use, &c., of Explosives.
.	.	.	.	.	.	.	.	.	.	.	.	.	.	55. Destroying Ships.
.	.	.	.	.	.	.	.	.	.	.	.	.	.	56. Destroying Railways.
.	.	[illegible]	.	[illegible]	.	.	[illegible]	[illegible]	.	.	.	.	.	57. Destroying Trees and Shrubs.
[illegible]	[illegible]	[illegible]	[illegible]	[illegible]	[illegible]	[illegible]	[illegible]	[illegible]	.	[illegible]	[illegible]	[illegible]	.	58. Other Malicious Injuries.
														Class V.—Forgery and Offences against the Currency.
[illegible]	.	[illegible]	.	.	.	.	.	[illegible]	[illegible]	.	.	.	.	59. Forgery and Uttering (felony).
.	.	[illegible]	.	[illegible]	.	.	.	.	.	[illegible]	.	.	[illegible]	60. Forgery (misdemeanour).
.	.	.	.	.	.	.	.	.	.	.	.	.	.	61. Coining.
.	.	[illegible]	[illegible]	.	.	.	.	.	.	.	.	[illegible]	[illegible]	62. Uttering or Possessing Counterfeit Coin.
														Class VI.—Other Offences not included in the above Classes.
.	.	.	.	.	.	.	.	.	.	.	.	.	.	63. High Treason. (Offences against the State and Public Order.)
.	.	.	.	.	.	.	.	.	.	.	.	.	.	64. Treason Felony.
.	.	[illegible]	.	.	.	.	.	.	.	[illegible]	[illegible]	.	.	65. Riot.
.	.	.	.	.	.	.	.	.	.	.	.	.	.	66. Unlawful Assembly.
.	[illegible]	[illegible]	[illegible]	[illegible]	[illegible]	.	[illegible]	[illegible]	.	[illegible]	[illegible]	[illegible]	[illegible]	67. Intimidation by Threatening Letters, Notices, or otherwise.
.	.	[illegible]	[illegible]	[illegible]	.	.	.	.	.	.	.	.	.	68. Demand or Robbery of Arms.
.	.	[illegible]	[illegible]	[illegible]	.	.	[illegible]	.	.	.	[illegible]	.	.	69. Assembling Dwelling-houses (by firing into the same).
.	.	[illegible]	[illegible]	.	[illegible]	.	.	[illegible]	.	.	.	.	.	70. Other Offences.
.	.	.	.	.	.	.	.	.	.	.	.	.	.	71. Extortion by Officers, &c. (Offences against Public Justice.)
.	.	[illegible]	.	.	[illegible]	.	.	.	.	.	.	.	.	72. Bribery, &c.
.	.	[illegible]	.	[illegible]	.	.	.	.	.	.	[illegible]	.	.	73. Perjury.
.	.	[illegible]	.	.	[illegible]	.	[illegible]	.	.	.	.	.	.	74. Escape and Rescue.
.	.	[illegible]	.	[illegible]	[illegible]	.	.	.	.	.	.	.	.	75. Other Offences.
.	.	.	.	.	.	.	.	.	.	.	.	.	.	76. Blasphemy, &c. (Offences against Religion.)
.	.	.	.	.	.	.	.	.	.	.	.	.	.	77. Piracy. (Offences against Law of Nations.)
.	.	.	.	.	.	.	.	.	.	.	.	.	.	78. Slave Trade.
.	.	[illegible]	.	[illegible]	.	.	.	.	.	.	.	.	.	79. Libel.
.	.	.	.	.	.	.	.	.	.	.	.	.	.	80. Poaching.
[illegible]	.	.	.	.	.	.	.	.	.	.	.	.	.	81. Indecent Exposure.
.	.	[illegible]	.	.	.	.	.	.	.	.	.	.	.	82. Keeping Disorderly Houses.
.	.	.	.	.	.	.	.	.	.	.	.	[illegible]	.	83. Other Nuisances.
[illegible]	[illegible]	[illegible]	[illegible]	.	[illegible]	[illegible]	[illegible]	[illegible]	[illegible]	.	.	.	[illegible]	84. Suicide (attempting to commit).
.	.	.	.	.	.	.	.	.	.	.	.	.	.	85. Other Misdemeanours.
[illegible]	[illegible]	[illegible]	[illegible]	[illegible]	[illegible]	[illegible]	[illegible]	[illegible]	[illegible]	[illegible]	[illegible]	[illegible]	[illegible]	TOTAL.

TABLE 24—*continued*.—RETURNS FROM THE SEVERAL COUNTIES.—County, and County

OFFENCES.	Towns									
	Total.	[illegible]	[illegible]	[illegible]	[illegible]	[illegible]	[illegible]	[illegible]	[illegible]	[illegible]
Class I.—Offences against the Person.										
1. Murder (of Persons aged above one Year),	4	.	1	1	.	.	1	.	.	.
Ditto (of Infants aged one Year and under),	4	1	.	1	.	1	.	1	1	.
2. Attempt to Murder,	[illegible]	.	.	.	.	.	.	.	.	.
3. Conspiracy or Incitement to Murder,	.	.	.	.	.	.	.	.	.	.
4. Manslaughter,	[illegible]	1	1	[illegible]	.	[illegible]	[illegible]	[illegible]	[illegible]	[illegible]
5. Felonious Wounding,	[illegible]	[illegible]	[illegible]	[illegible]	.	[illegible]	[illegible]	.	1	[illegible]
6. Endangering Railway Passengers,	[illegible]	[illegible]	.	.	.	.	[illegible]	.	.	.
7. Malicious Woundings (misdemeanours),	[illegible]	[illegible]	.	[illegible]	.	[illegible]	1	[illegible]	.	[illegible]
8. Assault,	[illegible]	.	[illegible]	.	.	[illegible]	[illegible]	[illegible]	1	[illegible]
9. Intimidation and Molestation,	.	.	.	.	.	.	.	.	.	.
10. Cruelty to or Neglect of Children,	[illegible]	.	.	1	.	.	1	.	.	.
11. Abandoning Children under two Years,	[illegible]	.	.	.	.	.	1	.	1	.
12. Child Stealing,	1	.	.	1	.	.	.	.	.	.
13. Procuring Abortion,	.	.	.	.	.	.	.	.	.	.
14. Concealment of Birth,	[illegible]	4	.	[illegible]	.	1	.	4	[illegible]	1
15. Unnatural Offences,	4	1	.	1	.	.	1	1	.	.
16. Attempts to commit Unnatural Offences,	.	.	.	.	.	.	.	.	.	.
17. Indecency with Males,	[illegible]	1	.	.	.	.	.	.	.	1
18. Rape,	4	1	.	[illegible]	.	.	.	1	.	.
19. Indecent Assaults on Females,	[illegible]	[illegible]	1	4	.	.	1	4	1	1
20. Defilement of Girls under 13,	[illegible]	.	.	[illegible]	.	1	.	1	.	.
21. Defilement of Girls under 16,	1	.	.	1	.	.	.	[illegible]	.	.
22. Householder permitting Defilement of Girls,	.	.	.	.	.	.	.	.	.	.
23. Procuration,	1	.	.	.	.	.	.	.	.	.
24. Abduction,	1	.	1	.	.	.	.	.	.	.
25. Bigamy,	[illegible]	.	.	4	.	.	.	.	.	.
26. Other Offences against the Person,	[illegible]	.	.	.	.	.	.	.	.	1
Class II.—Offences against Property with Violence.										
27. Sacrilege,	[illegible]	[illegible]	1	[illegible]	.	.	.	[illegible]	.	.
28. Burglary,	[illegible]	[illegible]	[illegible]	[illegible]	1	1	[illegible]	4	1	[illegible]
29. Housebreaking,	[illegible]	[illegible]	[illegible]	[illegible]	1	[illegible]	[illegible]	[illegible]	4	1
30. Breaking into Shops, Warehouses, &c.,	[illegible]	.	.	[illegible]	.	.	1	1	.	.
31. Attempts to break into Houses, Shops, &c.,	[illegible]	1	[illegible]	.	1	[illegible]	1	1	.	1
32. Entering with intent to commit Felony,	[illegible]	.	.	[illegible]	.	.	.	.	.	.
33. Possession of Housebreaking Tools, &c.,	1	.	.	1	.	.	.	.	.	.
34. Robbery and Assaults with intent to Rob,	[illegible]	.	.	[illegible]	.	1	1	4	.	.
35. Extortion by Threats to accuse of Crime,	.	.	.	.	.	.	.	.	.	.
36. Extortion by other Threats,	.	.	.	.	.	.	.	.	.	.
Class III.—Offences against Property without Violence.										
37. Larceny of Horses, Cattle, and Sheep,	[illegible]	[illegible]	1	[illegible]	1	[illegible]	4	[illegible]	[illegible]	1
38. Larceny from the Person,	[illegible]	[illegible]	1	[illegible]	.	[illegible]	[illegible]	[illegible]	[illegible]	4
39. Larceny in Houses,	[illegible]	[illegible]	.	[illegible]	.	1	1	4	.	1
40. Larceny by a Servant,	[illegible]	4	[illegible]	[illegible]	.	1	1	[illegible]	[illegible]	.
41. Embezzlement,	[illegible]	.	1	[illegible]	.	[illegible]	1	4	[illegible]	.
42. Larceny of Post Letters,	[illegible]	[illegible]	.	.	.	.	.	.	.	.
43. Other aggravated Larcenies,	[illegible]	.	.	.	.	.	.	4	.	.
44. Simple Larceny and Minor Larcenies,	[illegible]	[illegible]	[illegible]	[illegible]	[illegible]	[illegible]	[illegible]	[illegible]	[illegible]	[illegible]
45. Obtaining Goods, &c., by False Pretences,	[illegible]	[illegible]	1	[illegible]	1	1	4	[illegible]	[illegible]	1
46. Frauds by Bankers, Agents, Trustees, &c.,	[illegible]	.	.	.	.	.	.	.	.	.
47. Falsifying Accounts,	1	.	.	.	.	.	.	1	.	.
48. Other Frauds,	[illegible]	.	.	.	.	.	.	.	.	.
49. Receiving Stolen Goods,	[illegible]	.	.	[illegible]	.	.	.	[illegible]	.	.
50. Offences in connection with Bankruptcy,	[illegible]	.	.	[illegible]	.	.	.	.	.	.

				Class I.—Offences against the Person.
1	1	1	.	1. Murder (of Persons aged above one Year)
1	.	.	1	Ditto (of Infants aged one Year and under)
.	1	.	.	2. Attempt to Murder.
.	1	.	.	3. Conspiracy or Threatening to Murder.
7	7	6	1	4. Manslaughter.
2	4	4	2	5. Felonious Wounding.
3	3	1	.	6. Endangering Railway Passengers.
6	3	2	.	7. Malicious Wounding (misdemeanours).
8	8	1	1	8. Assaults.
.	.	.	.	9. Intimidation and Molestation.
1	.	.	.	10. Cruelty to or neglect of Children.
.	.	.	1	11. Abandoning Children under two Years.
.	.	.	.	12. Child Stealing.
.	.	.	.	13. Procuring Abortion.
.	1	1	1	14. Concealment of Birth.
.	.	.	.	15. Unnatural Offences.
.	.	.	.	16. Attempts to commit Unnatural Offences.
.	.	.	.	17. Indecency with Males.
.	1	.	.	18. Rape.
2	.	.	.	19. Indecent Assaults on Females.
.	1	.	.	20. Defilement of Girls under 13.
.	.	.	.	21. Defilement of Girls under 16.
.	.	.	.	22. Householder permitting Defilement of Girls.
.	.	.	.	23. Procuration.
.	.	.	.	24. Abduction.
.	.	1	.	25. Bigamy.
1	.	.	.	26. Other Offences against the Person.
				Class II.—Offences against Property with Violence.
.	.	.	.	27. Sacrilege.
1	1	1	.	28. Burglary.
6	.	.	.	29. Housebreaking.
1	.	.	.	30. Breaking into Shops, Warehouses, &c.
.	.	.	.	31. Attempts to break into Houses, Shops, &c.
.	.	.	.	32. Entering with intent to commit Felony.
.	.	.	.	33. Possession of Housebreaking Tools, &c.
.	1	1	1	34. Robbery and Assaults with intent to Rob.
.	.	.	.	35. Extortion by threats to accuse of Crime.
.	.	.	.	36. Extortion by other Threats.
				Class III.—Offences against Property without Violence.
7	4	6	5	37. Larceny of Horses, Cattle, and Sheep.
6	9	4	9	38. Larceny from the Person.
7	1	.	.	39. Larceny in House.
.	.	7	9	40. Larceny by a Servant.
.	.	.	.	41. Embezzlement.
1	1	.	1	42. Larceny of Post Letters.
.	.	.	.	43. Other aggravated Larcenies.
[illegible]	65	45	[illegible]	44. Simple Larceny and Minor Larcenies.
1	1	1	9	45. Obtaining Goods, &c., by False Pretences.
.	.	.	.	46. Frauds by Bankers, Agents, Trustees, &c.

OFFENCES.										
Class IV.—Malicious Injuries to Property.										
Arson,	[illegible]	[illegible]	6	1	.	[illegible]	[illegible]	[illegible]	.	[illegible]
Setting Fire to Crops, Plantations, &c.,	[illegible]	1	4	.	.	[illegible]	[illegible]	6	1	1
Killing and Maiming Cattle,	[illegible]	[illegible]	1	1	.	1	1	1	3	1
[illegible] &c., of Explosives,	1	.	.	.	.	.	.	1	.	.
Destroying Ships,	1	.	.	.	.	.	.	1	.	.
Destroying Railways,	.	.	.	.	.	.	.	.	.	.
Destroying Trees and Shrubs,	2	.	.	.	.	6	.	.	.	.
Other Malicious Injuries,	[illegible]	[illegible]	.	[illegible]	[illegible]	[illegible]	[illegible]	[illegible]	[illegible]	6
Class V.—Forgery and Offences against the Currency.										
Forgery and Uttering (felony),	[illegible]	.	.	1	.	.	.	.	.	.
Forgery (misdemeanour),	.	.	.	.	.	.	.	.	.	.
Coining,	.	.	.	.	.	.	.	.	.	.
Uttering or Possessing Counterfeit Coin,	1	.	1	.	.	.	.	.	.	.
Class VI.—Other Offences not included in the above Classes.										
Offences against the State and Public Order. 60. High Treason,	.	.	.	.	.	.	.	.	.	.
61. Treason Felony,	.	.	.	.	.	.	.	.	.	.
62. Riot,	4	.	.	1	.	[illegible]	1	.	1	.
63. Unlawful Assembly,	.	.	.	.	.	.	.	.	.	.
64. Intimidation by Threatening Letters, Notices, or other Ways,	[illegible]	[illegible]	.	.	.	[illegible]	[illegible]	[illegible]	[illegible]	.
65. Demand or Robbery of Arms,	.	.	.	.	.	.	.	.	.	.
66. Attacking Dwelling-houses (by firing shots into them),	1	.	.	.	.	.	.	.	.	.
67. Other Offences,	[illegible]	.	.	.	.	[illegible]	[illegible]	.	[illegible]	.
Offences against Public Justice. 71. [illegible] by Officers, &c.,	.	.	.	.	.	.	.	.	.	.
72. Bribery, &c.,	1	.	.	1	.	.	.	.	.	.
73. Perjury,	[illegible]	.	1	.	.	[illegible]	.	.	.	.
74. Escapes and Rescues,	[illegible]	1	.	.	.	[illegible]	.	.	.	.
75. Other Offences,	1	.	[illegible]	.	.	.	.	.	.	.
Offences against Religion. 76. Blasphemy, &c.,	.	.	.	.	.	.	.	.	.	.
Offences against Law of Nations. 77. Piracy,	.	.	.	.	.	.	.	.	.	.
78. Slave Trade,	.	.	.	.	.	.	.	.	.	.
79. Libel,	.	.	.	.	.	.	.	.	.	.
80. Poaching,	.	.	.	.	.	.	.	.	.	.
81. Indecent Exposure,	.	.	.	.	.	.	.	.	.	.
82. Keeping Disorderly Houses,	.	.	.	.	.	.	.	.	.	.
83. Other Nuisances,	.	.	.	.	.	.	.	.	.	.
84. Suicide (attempting to commit),	[illegible]	1	[illegible]	[illegible]	.	.	.	1	[illegible]	[illegible]
85. Other Misdemeanours,	.	.	.	.	.	.	.	.	.	.

INDICTABLE OFFENCES.—Nature of Crimes Committed in each of City or of Town.

[illegible]	[illegible]	[illegible]	[illegible]	[illegible]	[illegible]	[illegible]	[illegible]	[illegible]	[illegible]	[illegible]	OFFENCES.
											Class IV.—[illegible]
.	[illegible]	[illegible]	[illegible]	[illegible]	[illegible]	.	[illegible]	[illegible]	[illegible]	[illegible]	[illegible]
.	.	.	[illegible]	[illegible]	[illegible]	.	[illegible]	[illegible]	.	[illegible]	[illegible]
.	[illegible]	[illegible]	[illegible]	[illegible]	[illegible]	.	[illegible]	[illegible]	[illegible]	[illegible]	[illegible]
.	.	.	.	.	.	.	.	.	.	.	[illegible]
.	.	.	.	.	.	.	.	.	.	.	[illegible]
.	.	.	.	.	.	.	.	.	.	.	[illegible]
.	.	.	.	.	.	.	.	.	.	.	[illegible]
[illegible]	[illegible]	[illegible]	[illegible]	[illegible]	[illegible]	[illegible]	[illegible]	[illegible]	[illegible]	[illegible]	[illegible]
											Class V.—[illegible]
.	.	[illegible]	[illegible]	.	[illegible]	.	.	.	[illegible]	.	[illegible]
.	.	.	.	.	.	.	.	.	.	.	[illegible]
.	.	.	.	.	.	.	.	.	.	.	[illegible]
.	.	.	.	.	.	.	.	.	.	.	[illegible]
											Class VI.—[illegible]
.	.	.	.	.	.	.	.	.	.	.	[illegible]
.	.	.	.	.	.	.	.	.	.	.	[illegible]
.	.	.	[illegible]	.	.	.	.	.	.	[illegible]	[illegible]
.	.	.	.	.	.	.	.	.	.	.	[illegible]
.	[illegible]	.	[illegible]	[illegible]	[illegible]	.	[illegible]	[illegible]	[illegible]	[illegible]	[illegible]
.	.	.	.	.	.	.	.	.	.	.	[illegible]
.	.	[illegible]	[illegible]	[illegible]	.	.	.	[illegible]	.	[illegible]	[illegible]
.	.	.	[illegible]	.	[illegible]	.	.	[illegible]	.	[illegible]	[illegible]
.	.	.	.	.	.	.	.	.	.	.	[illegible]
.	.	.	[illegible]	[illegible]	.	.	.	.	.	.	[illegible]
.	.	.	.	.	.	.	.	.	.	.	[illegible]
.	.	[illegible]	[illegible]	.	[illegible]	.	[illegible]	[illegible]	[illegible]	[illegible]	[illegible]
.	.	.	[illegible]	.	.	.	.	.	.	[illegible]	[illegible]
.	.	.	.	.	.	.	.	.	.	.	[illegible]
.	.	.	.	.	.	.	.	.	.	.	[illegible]
.	.	.	.	.	.	.	.	.	.	.	[illegible]
.	.	.	.	.	.	.	.	.	.	.	[illegible]
.	.	.	.	.	.	.	.	.	.	.	[illegible]
.	.	.	[illegible]	.	.	.	.	[illegible]	.	.	[illegible]
.	.	.	.	.	.	.	.	.	.	.	[illegible]
.	.	.	.	.	.	.	.	.	.	.	[illegible]
[illegible]	.	.	[illegible]	.	.	.	[illegible]	[illegible]	[illegible]	[illegible]	[illegible]
.	.	.	.	.	.	.	.	.	.	.	[illegible]
[illegible]	[illegible]	[illegible]	[illegible]	[illegible]	[illegible]	[illegible]	[illegible]	[illegible]	[illegible]	[illegible]	TOTAL.

TABLE 25.—Character[illegible]

[illegible]

Province, County, County of City, or Town	[illegible]
Leinster.	
Carlow	[illegible]
Drogheda Town	[illegible]
Dublin County	[illegible]
Dublin Metropolitan Police District	[illegible]
Kildare	[illegible]
Kilkenny	[illegible]
Kilkenny City	[illegible]
King's County	[illegible]
Longford	[illegible]
Louth	[illegible]
Meath	[illegible]
Queen's County	[illegible]
Westmeath	[illegible]
Wexford	[illegible]
Wicklow	[illegible]
Total of Province	[illegible]
Munster.	
Clare	[illegible]
Cork, E.R.	[illegible]
Cork, W.R.	[illegible]
Cork City	[illegible]
Kerry	[illegible]
Limerick	[illegible]
Limerick City	[illegible]
Tipperary, N.R.	[illegible]
Tipperary, S.R.	[illegible]
Waterford	[illegible]
Waterford City	[illegible]
Total of Province	[illegible]
Ulster.	
Antrim	[illegible]
Armagh	[illegible]
Belfast, City of	[illegible]
Carrickfergus Town of	[illegible]
Cavan	[illegible]
Donegal	[illegible]
Down	[illegible]
Fermanagh	[illegible]
Londonderry	[illegible]
Londonderry City	[illegible]
Monaghan	[illegible]
Tyrone	[illegible]
Total of Province	[illegible]
Connaught.	
Galway, E.R.	[illegible]
Galway, W.R.	[illegible]
Galway, Town of	[illegible]
Leitrim	[illegible]
Mayo	[illegible]
Roscommon	[illegible]
Sligo	[illegible]
Total of Province	[illegible]
Grand Total	[illegible]
Grand Total of all Persons Proceeded Against	[illegible]

SEVERAL COUNTIES

of Persons Prosecuted.

[illegible]

																		Province, County, County of City, or of Town
																		LEINSTER.
[illegible]	[illegible]	[illegible]	[illegible]	[illegible]	[illegible]	[illegible]	[illegible]	[illegible]	[illegible]	[illegible]	[illegible]	[illegible]	[illegible]	[illegible]	[illegible]	[illegible]	[illegible]	Carlow.
[illegible]	[illegible]	[illegible]	[illegible]	[illegible]	[illegible]	[illegible]	[illegible]	[illegible]	[illegible]	[illegible]	[illegible]	[illegible]	[illegible]	[illegible]	[illegible]	[illegible]	[illegible]	Drogheda Town.
[illegible]	[illegible]	[illegible]	[illegible]	[illegible]	[illegible]	[illegible]	[illegible]	[illegible]	[illegible]	[illegible]	[illegible]	[illegible]	[illegible]	[illegible]	[illegible]	[illegible]	[illegible]	Dublin County.
[illegible]	[illegible]	[illegible]	[illegible]	[illegible]	[illegible]	[illegible]	[illegible]	[illegible]	[illegible]	[illegible]	[illegible]	[illegible]	[illegible]	[illegible]	[illegible]	[illegible]	[illegible]	Dublin Metropolitan Police District.
[illegible]	[illegible]	[illegible]	[illegible]	[illegible]	[illegible]	[illegible]	[illegible]	[illegible]	[illegible]	[illegible]	[illegible]	[illegible]	[illegible]	[illegible]	[illegible]	[illegible]	[illegible]	Kildare.
[illegible]	[illegible]	[illegible]	[illegible]	[illegible]	[illegible]	[illegible]	[illegible]	[illegible]	[illegible]	[illegible]	[illegible]	[illegible]	[illegible]	[illegible]	[illegible]	[illegible]	[illegible]	Kilkenny.
[illegible]	[illegible]	[illegible]	[illegible]	[illegible]	[illegible]	[illegible]	[illegible]	[illegible]	[illegible]	[illegible]	[illegible]	[illegible]	[illegible]	[illegible]	[illegible]	[illegible]	[illegible]	Kilkenny City.
[illegible]	[illegible]	[illegible]	[illegible]	[illegible]	[illegible]	[illegible]	[illegible]	[illegible]	[illegible]	[illegible]	[illegible]	[illegible]	[illegible]	[illegible]	[illegible]	[illegible]	[illegible]	King's County.
[illegible]	[illegible]	[illegible]	[illegible]	[illegible]	[illegible]	[illegible]	[illegible]	[illegible]	[illegible]	[illegible]	[illegible]	[illegible]	[illegible]	[illegible]	[illegible]	[illegible]	[illegible]	Longford.
[illegible]	[illegible]	[illegible]	[illegible]	[illegible]	[illegible]	[illegible]	[illegible]	[illegible]	[illegible]	[illegible]	[illegible]	[illegible]	[illegible]	[illegible]	[illegible]	[illegible]	[illegible]	Louth.
[illegible]	[illegible]	[illegible]	[illegible]	[illegible]	[illegible]	[illegible]	[illegible]	[illegible]	[illegible]	[illegible]	[illegible]	[illegible]	[illegible]	[illegible]	[illegible]	[illegible]	[illegible]	Meath.
[illegible]	[illegible]	[illegible]	[illegible]	[illegible]	[illegible]	[illegible]	[illegible]	[illegible]	[illegible]	[illegible]	[illegible]	[illegible]	[illegible]	[illegible]	[illegible]	[illegible]	[illegible]	Queen's County.
[illegible]	[illegible]	[illegible]	[illegible]	[illegible]	[illegible]	[illegible]	[illegible]	[illegible]	[illegible]	[illegible]	[illegible]	[illegible]	[illegible]	[illegible]	[illegible]	[illegible]	[illegible]	Westmeath.
[illegible]	[illegible]	[illegible]	[illegible]	[illegible]	[illegible]	[illegible]	[illegible]	[illegible]	[illegible]	[illegible]	[illegible]	[illegible]	[illegible]	[illegible]	[illegible]	[illegible]	[illegible]	Wexford.
[illegible]	[illegible]	[illegible]	[illegible]	[illegible]	[illegible]	[illegible]	[illegible]	[illegible]	[illegible]	[illegible]	[illegible]	[illegible]	[illegible]	[illegible]	[illegible]	[illegible]	[illegible]	Wicklow.
[illegible]	[illegible]	[illegible]	[illegible]	[illegible]	[illegible]	[illegible]	[illegible]	[illegible]	[illegible]	[illegible]	[illegible]	[illegible]	[illegible]	[illegible]	[illegible]	[illegible]	[illegible]	TOTAL OF PROVINCE.
																		MUNSTER.
[illegible]	[illegible]	[illegible]	[illegible]	[illegible]	[illegible]	[illegible]	[illegible]	[illegible]	[illegible]	[illegible]	[illegible]	[illegible]	[illegible]	[illegible]	[illegible]	[illegible]	[illegible]	Clare.
[illegible]	[illegible]	[illegible]	[illegible]	[illegible]	[illegible]	[illegible]	[illegible]	[illegible]	[illegible]	[illegible]	[illegible]	[illegible]	[illegible]	[illegible]	[illegible]	[illegible]	[illegible]	Cork, E.R.
[illegible]	[illegible]	[illegible]	[illegible]	[illegible]	[illegible]	[illegible]	[illegible]	[illegible]	[illegible]	[illegible]	[illegible]	[illegible]	[illegible]	[illegible]	[illegible]	[illegible]	[illegible]	Cork, W.R.
[illegible]	[illegible]	[illegible]	[illegible]	[illegible]	[illegible]	[illegible]	[illegible]	[illegible]	[illegible]	[illegible]	[illegible]	[illegible]	[illegible]	[illegible]	[illegible]	[illegible]	[illegible]	Cork City.
[illegible]	[illegible]	[illegible]	[illegible]	[illegible]	[illegible]	[illegible]	[illegible]	[illegible]	[illegible]	[illegible]	[illegible]	[illegible]	[illegible]	[illegible]	[illegible]	[illegible]	[illegible]	Kerry.
[illegible]	[illegible]	[illegible]	[illegible]	[illegible]	[illegible]	[illegible]	[illegible]	[illegible]	[illegible]	[illegible]	[illegible]	[illegible]	[illegible]	[illegible]	[illegible]	[illegible]	[illegible]	Limerick.
[illegible]	[illegible]	[illegible]	[illegible]	[illegible]	[illegible]	[illegible]	[illegible]	[illegible]	[illegible]	[illegible]	[illegible]	[illegible]	[illegible]	[illegible]	[illegible]	[illegible]	[illegible]	Limerick City.
[illegible]	[illegible]	[illegible]	[illegible]	[illegible]	[illegible]	[illegible]	[illegible]	[illegible]	[illegible]	[illegible]	[illegible]	[illegible]	[illegible]	[illegible]	[illegible]	[illegible]	[illegible]	Tipperary, N.R.
[illegible]	[illegible]	[illegible]	[illegible]	[illegible]	[illegible]	[illegible]	[illegible]	[illegible]	[illegible]	[illegible]	[illegible]	[illegible]	[illegible]	[illegible]	[illegible]	[illegible]	[illegible]	Tipperary, S.R.
[illegible]	[illegible]	[illegible]	[illegible]	[illegible]	[illegible]	[illegible]	[illegible]	[illegible]	[illegible]	[illegible]	[illegible]	[illegible]	[illegible]	[illegible]	[illegible]	[illegible]	[illegible]	Waterford.
[illegible]	[illegible]	[illegible]	[illegible]	[illegible]	[illegible]	[illegible]	[illegible]	[illegible]	[illegible]	[illegible]	[illegible]	[illegible]	[illegible]	[illegible]	[illegible]	[illegible]	[illegible]	Waterford City.
[illegible]	[illegible]	[illegible]	[illegible]	[illegible]	[illegible]	[illegible]	[illegible]	[illegible]	[illegible]	[illegible]	[illegible]	[illegible]	[illegible]	[illegible]	[illegible]	[illegible]	[illegible]	TOTAL OF PROVINCE.
																		ULSTER.
[illegible]	[illegible]	[illegible]	[illegible]	[illegible]	[illegible]	[illegible]	[illegible]	[illegible]	[illegible]	[illegible]	[illegible]	[illegible]	[illegible]	[illegible]	[illegible]	[illegible]	[illegible]	Antrim.
[illegible]	[illegible]	[illegible]	[illegible]	[illegible]	[illegible]	[illegible]	[illegible]	[illegible]	[illegible]	[illegible]	[illegible]	[illegible]	[illegible]	[illegible]	[illegible]	[illegible]	[illegible]	Armagh.
[illegible]	[illegible]	[illegible]	[illegible]	[illegible]	[illegible]	[illegible]	[illegible]	[illegible]	[illegible]	[illegible]	[illegible]	[illegible]	[illegible]	[illegible]	[illegible]	[illegible]	[illegible]	Belfast, City of.
[illegible]	[illegible]	[illegible]	[illegible]	[illegible]	[illegible]	[illegible]	[illegible]	[illegible]	[illegible]	[illegible]	[illegible]	[illegible]	[illegible]	[illegible]	[illegible]	[illegible]	[illegible]	Carrickfergus, Town of.
[illegible]	[illegible]	[illegible]	[illegible]	[illegible]	[illegible]	[illegible]	[illegible]	[illegible]	[illegible]	[illegible]	[illegible]	[illegible]	[illegible]	[illegible]	[illegible]	[illegible]	[illegible]	Cavan.
[illegible]	[illegible]	[illegible]	[illegible]	[illegible]	[illegible]	[illegible]	[illegible]	[illegible]	[illegible]	[illegible]	[illegible]	[illegible]	[illegible]	[illegible]	[illegible]	[illegible]	[illegible]	Donegal.
[illegible]	[illegible]	[illegible]	[illegible]	[illegible]	[illegible]	[illegible]	[illegible]	[illegible]	[illegible]	[illegible]	[illegible]	[illegible]	[illegible]	[illegible]	[illegible]	[illegible]	[illegible]	Down.
[illegible]	[illegible]	[illegible]	[illegible]	[illegible]	[illegible]	[illegible]	[illegible]	[illegible]	[illegible]	[illegible]	[illegible]	[illegible]	[illegible]	[illegible]	[illegible]	[illegible]	[illegible]	Fermanagh.
[illegible]	[illegible]	[illegible]	[illegible]	[illegible]	[illegible]	[illegible]	[illegible]	[illegible]	[illegible]	[illegible]	[illegible]	[illegible]	[illegible]	[illegible]	[illegible]	[illegible]	[illegible]	Londonderry.
[illegible]	[illegible]	[illegible]	[illegible]	[illegible]	[illegible]	[illegible]	[illegible]	[illegible]	[illegible]	[illegible]	[illegible]	[illegible]	[illegible]	[illegible]	[illegible]	[illegible]	[illegible]	Londonderry City.
[illegible]	[illegible]	[illegible]	[illegible]	[illegible]	[illegible]	[illegible]	[illegible]	[illegible]	[illegible]	[illegible]	[illegible]	[illegible]	[illegible]	[illegible]	[illegible]	[illegible]	[illegible]	Monaghan.
[illegible]	[illegible]	[illegible]	[illegible]	[illegible]	[illegible]	[illegible]	[illegible]	[illegible]	[illegible]	[illegible]	[illegible]	[illegible]	[illegible]	[illegible]	[illegible]	[illegible]	[illegible]	Tyrone.
[illegible]	[illegible]	[illegible]	[illegible]	[illegible]	[illegible]	[illegible]	[illegible]	[illegible]	[illegible]	[illegible]	[illegible]	[illegible]	[illegible]	[illegible]	[illegible]	[illegible]	[illegible]	TOTAL OF PROVINCE.
																		CONNAUGHT.
[illegible]	[illegible]	[illegible]	[illegible]	[illegible]	[illegible]	[illegible]	[illegible]	[illegible]	[illegible]	[illegible]	[illegible]	[illegible]	[illegible]	[illegible]	[illegible]	[illegible]	[illegible]	Galway, E.R.
[illegible]	[illegible]	[illegible]	[illegible]	[illegible]	[illegible]	[illegible]	[illegible]	[illegible]	[illegible]	[illegible]	[illegible]	[illegible]	[illegible]	[illegible]	[illegible]	[illegible]	[illegible]	Galway, W.R.
[illegible]	[illegible]	[illegible]	[illegible]	[illegible]	[illegible]	[illegible]	[illegible]	[illegible]	[illegible]	[illegible]	[illegible]	[illegible]	[illegible]	[illegible]	[illegible]	[illegible]	[illegible]	Galway, Town of.
[illegible]	[illegible]	[illegible]	[illegible]	[illegible]	[illegible]	[illegible]	[illegible]	[illegible]	[illegible]	[illegible]	[illegible]	[illegible]	[illegible]	[illegible]	[illegible]	[illegible]	[illegible]	Leitrim.
[illegible]	[illegible]	[illegible]	[illegible]	[illegible]	[illegible]	[illegible]	[illegible]	[illegible]	[illegible]	[illegible]	[illegible]	[illegible]	[illegible]	[illegible]	[illegible]	[illegible]	[illegible]	Mayo.
[illegible]	[illegible]	[illegible]	[illegible]	[illegible]	[illegible]	[illegible]	[illegible]	[illegible]	[illegible]	[illegible]	[illegible]	[illegible]	[illegible]	[illegible]	[illegible]	[illegible]	[illegible]	Roscommon.
[illegible]	[illegible]	[illegible]	[illegible]	[illegible]	[illegible]	[illegible]	[illegible]	[illegible]	[illegible]	[illegible]	[illegible]	[illegible]	[illegible]	[illegible]	[illegible]	[illegible]	[illegible]	Sligo.
[illegible]	[illegible]	[illegible]	[illegible]	[illegible]	[illegible]	[illegible]	[illegible]	[illegible]	[illegible]	[illegible]	[illegible]	[illegible]	[illegible]	[illegible]	[illegible]	[illegible]	[illegible]	TOTAL OF PROVINCE.
[illegible]	[illegible]	[illegible]	[illegible]	[illegible]	[illegible]	[illegible]	[illegible]	[illegible]	[illegible]	[illegible]	[illegible]	[illegible]	[illegible]	[illegible]	[illegible]	[illegible]	[illegible]	GRAND TOTAL.
[illegible]	[illegible]	[illegible]	[illegible]	[illegible]	[illegible]	[illegible]	[illegible]	[illegible]	[illegible]	[illegible]	[illegible]	[illegible]	[illegible]	[illegible]	[illegible]	[illegible]	[illegible]	GRAND TOTAL OF ALL THE FOUR PROVINCES

LEINSTER.		
...w,	44	45
...uda Town,		
...n County,	[illegible]	[illegible]
...n Metropolitan Police District,	[illegible]	[illegible]
...w,	1	4
...nty,	[illegible]	[illegible]
...nty City,	[illegible]	[illegible]
...'s County,		
...ford,		
...h,	[illegible]	[illegible]
...h,	[illegible]	[illegible]
...'s County,	[illegible]	[illegible]
...meath,	[illegible]	[illegible]
...ord,	4	[illegible]
...low,	[illegible]	[illegible]
TOTAL OF PROVINCE,	[illegible]	[illegible]
MUNSTER.		
...	[illegible]	[illegible]
...E.R.,	[illegible]	[illegible]
...W.R.,		
...City,	[illegible]	[illegible]
...	[illegible]	[illegible]
...ick,	[illegible]	[illegible]
...ick City,	[illegible]	[illegible]
...ary, N.R.,	[illegible]	[illegible]
...ary, S.R.,	[illegible]	[illegible]
...ford,	4	[illegible]
...ford City,	[illegible]	[illegible]
TOTAL OF PROVINCE,	[illegible]	[illegible]
ULSTER.		
...m,	[illegible]	[illegible]
...h,	[illegible]	[illegible]
..., City of,	[illegible]	[illegible]
...kfergus, Town of,	[illegible]	11
...	[illegible]	[illegible]
...al,	[illegible]	[illegible]
...	[illegible]	[illegible]
...nagh,	[illegible]	[illegible]
...donderry,	[illegible]	[illegible]
...donderry City,	[illegible]	[illegible]
...ghan,	[illegible]	[illegible]
...e,	[illegible]	[illegible]
TOTAL OF PROVINCE,	[illegible]	[illegible]

SEVERAL COUNTIES.

TABLE 27.—Numbers of Houses of Bad Character.

Persons (7) m.	f.	Licensed (8)	Spirit- (9)	Total Number (10)	Number of Residents (11)	Public Houses (12)	Beer-Shops (13)	Other Houses (14)	Province, County, County of City, or of Town (15)
									LEINSTER.
.	.	.	.	[illegible]	[illegible]	.	.	.	Carlow.
.	.	.	.	[illegible]	.	.	.	[illegible]	Drogheda Town.
.	.	[illegible]	.	.	.	.	.	.	Dublin County.
[illegible]	[illegible]	[illegible]	[illegible]	[illegible]	[illegible]	.	.	.	Dublin Metropolitan Police District.
.	.	[illegible]	.	.	.	.	.	.	Kildare.
.	.	[illegible]	.	.	.	.	.	.	Kilkenny.
.	.	.	.	.	.	.	.	.	Kilkenny City.
.	.	.	.	.	.	.	.	.	King's County.
.	.	.	.	.	.	.	.	.	Longford.
.	.	.	.	.	.	.	.	.	Louth.
[illegible]	.	[illegible]	.	[illegible]	[illegible]	.	.	[illegible]	Meath.
.	.	[illegible]	.	.	.	.	.	.	Queen's County.
.	.	.	.	.	.	.	.	.	Westmeath.
.	.	.	.	[illegible]	.	.	.	[illegible]	Wexford.
.	.	.	.	.	.	.	.	.	Wicklow.
[illegible]	[illegible]	[illegible]	[illegible]	[illegible]	[illegible]	.	.	[illegible]	TOTAL OF PROVINCE.
									MUNSTER.
.	.	[illegible]	.	[illegible]	[illegible]	.	.	[illegible]	Clare.
.	.	[illegible]	.	.	.	.	.	.	Cork, E.R.
.	.	[illegible]	.	.	.	.	.	.	Cork, W.R.
.	.	[illegible]	.	[illegible]	[illegible]	[illegible]	.	[illegible]	Cork City.
.	.	[illegible]	.	.	.	.	.	.	Kerry.
.	.	[illegible]	.	.	.	.	.	.	Limerick.
.	.	.	.	[illegible]	.	.	.	[illegible]	Limerick City.
.	.	[illegible]	.	[illegible]	[illegible]	.	.	.	Tipperary N.R.
.	.	[illegible]	1	[illegible]	[illegible]	.	.	.	Tipperary S.R.
.	.	[illegible]	.	.	.	.	.	.	Waterford.
.	.	.	.	[illegible]	.	.	.	[illegible]	Waterford City.
.	.	[illegible]	[illegible]	[illegible]	[illegible]	[illegible]	.	[illegible]	TOTAL OF PROVINCE.
									ULSTER.
.	.	[illegible]	[illegible]	[illegible]	[illegible]	.	.	.	Antrim.
.	.	[illegible]	[illegible]	[illegible]	[illegible]	.	.	[illegible]	Armagh.
[illegible]	[illegible]	[illegible]	[illegible]	[illegible]	[illegible]	[illegible]	1	[illegible]	Belfast, Town of.
.	.	.	.	[illegible]	.	.	.	[illegible]	Carrickfergus, Town of.
.	.	[illegible]	.	.	.	.	.	.	Cavan.
.	.	.	.	.	.	.	.	.	Donegal.
.	.	[illegible]	[illegible]	[illegible]	.	.	.	[illegible]	Down.
.	.	.	.	.	.	.	.	.	Fermanagh.
.	.	[illegible]	1	[illegible]	[illegible]	.	.	[illegible]	Londonderry.
.	.	[illegible]	.	.	.	.	.	.	Londonderry City.
.	.	[illegible]	.	[illegible]	[illegible]	.	.	[illegible]	Monaghan.
.	.	[illegible]	.	[illegible]	.	.	.	[illegible]	Tyrone.
[illegible]	[illegible]	[illegible]	[illegible]	[illegible]	[illegible]	[illegible]	1	[illegible]	TOTAL OF PROVINCE.
									CONNAUGHT.
.	.	.	.	[illegible]	[illegible]	.	.	.	Galway, E.R.
.	.	[illegible]	.	.	.	.	.	.	Galway, W.R.
.	.	.	.	.	.	.	.	.	Galway, Town of.
.	.	.	.	.	.	.	.	.	Leitrim.
.	.	[illegible]	.	1	.	.	.	1	Mayo.
.	.	.	.	[illegible]	[illegible]	.	.	[illegible]	Roscommon.
.	.	.	.	[illegible]	.	.	.	[illegible]	Sligo.
.	.	[illegible]	.	[illegible]	[illegible]	.	.	[illegible]	TOTAL OF PROVINCE.
[illegible]	[illegible]	[illegible]	[illegible]	[illegible]	[illegible]	[illegible]	1	[illegible]	TOTAL OF IRELAND.

[illegible] | [illegible] | [illegible]

TABLE 26.—POLICE RETURNS.—Crimes (Indictable Offences)

OFFENCES.	Crimes Committed											
	Jan.	Feb.	Mar.	April.	May.	June.	July.	Aug.	Sept.	Oct.	Nov.	Dec.
(1)	(2)	(3)	(4)	(5)	(6)	(7)	(8)	(9)	(10)	(11)	(12)	(13)
Class I.—Offences against the Person.												
1. Murder of persons aged above one Year	[illegible]	[illegible]	[illegible]	[illegible]	[illegible]	[illegible]	[illegible]	[illegible]	[illegible]	[illegible]	[illegible]	[illegible]
Ditto of Infants aged one Year and under	[illegible]	[illegible]	[illegible]	[illegible]	[illegible]	[illegible]	[illegible]	[illegible]	[illegible]	[illegible]	[illegible]	[illegible]
2. Attempt to Murder,	[illegible]	[illegible]	[illegible]	[illegible]	[illegible]	[illegible]	[illegible]	[illegible]	[illegible]	[illegible]	[illegible]	[illegible]
3. Conspiracy or Incitement to Murder,	[illegible]	[illegible]	[illegible]	[illegible]	[illegible]	[illegible]	[illegible]	[illegible]	[illegible]	[illegible]	[illegible]	[illegible]
4. Manslaughter,	[illegible]	[illegible]	[illegible]	[illegible]	[illegible]	[illegible]	[illegible]	[illegible]	[illegible]	[illegible]	[illegible]	[illegible]
5. Felonious Wounding,	[illegible]	[illegible]	[illegible]	[illegible]	[illegible]	[illegible]	[illegible]	[illegible]	[illegible]	[illegible]	[illegible]	[illegible]
6. Endangering Railway Passengers,	[illegible]	[illegible]	[illegible]	[illegible]	[illegible]	[illegible]	[illegible]	[illegible]	[illegible]	[illegible]	[illegible]	[illegible]
7. Malicious Wounding (misdemeanour),	[illegible]	[illegible]	[illegible]	[illegible]	[illegible]	[illegible]	[illegible]	[illegible]	[illegible]	[illegible]	[illegible]	[illegible]
8. Assaults,	[illegible]	[illegible]	[illegible]	[illegible]	[illegible]	[illegible]	[illegible]	[illegible]	[illegible]	[illegible]	[illegible]	[illegible]
9. Intimidation and Molestation,	[illegible]	[illegible]	[illegible]	[illegible]	[illegible]	[illegible]	[illegible]	[illegible]	[illegible]	[illegible]	[illegible]	[illegible]
10. Cruelty to or neglect of Children,	[illegible]	[illegible]	[illegible]	[illegible]	[illegible]	[illegible]	[illegible]	[illegible]	[illegible]	[illegible]	[illegible]	[illegible]
11. Abandoning Children under two years,	[illegible]	[illegible]	[illegible]	[illegible]	[illegible]	[illegible]	[illegible]	[illegible]	[illegible]	[illegible]	[illegible]	[illegible]
12. Child stealing,	[illegible]	[illegible]	[illegible]	[illegible]	[illegible]	[illegible]	[illegible]	[illegible]	[illegible]	[illegible]	[illegible]	[illegible]
13. Procuring Abortion,	[illegible]	[illegible]	[illegible]	[illegible]	[illegible]	[illegible]	[illegible]	[illegible]	[illegible]	[illegible]	[illegible]	[illegible]
14. Concealment of Birth,	[illegible]	[illegible]	[illegible]	[illegible]	[illegible]	[illegible]	[illegible]	[illegible]	[illegible]	[illegible]	[illegible]	[illegible]
15. Unnatural offences,	[illegible]	[illegible]	[illegible]	[illegible]	[illegible]	[illegible]	[illegible]	[illegible]	[illegible]	[illegible]	[illegible]	[illegible]
16. Attempts to commit unnatural offences,	[illegible]	[illegible]	[illegible]	[illegible]	[illegible]	[illegible]	[illegible]	[illegible]	[illegible]	[illegible]	[illegible]	[illegible]
17. Indecency with Males,	[illegible]	[illegible]	[illegible]	[illegible]	[illegible]	[illegible]	[illegible]	[illegible]	[illegible]	[illegible]	[illegible]	[illegible]
18. Rape,	[illegible]	[illegible]	[illegible]	[illegible]	[illegible]	[illegible]	[illegible]	[illegible]	[illegible]	[illegible]	[illegible]	[illegible]
19. Indecent Assaults on Females,	[illegible]	[illegible]	[illegible]	[illegible]	[illegible]	[illegible]	[illegible]	[illegible]	[illegible]	[illegible]	[illegible]	[illegible]
20. Defilement of Girls under 13,	[illegible]	[illegible]	[illegible]	[illegible]	[illegible]	[illegible]	[illegible]	[illegible]	[illegible]	[illegible]	[illegible]	[illegible]
21. Defilement of Girls under 16,	[illegible]	[illegible]	[illegible]	[illegible]	[illegible]	[illegible]	[illegible]	[illegible]	[illegible]	[illegible]	[illegible]	[illegible]
22. Householders permitting defilement of Girls,	[illegible]	[illegible]	[illegible]	[illegible]	[illegible]	[illegible]	[illegible]	[illegible]	[illegible]	[illegible]	[illegible]	[illegible]
23. Procuration,	[illegible]	[illegible]	[illegible]	[illegible]	[illegible]	[illegible]	[illegible]	[illegible]	[illegible]	[illegible]	[illegible]	[illegible]
24. Abduction,	[illegible]	[illegible]	[illegible]	[illegible]	[illegible]	[illegible]	[illegible]	[illegible]	[illegible]	[illegible]	[illegible]	[illegible]
25. Bigamy,	[illegible]	[illegible]	[illegible]	[illegible]	[illegible]	[illegible]	[illegible]	[illegible]	[illegible]	[illegible]	[illegible]	[illegible]
26. Other offences against the Person,	[illegible]	[illegible]	[illegible]	[illegible]	[illegible]	[illegible]	[illegible]	[illegible]	[illegible]	[illegible]	[illegible]	[illegible]
TOTAL OF CLASS I.,	[illegible]	[illegible]	[illegible]	[illegible]	[illegible]	[illegible]	[illegible]	[illegible]	[illegible]	[illegible]	[illegible]	[illegible]
Class II.—Offences against Property with Violence.												
27. Sacrilege,	[illegible]	[illegible]	[illegible]	[illegible]	[illegible]	[illegible]	[illegible]	[illegible]	[illegible]	[illegible]	[illegible]	[illegible]
28. Burglary,	[illegible]	[illegible]	[illegible]	[illegible]	[illegible]	[illegible]	[illegible]	[illegible]	[illegible]	[illegible]	[illegible]	[illegible]
29. Housebreaking,	[illegible]	[illegible]	[illegible]	[illegible]	[illegible]	[illegible]	[illegible]	[illegible]	[illegible]	[illegible]	[illegible]	[illegible]
30. Breaking into Shops, Warehouses, &c.	[illegible]	[illegible]	[illegible]	[illegible]	[illegible]	[illegible]	[illegible]	[illegible]	[illegible]	[illegible]	[illegible]	[illegible]
31. Attempts to break into Houses, Shops, &c.	[illegible]	[illegible]	[illegible]	[illegible]	[illegible]	[illegible]	[illegible]	[illegible]	[illegible]	[illegible]	[illegible]	[illegible]
32. Entering with intent to commit Felony,	[illegible]	[illegible]	[illegible]	[illegible]	[illegible]	[illegible]	[illegible]	[illegible]	[illegible]	[illegible]	[illegible]	[illegible]
33. Possession of Housebreaking Tools, &c.,	[illegible]	[illegible]	[illegible]	[illegible]	[illegible]	[illegible]	[illegible]	[illegible]	[illegible]	[illegible]	[illegible]	[illegible]
34. Robbery and Assaults with intent to rob,	[illegible]	[illegible]	[illegible]	[illegible]	[illegible]	[illegible]	[illegible]	[illegible]	[illegible]	[illegible]	[illegible]	[illegible]
35. Extortion by threats to accuse of crime,	[illegible]	[illegible]	[illegible]	[illegible]	[illegible]	[illegible]	[illegible]	[illegible]	[illegible]	[illegible]	[illegible]	[illegible]
36. Extortion by other threats,	[illegible]	[illegible]	[illegible]	[illegible]	[illegible]	[illegible]	[illegible]	[illegible]	[illegible]	[illegible]	[illegible]	[illegible]
TOTAL OF CLASS II.,	[illegible]	[illegible]	[illegible]	[illegible]	[illegible]	[illegible]	[illegible]	[illegible]	[illegible]	[illegible]	[illegible]	[illegible]
Class III.—Offences against Property without Violence.												
37. Larceny of Horses, Cattle, and Sheep,	[illegible]	[illegible]	[illegible]	[illegible]	[illegible]	[illegible]	[illegible]	[illegible]	[illegible]	[illegible]	[illegible]	[illegible]
38. Larceny from the Person,	[illegible]	[illegible]	[illegible]	[illegible]	[illegible]	[illegible]	[illegible]	[illegible]	[illegible]	[illegible]	[illegible]	[illegible]
39. Larceny in House,	[illegible]	[illegible]	[illegible]	[illegible]	[illegible]	[illegible]	[illegible]	[illegible]	[illegible]	[illegible]	[illegible]	[illegible]
40. Larceny by a Servant,	[illegible]	[illegible]	[illegible]	[illegible]	[illegible]	[illegible]	[illegible]	[illegible]	[illegible]	[illegible]	[illegible]	[illegible]
41. Embezzlement,	[illegible]	[illegible]	[illegible]	[illegible]	[illegible]	[illegible]	[illegible]	[illegible]	[illegible]	[illegible]	[illegible]	[illegible]
42. Larceny of Post Letters,	[illegible]	[illegible]	[illegible]	[illegible]	[illegible]	[illegible]	[illegible]	[illegible]	[illegible]	[illegible]	[illegible]	[illegible]
43. Other aggravated larcenies,	[illegible]	[illegible]	[illegible]	[illegible]	[illegible]	[illegible]	[illegible]	[illegible]	[illegible]	[illegible]	[illegible]	[illegible]
44. Simple larceny and minor larcenies,	[illegible]	[illegible]	[illegible]	[illegible]	[illegible]	[illegible]	[illegible]	[illegible]	[illegible]	[illegible]	[illegible]	[illegible]
45. Obtaining goods, &c., by false pretences,	[illegible]	[illegible]	[illegible]	[illegible]	[illegible]	[illegible]	[illegible]	[illegible]	[illegible]	[illegible]	[illegible]	[illegible]
46. Frauds by Bankers, Agents, Trustees, &c.,	[illegible]	[illegible]	[illegible]	[illegible]	[illegible]	[illegible]	[illegible]	[illegible]	[illegible]	[illegible]	[illegible]	[illegible]
47. Falsifying accounts,	[illegible]	[illegible]	[illegible]	[illegible]	[illegible]	[illegible]	[illegible]	[illegible]	[illegible]	[illegible]	[illegible]	[illegible]
48. Other Frauds,	[illegible]	[illegible]	[illegible]	[illegible]	[illegible]	[illegible]	[illegible]	[illegible]	[illegible]	[illegible]	[illegible]	[illegible]
49. Receiving Stolen Goods,	[illegible]	[illegible]	[illegible]	[illegible]	[illegible]	[illegible]	[illegible]	[illegible]	[illegible]	[illegible]	[illegible]	[illegible]
50. Offences in connection with Bankruptcy,	[illegible]	[illegible]	[illegible]	[illegible]	[illegible]	[illegible]	[illegible]	[illegible]	[illegible]	[illegible]	[illegible]	[illegible]
TOTAL OF CLASS III.,	[illegible]	[illegible]	[illegible]	[illegible]	[illegible]	[illegible]	[illegible]	[illegible]	[illegible]	[illegible]	[illegible]	[illegible]

NOTE.—"Crimes Committed" has the same meaning in this table as in Table [illegible]. "Apprehensions" denotes the Number of "Apprehended" [illegible]

Committed and Apprehensions in each Month of the Year.

Jan.	Feb.	Mar.	April	May	June	July	Aug.	Sept.	Oct.	Nov.	Dec.	OFFENCES.
												Class I.—Offences against the Person.
[illegible]	[illegible]	[illegible]	[illegible]	[illegible]	[illegible]	[illegible]	[illegible]	[illegible]	[illegible]	[illegible]	[illegible]	1. Murder (of persons aged above one Year)
[illegible]	[illegible]	[illegible]	[illegible]	[illegible]	[illegible]	[illegible]	[illegible]	[illegible]	[illegible]	[illegible]	[illegible]	1. Murder (of Infants aged one Year and under)
[illegible]	[illegible]	[illegible]	[illegible]	[illegible]	[illegible]	[illegible]	[illegible]	[illegible]	[illegible]	[illegible]	[illegible]	2. Attempts to Murder.
[illegible]	[illegible]	[illegible]	[illegible]	[illegible]	[illegible]	[illegible]	[illegible]	[illegible]	[illegible]	[illegible]	[illegible]	3. Conspiracy or incitement to Murder.
[illegible]	[illegible]	[illegible]	[illegible]	[illegible]	[illegible]	[illegible]	[illegible]	[illegible]	[illegible]	[illegible]	[illegible]	4. Manslaughter.
[illegible]	[illegible]	[illegible]	[illegible]	[illegible]	[illegible]	[illegible]	[illegible]	[illegible]	[illegible]	[illegible]	[illegible]	5. Felonious Wounding.
[illegible]	[illegible]	[illegible]	[illegible]	[illegible]	[illegible]	[illegible]	[illegible]	[illegible]	[illegible]	[illegible]	[illegible]	6. Endangering Railway Passengers.
[illegible]	[illegible]	[illegible]	[illegible]	[illegible]	[illegible]	[illegible]	[illegible]	[illegible]	[illegible]	[illegible]	[illegible]	7. Malicious Wounding (misdemeanour).
[illegible]	[illegible]	[illegible]	[illegible]	[illegible]	[illegible]	[illegible]	[illegible]	[illegible]	[illegible]	[illegible]	[illegible]	8. Assault.
[illegible]	[illegible]	[illegible]	[illegible]	[illegible]	[illegible]	[illegible]	[illegible]	[illegible]	[illegible]	[illegible]	[illegible]	9. Intimidation and Molestation.
[illegible]	[illegible]	[illegible]	[illegible]	[illegible]	[illegible]	[illegible]	[illegible]	[illegible]	[illegible]	[illegible]	[illegible]	10. Cruelty to or neglect of Children.
[illegible]	[illegible]	[illegible]	[illegible]	[illegible]	[illegible]	[illegible]	[illegible]	[illegible]	[illegible]	[illegible]	[illegible]	11. Abandoning Children under two years.
[illegible]	[illegible]	[illegible]	[illegible]	[illegible]	[illegible]	[illegible]	[illegible]	[illegible]	[illegible]	[illegible]	[illegible]	12. Child stealing.
[illegible]	[illegible]	[illegible]	[illegible]	[illegible]	[illegible]	[illegible]	[illegible]	[illegible]	[illegible]	[illegible]	[illegible]	13. Procuring abortion.
[illegible]	[illegible]	[illegible]	[illegible]	[illegible]	[illegible]	[illegible]	[illegible]	[illegible]	[illegible]	[illegible]	[illegible]	14. Concealment of birth.
[illegible]	[illegible]	[illegible]	[illegible]	[illegible]	[illegible]	[illegible]	[illegible]	[illegible]	[illegible]	[illegible]	[illegible]	15. Unnatural offences.
[illegible]	[illegible]	[illegible]	[illegible]	[illegible]	[illegible]	[illegible]	[illegible]	[illegible]	[illegible]	[illegible]	[illegible]	16. Attempts to commit unnatural offences.
[illegible]	[illegible]	[illegible]	[illegible]	[illegible]	[illegible]	[illegible]	[illegible]	[illegible]	[illegible]	[illegible]	[illegible]	17. Indecency with Males.
[illegible]	[illegible]	[illegible]	[illegible]	[illegible]	[illegible]	[illegible]	[illegible]	[illegible]	[illegible]	[illegible]	[illegible]	18. Rape.
[illegible]	[illegible]	[illegible]	[illegible]	[illegible]	[illegible]	[illegible]	[illegible]	[illegible]	[illegible]	[illegible]	[illegible]	19. Indecent assaults on Females.
[illegible]	[illegible]	[illegible]	[illegible]	[illegible]	[illegible]	[illegible]	[illegible]	[illegible]	[illegible]	[illegible]	[illegible]	20. Defilement of Girls under 13.
[illegible]	[illegible]	[illegible]	[illegible]	[illegible]	[illegible]	[illegible]	[illegible]	[illegible]	[illegible]	[illegible]	[illegible]	21. Defilement of Girls under 16.
[illegible]	[illegible]	[illegible]	[illegible]	[illegible]	[illegible]	[illegible]	[illegible]	[illegible]	[illegible]	[illegible]	[illegible]	22. Householder permitting defilement of Girls.
[illegible]	[illegible]	[illegible]	[illegible]	[illegible]	[illegible]	[illegible]	[illegible]	[illegible]	[illegible]	[illegible]	[illegible]	23. Procuration.
[illegible]	[illegible]	[illegible]	[illegible]	[illegible]	[illegible]	[illegible]	[illegible]	[illegible]	[illegible]	[illegible]	[illegible]	24. Abduction.
[illegible]	[illegible]	[illegible]	[illegible]	[illegible]	[illegible]	[illegible]	[illegible]	[illegible]	[illegible]	[illegible]	[illegible]	25. Bigamy.
[illegible]	[illegible]	[illegible]	[illegible]	[illegible]	[illegible]	[illegible]	[illegible]	[illegible]	[illegible]	[illegible]	[illegible]	26. Other offences against the Person.
[illegible]	[illegible]	[illegible]	[illegible]	[illegible]	[illegible]	[illegible]	[illegible]	[illegible]	[illegible]	[illegible]	[illegible]	TOTAL OF CLASS I.
												Class II.—Offences against Property with Violence.
[illegible]	[illegible]	[illegible]	[illegible]	[illegible]	[illegible]	[illegible]	[illegible]	[illegible]	[illegible]	[illegible]	[illegible]	27. Burglary.
[illegible]	[illegible]	[illegible]	[illegible]	[illegible]	[illegible]	[illegible]	[illegible]	[illegible]	[illegible]	[illegible]	[illegible]	28. Housebreaking.
[illegible]	[illegible]	[illegible]	[illegible]	[illegible]	[illegible]	[illegible]	[illegible]	[illegible]	[illegible]	[illegible]	[illegible]	29. Shopbreaking.
[illegible]	[illegible]	[illegible]	[illegible]	[illegible]	[illegible]	[illegible]	[illegible]	[illegible]	[illegible]	[illegible]	[illegible]	30. Breaking into Shops, Warehouses, &c.
[illegible]	[illegible]	[illegible]	[illegible]	[illegible]	[illegible]	[illegible]	[illegible]	[illegible]	[illegible]	[illegible]	[illegible]	31. Attempts to break into Houses, Shops, &c.
[illegible]	[illegible]	[illegible]	[illegible]	[illegible]	[illegible]	[illegible]	[illegible]	[illegible]	[illegible]	[illegible]	[illegible]	32. Entering with intent to commit Felony.
[illegible]	[illegible]	[illegible]	[illegible]	[illegible]	[illegible]	[illegible]	[illegible]	[illegible]	[illegible]	[illegible]	[illegible]	33. Possession of House breaking Tools, &c.
[illegible]	[illegible]	[illegible]	[illegible]	[illegible]	[illegible]	[illegible]	[illegible]	[illegible]	[illegible]	[illegible]	[illegible]	34. Robbery and Assault with intent to rob.
[illegible]	[illegible]	[illegible]	[illegible]	[illegible]	[illegible]	[illegible]	[illegible]	[illegible]	[illegible]	[illegible]	[illegible]	35. Extortion by threats to accuse of crimes.
[illegible]	[illegible]	[illegible]	[illegible]	[illegible]	[illegible]	[illegible]	[illegible]	[illegible]	[illegible]	[illegible]	[illegible]	36. Extortion by other menaces.
[illegible]	[illegible]	[illegible]	[illegible]	[illegible]	[illegible]	[illegible]	[illegible]	[illegible]	[illegible]	[illegible]	[illegible]	TOTAL OF CLASS II.
												Class III.—Offences against Property without Violence.
[illegible]	[illegible]	[illegible]	[illegible]	[illegible]	[illegible]	[illegible]	[illegible]	[illegible]	[illegible]	[illegible]	[illegible]	37. Larceny of Horses, Cattle, and Sheep.
[illegible]	[illegible]	[illegible]	[illegible]	[illegible]	[illegible]	[illegible]	[illegible]	[illegible]	[illegible]	[illegible]	[illegible]	38. Larceny from the Person.
[illegible]	[illegible]	[illegible]	[illegible]	[illegible]	[illegible]	[illegible]	[illegible]	[illegible]	[illegible]	[illegible]	[illegible]	39. Larceny in House.
[illegible]	[illegible]	[illegible]	[illegible]	[illegible]	[illegible]	[illegible]	[illegible]	[illegible]	[illegible]	[illegible]	[illegible]	40. Larceny by a Servant.
[illegible]	[illegible]	[illegible]	[illegible]	[illegible]	[illegible]	[illegible]	[illegible]	[illegible]	[illegible]	[illegible]	[illegible]	41. Embezzlement.
[illegible]	[illegible]	[illegible]	[illegible]	[illegible]	[illegible]	[illegible]	[illegible]	[illegible]	[illegible]	[illegible]	[illegible]	42. Larceny of Post Letters.
[illegible]	[illegible]	[illegible]	[illegible]	[illegible]	[illegible]	[illegible]	[illegible]	[illegible]	[illegible]	[illegible]	[illegible]	43. Other aggravated larcenies.
[illegible]	[illegible]	[illegible]	[illegible]	[illegible]	[illegible]	[illegible]	[illegible]	[illegible]	[illegible]	[illegible]	[illegible]	44. Simple larceny and minor larcenies.
[illegible]	[illegible]	[illegible]	[illegible]	[illegible]	[illegible]	[illegible]	[illegible]	[illegible]	[illegible]	[illegible]	[illegible]	45. Obtaining goods, &c., by false pretences.
[illegible]	[illegible]	[illegible]	[illegible]	[illegible]	[illegible]	[illegible]	[illegible]	[illegible]	[illegible]	[illegible]	[illegible]	46. Frauds by Bankers, Agents, Trustees, &c.
[illegible]	[illegible]	[illegible]	[illegible]	[illegible]	[illegible]	[illegible]	[illegible]	[illegible]	[illegible]	[illegible]	[illegible]	47. Falsifying accounts.
[illegible]	[illegible]	[illegible]	[illegible]	[illegible]	[illegible]	[illegible]	[illegible]	[illegible]	[illegible]	[illegible]	[illegible]	48. Other Frauds.
[illegible]	[illegible]	[illegible]	[illegible]	[illegible]	[illegible]	[illegible]	[illegible]	[illegible]	[illegible]	[illegible]	[illegible]	49. Receiving Stolen Goods.
[illegible]	[illegible]	[illegible]	[illegible]	[illegible]	[illegible]	[illegible]	[illegible]	[illegible]	[illegible]	[illegible]	[illegible]	50. Offences in connection with Bankruptcy.
[illegible]	[illegible]	[illegible]	[illegible]	[illegible]	[illegible]	[illegible]	[illegible]	[illegible]	[illegible]	[illegible]	[illegible]	TOTAL OF CLASS III.

Apprehensions for Indictable Offences actually effected in each Month, [illegible] from Table [illegible], which gives "[illegible] [illegible]" within the year.

TABLE 28—*continued*.—POLICE RETURNS.—Crimes (Indictable Offences)

OFFENCES. (1)	Jan. (2)	Feb. (3)	Mar. (4)	April (5)	May (6)	June (7)	July (8)	Aug. (9)	Sept. (10)	Oct. (11)	Nov. (12)	Dec. (13)
Class IV.—Malicious Injuries to Property.												
Arson,	[illegible]	[illegible]	[illegible]	[illegible]	[illegible]	[illegible]	[illegible]	[illegible]	[illegible]	[illegible]	[illegible]	[illegible]
Setting Fire to Crops, Plantations, &c.,	[illegible]	[illegible]	[illegible]	[illegible]	[illegible]	[illegible]	[illegible]	[illegible]	[illegible]	[illegible]	[illegible]	[illegible]
Killing and Maiming Cattle,	[illegible]	[illegible]	[illegible]	[illegible]	[illegible]	[illegible]	[illegible]	[illegible]	[illegible]	[illegible]	[illegible]	[illegible]
Malicious [illegible] of Explosives,	.	.	.	.	.	.	1	.	.	.	.	.
Destroying Ships,	.	.	.	.	.	.	.	.	[illegible]	.	.	.
Destroying Railways,	.	.	.	.	.	.	.	.	.	.	1	1
Destroying Trees and Shrubs,	1	.	1	.	1	1	.	1	.	1	1	.
Other malicious injuries,	[illegible]	[illegible]	[illegible]	[illegible]	[illegible]	[illegible]	[illegible]	[illegible]	[illegible]	[illegible]	[illegible]	[illegible]
TOTAL OF CLASS IV.,	[illegible]	[illegible]	[illegible]	[illegible]	[illegible]	[illegible]	[illegible]	[illegible]	[illegible]	[illegible]	[illegible]	[illegible]
Class V.—Forgery and Offences against the Currency.												
Forgery and uttering (felony),	[illegible]	[illegible]	[illegible]	[illegible]	[illegible]	.	1	1	[illegible]	1	.	.
Forgery (misdemeanour),	.	1	.	[illegible]	.	.	.	.	.	.	.	.
Coining,	.	.	.	.	.	.	1	.	.	.	.	.
Uttering or Possessing Counterfeit Coin,	.	1	.	1	1	.	[illegible]	1	.	.	.	.
TOTAL OF CLASS V.,	[illegible]	[illegible]	[illegible]	[illegible]	[illegible]	.	[illegible]	[illegible]	[illegible]	[illegible]	.	.
Class VI.—Other Offences not included in the above Classes.												
Offences against the State and Public Order. High Treason,	.	.	.	.	.	.	.	.	.	.	.	.
Treason Felony,	.	.	.	.	.	.	.	.	.	.	.	.
Riot,	1	.	.	1	.	[illegible]	1	[illegible]	1	.	.	.
Unlawful Assembly,	.	.	1	.	.	.	.	.	.	.	.	.
Intimidation by Threatening Letters, Notices, or otherwise,	14	[illegible]	[illegible]	[illegible]	[illegible]	[illegible]	[illegible]	[illegible]	[illegible]	[illegible]	[illegible]	[illegible]
[illegible] or Delivery of Arms,	.	.	1	.	.	1	.	1	.	.	.	.
Assaulting Dwelling-houses (by firing shots into them),	[illegible]	1	[illegible]	[illegible]	.	1	1	1	1	[illegible]	[illegible]	.
Other offences,	[illegible]	1	[illegible]	[illegible]	[illegible]	1	1	[illegible]	1	1	1	.
Offences against Public Justice. Extortion by Officers, &c.,	.	.	.	.	.	.	.	.	.	.	.	.
Bribery, &c.,	.	.	.	1	.	.	.	[illegible]	.	.	.	1
Perjury,	[illegible]	1	.	1	1	1	.	.	.	[illegible]	1	.
Escapes and Rescues,	1	[illegible]	.	[illegible]	1	[illegible]	[illegible]	[illegible]	1	[illegible]	.	.
Other offences,	.	.	.	.	1	.	.	[illegible]	.	1	.	.
Offences against Religion. Blasphemy, &c.,	.	.	.	.	.	.	.	.	.	.	.	.
Offences against Law of Nations. Piracy,	.	.	.	.	.	.	.	.	.	.	.	.
Slave Trade,	.	.	.	.	.	.	.	.	.	.	.	.
Libel,	.	.	.	1	.	.	.	.	.	.	.	.
Gambling,	.	.	.	.	.	.	.	.	.	.	.	.
Indecent Exposure,	.	1	1	.	[illegible]	.	[illegible]	.	.	.	1	1
Keeping Disorderly Houses,	.	.	.	.	.	.	.	.	.	.	.	.
Other Nuisances,	.	1	.	.	.	1	.	.	.	.	.	.
Suicide (attempting to commit),	[illegible]	[illegible]	[illegible]	[illegible]	[illegible]	[illegible]	[illegible]	[illegible]	[illegible]	[illegible]	7	[illegible]
Other misdemeanours,	.	.	.	.	1	.	.	1	.	.	.	.
TOTAL OF CLASS VI.,	[illegible]	[illegible]	[illegible]	[illegible]	[illegible]	[illegible]	[illegible]	[illegible]	[illegible]	[illegible]	[illegible]	[illegible]
GRAND TOTAL,	[illegible]	[illegible]	[illegible]	[illegible]	[illegible]	[illegible]	[illegible]	[illegible]	[illegible]	[illegible]	[illegible]	[illegible]

NOTE.—" Offences Committed " [illegible] table [illegible] Table [illegible]. " Apprehensions " [illegible]

Committed and Apprehensions in each Month of the Year.

Apprehensions.												OFFENCES.
Jan.	Feb.	Mar.	April	May.	June	July	Aug.	Sept.	Oct.	Nov.	Dec.	
[illegible]	[illegible]	[illegible]	[illegible]	[illegible]	[illegible]	[illegible]	[illegible]	[illegible]	[illegible]	[illegible]	[illegible]	
												Class IV.—Malicious Injuries to Property.
[illegible]	[illegible]	[illegible]	[illegible]	[illegible]	[illegible]	[illegible]	[illegible]	[illegible]	[illegible]	[illegible]	[illegible]	51. Arson.
[illegible]	.	.	.	.	.	2	.	.	1	[illegible]	.	52. Setting fire to Crops, Plantations, &c.
1	.	1	[illegible]	.	.	.	[illegible]	1	[illegible]	.	.	53. Killing and Maiming Cattle.
.	.	.	.	.	.	1	.	.	.	.	.	54. Malicious &c., of Fish ponds.
.	.	.	.	.	.	.	.	.	.	.	.	55. Destroying Ships.
.	.	.	.	.	.	.	.	.	.	.	.	56. Destroying Railways.
.	.	.	.	.	.	.	.	.	.	.	.	57. Destroying Trees and Plants.
[illegible]	[illegible]	[illegible]	[illegible]	[illegible]	[illegible]	[illegible]	[illegible]	[illegible]	[illegible]	[illegible]	[illegible]	58. Other Malicious Injuries.
[illegible]	[illegible]	7	[illegible]	[illegible]	[illegible]	[illegible]	[illegible]	4	[illegible]	[illegible]	[illegible]	Total of Class IV.
												Class V.—Forgery and Offences against the Currency.
3	[illegible]	1	[illegible]	[illegible]	1	1	[illegible]	1	.	1	.	59. Forgery and uttering (felony).
.	1	.	[illegible]	.	.	.	.	.	.	.	.	60. Forgery (misdemeanour).
.	.	.	.	.	.	.	3	.	.	.	.	61. Coining.
.	[illegible]	.	1	1	.	1	2	.	.	.	.	62. Uttering or Possessing Counterfeit Coin.
[illegible]	[illegible]	4	6	[illegible]	1	[illegible]	[illegible]	1	.	1	.	Total of Class V.
												Class VI.—Other Offences not Included in the above Classes.
.	.	.	.	.	.	.	.	.	.	.	.	63. High Treason. (Offences against the State and Public Order)
.	.	.	.	.	.	.	.	.	.	.	.	64. Treason Felony.
.	.	.	1	.	.	.	.	1	.	.	.	65. Riot.
.	.	4	.	.	.	.	.	.	.	.	.	66. Unlawful Assembly.
.	.	1	.	.	.	.	[illegible]	.	.	1	.	67. Intimidation by Threatening Letters, Menaces, or otherwise.
.	.	.	.	.	[illegible]	[illegible]	.	1	.	.	.	68. [illegible] of Arms.
.	.	.	[illegible]	.	[illegible]	.	.	.	.	.	.	69. [illegible]
[illegible]	[illegible]	.	[illegible]	[illegible]	.	.	[illegible]	1	.	.	.	70. Other Offences.
.	.	.	.	.	.	.	.	.	.	.	.	71. Extortion by Officers, &c. (Offences against Public Justice)
.	.	.	.	.	.	.	.	.	.	.	1	72. Bribery, &c.
.	1	.	[illegible]	1	.	.	.	.	.	.	.	73. Perjury.
[illegible]	4	.	[illegible]	.	1	1	1	2	.	.	.	74. Escape and Rescue.
.	.	.	.	.	.	.	.	.	1	.	.	75. Other offences.
.	.	.	.	.	.	.	.	.	.	.	.	76. [illegible], &c. (Offences against Religion)
.	.	.	.	.	.	.	.	.	.	.	.	77. Piracy. (Offences against Law of Nations)
.	.	.	.	.	.	.	.	.	.	.	.	78. Slave Trade.
.	.	.	.	.	.	1	.	.	.	.	.	79. Libel.
.	.	.	.	.	.	.	.	.	.	.	.	80. Poaching.
.	.	1	.	1	.	1	.	.	.	1	1	81. Indecent Exposure.
.	.	.	.	.	.	.	.	.	.	.	.	82. Keeping Disorderly Houses.
.	.	.	.	.	.	.	.	.	.	.	.	83. Other Nuisances.
[illegible]	[illegible]	[illegible]	[illegible]	11	[illegible]	[illegible]	[illegible]	[illegible]	[illegible]	6	11	84. Suicide (attempting to commit).
.	.	.	.	.	.	.	1	.	.	.	.	85. Other misdemeanours.
[illegible]	[illegible]	[illegible]	[illegible]	[illegible]	[illegible]	[illegible]	[illegible]	[illegible]	[illegible]	[illegible]	[illegible]	Total of Class VI.
[illegible]	[illegible]	[illegible]	[illegible]	[illegible]	[illegible]	[illegible]	[illegible]	[illegible]	[illegible]	[illegible]	[illegible]	Grand Total.

Apprehensions for Indictable Offences actually effected in each Month, this differing from Table [illegible], which gives "Persons disposed of within the year.

TABLE 29.—Return of Persons Convicted three times and upwards, of being Drunk, or Drunk and Disorderly, during the year ended 31st December, 1895 (so far as known to the Police).

Province, County, County of City and of Town, and Police District.	No. Convicted 3 times and less than 7.	No. Convicted 7 times and less than 30.	No. Convicted 30 times and upwards.	Total.
LEINSTER.				
Carlow,	[illegible]	[illegible]	–	[illegible]
Drogheda, Town of,	[illegible]	[illegible]	–	[illegible]
Dublin,	[illegible]	[illegible]	[illegible]	[illegible]
Dublin Metropolitan Police District,	[illegible]	[illegible]	[illegible]	[illegible]
Kildare,	[illegible]	[illegible]	[illegible]	[illegible]
Kilkenny,	[illegible]	[illegible]	[illegible]	[illegible]
Kilkenny City,	[illegible]	[illegible]	–	[illegible]
King's Co.,	[illegible]	[illegible]	[illegible]	[illegible]
Longford,	[illegible]	[illegible]	[illegible]	[illegible]
Louth,	[illegible]	[illegible]	[illegible]	[illegible]
Meath,	[illegible]	[illegible]	[illegible]	[illegible]
Queen's Co.,	[illegible]	[illegible]	[illegible]	[illegible]
Westmeath,	[illegible]	[illegible]	[illegible]	[illegible]
Wexford,	[illegible]	[illegible]	[illegible]	[illegible]
Wicklow,	[illegible]	[illegible]	[illegible]	[illegible]
TOTAL OF PROVINCE,	[illegible]	[illegible]	[illegible]	[illegible]

PRISONS

Notes to Tables 30 to 40.

Notes to Table 30.

(a.) This table gives the numbers of each class of prisoners received in each prison during the year. In the case of prisoners committed for trial it is necessary to distinguish those who were and those who were not previously in prison on remand; otherwise in making up the total the same person would, in many cases, count twice—as a remand prisoner and as a prisoner committed for trial. Similarly, convicted prisoners have to be divided into those who were and those who were not in detention before trial. The figures of the cases which thus appear a second or a third time are printed in old face type, columns 3, 5, and 7. The total of criminal prisoners, column 10, is obtained by adding the figures in the other columns 2, 4, 6, 8, and 9.

The table gives only the *first* receptions of prisoners on remand, committed for trial, &c. When prisoners are transferred from one prison to another they appear only in the return from the prison in which they are first received, not in that from the prison to which they are removed. As convicts, as a rule, undergo some detention in local prisons before transfer to a convict prison, they appear as receptions only in the local prison returns.

(b.) Column 11, "Surety Prisoners," includes only *unconvicted* persons imprisoned in default of finding sureties to keep the peace or to be of good behaviour.

(c.) Column 12, "Debtors," comprises all persons who are treated as debtors in prison, including bankrupts imprisoned to prevent absconding, &c.

Notes to Table 31.

Section (a).

(d.) This table gives, in columns 2 to 5, the numbers of prisoners on remand who are *disposed of within the year*. It therefore includes those in prison on remand on 1st January, but not those on remand and still undisposed of on 31st December. Those who after remand are discharged appear in column 3, those convicted summarily in column 4, those committed for trial in column 5.

(e.) Similar remarks apply to columns 6 to 15. Prisoners waiting trial on 1st January are included, those awaiting trial and not disposed of on 31st December are excluded.

Section (b).

(f.) This table shows only the final disposal of each convicted prisoner released or removed during the year. Each case appears only under the prison from which the prisoner is finally discharged or removed. If a prisoner has been removed from one prison to another, his case is included in the figures for the last prison only.

Notes to Table 32.

(g.) This table includes all cases *received under sentence* during the year from 1st January to 31st December, whether in prison before conviction or not.

(h.) All prisoners appear in the return from the prison in which they are *first received after sentence*, and not in the return for any prison to which they may be subsequently removed.

(i.) Column 6 contains only cases where a license is *forfeited* on conviction by a Court of Summary Jurisdiction for an offence under section 3 of the Prevention of Crimes Act, 1871. Other cases of forfeiture and all cases of revocation of license are included in column 31.

PRISONS.

30.—PRISONERS.—Receptions of Prisoners in each Prison.

31.—PRISONERS.—Disposal of Prisoners in each Prison.

32.—CONVICTED PRISONERS.—Nature of Sentences of Prisoners received in each Prison.

33.—CONVICTED PRISONERS.—Length of Sentences.

34.—CONVICTED PRISONERS.—Previous Convictions.

35.—CONVICTED PRISONERS.—Age and Sex.

36.—CONVICTED PRISONERS.—Birthplace.

37.—CONVICTED PRISONERS.—Degrees of Instruction.

38.—CONVICTED PRISONERS.—Previous Occupations.

39.—CRIMINAL PRISONERS.—Numbers received in Prison in each Month of the Year.

40.—CONVICTS.—Length of Sentences of Convicts under Detention on 31st. December, 1896.

TABLE 30.—PRISONERS,—

(See [illegible] a, b

On Remand. (1)		Previously in Prison on Remand. (2)		Not previously in Prison on Remand. (3)		Previously in Prison on Remand. (4)		Not previously in Prison on Remand. (5)		Previously in Prison on Remand or Committed for Trial. (6)		Not previously in Prison on Remand or Committed for Trial. (7)		Convicted by Court-Martial (8)
M.	F.	M.	F.	M.	F.	M.	F.	M.	F.	M.	F.	M.	F.	M.
[illegible]	[illegible]	[illegible]	[illegible]	[illegible]	[illegible]	[illegible]	[illegible]	[illegible]	[illegible]	[illegible]	[illegible]	[illegible]	[illegible]	[illegible]
[illegible]	[illegible]	[illegible]	[illegible]	[illegible]	[illegible]	[illegible]	[illegible]	[illegible]	[illegible]	[illegible]	[illegible]	[illegible]	[illegible]	[illegible]
[illegible]	[illegible]	[illegible]	[illegible]	[illegible]	[illegible]	[illegible]	[illegible]	[illegible]	[illegible]	[illegible]	[illegible]	[illegible]	[illegible]	[illegible]
[illegible]	[illegible]	[illegible]	[illegible]	[illegible]	[illegible]	[illegible]	[illegible]	[illegible]	[illegible]	[illegible]	[illegible]	[illegible]	[illegible]	[illegible]
[illegible]	[illegible]	[illegible]	[illegible]	[illegible]	[illegible]	[illegible]	[illegible]	[illegible]	[illegible]	[illegible]	[illegible]	[illegible]	[illegible]	[illegible]
[illegible]	[illegible]	[illegible]	[illegible]	[illegible]	[illegible]	[illegible]	[illegible]	[illegible]	[illegible]	[illegible]	[illegible]	[illegible]	[illegible]	[illegible]
[illegible]	[illegible]	[illegible]	[illegible]	[illegible]	[illegible]	[illegible]	[illegible]	[illegible]	[illegible]	[illegible]	[illegible]	[illegible]	[illegible]	[illegible]
[illegible]	[illegible]	[illegible]	[illegible]	[illegible]	[illegible]	[illegible]	[illegible]	[illegible]	[illegible]	[illegible]	[illegible]	[illegible]	[illegible]	[illegible]
[illegible]	[illegible]	[illegible]	[illegible]	[illegible]	[illegible]	[illegible]	[illegible]	[illegible]	[illegible]	[illegible]	[illegible]	[illegible]	[illegible]	[illegible]
[illegible]	[illegible]	[illegible]	[illegible]	[illegible]	[illegible]	[illegible]	[illegible]	[illegible]	[illegible]	[illegible]	[illegible]	[illegible]	[illegible]	[illegible]
[illegible]	[illegible]	[illegible]	[illegible]	[illegible]	[illegible]	[illegible]	[illegible]	[illegible]	[illegible]	[illegible]	[illegible]	[illegible]	[illegible]	[illegible]
[illegible]	[illegible]	[illegible]	[illegible]	[illegible]	[illegible]	[illegible]	[illegible]	[illegible]	[illegible]	[illegible]	[illegible]	[illegible]	[illegible]	[illegible]
[illegible]	[illegible]	[illegible]	[illegible]	[illegible]	[illegible]	[illegible]	[illegible]	[illegible]	[illegible]	[illegible]	[illegible]	[illegible]	[illegible]	[illegible]
[illegible]	[illegible]	[illegible]	[illegible]	[illegible]	[illegible]	[illegible]	[illegible]	[illegible]	[illegible]	[illegible]	[illegible]	[illegible]	[illegible]	[illegible]
[illegible]	[illegible]	[illegible]	[illegible]	[illegible]	[illegible]	[illegible]	[illegible]	[illegible]	[illegible]	[illegible]	[illegible]	[illegible]	[illegible]	[illegible]
[illegible]	[illegible]	[illegible]	[illegible]	[illegible]	[illegible]	[illegible]	[illegible]	[illegible]	[illegible]	[illegible]	[illegible]	[illegible]	[illegible]	[illegible]
[illegible]	[illegible]	[illegible]	[illegible]	[illegible]	[illegible]	[illegible]	[illegible]	[illegible]	[illegible]	[illegible]	[illegible]	[illegible]	[illegible]	[illegible]
[illegible]	[illegible]	[illegible]	[illegible]	[illegible]	[illegible]	[illegible]	[illegible]	[illegible]	[illegible]	[illegible]	[illegible]	[illegible]	[illegible]	[illegible]
[illegible]	[illegible]	[illegible]	[illegible]	[illegible]	[illegible]	[illegible]	[illegible]	[illegible]	[illegible]	[illegible]	[illegible]	[illegible]	[illegible]	[illegible]
[illegible]	[illegible]	[illegible]	[illegible]	[illegible]	[illegible]	[illegible]	[illegible]	[illegible]	[illegible]	[illegible]	[illegible]	[illegible]	[illegible]	[illegible]
[illegible]	[illegible]	[illegible]	[illegible]	[illegible]	[illegible]	[illegible]	[illegible]	[illegible]	[illegible]	[illegible]	[illegible]	[illegible]	[illegible]	[illegible]
[illegible]	[illegible]	[illegible]	[illegible]	[illegible]	[illegible]	[illegible]	[illegible]	[illegible]	[illegible]	[illegible]	[illegible]	[illegible]	[illegible]	[illegible]
[illegible]	[illegible]	[illegible]	[illegible]	[illegible]	[illegible]	[illegible]	[illegible]	[illegible]	[illegible]	[illegible]	[illegible]	[illegible]	[illegible]	[illegible]
[illegible]	[illegible]	[illegible]	[illegible]	[illegible]	[illegible]	[illegible]	[illegible]	[illegible]	[illegible]	[illegible]	[illegible]	[illegible]	[illegible]	[illegible]
[illegible]	[illegible]	[illegible]	[illegible]	[illegible]	[illegible]	[illegible]	[illegible]	[illegible]	[illegible]	[illegible]	[illegible]	[illegible]	[illegible]	[illegible]
[illegible]	[illegible]	[illegible]	[illegible]	[illegible]	[illegible]	[illegible]	[illegible]	[illegible]	[illegible]	[illegible]	[illegible]	[illegible]	[illegible]	[illegible]

Receptions of Prisoners.

and c, on page 128.)

Total [illegible] (10)			[illegible] (11)		[illegible] (12)		[illegible] (13)		Total [illegible] (14)			PRISONS. (15)
Total.	M.	F.	M.	F.	M.	F.	M.	F.	Total.	M.	F.	
												Larger Prisons.
[illegible]	[illegible]	[illegible]	[illegible]	[illegible]	[illegible]	.	[illegible]	[illegible]	[illegible]	[illegible]	[illegible]	Armagh.
[illegible]	[illegible]	[illegible]	[illegible]	[illegible]	[illegible]	.	[illegible]	[illegible]	[illegible]	[illegible]	[illegible]	[illegible]
[illegible]	[illegible]	[illegible]	7	4	.	.	[illegible]	.	[illegible]	[illegible]	[illegible]	Castlebar.
[illegible]	[illegible]	.	[illegible]	.	[illegible]	.	1	.	[illegible]	[illegible]	.	Clonmel.
[illegible]	[illegible]	.	[illegible]	.	[illegible]	.	[illegible]	.	[illegible]	[illegible]	.	Cork, Male.
[illegible]	.	[illegible]	.	[illegible]	.	[illegible]	.	[illegible]	[illegible]	.	[illegible]	Cork, Female.
[illegible]	[illegible]	.	[illegible]	.	[illegible]	.	[illegible]		[illegible]	[illegible]	.	[illegible]
[illegible]	[illegible]	[illegible]	[illegible]	4	[illegible]	.	[illegible]	.	[illegible]	[illegible]	[illegible]	Galway.
[illegible]	.	[illegible]	.	[illegible]	.	[illegible]		[illegible]	[illegible]	.	[illegible]	[illegible], Female.
[illegible]	[illegible]	.	[illegible]	.	.	.	[illegible]	.	[illegible]	[illegible]	.	[illegible]
[illegible]	[illegible]	.	[illegible]	.	11	.	[illegible]	.	[illegible]	[illegible]	.	[illegible]
[illegible]	[illegible]	.	[illegible]	.	[illegible]	.	[illegible]	.	[illegible]	[illegible]	.	Limerick, Male.
[illegible]		[illegible]		[illegible]	.		.	[illegible]	[illegible]	.	[illegible]	Limerick, Female.
[illegible]	[illegible]	[illegible]	[illegible]	[illegible]	[illegible]	[illegible]	1	.	[illegible]	[illegible]	[illegible]	Londonderry.
[illegible]	[illegible]	.	[illegible]	.	.	.	[illegible]	.	[illegible]	[illegible]	.	[illegible]
[illegible]	[illegible]	[illegible]	[illegible]	7	[illegible]	.	.	[illegible]	[illegible]	[illegible]	[illegible]	[illegible]
[illegible]	[illegible]	[illegible]	[illegible]	[illegible]	[illegible]	[illegible]	[illegible]	[illegible]	[illegible]	[illegible]	[illegible]	[illegible]
[illegible]	[illegible]	[illegible]	[illegible]	11	[illegible]	.	[illegible]	.	[illegible]	[illegible]	[illegible]	[illegible]
[illegible]	[illegible]	[illegible]	[illegible]	[illegible]	.	[illegible]	[illegible]	[illegible]	[illegible]	[illegible]	[illegible]	Waterford.
[illegible]	[illegible]	[illegible]	[illegible]	[illegible]	[illegible]	.	[illegible]	[illegible]	[illegible]	[illegible]	[illegible]	Wexford.
												[illegible] Prisons.
[illegible]	[illegible]	[illegible]	.	.	.	.	.	.	[illegible]	[illegible]	[illegible]	[illegible]
[illegible]	[illegible]	[illegible]	[illegible]	.	.	.	.	.	[illegible]	[illegible]	[illegible]	[illegible]
[illegible]	[illegible]	[illegible]	.	.	.	.	.	.	[illegible]	[illegible]	[illegible]	[illegible]
[illegible]	[illegible]	[illegible]	[illegible]	.	.	.	.	.	[illegible]	[illegible]	[illegible]	[illegible]
[illegible]	[illegible]	[illegible]	.	[illegible]	[illegible]	.	[illegible]	.	[illegible]	[illegible]	[illegible]	[illegible]
[illegible]	[illegible]	[illegible]	.	.	.	.	.	.	[illegible]	[illegible]	[illegible]	[illegible]
[illegible]	[illegible]	[illegible]	.	.	.	.	.	.	[illegible]	[illegible]	[illegible]	[illegible] Bridewells and [illegible]
[illegible]	[illegible]	[illegible]	[illegible]	[illegible]	[illegible]	[illegible]	[illegible]	[illegible]	[illegible]	[illegible]	[illegible]	TOTAL.
			[illegible]		[illegible]		[illegible]					

	M.	F.
[illegible]	[illegible]	[illegible]
[illegible]	[illegible]	[illegible]
[illegible]	[illegible]	[illegible]
[illegible]	[illegible]	[illegible]
Other orders,	[illegible]	[illegible]
Total,	[illegible]	[illegible]

TABLE 31.—DISPOSAL

(a.)—Disposal of

(See notes at end a

Prisons.	Total Number. (2) Total	M.	F.	Discharged. (3) M.	F.	Convicted Summarily. (4) M.	F.	Committed for Trial. (5) M.	F.	Absconded. (6) M.	F.	Dead. (7) M.	F.	Handed over to Naval and Military Authorities, &c. (8) M.	Removed to Asylums. (9) M.	F.
(1)																
Larger Prisons.																
Armagh,	171	142	[illegible]	[illegible]	[illegible]	[illegible]	[illegible]	[illegible]	.	1	.	1	.	[illegible]	1	.
Belfast,	[illegible]	735	[illegible]	771	[illegible]	[illegible]	[illegible]	[illegible]	[illegible]	.	.	.	.	13	1	.
Castlebar,	[illegible]	[illegible]	7	[illegible]	[illegible]	[illegible]	1	[illegible]	.	.	.	.	.	[illegible]	.	.
Clonmel,	113	113	.	[illegible]	.	[illegible]	.	[illegible]	.	.	.	.	.	[illegible]	.	.
Cork, Male,	227	[illegible]	.	112	.	[illegible]	.	[illegible]	.	.	.	.	.	4	3	.
Cork, Female,	[illegible]	.	[illegible]	.	[illegible]	.	[illegible]	.	[illegible]	.	.	.	.	.	.	1
Dundalk,	[illegible]	[illegible]	.	[illegible]	.	[illegible]	.	[illegible]	.	1	.	.	.	4	.	.
Galway,	[illegible]	[illegible]	14	[illegible]	4	[illegible]	[illegible]	[illegible]	1	.	.	.	.	4	5	.
Grangegorman, Female,	[illegible]	.	[illegible]	.	[illegible]	.	[illegible]	.	[illegible]	.	.	.	.	.	.	[illegible]
Kilkenny,	[illegible]	177	.	[illegible]	.	[illegible]	.	[illegible]	.	.	.	.	.	4	.	.
Kilmainham,	[illegible]	[illegible]	.	[illegible]	.	[illegible]	.	[illegible]	.	[illegible]	.	[illegible]	.	77	4	.
Limerick, Male,	[illegible]	[illegible]	.	[illegible]	.	[illegible]	.	[illegible]	.	.	.	.	.	[illegible]	[illegible]	.
Limerick, Female,	[illegible]	.	[illegible]	.	[illegible]	.	[illegible]	.	[illegible]	.	.	.	.	.	.	1
Londonderry,	[illegible]	[illegible]	[illegible]	[illegible]	[illegible]	[illegible]	[illegible]	[illegible]	[illegible]	.	.	.	.	[illegible]	.	.
Mountjoy,	.	.	.	.	.	.	.	.	.	.	.	.	.	.	.	.
Sligo,	[illegible]	[illegible]	[illegible]	[illegible]	[illegible]	17	[illegible]	[illegible]	[illegible]	.	.	.	.	[illegible]	.	.
Tralee,	[illegible]	[illegible]	[illegible]	[illegible]	[illegible]	[illegible]	[illegible]	[illegible]	[illegible]	.	.	.	.	1	1	.
Tullamore,	113	[illegible]	[illegible]	[illegible]	[illegible]	[illegible]	[illegible]	[illegible]	[illegible]	.	.	.	.	[illegible]	.	.
Waterford,	[illegible]	[illegible]	[illegible]	[illegible]	7	[illegible]	[illegible]	[illegible]	[illegible]	.	.	.	.	[illegible]	.	.
Wexford,	[illegible]	[illegible]	[illegible]	[illegible]	[illegible]	[illegible]	[illegible]	[illegible]	[illegible]	.	.	.	.	1	.	.
Minor Prisons.																
Carrick-on-Shannon,	[illegible]	[illegible]	[illegible]	[illegible]	[illegible]	[illegible]	[illegible]	[illegible]	1	.	.	.	.	[illegible]	.	.
[illegible],	[illegible]	[illegible]	[illegible]	[illegible]	[illegible]	[illegible]	[illegible]	[illegible]	[illegible]	.	.	.	.	[illegible]	.	.
Enniskillen,	[illegible]	[illegible]	[illegible]	[illegible]	1	[illegible]	[illegible]	[illegible]	[illegible]	.	.	.	.	[illegible]	.	.
[illegible],	[illegible]	[illegible]	[illegible]	[illegible]	[illegible]	[illegible]	7	.	.	.	.	.	.	[illegible]	.	.
Omagh,	[illegible]	[illegible]	[illegible]	[illegible]	[illegible]	1	1	.	.	.	.	.	.	[illegible]	.	.
Wicklow,	[illegible]	[illegible]	[illegible]	[illegible]	[illegible]	[illegible]	1	[illegible]	1	.	.	.	.	[illegible]	.	.
Fifteen Bridewells and one Lockup,	[illegible]	[illegible]	[illegible]	[illegible]	[illegible]	[illegible]	[illegible]	[illegible]	[illegible]	.	.	.	.	[illegible]	[illegible]	.
Total,	[illegible]	[illegible]	[illegible]	[illegible]	[illegible]	[illegible]	[illegible]	[illegible]	[illegible]	[illegible]	.	[illegible]	.	[illegible]	[illegible]	4
				[illegible]		[illegible]		[illegible]		[illegible]		[illegible]				

OF PRISONERS.

Unconvicted Prisoners.

on page 138.)

Prisoners Committed for Trial. Total Number. Total	M.	F.	Acquitted. M.	F.	Convicted. M.	F.	Absconded while awaiting Trial. M.	F.	Died while awaiting Trial. M.	F.	Removed to Asylums. M.	F.	Prisons.
													Larger Prisons.
[illegible]	[illegible]	[illegible]	[illegible]	[illegible]	[illegible]	[illegible]		.	.	.	.	.	Armagh.
[illegible]	[illegible]	[illegible]	[illegible]	[illegible]	[illegible]	[illegible]		.	.	.	[illegible]	[illegible]	Belfast.
[illegible]	[illegible]	[illegible]	.	.	[illegible]	[illegible]	.	.	.	.	[illegible]	.	Castlebar (?).
[illegible]	[illegible]	.	[illegible]	.	[illegible]	.	.	.	.	.	.		Clonmel (?).
[illegible]	[illegible]	.	[illegible]	.	[illegible]	.	.	.	.	.	.		Cork, Male.
[illegible]	.	[illegible]	.	[illegible]	.	[illegible]	.	.	.	.	.	[illegible]	Cork, Female.
[illegible]	[illegible]	.	[illegible]	.	[illegible]	.	.	.	.	.	.	.	Dundalk.
[illegible]	[illegible]	[illegible]	[illegible]	[illegible]	[illegible]	[illegible]	.	.	.	.	.	.	Galway.
[illegible]	.	[illegible]	.	[illegible]	.	[illegible]	.	.	.	.	.	.	Grangegorman, Female.
[illegible]	[illegible]	.	[illegible]	.	[illegible]	.	.	.	.	.	.	.	Kilkenny.
[illegible]	[illegible]	.	[illegible]	.	[illegible]	.	[illegible]	.	.	.	[illegible]	.	Kilmainham.
[illegible]	[illegible]	.	[illegible]	.	[illegible]	.	.	.	.	.	[illegible]	.	Limerick, Male.
[illegible]	.	[illegible]	.	[illegible]	.	[illegible]	.	.	.	.	.	.	Limerick, Female.
[illegible]	[illegible]	[illegible]	[illegible]	[illegible]	[illegible]	[illegible]	.	.	.	.	.	.	Londonderry.
.	.	.	.	.	.	.	.	.	.	.	.	.	Mountjoy (?).
[illegible]	[illegible]	[illegible]	[illegible]	[illegible]	[illegible]	[illegible]	.	.	.	.	.	[illegible]	Sligo.
[illegible]	[illegible]	[illegible]	[illegible]	.	[illegible]	[illegible]	.	.	.	.	[illegible]	.	Tralee.
[illegible]	[illegible]	[illegible]	[illegible]	[illegible]	[illegible]	[illegible]	[illegible]	.	.	.	[illegible]	.	Tullamore.
[illegible]	[illegible]	[illegible]	[illegible]	[illegible]	[illegible]	[illegible]	.	.	.	.	.	.	Waterford.
[illegible]	[illegible]	[illegible]	[illegible]	[illegible]	[illegible]	.	[illegible]	.	.	.	[illegible]	.	Wexford.
													Minor Prisons.
.	.	.	.	.	.	.	.	.	.	.	.	.	[illegible]
.	.	.	.	.	.	.	.	.	.	.	[illegible]	.	[illegible]
.	.	.	.	.	.	.	.	.	.	.	.	.	[illegible]
.	.	.	.	.	.	.	.	.	.	.	.	.	[illegible]
[illegible]	[illegible]	.	[illegible]	.	.	.	.	.	.	.	.	.	[illegible]
.	.	.	.	.	.	.	.	.	.	.	.	.	Wicklow.
.	.	.	.	.	.	.	.	.	.	.	.	.	[illegible] Bridewells and Lock-ups.
[illegible]	[illegible]	[illegible]	[illegible]	[illegible]	[illegible]	[illegible]	[illegible]	.	.	.	[illegible]	[illegible]	Total.
			[illegible]		[illegible]		[illegible]		.		[illegible]		

TABLE 31.—DISPOSAL

(b)—Disposal of

(See note f

Prisons.	Total.	Released: On expiration of Sentence.	On Payment of Fine.	On Finding Bail.	On Pardon or Reduction of Sentence.	On Licence: In ordinary Course.	On Medical or other special Grounds.
(1)	(2)	(3)	(4)	(5)	(6)	(7)	(8)
Larger Prisons.							
[illegible]	[illegible]	[illegible]	[illegible]	7	6	.	.
[illegible]	[illegible]	[illegible]	[illegible]	[illegible]	17	.	.
[illegible]	[illegible]	[illegible]	[illegible]	-	[illegible]	.	.
[illegible]	[illegible]	[illegible]	[illegible]	[illegible]	[illegible]	.	.
[illegible], Male,	[illegible]	[illegible]	[illegible]	[illegible]	[illegible]	[illegible]	.
[illegible], Female,	[illegible]	[illegible]	[illegible]	-	[illegible]	.	.
[illegible]	[illegible]	[illegible]	[illegible]	-	[illegible]	.	.
[illegible]	[illegible]	[illegible]	[illegible]	[illegible]	11	.	.
[illegible], Female,	[illegible]	[illegible]	[illegible]	-	[illegible]	.	.
[illegible]	[illegible]	[illegible]	[illegible]	[illegible]	[illegible]	.	.
[illegible]	[illegible]	[illegible]	[illegible]	[illegible]	[illegible]	.	.
[illegible], Male,	[illegible]	[illegible]	[illegible]	[illegible]	[illegible]	.	.
[illegible], Female,	[illegible]	[illegible]	[illegible]	-	[illegible]	.	.
[illegible]	[illegible]	[illegible]	[illegible]	[illegible]	[illegible]	.	.
[illegible]	[illegible]	[illegible]	[illegible]	[illegible]	[illegible]	.	.
[illegible]	[illegible]	[illegible]	[illegible]	[illegible]	[illegible]	.	.
[illegible]	[illegible]	[illegible]	[illegible]	[illegible]	[illegible]	.	.
[illegible]	[illegible]	[illegible]	[illegible]	[illegible]	[illegible]	.	.
[illegible]	[illegible]	[illegible]	[illegible]	-	[illegible]	.	.
[illegible]	[illegible]	[illegible]	[illegible]	[illegible]	[illegible]	.	.
Minor Prisons.							
[illegible]	[illegible]	[illegible]	[illegible]	.	.	.	.
[illegible]	[illegible]	[illegible]	[illegible]	.	.	.	.
[illegible]	[illegible]	[illegible]	[illegible]	.	.	.	.
[illegible]	[illegible]	[illegible]	[illegible]	[illegible]	[illegible]	.	.
[illegible]	[illegible]	[illegible]	[illegible]	.	.	.	.
[illegible]	[illegible]	[illegible]	[illegible]	.	.	.	.

OF PRISONERS.

Convicted Prisoners.

on page 12[illegible])

Removed.				Escaped.	Committed Suicide.	Died.	Executed.	PRISONS.
To Gaols or Convict Prisons.	To Reformatories.	To Asylums.	To England, Scotland, &c.					
(9)	(10)	(11)	(12)	(13)	(14)	(15)	(16)	
								Local Prisons.
.	.	.	.	.	.	.	.	Armagh.
.	[illegible]	[illegible]	.	.	.	1	.	Belfast.
.	.	[illegible]	.	.	.	1	.	Castlebar.
.	.	[illegible]	.	.	.	.	.	Clonmel.
.	[illegible]	[illegible]	.	.	.	.	.	Cork, Male.
.	.	[illegible]	.	.	.	.	.	Cork, Female.
.	.	1	.	.	.	.	.	Dundalk.
.	[illegible]	[illegible]		.	.	.	.	Galway.
.	[illegible]	[illegible]		.	.	.	.	Grangegorman, Female.
.	.	[illegible]		.	.	.	.	Kilkenny.
.	[illegible]	[illegible]		.	.	.	.	Kilmainham.
.	[illegible]	[illegible]		.	.	.	.	Limerick, Male.
.	[illegible]	[illegible]	.	.	.	.	.	Limerick, Female.
.	[illegible]	[illegible]	.	.	.	.	.	Londonderry.
.	[illegible]	[illegible]	.	.	.	.	.	Mountjoy.
.	1	[illegible]	.	.	.	.	.	Sligo.
.	[illegible]	[illegible]	.	.	.	.	.	Tralee.
.	[illegible]	.	.	.	.	.	.	Tullamore.
.	[illegible]	[illegible]	.	.	.	.	.	Waterford.
.	.	[illegible]	.	.	1	1	.	Wexford.
								Minor Prisons.
.	.	.	.	.	.	.	.	Carrick-on-Shannon.
.	.	.	.	.	.	.	.	Drogheda.
.	1	1	.	.	.	.	.	Enniskillen.
.	.	.	.	.	.	.	.	Mullingar.
.	.	.	.	.	.	.	.	Omagh.
.	.	.	.	.	.	.	.	Wicklow.
.	.	.	.	.	.	.	.	11 Bridewells.
.	[illegible]	[illegible]	.	.	1	[illegible]	.	Total Local Prisons.
								Convict Prisons.
.	.	.	.	.	.	.	.	Grangegorman, Female.
.	.	[illegible]	.	.	.	.	.	Maryborough.
.	.	[illegible]	.	.	.	1	.	Mountjoy, Male.
	.	[illegible]	.	.	.	1	.	Total Convict Prisons.
	[illegible]	[illegible]	.	.	[illegible]	[illegible]	.	GRAND TOTAL.

TABLE 32.—CONVICTED PRISONERS.—

(See notes p. 3,

Prisons.	Number Received in Prison after Conviction.	Death.		Penal Servitude.			Detention of Lunatic (with or without other Punishment.)			Imprisonment: Total Imprisonment.			Imprisonment without option of Fine: Total	With Hard Labour.		Without Hard Labour.	
		(3)		(4)			(5)			(6)				(7)		(8)	
(1)	(2)	M.	F.	Total	M.	F.	Total	M.	F.	Total	M.	F.	(7)	M.	F.	M.	F.
Larger Prisons.																	
Armagh,	[illegible]	[illegible]	.	[illegible]	[illegible]	.	[illegible]	[illegible]	.	[illegible]	[illegible]	[illegible]	[illegible]	[illegible]	[illegible]	[illegible]	[illegible]
Belfast,	[illegible]	.	.	[illegible]	[illegible]	.	.	.	.	[illegible]	[illegible]	[illegible]	[illegible]	[illegible]	[illegible]	[illegible]	[illegible]
Castlebar,	[illegible]	.	.	[illegible]	[illegible]	.	.	.	.	[illegible]	[illegible]	[illegible]	[illegible]	[illegible]	[illegible]	[illegible]	[illegible]
Clonmel,	[illegible]	.	.	[illegible]	[illegible]	.	[illegible]	[illegible]	.	[illegible]	[illegible]	.	[illegible]	[illegible]	.	[illegible]	.
Cork, Male,	[illegible]	[illegible]	.	[illegible]	[illegible]	.	[illegible]	[illegible]	.	[illegible]	[illegible]	.	[illegible]	[illegible]	.	[illegible]	.
Cork, Female,	[illegible]	.	.	[illegible]	.	[illegible]	.	.	.	[illegible]	.	[illegible]	[illegible]	.	[illegible]	.	[illegible]
Dundalk,	[illegible]	.	.	[illegible]	[illegible]	.	.	.	.	[illegible]	[illegible]	.	[illegible]	[illegible]	.	[illegible]	.
Galway,	[illegible]	.	.	[illegible]	[illegible]	.	[illegible]	[illegible]	.	[illegible]	[illegible]	[illegible]	[illegible]	[illegible]	[illegible]	[illegible]	[illegible]
Grangegorman, Female,	[illegible]	.	.	[illegible]	.	[illegible]	.	.	.	[illegible]	.	[illegible]	[illegible]	.	[illegible]	.	[illegible]
Kilkenny,	[illegible]	.	.	[illegible]	[illegible]	.	.	.	.	[illegible]	[illegible]	.	[illegible]	[illegible]	.	[illegible]	.
Kilmainham,	[illegible]	.	.	[illegible]	[illegible]	.	.	.	.	[illegible]	[illegible]	.	[illegible]	[illegible]	.	[illegible]	.
Limerick, Male,	[illegible]	.	.	[illegible]	[illegible]	.	.	.	.	[illegible]	[illegible]	.	[illegible]	[illegible]	.	[illegible]	.
Limerick, Female,	[illegible]	.	.	[illegible]	.	[illegible]	.	.	.	[illegible]	.	[illegible]	[illegible]	.	[illegible]	.	[illegible]
Londonderry,	[illegible]	.	.	[illegible]	[illegible]	.	.	.	.	[illegible]	[illegible]	[illegible]	[illegible]	[illegible]	[illegible]	[illegible]	[illegible]
Mountjoy,	[illegible]	.	.	[illegible]	[illegible]	.	[illegible]	[illegible]	.	[illegible]	[illegible]	.	[illegible]	[illegible]	.	[illegible]	.
Sligo,	[illegible]	.	.	[illegible]	[illegible]	.	.	.	.	[illegible]	[illegible]	[illegible]	[illegible]	[illegible]	[illegible]	[illegible]	[illegible]
Tralee,	[illegible]	.	.	[illegible]	.	[illegible]	.	.	.	[illegible]	[illegible]	[illegible]	[illegible]	[illegible]	[illegible]	[illegible]	[illegible]
Tullamore,	[illegible]	.	.	[illegible]	[illegible]	.	.	.	.	[illegible]	[illegible]	[illegible]	[illegible]	[illegible]	[illegible]	[illegible]	[illegible]
Waterford,	[illegible]	.	.	.	.	.	.	.	.	[illegible]	[illegible]	[illegible]	[illegible]	[illegible]	[illegible]	[illegible]	[illegible]
Wexford,	[illegible]	.	.	[illegible]	[illegible]	.	.	.	.	[illegible]	[illegible]	[illegible]	[illegible]	[illegible]	[illegible]	[illegible]	[illegible]
Minor Prisons.																	
Carrick-on-Shannon,	[illegible]	.	.	.	.	.	.	.	.	[illegible]	[illegible]	[illegible]	[illegible]	[illegible]	[illegible]	[illegible]	[illegible]
[illegible],	[illegible]	.	.	.	.	.	.	.	.	[illegible]	[illegible]	[illegible]	[illegible]	[illegible]	[illegible]	[illegible]	[illegible]
Enniskillen,	[illegible]	.	.	.	.	.	.	.	.	[illegible]	[illegible]	[illegible]	[illegible]	[illegible]	[illegible]	[illegible]	[illegible]
[illegible],	[illegible]	.	.	.	.	.	.	.	.	[illegible]	[illegible]	[illegible]	[illegible]	[illegible]	[illegible]	[illegible]	[illegible]
Omagh,	[illegible]	.	.	.	.	.	.	.	.	[illegible]	[illegible]	[illegible]	[illegible]	[illegible]	[illegible]	[illegible]	[illegible]
Wicklow,	[illegible]	.	.	.	.	.	.	.	.	[illegible]	[illegible]	[illegible]	[illegible]	[illegible]	.	[illegible]	.
13 Bridewells,	[illegible]	.	.	.	.	.	.	.	.	[illegible]	[illegible]	[illegible]	[illegible]	.	.	[illegible]	[illegible]
Total,	*[illegible]	[illegible]	.	[illegible]	[illegible]	[illegible]	[illegible]	[illegible]	.	[illegible]	[illegible]	[illegible]	[illegible]	[illegible]	[illegible]	[illegible]	[illegible]
		[illegible]												[illegible]		[illegible]	

* Including 7 male prisoners, against whom special verdicts of "guilty, but insane," were returned.

Nature of Sentences of Prisoners Received.

(… and [illegible], on page 128.)

Imprisonment: Total (11)	In default of Payment of Fines, With Hard Labour, m.	With Hard Labour, f.	Without Hard Labour, m.	Without Hard Labour, f.	Imprisonment in default of Bail: Total	m.	f.	Total Hard Labour (14)	Total without Hard Labour (15)	First-class Misdemeanants, m.	f.	Sentenced to Penal Servitude (17)	Flogged (18)	Whipped (19)	[illegible] (20)	[illegible] (21)	PRISONS. (22)
																	County Prisons.
[illegible]	[illegible]	[illegible]	[illegible]	[illegible]	.	.	.	[illegible]	[illegible]	.	.	[illegible]	.	.	.	[illegible]	Armagh.
[illegible]	[illegible]	[illegible]	[illegible]	[illegible]	[illegible]	[illegible]	[illegible]	[illegible]	[illegible]	1	1	[illegible]	.	.	[illegible]	1	Belfast.
[illegible]	[illegible]	[illegible]	[illegible]	[illegible]	.	.	.	[illegible]	[illegible]	.	.	1	.	.	.	.	Castlebar.
[illegible]	[illegible]	.	[illegible]	.	6	[illegible]	.	[illegible]	[illegible]	.	.	[illegible]	.	.	.	1	Clonmel.
[illegible]	[illegible]	.	[illegible]	.	[illegible]	[illegible]	.	[illegible]	[illegible]	.	.	[illegible]	.	.	.	1	Cork, Male.
[illegible]	.	[illegible]	.	[illegible]	.	.	.	[illegible]	[illegible]	.	.	.	.	.	.	.	Cork, Female.
[illegible]	[illegible]	.	[illegible]	.	.	.	.	[illegible]	[illegible]	.	.	[illegible]	.	.	.	.	Dundalk.
[illegible]	[illegible]	[illegible]	[illegible]	[illegible]	[illegible]	[illegible]	[illegible]	[illegible]	[illegible]	.	.	6	.	.	.	.	Galway.
[illegible]	.	[illegible]	.	[illegible]	.	.	.	[illegible]	[illegible]	.	.	.	.	.	.	1	Grangegorman, Female.
[illegible]	[illegible]	.	[illegible]	.	[illegible]	[illegible]	.	[illegible]	[illegible]	.	.	[illegible]	.	.	.	.	Kilkenny.
[illegible]	[illegible]	.	[illegible]	.	.	.	.	[illegible]	[illegible]	.	.	1	.	.	.	1	Kilmainham.
[illegible]	[illegible]	.	[illegible]	.	.	.	.	[illegible]	[illegible]	.	.	[illegible]	.	.	.	.	Limerick, Male.
[illegible]	.	[illegible]	.	[illegible]	.	.	.	[illegible]	[illegible]	.	.	.	.	.	1	.	Limerick, Female.
[illegible]	[illegible]	[illegible]	[illegible]	[illegible]	[illegible]	[illegible]	[illegible]	[illegible]	[illegible]	.	.	[illegible]	.	.	.	1	Londonderry.
[illegible]	[illegible]	.	[illegible]	.	.	.	.	[illegible]	[illegible]	.	.	[illegible]	.	.	.	[illegible]	Mountjoy.
[illegible]	[illegible]	[illegible]	[illegible]	[illegible]	.	.	.	[illegible]	[illegible]	.	.	.	.	.	.	[illegible]	Sligo.
[illegible]	[illegible]	[illegible]	[illegible]	[illegible]	.	.	.	[illegible]	[illegible]	1	.	[illegible]	.	.	.	.	Tralee.
[illegible]	[illegible]	[illegible]	[illegible]	[illegible]	.	.	.	[illegible]	[illegible]	.	.	[illegible]	.	.	.	1	Tullamore.
[illegible]	[illegible]	[illegible]	[illegible]	[illegible]	.	.	.	[illegible]	[illegible]	.	.	1	.	.	.	.	Waterford.
[illegible]	[illegible]	[illegible]	[illegible]	[illegible]	.	.	.	[illegible]	[illegible]	.	.	[illegible]	.	.	.	.	Wexford.
																	Bridewells.
[illegible]	[illegible]	[illegible]	[illegible]	[illegible]	.	.	.	[illegible]	[illegible]	.	.	.	.	.	.	.	Carrick-on-Shannon.
[illegible]	[illegible]	[illegible]	[illegible]	[illegible]	.	.	.	[illegible]	[illegible]	.	.	.	.	.	.	.	Drogheda.
[illegible]	[illegible]	[illegible]	[illegible]	[illegible]	.	.	.	[illegible]	[illegible]	.	.	.	.	.	.	.	[illegible]
[illegible]	[illegible]	[illegible]	[illegible]	[illegible]	.	.	.	[illegible]	[illegible]	.	.	.	.	.	.	.	Mullingar.
[illegible]	[illegible]	[illegible]	[illegible]	[illegible]	.	.	.	[illegible]	[illegible]	.	.	.	.	.	.	.	Omagh.
[illegible]	[illegible]	[illegible]	[illegible]	[illegible]	.	.	.	[illegible]	[illegible]	.	.	[illegible]	.	.	.	.	Wicklow.
[illegible]	[illegible]	[illegible]	[illegible]	[illegible]	.	.	.	[illegible]	[illegible]	.	.	.	.	.	.	.	13 Bridewells.
[illegible]	[illegible]	[illegible]	[illegible]	[illegible]	[illegible]	[illegible]	[illegible]	[illegible]	[illegible]	[illegible]	[illegible]	[illegible]	.	.	[illegible]	[illegible]	TOTAL.
	[illegible]		[illegible]														

[illegible] Including [illegible] prisoners sentenced to Hard Labour.

TABLE 33.—CONVICTED PRISONERS.—

See note [illegible]

LENGTH OF SENTENCE. (1)	Penal Servitude. (2) Total	M.	F.	[illegible] of Licence [illegible] (3) Total	M.	F.	Total [illegible] (4) Total	M.	F.	Imprisonment, without option of Fine. Total (5)	With Hard Labour. (6) M.	F.	Without Hard Labour. (7) M.	F.
Death (commuted),	[illegible]	[illegible]	.	.	.	.	.	.	.	.	.	.	.	.
Penal Servitude: Life,	.	.	.	.	.	.	.	.	.	.	.	.	.	.
" 20 Years,	.	.	.	.	.	.	.	.	.	.	.	.	.	.
" [illegible]	[illegible]	[illegible]	.	.	.	.	.	.	.	.	.	.	.	.
" [illegible]	[illegible]	[illegible]	.	.	.	.	.	.	.	.	.	.	.	.
" [illegible]	[illegible]	[illegible]	.	.	.	.	.	.	.	.	.	.	.	.
" [illegible]	[illegible]	[illegible]	[illegible]	.	.	.	.	.	.	.	.	.	.	.
" [illegible]	[illegible]	[illegible]	.	.	.	.	.	.	.	.	.	.	.	.
" [illegible]	[illegible]	[illegible]	[illegible]	.	.	.	.	.	.	.	.	.	.	.
" [illegible]	[illegible]	[illegible]	[illegible]	.	.	.	.	.	.	.	.	.	.	.
Total Penal Servitude Sentences,	[illegible]	[illegible]	[illegible]	.	.	.	.	.	.	.	.	.	.	.
Imprisonment: Over 2 years,	.	.	.	[illegible]	[illegible]	.	.	.	.	.	.	.	.	.
" 18 Months, and over 12 Months,	.	.	.	.	.	.	[illegible]	[illegible]	[illegible]	[illegible]	[illegible]	[illegible]	[illegible]	.
" [illegible]	.	.	.	[illegible]	[illegible]	.	[illegible]	[illegible]	[illegible]	[illegible]	[illegible]	[illegible]	[illegible]	[illegible]
" [illegible]	.	.	.	[illegible]	[illegible]	.	[illegible]	[illegible]	[illegible]	[illegible]	[illegible]	[illegible]	[illegible]	[illegible]
" [illegible] Weeks	.	.	.	.	.	.	[illegible]	[illegible]	[illegible]	[illegible]	[illegible]	[illegible]	[illegible]	[illegible]
" [illegible]	.	.	.	[illegible]	[illegible]	.	[illegible]	[illegible]	[illegible]	[illegible]	[illegible]	[illegible]	[illegible]	[illegible]

Length of Sentences.

(… on page 138.)

Imprisonment: In default of Payment of Fine: Total (6)	With Hard Labour (7) M.	With Hard Labour (7) F.	Without Hard Labour (8) M.	Without Hard Labour (8) F.	In default of Bail (11): Total	M.	F.	Total Hard Labour (12)	Total Without Hard Labour (13)	Fine, Cum Pœna (14): M	F	(15)	(16)	LENGTH OF SENTENCE.
[illegible]	[illegible]	[illegible]	[illegible]	[illegible]	[illegible]	[illegible]	[illegible]	[illegible]	[illegible]	[illegible]	[illegible]	[illegible]	[illegible]	Death sentence.
[illegible]	[illegible]	[illegible]	[illegible]	[illegible]	[illegible]	[illegible]	[illegible]	[illegible]	[illegible]	[illegible]	[illegible]	[illegible]	[illegible]	Penal Servitude: Life.
[illegible]	[illegible]	[illegible]	[illegible]	[illegible]	[illegible]	[illegible]	[illegible]	[illegible]	[illegible]	[illegible]	[illegible]	[illegible]	[illegible]	[illegible] Years.
[illegible]	[illegible]	[illegible]	[illegible]	[illegible]	[illegible]	[illegible]	[illegible]	[illegible]	[illegible]	[illegible]	[illegible]	[illegible]	[illegible]	Total Penal Servitude Sentences.
[illegible]	[illegible]	[illegible]	[illegible]	[illegible]	[illegible]	[illegible]	[illegible]	[illegible]	[illegible]	[illegible]	[illegible]	[illegible]	[illegible]	Imprisonment: Over 2 years.
[illegible]	[illegible]	[illegible]	[illegible]	[illegible]	[illegible]	[illegible]	[illegible]	[illegible]	[illegible]	[illegible]	[illegible]	[illegible]	[illegible]	[illegible] months, and over [illegible] months.
[illegible]	[illegible]	[illegible]	[illegible]	[illegible]	[illegible]	[illegible]	[illegible]	[illegible]	[illegible]	[illegible]	[illegible]	[illegible]	[illegible]	[illegible] weeks.
[illegible]	[illegible]	[illegible]	[illegible]	[illegible]	[illegible]	[illegible]	[illegible]	[illegible]	[illegible]	[illegible]	[illegible]	[illegible]	[illegible]	1 week.
[illegible]	[illegible]	[illegible]	[illegible]	[illegible]	[illegible]	[illegible]	[illegible]	[illegible]	[illegible]	[illegible]	[illegible]	[illegible]	[illegible]	[illegible] days.
[illegible]	[illegible]	[illegible]	[illegible]	[illegible]	[illegible]	[illegible]	[illegible]	[illegible]	[illegible]	[illegible]	[illegible]	[illegible]	[illegible]	Total Sentences of Imprisonment.

† Including five Bail prisoners sentenced to Hard Labour.

IRELAND.

TABLE 34.—CONVICTED

(Court Martial Prisoners are

PRISONS. (1)	Total. (2)			One. (3)		Two. (4)		Three. (5)		Four Times. (6)		Five Times. (7)		Six to ten Times. (8)	
	Total.	M.	F.	M.	F.	M.	F.	M.	F.	M.	F.	M.	F.	M.	F.
[illegible]															
[illegible]	[illegible]	[illegible]	[illegible]	[illegible]	[illegible]	[illegible]	[illegible]	[illegible]	[illegible]	[illegible]	[illegible]	[illegible]	[illegible]	[illegible]	[illegible]
[illegible]	[illegible]	[illegible]	[illegible]	[illegible]	[illegible]	[illegible]	[illegible]	[illegible]	[illegible]	[illegible]	[illegible]	[illegible]	[illegible]	[illegible]	[illegible]
[illegible]	[illegible]	[illegible]	[illegible]	[illegible]	[illegible]	[illegible]	[illegible]	[illegible]	[illegible]	[illegible]	[illegible]	[illegible]	[illegible]	[illegible]	[illegible]
[illegible]	[illegible]	[illegible]	.	[illegible]	.	[illegible]	.	[illegible]	.	[illegible]	.	[illegible]	.	[illegible]	.
Male,	[illegible]	[illegible]	.	[illegible]	.	[illegible]	.	[illegible]	.	[illegible]		[illegible]	.	[illegible]	.
Female,	[illegible]	.	[illegible]	.	[illegible]	.	[illegible]	.	[illegible]		[illegible]	.	[illegible]	.	[illegible]
[illegible]	[illegible]	[illegible]	.	[illegible]	.	[illegible]	.	[illegible]	.	[illegible]		[illegible]	.	[illegible]	.
[illegible]	[illegible]	[illegible]	[illegible]	[illegible]	[illegible]	[illegible]	[illegible]	[illegible]	[illegible]	[illegible]	[illegible]	[illegible]	[illegible]	[illegible]	[illegible]
[illegible] Female,	[illegible]	.	[illegible]	.	[illegible]	.	[illegible]		[illegible]	.	[illegible]	.	[illegible]	.	[illegible]
[illegible]	[illegible]	[illegible]	.	[illegible]	.	[illegible]	.	[illegible]	.	[illegible]	.	[illegible]	.	[illegible]	.
[illegible]	[illegible]	[illegible]	.	[illegible]	.	[illegible]	.	[illegible]		[illegible]	.	[illegible]	.	[illegible]	.
[illegible] Male,	[illegible]	[illegible]	.	[illegible]	.	[illegible]	.	[illegible]	.	[illegible]	.	[illegible]	.	[illegible]	.
[illegible] Female,	[illegible]	.	[illegible]	.	[illegible]	.	[illegible]	.	[illegible]	.	[illegible]	.	[illegible]	.	[illegible]
[illegible]	[illegible]	[illegible]	[illegible]	[illegible]	[illegible]	[illegible]	[illegible]	[illegible]	[illegible]	[illegible]	[illegible]	[illegible]	[illegible]	[illegible]	[illegible]
[illegible]	[illegible]	[illegible]	.	[illegible]	.	[illegible]	.	[illegible]	.	[illegible]	.	[illegible]	.	[illegible]	.
[illegible]	[illegible]	[illegible]	[illegible]	[illegible]	[illegible]	[illegible]	[illegible]	[illegible]	[illegible]	[illegible]	[illegible]	[illegible]	[illegible]	[illegible]	[illegible]
[illegible]	[illegible]	[illegible]	[illegible]	[illegible]	[illegible]	[illegible]	[illegible]	[illegible]	[illegible]	[illegible]	[illegible]	[illegible]	[illegible]	[illegible]	[illegible]
[illegible]	[illegible]	[illegible]	[illegible]	[illegible]	[illegible]	[illegible]	[illegible]	[illegible]	[illegible]	[illegible]	[illegible]	[illegible]	[illegible]	[illegible]	[illegible]
[illegible]	[illegible]	[illegible]	[illegible]	[illegible]	[illegible]	[illegible]	[illegible]	[illegible]	[illegible]	[illegible]	[illegible]	[illegible]	[illegible]	[illegible]	[illegible]
[illegible]	[illegible]	[illegible]	[illegible]	[illegible]	[illegible]	[illegible]	[illegible]	[illegible]	[illegible]	[illegible]	[illegible]	[illegible]	[illegible]	[illegible]	[illegible]
[illegible]															
[illegible]	[illegible]	[illegible]	[illegible]	[illegible]	[illegible]	[illegible]	[illegible]	[illegible]	[illegible]	[illegible]	[illegible]	[illegible]	[illegible]	[illegible]	[illegible]
[illegible]	[illegible]	[illegible]	[illegible]	[illegible]	[illegible]	[illegible]	[illegible]	[illegible]	[illegible]	[illegible]	[illegible]	[illegible]	[illegible]	[illegible]	[illegible]
[illegible]	[illegible]	[illegible]	[illegible]	[illegible]	[illegible]	[illegible]	[illegible]	[illegible]	[illegible]	[illegible]	[illegible]	[illegible]	[illegible]	[illegible]	[illegible]
[illegible]	[illegible]	[illegible]	[illegible]	[illegible]	[illegible]	[illegible]	[illegible]	[illegible]	[illegible]	[illegible]	[illegible]	[illegible]	[illegible]	[illegible]	[illegible]
[illegible]	[illegible]	[illegible]	[illegible]	[illegible]	[illegible]	[illegible]	[illegible]	[illegible]	[illegible]	[illegible]	[illegible]	[illegible]	[illegible]	[illegible]	[illegible]
[illegible]	[illegible]	[illegible]	[illegible]	[illegible]	[illegible]	[illegible]	[illegible]	[illegible]	[illegible]	[illegible]	[illegible]	[illegible]	[illegible]	[illegible]	[illegible]
[illegible]	[illegible]	[illegible]	[illegible]	[illegible]	[illegible]	[illegible]	[illegible]	[illegible]	[illegible]	[illegible]	[illegible]	[illegible]	[illegible]	[illegible]	[illegible]

PRISONERS.—Previous Convictions.

[illegible] included in this Table)

[illegible] Convictions				Number of Prisoners who had previously undergone Sentences of Penal Servitude												
Seven to Twenty Years		Above Twenty Years		Total			One		Two		Three		Four		Five or More	
M.	F.	M.	F.	Total	M.	F.	M.	F.	M.	F.	M.	F.	M.	F.	M.	F.
[illegible]	[illegible]	[illegible]	[illegible]	[illegible]	[illegible]	[illegible]	[illegible]	[illegible]	[illegible]	[illegible]	[illegible]	[illegible]	[illegible]	[illegible]	[illegible]	[illegible]
[illegible]	[illegible]	[illegible]	[illegible]	[illegible]	[illegible]	[illegible]	[illegible]	[illegible]	[illegible]	[illegible]	[illegible]	[illegible]	[illegible]	[illegible]	[illegible]	[illegible]
[illegible]	[illegible]	[illegible]	[illegible]	[illegible]	[illegible]	[illegible]	[illegible]	[illegible]	[illegible]	[illegible]	[illegible]	[illegible]	[illegible]	[illegible]	[illegible]	[illegible]
[illegible]	[illegible]	[illegible]	[illegible]	[illegible]	[illegible]	[illegible]	[illegible]	[illegible]	[illegible]	[illegible]	[illegible]	[illegible]	[illegible]	[illegible]	[illegible]	[illegible]
[illegible]	[illegible]	[illegible]	[illegible]	[illegible]	[illegible]	[illegible]	[illegible]	[illegible]	[illegible]	[illegible]	[illegible]	[illegible]	[illegible]	[illegible]	[illegible]	[illegible]
[illegible]	[illegible]	[illegible]	[illegible]	[illegible]	[illegible]	[illegible]	[illegible]	[illegible]	[illegible]	[illegible]	[illegible]	[illegible]	[illegible]	[illegible]	[illegible]	[illegible]
[illegible]	[illegible]	[illegible]	[illegible]	[illegible]	[illegible]	[illegible]	[illegible]	[illegible]	[illegible]	[illegible]	[illegible]	[illegible]	[illegible]	[illegible]	[illegible]	[illegible]
[illegible]	[illegible]	[illegible]	[illegible]	[illegible]	[illegible]	[illegible]	[illegible]	[illegible]	[illegible]	[illegible]	[illegible]	[illegible]	[illegible]	[illegible]	[illegible]	[illegible]
[illegible]	[illegible]	[illegible]	[illegible]	[illegible]	[illegible]	[illegible]	[illegible]	[illegible]	[illegible]	[illegible]	[illegible]	[illegible]	[illegible]	[illegible]	[illegible]	[illegible]
[illegible]	[illegible]	[illegible]	[illegible]	[illegible]	[illegible]	[illegible]	[illegible]	[illegible]	[illegible]	[illegible]	[illegible]	[illegible]	[illegible]	[illegible]	[illegible]	[illegible]
[illegible]	[illegible]	[illegible]	[illegible]	[illegible]	[illegible]	[illegible]	[illegible]	[illegible]	[illegible]	[illegible]	[illegible]	[illegible]	[illegible]	[illegible]	[illegible]	[illegible]
[illegible]	[illegible]	[illegible]	[illegible]	[illegible]	[illegible]	[illegible]	[illegible]	[illegible]	[illegible]	[illegible]	[illegible]	[illegible]	[illegible]	[illegible]	[illegible]	[illegible]
[illegible]	[illegible]	[illegible]	[illegible]	[illegible]	[illegible]	[illegible]	[illegible]	[illegible]	[illegible]	[illegible]	[illegible]	[illegible]	[illegible]	[illegible]	[illegible]	[illegible]
[illegible]	[illegible]	[illegible]	[illegible]	[illegible]	[illegible]	[illegible]	[illegible]	[illegible]	[illegible]	[illegible]	[illegible]	[illegible]	[illegible]	[illegible]	[illegible]	[illegible]
[illegible]	[illegible]	[illegible]	[illegible]	[illegible]	[illegible]	[illegible]	[illegible]	[illegible]	[illegible]	[illegible]	[illegible]	[illegible]	[illegible]	[illegible]	[illegible]	[illegible]
[illegible]	[illegible]	[illegible]	[illegible]	[illegible]	[illegible]	[illegible]	[illegible]	[illegible]	[illegible]	[illegible]	[illegible]	[illegible]	[illegible]	[illegible]	[illegible]	[illegible]
[illegible]	[illegible]	[illegible]	[illegible]	[illegible]	[illegible]	[illegible]	[illegible]	[illegible]	[illegible]	[illegible]	[illegible]	[illegible]	[illegible]	[illegible]	[illegible]	[illegible]
[illegible]	[illegible]	[illegible]	[illegible]	[illegible]	[illegible]	[illegible]	[illegible]	[illegible]	[illegible]	[illegible]	[illegible]	[illegible]	[illegible]	[illegible]	[illegible]	[illegible]
[illegible]	[illegible]	[illegible]	[illegible]	[illegible]	[illegible]	[illegible]	[illegible]	[illegible]	[illegible]	[illegible]	[illegible]	[illegible]	[illegible]	[illegible]	[illegible]	[illegible]
[illegible]	[illegible]	[illegible]	[illegible]	[illegible]	[illegible]	[illegible]	[illegible]	[illegible]	[illegible]	[illegible]	[illegible]	[illegible]	[illegible]	[illegible]	[illegible]	[illegible]
[illegible]	[illegible]	[illegible]	[illegible]	[illegible]	[illegible]	[illegible]	[illegible]	[illegible]	[illegible]	[illegible]	[illegible]	[illegible]	[illegible]	[illegible]	[illegible]	[illegible]
[illegible]	[illegible]	[illegible]	[illegible]	[illegible]	[illegible]	[illegible]	[illegible]	[illegible]	[illegible]	[illegible]	[illegible]	[illegible]	[illegible]	[illegible]	[illegible]	[illegible]
[illegible]	[illegible]	[illegible]	[illegible]	[illegible]	[illegible]	[illegible]	[illegible]	[illegible]	[illegible]	[illegible]	[illegible]	[illegible]	[illegible]	[illegible]	[illegible]	[illegible]
[illegible]	[illegible]	[illegible]	[illegible]	[illegible]	[illegible]	[illegible]	[illegible]	[illegible]	[illegible]	[illegible]	[illegible]	[illegible]	[illegible]	[illegible]	[illegible]	[illegible]
[illegible]	[illegible]	[illegible]	[illegible]	[illegible]	[illegible]	[illegible]	[illegible]	[illegible]	[illegible]	[illegible]	[illegible]	[illegible]	[illegible]	[illegible]	[illegible]	[illegible]
[illegible]	[illegible]	[illegible]	[illegible]	[illegible]	[illegible]	[illegible]	[illegible]	[illegible]	[illegible]	[illegible]	[illegible]	[illegible]	[illegible]	[illegible]	[illegible]	[illegible]
[illegible]	[illegible]	[illegible]	[illegible]	[illegible]	[illegible]	[illegible]	[illegible]	[illegible]	[illegible]	[illegible]	[illegible]	[illegible]	[illegible]	[illegible]	[illegible]	[illegible]

TABLE 35.—CONVICTED PRISONERS.—Age and Sex.

(See note A

(Court Martial Prisoners are

Prisons. (1)	Total Number. (2) Total.	M.	F.	Under 12 Years. (3) M.	F.	12 Years and under 16. (4) M.	F.	16 and under 21. (5) M.	F.	21 and under 30. (6) M.	F.	30 and under 40. (7) M.	F.	40 and under 50. (8) M.	F.	50 and under 60. (9) M.	F.
Larger Prisons.																	
Armagh,	[illegible]	[illegible]	[illegible]	.	.	[illegible]	[illegible]	[illegible]	[illegible]	[illegible]	[illegible]	[illegible]	[illegible]	[illegible]	[illegible]	[illegible]	[illegible]
Belfast,	[illegible]	[illegible]	[illegible]	3	.	[illegible]	[illegible]	[illegible]	[illegible]	[illegible]	[illegible]	[illegible]	[illegible]	[illegible]	[illegible]	[illegible]	[illegible]
Castlebar,	[illegible]	[illegible]	[illegible]	.	.	[illegible]	[illegible]	[illegible]	[illegible]	[illegible]	[illegible]	[illegible]	[illegible]	[illegible]	[illegible]	[illegible]	[illegible]
Clonmel,	[illegible]	[illegible]	.	.	.	.	.	[illegible]	.	[illegible]	.	[illegible]	.	[illegible]	.	[illegible]	
Cork, Male,	[illegible]	[illegible]	.	1	.	[illegible]	.	[illegible]	.	[illegible]	.	[illegible]	.	[illegible]	.	[illegible]	.
Cork, Female,	[illegible]	.	[illegible]	.	.	.	[illegible]	.	[illegible]	.	[illegible]	.	[illegible]	.	[illegible]	.	[illegible]
Dundalk,	[illegible]	[illegible]	.	.	.	[illegible]	.	[illegible]	.	[illegible]	.	[illegible]	.	[illegible]	.	[illegible]	.
Galway,	[illegible]	[illegible]	[illegible]	[illegible]	.	[illegible]	.	[illegible]	[illegible]	[illegible]	[illegible]	[illegible]	[illegible]	[illegible]	[illegible]	[illegible]	[illegible]
Grangegorman, Female,	[illegible]	.	[illegible]		[illegible]	.	[illegible]	.	[illegible]	.	[illegible]	.	[illegible]	.	[illegible]	.	[illegible]
Kilkenny,	[illegible]	[illegible]	.		.	[illegible]	.	[illegible]	.	[illegible]	.	[illegible]	.	[illegible]	.	[illegible]	.
Kilmainham,	[illegible]	[illegible]	.	.	.	[illegible]	.	[illegible]	.	[illegible]	.	[illegible]	.	[illegible]	.	[illegible]	.
Limerick, Male,	[illegible]	[illegible]	.	.	.	[illegible]	.	[illegible]	.	[illegible]	.	[illegible]		[illegible]	.	[illegible]	.
Limerick, Female,	[illegible]	.	[illegible]	.	.	.	[illegible]	.	[illegible]	.	[illegible]	.	[illegible]	.	[illegible]	.	[illegible]
Londonderry,	[illegible]	[illegible]	[illegible]	[illegible]	.	[illegible]	[illegible]	[illegible]	[illegible]	[illegible]	[illegible]	[illegible]	[illegible]	[illegible]	[illegible]	[illegible]	[illegible]
Mountjoy,	[illegible]	[illegible]	.	[illegible]	.	[illegible]	.	[illegible]	.	[illegible]	.	[illegible]	.	[illegible]	.	[illegible]	.
Sligo,	[illegible]	[illegible]	[illegible]	.	.	[illegible]	.	[illegible]	[illegible]	[illegible]	[illegible]	[illegible]	[illegible]	[illegible]	[illegible]	[illegible]	[illegible]
Tralee,	[illegible]	[illegible]	[illegible]	1	.	[illegible]	[illegible]	[illegible]	[illegible]	[illegible]	[illegible]	[illegible]	[illegible]	[illegible]	[illegible]	[illegible]	[illegible]
Tullamore,	[illegible]	[illegible]	[illegible]	.	[illegible]	1	.	[illegible]	[illegible]	[illegible]	[illegible]	[illegible]	[illegible]	[illegible]	[illegible]	[illegible]	[illegible]
Waterford,	[illegible]	[illegible]	[illegible]	.	.	[illegible]	[illegible]	[illegible]	[illegible]	[illegible]	[illegible]	[illegible]	[illegible]	[illegible]	[illegible]	[illegible]	[illegible]
Wexford,	[illegible]	[illegible]	[illegible]	.	.	[illegible]	[illegible]	[illegible]	[illegible]	[illegible]	[illegible]	[illegible]	[illegible]	[illegible]	[illegible]	[illegible]	[illegible]
Minor Prisons.																	
Carrick-on-Shannon,	[illegible]	[illegible]	[illegible]	.	.	.	.	[illegible]	[illegible]	[illegible]	[illegible]	[illegible]	[illegible]	[illegible]	[illegible]	[illegible]	[illegible]
Downpatrick,	[illegible]	[illegible]	[illegible]	.	.	[illegible]	.	[illegible]	[illegible]	[illegible]	[illegible]	[illegible]	[illegible]	[illegible]	[illegible]	[illegible]	[illegible]
Enniskillen,	[illegible]	[illegible]	[illegible]	1	.	.	.	[illegible]	[illegible]	[illegible]	[illegible]	[illegible]	[illegible]	[illegible]	[illegible]	[illegible]	[illegible]
Mullingar,	[illegible]	[illegible]	[illegible]	.	.	.	.	[illegible]	[illegible]	[illegible]	[illegible]	[illegible]	[illegible]	[illegible]	[illegible]	[illegible]	[illegible]
Omagh,	[illegible]	[illegible]	[illegible]	.	.	[illegible]	.	[illegible]	[illegible]	[illegible]	[illegible]	[illegible]	[illegible]	[illegible]	[illegible]	[illegible]	[illegible]
Wicklow,	[illegible]	[illegible]	[illegible]	.	.	[illegible]	.	[illegible]	.	[illegible]	[illegible]	[illegible]	[illegible]	[illegible]	[illegible]	[illegible]	[illegible]
[illegible] Bridewells,	[illegible]	[illegible]	[illegible]	.	.	.	.	[illegible]	3	[illegible]	[illegible]	[illegible]	[illegible]	[illegible]	[illegible]	[illegible]	[illegible]
Total,	[illegible]	[illegible]	[illegible]	[illegible]	[illegible]	[illegible]	[illegible]	[illegible]	[illegible]	[illegible]	[illegible]	[illegible]	[illegible]	[illegible]	[illegible]	[illegible]	[illegible]
				[illegible]		[illegible]		[illegible]		[illegible]		[illegible]		[illegible]		[illegible]	

TABLE 36.—CONVICTED PRISONERS.—Birthplace.

[illegible] page 138.)

[illegible] included in these Tables.)

Age. 61 and upwards. M.	F.	Age not ascertained. M.	F.	Birthplace. England. M.	F.	Wales. M.	F.	Scotland. M.	F.	Ireland. M.	F.	Colonies and India. M.	F.	Foreign Countries. M.	F.	Not ascertained. M.	F.	PRISONS.
																		Larger Prisons.
[illegible]	[illegible]	.	.	[illegible]	.	.	.	[illegible]	[illegible]	[illegible]	[illegible]	.	.	[illegible]	.	[illegible]		Armagh.
[illegible]	[illegible]	[illegible]	.	[illegible]	[illegible]	.	[illegible]	[illegible]	[illegible]	[illegible]	[illegible]	[illegible]	[illegible]	[illegible]	.	[illegible]		Belfast.
[illegible]	[illegible]	.	.	.	.	.	.	[illegible]	.	[illegible]	[illegible]	[illegible]	.	.	.	.		Castlebar.
[illegible]	.	.	.	[illegible]	.	[illegible]	.	[illegible]	.	[illegible]	.	.	.	.	.	.	.	Clonmel.
[illegible]	.	.	.	[illegible]	.	[illegible]	.	[illegible]	.	[illegible]	.	[illegible]	.	[illegible]	.	.	.	Cork, Male.
.	[illegible]	.	.	.	[illegible]	.	.	.	.	.	[illegible]	.	[illegible]	.	.	.		Cork, Female.
[illegible]	.	.	.	[illegible]	.	.	.	[illegible]	.	[illegible]	.	[illegible]	.	[illegible]	.	.	.	Dundalk.
[illegible]	[illegible]	.	.	[illegible]	.	.	.	[illegible]	.	[illegible]	[illegible]	[illegible]	.	[illegible]	[illegible]	.		Galway.
.	[illegible]	.	.	.	[illegible]	.	.	.	[illegible]	.	[illegible]		[illegible]	.	[illegible]	.		Grangegorman, Female.
[illegible]		.	.	[illegible]	.	[illegible]	.	[illegible]	.	[illegible]	.	[illegible]	.	[illegible]	.	.		Kilkenny.
[illegible]	.	.	.	[illegible]	.	[illegible]	.	[illegible]	.	[illegible]	.	[illegible]	.	[illegible]	.	.	.	Kilmainham.
[illegible]	.	.	.	[illegible]	.	.	.	.	.	[illegible]	.	[illegible]	.	[illegible]	.	.	.	Limerick, Male.
.	[illegible]			.	[illegible]	.	.	.	.	.	[illegible]	.	.	.	[illegible]		[illegible]	Limerick, Female.
[illegible]	[illegible]	.	.	[illegible]	[illegible]	[illegible]	.	[illegible]	[illegible]	[illegible]	[illegible]	[illegible]		[illegible]		.	.	Londonderry.
[illegible]	.	.	.	[illegible]		[illegible]	.	[illegible]	.	[illegible]	.	[illegible]		[illegible]	.	.		Mountjoy.
[illegible]	[illegible]	.	.	[illegible]	.	.	.	[illegible]	.	[illegible]	[illegible]	[illegible]	[illegible]	.	.	.	.	Naas.
[illegible]	[illegible]	.	.	[illegible]	.	.	.	.	.	[illegible]	[illegible]	[illegible]	.	[illegible]	.	.	.	Tralee.
[illegible]	[illegible]	.	.	[illegible]	[illegible]	[illegible]	.	[illegible]	.	[illegible]	[illegible]	[illegible]	[illegible]	[illegible]	[illegible]	.	.	Tullamore.
[illegible]	[illegible]	.	.	[illegible]	.	.	.	[illegible]	.	[illegible]	[illegible]	.	.	[illegible]	.	.	.	Waterford.
[illegible]	[illegible]	.	.	.	.	.	.	.	.	[illegible]	[illegible]	.	.	.	.	.	.	Wexford.
																		Minor Prisons.
[illegible]		.	.	.	.	.	.	.	.	[illegible]	[illegible]	.	.	.	.	.	.	Carrick-on-Shannon.
[illegible]	[illegible]	[illegible]	[illegible]	[illegible]	[illegible]	.	.	[illegible]	.	[illegible]	[illegible]	.	.	.	.	.	.	Drogheda.
[illegible]	[illegible]		.	[illegible]	.	.	.	[illegible]	.	[illegible]	[illegible]	[illegible]	.	[illegible]	.	[illegible]	.	Enniskillen.
[illegible]	[illegible]	.	.	.	.	.	.	.	.	[illegible]	[illegible]	.	.	.	.	.	.	[illegible]
[illegible]	[illegible]	.	.	.	.	.	.	.	.	[illegible]	[illegible]	.	.	.	.	.		Omagh.
[illegible]	[illegible]	.	.	.	.	.	.	.	.	[illegible]	[illegible]	.	.	.	.	.		Wicklow.
[illegible]	[illegible]	[illegible]	[illegible]	[illegible]	.	.	.	[illegible]	.	[illegible]	[illegible]	.	.	[illegible]	[illegible]	.	.	[illegible] Bridewells.
[illegible]	[illegible]	[illegible]	[illegible]	[illegible]	[illegible]	[illegible]	[illegible]	[illegible]	[illegible]	[illegible]	[illegible]	[illegible]	[illegible]	[illegible]	[illegible]	[illegible]	[illegible]	TOTAL.
[illegible]		[illegible]		[illegible]		[illegible]		[illegible]		[illegible]		[illegible]		[illegible]		[illegible]		

TABLE 67.—CONVICTED PRISONERS.—Degrees of Instruction.

([illegible]) Prisoners, &c.

Prisons. (1)	Total Number (2)			Degrees of Instruction: Neither Read nor Write (3)		Read, or Read and Write imperfectly (4)		Read and Write well (5)		Superior Instruction (6)		Instruction not ascertained (7)	
	Total.	M.	F.	M.	F.	M.	F.	M.	F.	M.	F.	M.	F.
[illegible] Prisons.													
Armagh,	[illegible]	776	[illegible]	[illegible]	[illegible]	[illegible]	[illegible]	[illegible]	[illegible]	[illegible]	.	.	.
Belfast,	[illegible]	[illegible]	[illegible]	[illegible]	[illegible]	[illegible]	[illegible]	[illegible]	[illegible]	[illegible]	.	[illegible]	.
Castlebar,	[illegible]	[illegible]	[illegible]	[illegible]	[illegible]	[illegible]	[illegible]	[illegible]	[illegible]	[illegible]	[illegible]	.	.
Clonmel,	[illegible]	[illegible]	.	[illegible]	.	[illegible]	.	[illegible]	.	[illegible]	.	.	.
Cork, Male,	[illegible]	[illegible]	.	[illegible]	.	[illegible]	.	[illegible]	.	[illegible]	.	.	.
Cork, Female,	[illegible]	.	[illegible]	.	[illegible]	.	[illegible]	.	[illegible]	.	.	.	.
Dundalk,	[illegible]	[illegible]	.	[illegible]	.	[illegible]	.	[illegible]	.	.	.	.	.
Galway,	[illegible]	[illegible]	[illegible]	[illegible]	[illegible]	[illegible]	[illegible]	[illegible]	[illegible]	[illegible]	.	.	.
Grangegorman, Female,	[illegible]	.	[illegible]	.	[illegible]	.	[illegible]	.	[illegible]	.	[illegible]	.	.
Kilkenny,	[illegible]	[illegible]	.	[illegible]	.	[illegible]	.	[illegible]	.	[illegible]	.	[illegible]	.
[illegible]	[illegible]	[illegible]	.	[illegible]	.	[illegible]	.	[illegible]	.	[illegible]	.	[illegible]	.
Limerick, Male,	[illegible]	[illegible]	.	[illegible]	.	[illegible]	.	[illegible]	.	[illegible]	.	.	.
Limerick, Female,	[illegible]	.	[illegible]	.	[illegible]	.	[illegible]	.	[illegible]	.	[illegible]	.	.
Londonderry,	[illegible]	[illegible]	[illegible]	[illegible]	[illegible]	[illegible]	[illegible]	[illegible]	[illegible]	[illegible]	.	.	.
Mountjoy,	[illegible]	[illegible]	.	[illegible]	.	[illegible]	.	[illegible]	.	[illegible]	.	.	.
Sligo,	[illegible]	[illegible]	[illegible]	[illegible]	[illegible]	[illegible]	[illegible]	[illegible]	[illegible]	[illegible]	.	.	.
Tralee,	[illegible]	[illegible]	[illegible]	[illegible]	[illegible]	[illegible]	[illegible]	[illegible]	[illegible]	[illegible]	.	.	.
Tullamore,	[illegible]	[illegible]	[illegible]	[illegible]	[illegible]	[illegible]	[illegible]	[illegible]	[illegible]	[illegible]	[illegible]	.	.
Waterford,	[illegible]	[illegible]	[illegible]	[illegible]	[illegible]	[illegible]	[illegible]	[illegible]	[illegible]	[illegible]	.	.	.
Wexford,	[illegible]	[illegible]	[illegible]	[illegible]	[illegible]	[illegible]	[illegible]	[illegible]	[illegible]	[illegible]	.	.	.
Military Prisons.													
[illegible]	[illegible]	[illegible]	[illegible]	[illegible]	[illegible]	[illegible]	[illegible]	[illegible]	[illegible]	.	.	.	.
[illegible]	[illegible]	[illegible]	[illegible]	[illegible]	[illegible]	[illegible]	[illegible]	[illegible]	[illegible]	[illegible]	.	[illegible]	[illegible]
[illegible]	[illegible]	[illegible]	[illegible]	[illegible]	[illegible]	[illegible]	[illegible]	[illegible]	[illegible]	[illegible]	.	.	.
[illegible]	[illegible]	[illegible]	[illegible]	[illegible]	[illegible]	[illegible]	[illegible]	[illegible]	.	.	.	.	.
Omagh,	[illegible]	[illegible]	[illegible]	[illegible]	[illegible]	[illegible]	[illegible]	[illegible]	[illegible]	.	.	.	.
[illegible]	[illegible]	[illegible]	[illegible]	[illegible]	[illegible]	[illegible]	[illegible]	[illegible]	[illegible]	.	.	.	.
[illegible]	[illegible]	[illegible]	[illegible]	[illegible]	[illegible]	[illegible]	[illegible]	[illegible]	[illegible]	[illegible]	.	.	.
TOTAL,	[illegible]	[illegible]	[illegible]	[illegible]	[illegible]	[illegible]	[illegible]	[illegible]	[illegible]	[illegible]	[illegible]	[illegible]	[illegible]
				[illegible]		[illegible]		[illegible]		[illegible]		[illegible]	

TABLE 38.—CONVICTED PRISONERS.—Previous Occupations.

[illegible] not included in these Tables.)

[illegible]		[illegible]		[illegible]		[illegible]		[illegible]		[illegible]		[illegible]		[illegible]		[illegible]	[illegible]	[illegible]		[illegible]		PRISONS.
M.	F.	M.	F.	M.	F.	M.	F.	M.	F.	M.	F.	M.	F.	M.	F.	M.	F.	M.	F.	M.	F.	
																						[illegible]
[illegible]	[illegible]	[illegible]	[illegible]	[illegible]	[illegible]	[illegible]	[illegible]	[illegible]	[illegible]	[illegible]	[illegible]	[illegible]	[illegible]	[illegible]	[illegible]	[illegible]	[illegible]	[illegible]	[illegible]	[illegible]	[illegible]	Armagh.
[illegible]	[illegible]	[illegible]	[illegible]	[illegible]	[illegible]	[illegible]	[illegible]	[illegible]	[illegible]	[illegible]	[illegible]	[illegible]	[illegible]	[illegible]	[illegible]	[illegible]	[illegible]	[illegible]	[illegible]	[illegible]	[illegible]	Belfast.
[illegible]	[illegible]	[illegible]	[illegible]	[illegible]	[illegible]	[illegible]	[illegible]	[illegible]	[illegible]	[illegible]	[illegible]	[illegible]	[illegible]	[illegible]	[illegible]	[illegible]	[illegible]	[illegible]	[illegible]	[illegible]	[illegible]	Castlebar.
[illegible]	[illegible]	[illegible]	[illegible]	[illegible]	[illegible]	[illegible]	[illegible]	[illegible]	[illegible]	[illegible]	[illegible]	[illegible]	[illegible]	[illegible]	[illegible]	[illegible]	[illegible]	[illegible]	[illegible]	[illegible]	[illegible]	Clonmel.
[illegible]	[illegible]	[illegible]	[illegible]	[illegible]	[illegible]	[illegible]	[illegible]	[illegible]	[illegible]	[illegible]	[illegible]	[illegible]	[illegible]	[illegible]	[illegible]	[illegible]	[illegible]	[illegible]	[illegible]	[illegible]	[illegible]	Cork, Male.
[illegible]	[illegible]	[illegible]	[illegible]	[illegible]	[illegible]	[illegible]	[illegible]	[illegible]	[illegible]	[illegible]	[illegible]	[illegible]	[illegible]	[illegible]	[illegible]	[illegible]	[illegible]	[illegible]	[illegible]	[illegible]	[illegible]	Cork, Female.
[illegible]	[illegible]	[illegible]	[illegible]	[illegible]	[illegible]	[illegible]	[illegible]	[illegible]	[illegible]	[illegible]	[illegible]	[illegible]	[illegible]	[illegible]	[illegible]	[illegible]	[illegible]	[illegible]	[illegible]	[illegible]	[illegible]	Dundalk.
[illegible]	[illegible]	[illegible]	[illegible]	[illegible]	[illegible]	[illegible]	[illegible]	[illegible]	[illegible]	[illegible]	[illegible]	[illegible]	[illegible]	[illegible]	[illegible]	[illegible]	[illegible]	[illegible]	[illegible]	[illegible]	[illegible]	Galway.
[illegible]	[illegible]	[illegible]	[illegible]	[illegible]	[illegible]	[illegible]	[illegible]	[illegible]	[illegible]	[illegible]	[illegible]	[illegible]	[illegible]	[illegible]	[illegible]	[illegible]	[illegible]	[illegible]	[illegible]	[illegible]	[illegible]	Grangegorman, Female.
[illegible]	[illegible]	[illegible]	[illegible]	[illegible]	[illegible]	[illegible]	[illegible]	[illegible]	[illegible]	[illegible]	[illegible]	[illegible]	[illegible]	[illegible]	[illegible]	[illegible]	[illegible]	[illegible]	[illegible]	[illegible]	[illegible]	Kilkenny.
[illegible]	[illegible]	[illegible]	[illegible]	[illegible]	[illegible]	[illegible]	[illegible]	[illegible]	[illegible]	[illegible]	[illegible]	[illegible]	[illegible]	[illegible]	[illegible]	[illegible]	[illegible]	[illegible]	[illegible]	[illegible]	[illegible]	Kilmainham.
[illegible]	[illegible]	[illegible]	[illegible]	[illegible]	[illegible]	[illegible]	[illegible]	[illegible]	[illegible]	[illegible]	[illegible]	[illegible]	[illegible]	[illegible]	[illegible]	[illegible]	[illegible]	[illegible]	[illegible]	[illegible]	[illegible]	Limerick, Male.
[illegible]	[illegible]	[illegible]	[illegible]	[illegible]	[illegible]	[illegible]	[illegible]	[illegible]	[illegible]	[illegible]	[illegible]	[illegible]	[illegible]	[illegible]	[illegible]	[illegible]	[illegible]	[illegible]	[illegible]	[illegible]	[illegible]	Limerick, Female.
[illegible]	[illegible]	[illegible]	[illegible]	[illegible]	[illegible]	[illegible]	[illegible]	[illegible]	[illegible]	[illegible]	[illegible]	[illegible]	[illegible]	[illegible]	[illegible]	[illegible]	[illegible]	[illegible]	[illegible]	[illegible]	[illegible]	Londonderry.
[illegible]	[illegible]	[illegible]	[illegible]	[illegible]	[illegible]	[illegible]	[illegible]	[illegible]	[illegible]	[illegible]	[illegible]	[illegible]	[illegible]	[illegible]	[illegible]	[illegible]	[illegible]	[illegible]	[illegible]	[illegible]	[illegible]	Mountjoy.
[illegible]	[illegible]	[illegible]	[illegible]	[illegible]	[illegible]	[illegible]	[illegible]	[illegible]	[illegible]	[illegible]	[illegible]	[illegible]	[illegible]	[illegible]	[illegible]	[illegible]	[illegible]	[illegible]	[illegible]	[illegible]	[illegible]	Sligo.
[illegible]	[illegible]	[illegible]	[illegible]	[illegible]	[illegible]	[illegible]	[illegible]	[illegible]	[illegible]	[illegible]	[illegible]	[illegible]	[illegible]	[illegible]	[illegible]	[illegible]	[illegible]	[illegible]	[illegible]	[illegible]	[illegible]	Tralee.
[illegible]	[illegible]	[illegible]	[illegible]	[illegible]	[illegible]	[illegible]	[illegible]	[illegible]	[illegible]	[illegible]	[illegible]	[illegible]	[illegible]	[illegible]	[illegible]	[illegible]	[illegible]	[illegible]	[illegible]	[illegible]	[illegible]	Tullamore.
[illegible]	[illegible]	[illegible]	[illegible]	[illegible]	[illegible]	[illegible]	[illegible]	[illegible]	[illegible]	[illegible]	[illegible]	[illegible]	[illegible]	[illegible]	[illegible]	[illegible]	[illegible]	[illegible]	[illegible]	[illegible]	[illegible]	Waterford.
[illegible]	[illegible]	[illegible]	[illegible]	[illegible]	[illegible]	[illegible]	[illegible]	[illegible]	[illegible]	[illegible]	[illegible]	[illegible]	[illegible]	[illegible]	[illegible]	[illegible]	[illegible]	[illegible]	[illegible]	[illegible]	[illegible]	Wexford.
																						[illegible]
[illegible]	[illegible]	[illegible]	[illegible]	[illegible]	[illegible]	[illegible]	[illegible]	[illegible]	[illegible]	[illegible]	[illegible]	[illegible]	[illegible]	[illegible]	[illegible]	[illegible]	[illegible]	[illegible]	[illegible]	[illegible]	[illegible]	Carrick-on-Shannon.
[illegible]	[illegible]	[illegible]	[illegible]	[illegible]	[illegible]	[illegible]	[illegible]	[illegible]	[illegible]	[illegible]	[illegible]	[illegible]	[illegible]	[illegible]	[illegible]	[illegible]	[illegible]	[illegible]	[illegible]	[illegible]	[illegible]	[illegible]
[illegible]	[illegible]	[illegible]	[illegible]	[illegible]	[illegible]	[illegible]	[illegible]	[illegible]	[illegible]	[illegible]	[illegible]	[illegible]	[illegible]	[illegible]	[illegible]	[illegible]	[illegible]	[illegible]	[illegible]	[illegible]	[illegible]	[illegible]
[illegible]	[illegible]	[illegible]	[illegible]	[illegible]	[illegible]	[illegible]	[illegible]	[illegible]	[illegible]	[illegible]	[illegible]	[illegible]	[illegible]	[illegible]	[illegible]	[illegible]	[illegible]	[illegible]	[illegible]	[illegible]	[illegible]	[illegible]
[illegible]	[illegible]	[illegible]	[illegible]	[illegible]	[illegible]	[illegible]	[illegible]	[illegible]	[illegible]	[illegible]	[illegible]	[illegible]	[illegible]	[illegible]	[illegible]	[illegible]	[illegible]	[illegible]	[illegible]	[illegible]	[illegible]	Omagh.
[illegible]	[illegible]	[illegible]	[illegible]	[illegible]	[illegible]	[illegible]	[illegible]	[illegible]	[illegible]	[illegible]	[illegible]	[illegible]	[illegible]	[illegible]	[illegible]	[illegible]	[illegible]	[illegible]	[illegible]	[illegible]	[illegible]	Wicklow.
[illegible]	[illegible]	[illegible]	[illegible]	[illegible]	[illegible]	[illegible]	[illegible]	[illegible]	[illegible]	[illegible]	[illegible]	[illegible]	[illegible]	[illegible]	[illegible]	[illegible]	[illegible]	[illegible]	[illegible]	[illegible]	[illegible]	[illegible]
[illegible]	[illegible]	[illegible]	[illegible]	[illegible]	[illegible]	[illegible]	[illegible]	[illegible]	[illegible]	[illegible]	[illegible]	[illegible]	[illegible]	[illegible]	[illegible]	[illegible]	[illegible]	[illegible]	[illegible]	[illegible]	[illegible]	TOTAL.
[illegible]		[illegible]		[illegible]		[illegible]		[illegible]		[illegible]		[illegible]		[illegible]				[illegible]		[illegible]		

TABLE 89.—CRIMINAL PRISONERS.—Numbers

(Court Martial Prisoners are

PRISONS (1)	January. (2)	February. (3)	March. (4)	April. (5)	May. (6)	June. (7)
Larger Prisons.						
Armagh,	[illegible]	[illegible]	[illegible]	[illegible]	[illegible]	[illegible]
Belfast,	[illegible]	[illegible]	[illegible]	[illegible]	[illegible]	[illegible]
Castlebar,	[illegible]	[illegible]	[illegible]	[illegible]	[illegible]	[illegible]
Clonmel,	[illegible]	[illegible]	[illegible]	[illegible]	[illegible]	[illegible]
Cork, Male,	[illegible]	[illegible]	[illegible]	[illegible]	[illegible]	[illegible]
Cork, Female,	[illegible]	[illegible]	[illegible]	[illegible]	[illegible]	[illegible]
Dundalk,	[illegible]	[illegible]	[illegible]	[illegible]	[illegible]	[illegible]
Galway,	[illegible]	[illegible]	[illegible]	[illegible]	[illegible]	[illegible]
Grangegorman, Female,	[illegible]	[illegible]	[illegible]	[illegible]	[illegible]	[illegible]
Kilkenny,	[illegible]	[illegible]	[illegible]	[illegible]	[illegible]	[illegible]
Kilmainham,	[illegible]	[illegible]	[illegible]	[illegible]	[illegible]	[illegible]
Limerick, Male,	[illegible]	[illegible]	[illegible]	[illegible]	[illegible]	[illegible]
Limerick, Female,	[illegible]	[illegible]	[illegible]	[illegible]	[illegible]	[illegible]
Londonderry	[illegible]	[illegible]	[illegible]	[illegible]	[illegible]	[illegible]
Mountjoy,	[illegible]	[illegible]	[illegible]	[illegible]	[illegible]	[illegible]
Sligo,	[illegible]	[illegible]	[illegible]	[illegible]	[illegible]	[illegible]
Tralee,	[illegible]	[illegible]	[illegible]	[illegible]	[illegible]	[illegible]
Tullamore	[illegible]	[illegible]	[illegible]	[illegible]	[illegible]	[illegible]
Waterford,	[illegible]	[illegible]	[illegible]	[illegible]	[illegible]	[illegible]
Wexford,	[illegible]	[illegible]	[illegible]	[illegible]	[illegible]	[illegible]
Minor Prisons.						
Carrick-on-Shannon,	[illegible]	[illegible]	[illegible]	[illegible]	[illegible]	[illegible]
Drogheda,	[illegible]	[illegible]	[illegible]	[illegible]	[illegible]	[illegible]
[illegible]	[illegible]	[illegible]	[illegible]	[illegible]	[illegible]	[illegible]
Mullingar,	[illegible]	[illegible]	[illegible]	[illegible]	[illegible]	[illegible]
Omagh,	[illegible]	[illegible]	[illegible]	[illegible]	[illegible]	[illegible]
Wicklow,	[illegible]	[illegible]	[illegible]	[illegible]	[illegible]	[illegible]
Prison Bridewells and Lock-ups	[illegible]	[illegible]	[illegible]	[illegible]	[illegible]	[illegible]
TOTAL,	[illegible]	[illegible]	[illegible]	[illegible]	[illegible]	[illegible]

received in Prison in each Month of the Year.

(not included in this Table.)

July. ([illegible])	August. ([illegible])	September. ([illegible])	October. ([illegible])	November. ([illegible])	December. ([illegible])	PRISONS.
						Larger Prisons.
[illegible]	[illegible]	[illegible]	[illegible]	[illegible]	[illegible]	Armagh.
[illegible]	[illegible]	[illegible]	[illegible]	[illegible]	[illegible]	Belfast.
[illegible]	[illegible]	[illegible]	[illegible]	[illegible]	[illegible]	Castlebar.
[illegible]	[illegible]	[illegible]	[illegible]	[illegible]	[illegible]	Clonmel.
[illegible]	[illegible]	[illegible]	[illegible]	[illegible]	[illegible]	Cork, Male.
[illegible]	[illegible]	[illegible]	[illegible]	[illegible]	[illegible]	Cork, Female.
[illegible]	[illegible]	[illegible]	[illegible]	[illegible]	[illegible]	Dundalk.
[illegible]	[illegible]	[illegible]	71	[illegible]	[illegible]	Galway.
[illegible]	[illegible]	[illegible]	[illegible]	[illegible]	[illegible]	Grangegorman, Female.
[illegible]	[illegible]	[illegible]	[illegible]	[illegible]	[illegible]	Kilkenny.
[illegible]	[illegible]	[illegible]	[illegible]	[illegible]	[illegible]	Kilmainham.
[illegible]	[illegible]	[illegible]	[illegible]	[illegible]	[illegible]	Limerick, Male.
[illegible]	[illegible]	[illegible]	[illegible]	[illegible]	[illegible]	Limerick, Female.
[illegible]	[illegible]	[illegible]	[illegible]	[illegible]	[illegible]	Londonderry.
[illegible]	[illegible]	[illegible]	[illegible]	[illegible]	[illegible]	Mountjoy.
[illegible]	[illegible]	[illegible]	[illegible]	[illegible]	[illegible]	Sligo.
[illegible]	[illegible]	[illegible]	[illegible]	[illegible]	[illegible]	Tralee.
[illegible]	[illegible]	[illegible]	[illegible]	[illegible]	[illegible]	Tullamore.
[illegible]	[illegible]	[illegible]	[illegible]	[illegible]	[illegible]	Waterford.
[illegible]	[illegible]	[illegible]	[illegible]	[illegible]	[illegible]	Wexford.
						Minor Prisons.
[illegible]	[illegible]	[illegible]	[illegible]	[illegible]	[illegible]	Carrick-on-Shannon.
[illegible]	[illegible]	[illegible]	[illegible]	[illegible]	[illegible]	Drogheda.
[illegible]	[illegible]	[illegible]	[illegible]	[illegible]	[illegible]	Enniskillen.
[illegible]	[illegible]	[illegible]	[illegible]	[illegible]	[illegible]	Mullingar.
[illegible]	[illegible]	[illegible]	[illegible]	[illegible]	[illegible]	Omagh.
[illegible]	[illegible]	[illegible]	[illegible]	[illegible]	[illegible]	Wicklow.
[illegible]	[illegible]	[illegible]	[illegible]	[illegible]	[illegible]	Prisons, Bridewells and one Lock-up.
[illegible]	[illegible]	[illegible]	[illegible]	[illegible]	[illegible]	TOTAL.

TABLE 40.—CONVICTS.—Length of Sentences of Convicts under detention on December 31st, 1896.

Length of Sentences. (1)	Total. (2)	[illegible] (3) Over 3 Years.	3 Years and over 1 Year.	1 Year and under.	[illegible] (4)
Life (Death commuted),	[illegible]	-	-		
Life,	[illegible]	-	-		
20 Years,	[illegible]	-	-		
[illegible]	[illegible]	-	-		
[illegible]	[illegible]	-	[illegible]		
[illegible]	-	-	-		
[illegible]	[illegible]	-	-		
[illegible]	-	-	-		
[illegible]	-	-	-		
[illegible]	[illegible]	-	-		
[illegible]	[illegible]	-	-		
[illegible]	-	-	-		
[illegible]	[illegible]	-	-	-	
[illegible]	-	-	-	-	
[illegible]	[illegible]	[illegible]	[illegible]	[illegible]	
9	-	-	-	-	
[illegible]	-	-	-	-	
[illegible]	[illegible]	[illegible]	[illegible]	[illegible]	
[illegible]	[illegible]	-	-	-	
[illegible]	[illegible]	-	[illegible]	[illegible]	
[illegible]	[illegible]	[illegible]	-	-	
3	[illegible]	[illegible]	-	[illegible]	-
[illegible] Licence only. Over 3 Years,	[illegible]	-	-	-	-
3 Years and over 1 Year,	[illegible]	-	-	-	-
1 Year and under,	[illegible]	-	-	-	-
TOTAL,	[illegible]	[illegible]	[illegible]	[illegible]	-

REFORMATORY AND INDUSTRIAL SCHOOLS.

REFORMATORY AND INDUSTRIAL SCHOOLS.

41.—REFORMATORY SCHOOLS.—Committals and Sentences.

42.—REFORMATORY SCHOOLS.—Offences.

43.—REFORMATORY SCHOOLS.—Age, Sex, State of Instruction and previous Commitments of Offenders.

44.—REFORMATORY SCHOOLS.—Numbers under Detention, Committed, Discharged, and Removed.

45.—INDUSTRIAL SCHOOLS.—Numbers under Detention, Committed, Discharged, and Removed, with Age, Sex, and State of Instruction.

46.—INDUSTRIAL SCHOOLS.—Discharges, and Terms of Detention actually served.

47.—INDUSTRIAL SCHOOLS.—Grounds of Committal.

TABLE 41.—REFORMATORY SCHOOLS.—Return showing Occasion of Committals and Sentences passed upon Boys and Girls Received during the Year 1896. Made by the Inspector of Reformatories and Industrial Schools.

Certified Schools. [illegible]	Committals: [illegible]	[illegible]	Total Committed [illegible]	Previous Imprisonment: [illegible]	[illegible]	[illegible]	[illegible]	[illegible]	[illegible]	Term of Committal: 2 Years.	3 [illegible]	4 [illegible]	5 [illegible]
Boys.													
[illegible] (Protestant)	[illegible]	[illegible]	[illegible]	[illegible]	[illegible]	[illegible]	.	.	.	.	[illegible]	[illegible]	[illegible]
[illegible] (Roman Catholic)	.	[illegible]	[illegible]	[illegible]	[illegible]	.	.	.	.	.	[illegible]	[illegible]	[illegible]
St. Kevin's, Glencree, [illegible] April, [illegible] (Roman Catholic)	[illegible]	[illegible]	[illegible]	[illegible]	[illegible]	.	.	.	.	.	[illegible]	[illegible]	[illegible]
Total Boys,	[illegible]	[illegible]	[illegible]	[illegible]	[illegible]	[illegible]				.	[illegible]	[illegible]	[illegible]
Girls.													
[illegible] (Roman Catholic)	.	[illegible]	[illegible]	[illegible]	.	.	.	.	.	.	.	[illegible]	.
St. Joseph's, Limerick, [illegible] January, [illegible] (Roman Catholic)	.	[illegible]	[illegible]	[illegible]	[illegible]	.	.	.	.	.	[illegible]	[illegible]	[illegible]
[illegible] (Roman Catholic)	.	[illegible]	[illegible]	[illegible]	.	.	.	.	.	.	.	.	[illegible]
Total Girls,	.	9	[illegible]	[illegible]	[illegible]	.	.	.	.	.	[illegible]	[illegible]	[illegible]
Total Boys and Girls,	[illegible]	[illegible]	113	[illegible]	[illegible]	[illegible]	.	.	.	.	[illegible]	[illegible]	[illegible]
Total Protestants,	[illegible]	[illegible]	[illegible]	17	[illegible]	[illegible]	.	.	.	.	[illegible]	[illegible]	[illegible]
Total Roman Catholics,	[illegible]	[illegible]	[illegible]	[illegible]	[illegible]	.	.	.	.	.	[illegible]	[illegible]	[illegible]

TABLE 42.—REFORMATORY SCHOOLS.—Return of Offences of which the Boys and Girls were Convicted, who were Received under Stat. 31 & 32 Vic., c. 59, into Reformatory Schools during the Year 1896. Made by the Inspector of Reformatories and Industrial Schools.

Offences.	Boys. [illegible]	[illegible]	[illegible]	Girls. [illegible]	[illegible]	[illegible]	Total: B.	G.	B. & G.
Larceny and Petty Theft,	[illegible]	[illegible]	[illegible]	.	[illegible]	[illegible]	[illegible]	[illegible]	[illegible]
" of Firearms,	.	.	.	.	.	.	.	.	.
" by Servants,	.	[illegible]	.	.	.	.	[illegible]	.	[illegible]
" from Person,	.	[illegible]	[illegible]	.	.	.	[illegible]	.	[illegible]
" in Dwelling-house,	.	[illegible]	.	.	.	.	[illegible]	.	[illegible]
Attempt to Steal,	.	.	[illegible]	.	.	.	[illegible]	.	[illegible]
Unlawful Possession of Goods,	.	[illegible]	[illegible]	.	.	.	[illegible]	.	[illegible]
Receiving Stolen Goods,	.	.	.	.	.	.	.	.	.
Fraudulent Offences,	.	.	[illegible]	.	.	.	[illegible]	.	[illegible]
Embezzlement,	.	.	.	.	.	.	.	.	.
Horse Stealing,	.	.	.	.	.	.	.	.	.
Sheep Stealing,	.	.	.	.	.	.	.	.	.
Cattle Stealing,	.	.	.	.	.	.	.	.	.
Housebreaking, Shopbreaking, &c.,	[illegible]	.	[illegible]	.	.	.	[illegible]	.	[illegible]
Burglary,	.	.	.	[illegible]	.	.	.	.	.
Robbery on the Highway,	.	.	.	.	.	.	.	.	.
Attempt to Break into Houses, &c.,	.	.	.	.	.	.	.	.	.
Arson and Wilful Burning,	.	.	.	.	.	.	.	.	.
Wilful Damage and other Malicious Offences,	.	[illegible]	[illegible]	.	.	.	[illegible]	.	[illegible]
Assaults,	[illegible]	[illegible]	[illegible]	.	.	.	[illegible]	.	[illegible]
Assaults with Intent to Ravish,	.	.	.	.	.	.	.	.	.
Forgery,	.	.	.	.	.	.	.	.	.
Uttering Counterfeit Coin,	.	.	.	.	.	.	.	.	.
Vagrancy,	.	[illegible]	[illegible]	[illegible]	[illegible]	.	[illegible]	[illegible]	[illegible]
Other Offences,	.	[illegible]	[illegible]	.	.	.	[illegible]	.	[illegible]
Total,	[illegible]	[illegible]	[illegible]	[illegible]	[illegible]	[illegible]	[illegible]	[illegible]	[illegible]

TABLE 4[illegible].—REFORMATORY SCHOOLS.—Return showing Age, State of Instruction, [illegible] Stat. 21 & 22 Vic., c. [illegible], into Reformatory Schools during the Year

SCHOOLS.	Total	Age when admitted: [illegible]	[illegible]	[illegible]	[illegible]	State of Instruction on Admission: [illegible]	[illegible]	[illegible]	[illegible]	[illegible]
BOYS.										
Malone, Belfast,	[illegible]	1	7	[illegible]	[illegible]	[illegible]	[illegible]	[illegible]	1	.
Philipstown, King's Co.,	[illegible]	1	11	[illegible]	[illegible]	[illegible]	[illegible]	.	.	.
Glencree, Co. Wicklow,	[illegible]		1	15	[illegible]	[illegible]	15	1	.	.
TOTAL,	[illegible]	1	[illegible]	[illegible]	[illegible]	[illegible]	[illegible]	[illegible]	1	.
GIRLS.										
High Park, Dublin,	1	.	.	.	1	1	.	.	.	.
Limerick,	7	1	[illegible]	[illegible]	[illegible]	[illegible]	3	.	.	.
[illegible],	1	.	.	1	.	1	.	.	.	.
TOTAL,	[illegible]	1	[illegible]	[illegible]	1	[illegible]	3	.	.	.
TOTAL BOYS AND GIRLS,	[illegible]	[illegible]	[illegible]	[illegible]	[illegible]	[illegible]	[illegible]	[illegible]	1	.

previous Commitments, and Social Condition of the Boys and Girls received, under 1896. Made by the Inspector of Reformatories and Industrial Schools.

Previously committed to ... Prison: Once	Twice	Three and upwards	Not previously committed	Social Condition of Applicants: Illegitimate	Both Parents dead	Father dead	Mother dead	Deserted by Parents	Both Parents destitute or ...	Both Parents alive, and ...	SCHOOLS.
											BOYS.
[illegible]	..	..	17	..	[illegible]	[illegible]	[illegible]	..	..	[illegible]	[illegible], Belfast.
7	4	..	[illegible]	1	6	6	[illegible]	..	..	[illegible]	Philipstown, King's Co.
5	1	..	[illegible]	1	[illegible]	[illegible]	4	1	..	[illegible]	Glencree, Co. Wicklow.
[illegible]	4	..	[illegible]	[illegible]	[illegible]	[illegible]	[illegible]	1	..	[illegible]	TOTAL.
											GIRLS.
..	..	..	[illegible]	..	..	..	..	..	..	1	High Park, Dublin.
1	..	..	[illegible]	..	1	[illegible]	[illegible]	..	1	1	Limerick.
..	..	..	[illegible]	..	..	..	..	..	..	1	Monaghan.
[illegible]	..	..	[illegible]	..	[illegible]	3	1	..	1	[illegible]	TOTAL.
[illegible]	[illegible]	..	[illegible]	[illegible]	[illegible]	[illegible]	[illegible]	[illegible]	1	[illegible]	TOTAL BOYS AND GIRLS.

Girls under Detention, Committed, Discharged, and Removed in the Year 1896
and Industrial Schools.

Remaining under Detention at end of Year.				Discharged or	

TABLE 46.—INDUSTRIAL SCHOOLS.—Return showing the Number under Detention, ... Stat. 31 Vic., c. 25. Made by the Inspector

INDUSTRIAL SCHOOLS, ARRANGED IN COUNTIES.	Under Detention ... Year: In School	On Licence	Absconded	[illegible]	Total	Admitted ... Year: Committed during the Year	Received from other Industrial Schools	[illegible]	Discharged, ... Year: [illegible]	[illegible]	[illegible]	Dead	Total [illegible]
GIRLS.													
Antrim:													
Hampton House (Protestant),	[illegible]	[illegible]	[illegible]	[illegible]	[illegible]	[illegible]	[illegible]	[illegible]	[illegible]	[illegible]	[illegible]	[illegible]	[illegible]
St. Patrick's (R.C.), Belfast,	[illegible]	[illegible]	[illegible]	[illegible]	[illegible]	[illegible]	[illegible]	[illegible]	[illegible]	[illegible]	[illegible]	[illegible]	[illegible]
Abbeyville (R.C.), Belfast,	[illegible]	[illegible]	[illegible]	[illegible]	[illegible]	[illegible]	[illegible]	[illegible]	[illegible]	[illegible]	[illegible]	[illegible]	[illegible]
[illegible] Lodge (Protestant),	[illegible]	[illegible]	[illegible]	[illegible]	[illegible]	[illegible]	[illegible]	[illegible]	[illegible]	[illegible]	[illegible]	[illegible]	[illegible]
Armagh:													
[illegible] (R.C.),	[illegible]	[illegible]	[illegible]	[illegible]	[illegible]	[illegible]	[illegible]	[illegible]	[illegible]	[illegible]	[illegible]	[illegible]	[illegible]
Cavan:													
[illegible],	[illegible]	[illegible]	[illegible]	[illegible]	[illegible]	[illegible]	[illegible]	[illegible]	[illegible]	[illegible]	[illegible]	[illegible]	[illegible]
St. Joseph's, Cavan (R.C.),	[illegible]	[illegible]	[illegible]	[illegible]	[illegible]	[illegible]	[illegible]	[illegible]	[illegible]	[illegible]	[illegible]	[illegible]	[illegible]
Clare:													
Ennis,	[illegible]	[illegible]	[illegible]	[illegible]	[illegible]	[illegible]	[illegible]	[illegible]	[illegible]	[illegible]	[illegible]	[illegible]	[illegible]
Cork:													
St. Aloysius', Clonakilty (R.C.),	[illegible]	[illegible]	[illegible]	[illegible]	[illegible]	[illegible]	[illegible]	[illegible]	[illegible]	[illegible]	[illegible]	[illegible]	[illegible]
St. [illegible], Queenstown (R.C.),	[illegible]	[illegible]	[illegible]	[illegible]	[illegible]	[illegible]	[illegible]	[illegible]	[illegible]	[illegible]	[illegible]	[illegible]	[illegible]
Our Lady of Mercy, [illegible] (R.C.),	[illegible]	[illegible]	[illegible]	[illegible]	[illegible]	[illegible]	[illegible]	[illegible]	[illegible]	[illegible]	[illegible]	[illegible]	[illegible]
St. [illegible] House, [illegible] (Protestant),	[illegible]	[illegible]	[illegible]	[illegible]	[illegible]	[illegible]	[illegible]	[illegible]	[illegible]	[illegible]	[illegible]	[illegible]	[illegible]
Mallow,	[illegible]	[illegible]	[illegible]	[illegible]	[illegible]	[illegible]	[illegible]	[illegible]	[illegible]	[illegible]	[illegible]	[illegible]	[illegible]
St. Finbar's, Cork (R.C.),	[illegible]	[illegible]	[illegible]	[illegible]	[illegible]	[illegible]	[illegible]	[illegible]	[illegible]	[illegible]	[illegible]	[illegible]	[illegible]
[illegible] Home, Cork (Protestant),	[illegible]	[illegible]	[illegible]	[illegible]	[illegible]	[illegible]	[illegible]	[illegible]	[illegible]	[illegible]	[illegible]	[illegible]	[illegible]
Dublin:													
[illegible], Dublin (R.C.),	[illegible]	[illegible]	[illegible]	[illegible]	[illegible]	[illegible]	[illegible]	[illegible]	[illegible]	[illegible]	[illegible]	[illegible]	[illegible]
[illegible] (R.C.),	[illegible]	[illegible]	[illegible]	[illegible]	[illegible]	[illegible]	[illegible]	[illegible]	[illegible]	[illegible]	[illegible]	[illegible]	[illegible]
[illegible],	[illegible]	[illegible]	[illegible]	[illegible]	[illegible]	[illegible]	[illegible]	[illegible]	[illegible]	[illegible]	[illegible]	[illegible]	[illegible]
[illegible] (R.C.),	[illegible]	[illegible]	[illegible]	[illegible]	[illegible]	[illegible]	[illegible]	[illegible]	[illegible]	[illegible]	[illegible]	[illegible]	[illegible]
[illegible] (R.C.),	[illegible]	[illegible]	[illegible]	[illegible]	[illegible]	[illegible]	[illegible]	[illegible]	[illegible]	[illegible]	[illegible]	[illegible]	[illegible]
[illegible], Dublin (Protestant),	[illegible]	[illegible]	[illegible]	[illegible]	[illegible]	[illegible]	[illegible]	[illegible]	[illegible]	[illegible]	[illegible]	[illegible]	[illegible]
Galway:													
Ballinasloe (R.C.),	[illegible]	[illegible]	[illegible]	[illegible]	[illegible]	[illegible]	[illegible]	[illegible]	[illegible]	[illegible]	[illegible]	[illegible]	[illegible]
Loughrea (R.C.),	[illegible]	[illegible]	[illegible]	[illegible]	[illegible]	[illegible]	[illegible]	[illegible]	[illegible]	[illegible]	[illegible]	[illegible]	[illegible]
Clifden (R.C.),	[illegible]	[illegible]	[illegible]	[illegible]	[illegible]	[illegible]	[illegible]	[illegible]	[illegible]	[illegible]	[illegible]	[illegible]	[illegible]
[illegible] (R.C.),	[illegible]	[illegible]	[illegible]	[illegible]	[illegible]	[illegible]	[illegible]	[illegible]	[illegible]	[illegible]	[illegible]	[illegible]	[illegible]
St. Anne's, Galway (R.C.),	[illegible]	[illegible]	[illegible]	[illegible]	[illegible]	[illegible]	[illegible]	[illegible]	[illegible]	[illegible]	[illegible]	[illegible]	[illegible]
Kerry:													
[illegible] (R.C.),	[illegible]	[illegible]	[illegible]	[illegible]	[illegible]	[illegible]	[illegible]	[illegible]	[illegible]	[illegible]	[illegible]	[illegible]	[illegible]
[illegible] (R.C.),	[illegible]	[illegible]	[illegible]	[illegible]	[illegible]	[illegible]	[illegible]	[illegible]	[illegible]	[illegible]	[illegible]	[illegible]	[illegible]
Kilkenny:													
Kilkenny (R.C.),	[illegible]	[illegible]	[illegible]	[illegible]	[illegible]	[illegible]	[illegible]	[illegible]	[illegible]	[illegible]	[illegible]	[illegible]	[illegible]
King's County:													
[illegible] (R.C.),	[illegible]	[illegible]	[illegible]	[illegible]	[illegible]	[illegible]	[illegible]	[illegible]	[illegible]	[illegible]	[illegible]	[illegible]	[illegible]
Limerick:													
St. George's, Limerick (R.C.),	[illegible]	[illegible]	[illegible]	[illegible]	[illegible]	[illegible]	[illegible]	[illegible]	[illegible]	[illegible]	[illegible]	[illegible]	[illegible]
St. Vincent's, " (R.C.),	[illegible]	[illegible]	[illegible]	[illegible]	[illegible]	[illegible]	[illegible]	[illegible]	[illegible]	[illegible]	[illegible]	[illegible]	[illegible]
Longford:													
[illegible] (R.C.),	[illegible]	[illegible]	[illegible]	[illegible]	[illegible]	[illegible]	[illegible]	[illegible]	[illegible]	[illegible]	[illegible]	[illegible]	[illegible]
Louth:													
Dundalk (R.C.),	[illegible]	[illegible]	[illegible]	[illegible]	[illegible]	[illegible]	[illegible]	[illegible]	[illegible]	[illegible]	[illegible]	[illegible]	[illegible]
Mayo:													
[illegible],	[illegible]	[illegible]	[illegible]	[illegible]	[illegible]	[illegible]	[illegible]	[illegible]	[illegible]	[illegible]	[illegible]	[illegible]	[illegible]
Westport (R.C.),	[illegible]	[illegible]	[illegible]	[illegible]	[illegible]	[illegible]	[illegible]	[illegible]	[illegible]	[illegible]	[illegible]	[illegible]	[illegible]
Monaghan:													
Monaghan (R.C.),	[illegible]	[illegible]	[illegible]	[illegible]	[illegible]	[illegible]	[illegible]	[illegible]	[illegible]	[illegible]	[illegible]	[illegible]	[illegible]
Roscommon:													
[illegible] (R.C.),	[illegible]	[illegible]	[illegible]	[illegible]	[illegible]	[illegible]	[illegible]	[illegible]	[illegible]	[illegible]	[illegible]	[illegible]	[illegible]
[illegible], Athlone (R.C.),	[illegible]	[illegible]	[illegible]	[illegible]	[illegible]	[illegible]	[illegible]	[illegible]	[illegible]	[illegible]	[illegible]	[illegible]	[illegible]
Sligo:													
[illegible] Abbey (R.C.),	[illegible]	[illegible]	[illegible]	[illegible]	[illegible]	[illegible]	[illegible]	[illegible]	[illegible]	[illegible]	[illegible]	[illegible]	[illegible]
Sligo (R.C.),	[illegible]	[illegible]	[illegible]	[illegible]	[illegible]	[illegible]	[illegible]	[illegible]	[illegible]	[illegible]	[illegible]	[illegible]	[illegible]

Committed, Discharged, Removed, or Transferred in the Year 1896, with the Costs, under [illegible] of Reformatories and Industrial Schools.

[illegible]	[illegible]	[illegible]	[illegible]	[illegible]	[illegible]	[illegible]	[illegible]	[illegible]	[illegible]	[illegible]	[illegible]	[illegible]	[illegible]	Total Cost.	Imperial [illegible]	Local [illegible]	Other [illegible]	Fees	INDUSTRIAL SCHOOLS, ARRANGED IN COUNTIES.
														£	£	£	£	£	[illegible]
																			Antrim:
[illegible]	[illegible]	[illegible]	[illegible]	[illegible]	[illegible]	[illegible]	[illegible]	[illegible]	[illegible]	[illegible]	[illegible]	[illegible]	[illegible]	[illegible]	[illegible]	[illegible]	[illegible]	[illegible]	[illegible] (Protestant).
[illegible]	[illegible]	[illegible]	[illegible]	[illegible]	[illegible]	[illegible]	[illegible]	[illegible]	[illegible]	[illegible]	[illegible]	[illegible]	[illegible]	[illegible]	[illegible]	[illegible]	[illegible]	[illegible]	St. Patrick's (R.C.), Belfast.
[illegible]	[illegible]	[illegible]	[illegible]	[illegible]	[illegible]	[illegible]	[illegible]	[illegible]	[illegible]	[illegible]	[illegible]	[illegible]	[illegible]	[illegible]	[illegible]	[illegible]	[illegible]	[illegible]	[illegible] (R.C.), (Females).
[illegible]	[illegible]	[illegible]	[illegible]	[illegible]	[illegible]	[illegible]	[illegible]	[illegible]	[illegible]	[illegible]	[illegible]	[illegible]	[illegible]	[illegible]	[illegible]	[illegible]	[illegible]	[illegible]	[illegible] Lodge (Protestant).
																			Armagh:
[illegible]	[illegible]	[illegible]	[illegible]	[illegible]	[illegible]	[illegible]	[illegible]	[illegible]	[illegible]	[illegible]	[illegible]	[illegible]	[illegible]	[illegible]	[illegible]	[illegible]	[illegible]	[illegible]	[illegible] (R.C.)
																			Cavan:
[illegible]	[illegible]	[illegible]	[illegible]	[illegible]	[illegible]	[illegible]	[illegible]	[illegible]	[illegible]	[illegible]	[illegible]	[illegible]	[illegible]	[illegible]	[illegible]	[illegible]	[illegible]	[illegible]	[illegible]
[illegible]	[illegible]	[illegible]	[illegible]	[illegible]	[illegible]	[illegible]	[illegible]	[illegible]	[illegible]	[illegible]	[illegible]	[illegible]	[illegible]	[illegible]	[illegible]	[illegible]	[illegible]	[illegible]	St. Joseph's, Cavan (R.C.)
																			Clare:
[illegible]	[illegible]	[illegible]	[illegible]	[illegible]	[illegible]	[illegible]	[illegible]	[illegible]	[illegible]	[illegible]	[illegible]	[illegible]	[illegible]	[illegible]	[illegible]	[illegible]	[illegible]	[illegible]	Ennis.
																			Cork:
[illegible]	[illegible]	[illegible]	[illegible]	[illegible]	[illegible]	[illegible]	[illegible]	[illegible]	[illegible]	[illegible]	[illegible]	[illegible]	[illegible]	[illegible]	[illegible]	[illegible]	[illegible]	[illegible]	St. [illegible], [illegible] (R.C.)
[illegible]	[illegible]	[illegible]	[illegible]	[illegible]	[illegible]	[illegible]	[illegible]	[illegible]	[illegible]	[illegible]	[illegible]	[illegible]	[illegible]	[illegible]	[illegible]	[illegible]	[illegible]	[illegible]	St. Colman's, Queenstown (R.C.)
[illegible]	[illegible]	[illegible]	[illegible]	[illegible]	[illegible]	[illegible]	[illegible]	[illegible]	[illegible]	[illegible]	[illegible]	[illegible]	[illegible]	[illegible]	[illegible]	[illegible]	[illegible]	[illegible]	Our Lady of Mercy, Kinsale (R.C.)
[illegible]	[illegible]	[illegible]	[illegible]	[illegible]	[illegible]	[illegible]	[illegible]	[illegible]	[illegible]	[illegible]	[illegible]	[illegible]	[illegible]	[illegible]	[illegible]	[illegible]	[illegible]	[illegible]	St. John's Home, [illegible] (Protestant)
[illegible]	[illegible]	[illegible]	[illegible]	[illegible]	[illegible]	[illegible]	[illegible]	[illegible]	[illegible]	[illegible]	[illegible]	[illegible]	[illegible]	[illegible]	[illegible]	[illegible]	[illegible]	[illegible]	Mallow.
[illegible]	[illegible]	[illegible]	[illegible]	[illegible]	[illegible]	[illegible]	[illegible]	[illegible]	[illegible]	[illegible]	[illegible]	[illegible]	[illegible]	[illegible]	[illegible]	[illegible]	[illegible]	[illegible]	St. Finbarr's, Cork (R.C.)
[illegible]	[illegible]	[illegible]	[illegible]	[illegible]	[illegible]	[illegible]	[illegible]	[illegible]	[illegible]	[illegible]	[illegible]	[illegible]	[illegible]	[illegible]	[illegible]	[illegible]	[illegible]	[illegible]	Training Home, Cork (Protestant).
																			Dublin:
[illegible]	[illegible]	[illegible]	[illegible]	[illegible]	[illegible]	[illegible]	[illegible]	[illegible]	[illegible]	[illegible]	[illegible]	[illegible]	[illegible]	[illegible]	[illegible]	[illegible]	[illegible]	[illegible]	[illegible], Dublin (R.C.)
[illegible]	[illegible]	[illegible]	[illegible]	[illegible]	[illegible]	[illegible]	[illegible]	[illegible]	[illegible]	[illegible]	[illegible]	[illegible]	[illegible]	[illegible]	[illegible]	[illegible]	[illegible]	[illegible]	[illegible] (R.C.)
[illegible]	[illegible]	[illegible]	[illegible]	[illegible]	[illegible]	[illegible]	[illegible]	[illegible]	[illegible]	[illegible]	[illegible]	[illegible]	[illegible]	[illegible]	[illegible]	[illegible]	[illegible]	[illegible]	Golden Bridge.
[illegible]	[illegible]	[illegible]	[illegible]	[illegible]	[illegible]	[illegible]	[illegible]	[illegible]	[illegible]	[illegible]	[illegible]	[illegible]	[illegible]	[illegible]	[illegible]	[illegible]	[illegible]	[illegible]	Lakelands, Sandymount (R.C.)
[illegible]	[illegible]	[illegible]	[illegible]	[illegible]	[illegible]	[illegible]	[illegible]	[illegible]	[illegible]	[illegible]	[illegible]	[illegible]	[illegible]	[illegible]	[illegible]	[illegible]	[illegible]	[illegible]	[illegible] (R.C.)
[illegible]	[illegible]	[illegible]	[illegible]	[illegible]	[illegible]	[illegible]	[illegible]	[illegible]	[illegible]	[illegible]	[illegible]	[illegible]	[illegible]	[illegible]	[illegible]	[illegible]	[illegible]	[illegible]	[illegible], Dublin (Protestant)
																			Galway:
[illegible]	[illegible]	[illegible]	[illegible]	[illegible]	[illegible]	[illegible]	[illegible]	[illegible]	[illegible]	[illegible]	[illegible]	[illegible]	[illegible]	[illegible]	[illegible]	[illegible]	[illegible]	[illegible]	[illegible] (R.C.)
[illegible]	[illegible]	[illegible]	[illegible]	[illegible]	[illegible]	[illegible]	[illegible]	[illegible]	[illegible]	[illegible]	[illegible]	[illegible]	[illegible]	[illegible]	[illegible]	[illegible]	[illegible]	[illegible]	Ballinasloe (R.C.)
[illegible]	[illegible]	[illegible]	[illegible]	[illegible]	[illegible]	[illegible]	[illegible]	[illegible]	[illegible]	[illegible]	[illegible]	[illegible]	[illegible]	[illegible]	[illegible]	[illegible]	[illegible]	[illegible]	Clifden (R.C.)
[illegible]	[illegible]	[illegible]	[illegible]	[illegible]	[illegible]	[illegible]	[illegible]	[illegible]	[illegible]	[illegible]	[illegible]	[illegible]	[illegible]	[illegible]	[illegible]	[illegible]	[illegible]	[illegible]	Oughterard (R.C.)
[illegible]	[illegible]	[illegible]	[illegible]	[illegible]	[illegible]	[illegible]	[illegible]	[illegible]	[illegible]	[illegible]	[illegible]	[illegible]	[illegible]	[illegible]	[illegible]	[illegible]	[illegible]	[illegible]	St. Anne's, Galway (R.C.)
																			Kerry:
[illegible]	[illegible]	[illegible]	[illegible]	[illegible]	[illegible]	[illegible]	[illegible]	[illegible]	[illegible]	[illegible]	[illegible]	[illegible]	[illegible]	[illegible]	[illegible]	[illegible]	[illegible]	[illegible]	Killarney (R.C.)
[illegible]	[illegible]	[illegible]	[illegible]	[illegible]	[illegible]	[illegible]	[illegible]	[illegible]	[illegible]	[illegible]	[illegible]	[illegible]	[illegible]	[illegible]	[illegible]	[illegible]	[illegible]	[illegible]	[illegible] (R.C.)
																			Kilkenny:
[illegible]	[illegible]	[illegible]	[illegible]	[illegible]	[illegible]	[illegible]	[illegible]	[illegible]	[illegible]	[illegible]	[illegible]	[illegible]	[illegible]	[illegible]	[illegible]	[illegible]	[illegible]	[illegible]	Kilkenny (R.C.)
																			King's County:
[illegible]	[illegible]	[illegible]	[illegible]	[illegible]	[illegible]	[illegible]	[illegible]	[illegible]	[illegible]	[illegible]	[illegible]	[illegible]	[illegible]	[illegible]	[illegible]	[illegible]	[illegible]	[illegible]	[illegible] (R.C.)
																			Limerick:
[illegible]	[illegible]	[illegible]	[illegible]	[illegible]	[illegible]	[illegible]	[illegible]	[illegible]	[illegible]	[illegible]	[illegible]	[illegible]	[illegible]	[illegible]	[illegible]	[illegible]	[illegible]	[illegible]	St. George's, Limerick (R.C.)
[illegible]	[illegible]	[illegible]	[illegible]	[illegible]	[illegible]	[illegible]	[illegible]	[illegible]	[illegible]	[illegible]	[illegible]	[illegible]	[illegible]	[illegible]	[illegible]	[illegible]	[illegible]	[illegible]	St. Vincent's „ (R.C.)
																			Longford:
[illegible]	[illegible]	[illegible]	[illegible]	[illegible]	[illegible]	[illegible]	[illegible]	[illegible]	[illegible]	[illegible]	[illegible]	[illegible]	[illegible]	[illegible]	[illegible]	[illegible]	[illegible]	[illegible]	[illegible] (R.C.)
																			Louth:
[illegible]	[illegible]	[illegible]	[illegible]	[illegible]	[illegible]	[illegible]	[illegible]	[illegible]	[illegible]	[illegible]	[illegible]	[illegible]	[illegible]	[illegible]	[illegible]	[illegible]	[illegible]	[illegible]	Dundalk (R.C.)
																			Mayo:
[illegible]	[illegible]	[illegible]	[illegible]	[illegible]	[illegible]	[illegible]	[illegible]	[illegible]	[illegible]	[illegible]	[illegible]	[illegible]	[illegible]	[illegible]	[illegible]	[illegible]	[illegible]	[illegible]	[illegible]
[illegible]	[illegible]	[illegible]	[illegible]	[illegible]	[illegible]	[illegible]	[illegible]	[illegible]	[illegible]	[illegible]	[illegible]	[illegible]	[illegible]	[illegible]	[illegible]	[illegible]	[illegible]	[illegible]	Westport (R.C.)
																			Monaghan:
[illegible]	[illegible]	[illegible]	[illegible]	[illegible]	[illegible]	[illegible]	[illegible]	[illegible]	[illegible]	[illegible]	[illegible]	[illegible]	[illegible]	[illegible]	[illegible]	[illegible]	[illegible]	[illegible]	Monaghan (R.C.)
																			Roscommon:
[illegible]	[illegible]	[illegible]	[illegible]	[illegible]	[illegible]	[illegible]	[illegible]	[illegible]	[illegible]	[illegible]	[illegible]	[illegible]	[illegible]	[illegible]	[illegible]	[illegible]	[illegible]	[illegible]	Roscommon (R.C.)
[illegible]	[illegible]	[illegible]	[illegible]	[illegible]	[illegible]	[illegible]	[illegible]	[illegible]	[illegible]	[illegible]	[illegible]	[illegible]	[illegible]	[illegible]	[illegible]	[illegible]	[illegible]	[illegible]	Summerhill, Athlone (R.C.)
																			Sligo:
[illegible]	[illegible]	[illegible]	[illegible]	[illegible]	[illegible]	[illegible]	[illegible]	[illegible]	[illegible]	[illegible]	[illegible]	[illegible]	[illegible]	[illegible]	[illegible]	[illegible]	[illegible]	[illegible]	Benada Abbey (R.C.)
[illegible]	[illegible]	[illegible]	[illegible]	[illegible]	[illegible]	[illegible]	[illegible]	[illegible]	[illegible]	[illegible]	[illegible]	[illegible]	[illegible]	[illegible]	[illegible]	[illegible]	[illegible]	[illegible]	Sligo (R.C.)

TABLE 44.—continued.—INDUSTRIAL SCHOOLS.—Return showing the Number [illegible]
Courts, under Stat. 31 Vic., c. 25. Made by [illegible]

INDUSTRIAL SCHOOLS, ARRANGED IN COUNTIES.	[illegible]					[illegible]			[illegible]			
	[illegible]	[illegible]	[illegible]	[illegible]	[illegible]	[illegible]	[illegible]	[illegible]	[illegible]	[illegible]	[illegible]	[illegible]
[illegible]—continued.												
[illegible]:												
[illegible] (R.C.)	[illegible]	[illegible]	[illegible]	[illegible]	[illegible]	[illegible]	[illegible]	[illegible]	[illegible]	[illegible]	[illegible]	[illegible]
[illegible] (R.C.)	[illegible]	[illegible]	[illegible]	[illegible]	[illegible]	[illegible]	[illegible]	[illegible]	[illegible]	[illegible]	[illegible]	[illegible]
[illegible] (R.C.)	[illegible]	[illegible]	[illegible]	[illegible]	[illegible]	[illegible]	[illegible]	[illegible]	[illegible]	[illegible]	[illegible]	[illegible]
[illegible] (R.C.)	[illegible]	[illegible]	[illegible]	[illegible]	[illegible]	[illegible]	[illegible]	[illegible]	[illegible]	[illegible]	[illegible]	[illegible]
[illegible]:												
[illegible] (R.C.)	[illegible]	[illegible]	[illegible]	[illegible]	[illegible]	[illegible]	[illegible]	[illegible]	[illegible]	[illegible]	[illegible]	[illegible]
[illegible]:												
[illegible] (R.C.)	[illegible]	[illegible]	[illegible]	[illegible]	[illegible]	[illegible]	[illegible]	[illegible]	[illegible]	[illegible]	[illegible]	[illegible]
[illegible]:												
[illegible] (R.C.)	[illegible]	[illegible]	[illegible]	[illegible]	[illegible]	[illegible]	[illegible]	[illegible]	[illegible]	[illegible]	[illegible]	[illegible]
[illegible]:												
[illegible] (R.C.)	[illegible]	[illegible]	[illegible]	[illegible]	[illegible]	[illegible]	[illegible]	[illegible]	[illegible]	[illegible]	[illegible]	[illegible]
[illegible] (R.C.)	[illegible]	[illegible]	[illegible]	[illegible]	[illegible]	[illegible]	[illegible]	[illegible]	[illegible]	[illegible]	[illegible]	[illegible]
[illegible]:												
[illegible]	[illegible]	[illegible]	[illegible]	[illegible]	[illegible]	[illegible]	[illegible]	[illegible]	[illegible]	[illegible]	[illegible]	[illegible]
[illegible]	[illegible]	[illegible]	[illegible]	[illegible]	[illegible]	[illegible]	[illegible]	[illegible]	[illegible]	[illegible]	[illegible]	[illegible]
[illegible]												
[illegible]:												
[illegible]	[illegible]	[illegible]	[illegible]	[illegible]	[illegible]	[illegible]	[illegible]	[illegible]	[illegible]	[illegible]	[illegible]	[illegible]
[illegible]	[illegible]	[illegible]	[illegible]	[illegible]	[illegible]	[illegible]	[illegible]	[illegible]	[illegible]	[illegible]	[illegible]	[illegible]
[illegible] (R.C.)	[illegible]	[illegible]	[illegible]	[illegible]	[illegible]	[illegible]	[illegible]	[illegible]	[illegible]	[illegible]	[illegible]	[illegible]
[illegible]:												
[illegible]	[illegible]	[illegible]	[illegible]	[illegible]	[illegible]	[illegible]	[illegible]	[illegible]	[illegible]	[illegible]	[illegible]	[illegible]
[illegible]	[illegible]	[illegible]	[illegible]	[illegible]	[illegible]	[illegible]	[illegible]	[illegible]	[illegible]	[illegible]	[illegible]	[illegible]
[illegible] (R.C.)	[illegible]	[illegible]	[illegible]	[illegible]	[illegible]	[illegible]	[illegible]	[illegible]	[illegible]	[illegible]	[illegible]	[illegible]
[illegible] (R.C.)	[illegible]	[illegible]	[illegible]	[illegible]	[illegible]	[illegible]	[illegible]	[illegible]	[illegible]	[illegible]	[illegible]	[illegible]
[illegible] (R.C.)	[illegible]	[illegible]	[illegible]	[illegible]	[illegible]	[illegible]	[illegible]	[illegible]	[illegible]	[illegible]	[illegible]	[illegible]
[illegible]:												
[illegible] (R.C.)	[illegible]	[illegible]	[illegible]	[illegible]	[illegible]	[illegible]	[illegible]	[illegible]	[illegible]	[illegible]	[illegible]	[illegible]
[illegible]:												
[illegible] (R.C.)	[illegible]	[illegible]	[illegible]	[illegible]	[illegible]	[illegible]	[illegible]	[illegible]	[illegible]	[illegible]	[illegible]	[illegible]
[illegible] (R.C.)	[illegible]	[illegible]	[illegible]	[illegible]	[illegible]	[illegible]	[illegible]	[illegible]	[illegible]	[illegible]	[illegible]	[illegible]
[illegible]	[illegible]	[illegible]	[illegible]	[illegible]	[illegible]	[illegible]	[illegible]	[illegible]	[illegible]	[illegible]	[illegible]	[illegible]
[illegible]:												
[illegible] (R.C.)	[illegible]	[illegible]	[illegible]	[illegible]	[illegible]	[illegible]	[illegible]	[illegible]	[illegible]	[illegible]	[illegible]	[illegible]
[illegible] (R.C.)	[illegible]	[illegible]	[illegible]	[illegible]	[illegible]	[illegible]	[illegible]	[illegible]	[illegible]	[illegible]	[illegible]	[illegible]
[illegible]:												
[illegible] (R.C.)	[illegible]	[illegible]	[illegible]	[illegible]	[illegible]	[illegible]	[illegible]	[illegible]	[illegible]	[illegible]	[illegible]	[illegible]
[illegible] (R.C.)	[illegible]	[illegible]	[illegible]	[illegible]	[illegible]	[illegible]	[illegible]	[illegible]	[illegible]	[illegible]	[illegible]	[illegible]
[illegible]:												
[illegible] (R.C.)	[illegible]	[illegible]	[illegible]	[illegible]	[illegible]	[illegible]	[illegible]	[illegible]	[illegible]	[illegible]	[illegible]	[illegible]
[illegible]:												
[illegible] (R.C.)	[illegible]	[illegible]	[illegible]	[illegible]	[illegible]	[illegible]	[illegible]	[illegible]	[illegible]	[illegible]	[illegible]	[illegible]
[illegible]:												
[illegible] (R.C.)	[illegible]	[illegible]	[illegible]	[illegible]	[illegible]	[illegible]	[illegible]	[illegible]	[illegible]	[illegible]	[illegible]	[illegible]

[illegible] Detention, Committed, Discharged, Removed, or Transferred in the Year 1896, with the [illegible] Inspector of Reformatories and Industrial Schools.

[illegible]	[illegible]	[illegible]	[illegible]	[illegible]	[illegible]	[illegible]	[illegible]	[illegible]	[illegible]	[illegible]	[illegible]	[illegible]	[illegible]	[illegible]	Total Cost	Contributions to: Imperial Treasury	Local Rates	Other Sources	[illegible]	INDUSTRIAL SCHOOLS, ARRANGED IN COUNTIES
																				GIRLS—continued.
																				Tipperary:
[illegible]	[illegible]	[illegible]	[illegible]	[illegible]	[illegible]	[illegible]	[illegible]	[illegible]	[illegible]	[illegible]	[illegible]	[illegible]	[illegible]	[illegible]	[illegible]	[illegible]	[illegible]	[illegible]	[illegible]	Templemore (R.C.)
[illegible]	[illegible]	[illegible]	[illegible]	[illegible]	[illegible]	[illegible]	[illegible]	[illegible]	[illegible]	[illegible]	[illegible]	[illegible]	[illegible]	[illegible]	[illegible]	[illegible]	[illegible]	[illegible]	[illegible]	Cashel (R.C.)
[illegible]	[illegible]	[illegible]	[illegible]	[illegible]	[illegible]	[illegible]	[illegible]	[illegible]	[illegible]	[illegible]	[illegible]	[illegible]	[illegible]	[illegible]	[illegible]	[illegible]	[illegible]	[illegible]	[illegible]	Thurles (R.C.)
[illegible]	[illegible]	[illegible]	[illegible]	[illegible]	[illegible]	[illegible]	[illegible]	[illegible]	[illegible]	[illegible]	[illegible]	[illegible]	[illegible]	[illegible]	[illegible]	[illegible]	[illegible]	[illegible]	[illegible]	Tipperary (R.C.)
																				Tyrone:
[illegible]	[illegible]	[illegible]	[illegible]	[illegible]	[illegible]	[illegible]	[illegible]	[illegible]	[illegible]	[illegible]	[illegible]	[illegible]	[illegible]	[illegible]	[illegible]	[illegible]	[illegible]	[illegible]	[illegible]	Strabane (R.C.)
																				Waterford:
[illegible]	[illegible]	[illegible]	[illegible]	[illegible]	[illegible]	[illegible]	[illegible]	[illegible]	[illegible]	[illegible]	[illegible]	[illegible]	[illegible]	[illegible]	[illegible]	[illegible]	[illegible]	[illegible]	[illegible]	Waterford (R.C.)
																				Westmeath:
[illegible]	[illegible]	[illegible]	[illegible]	[illegible]	[illegible]	[illegible]	[illegible]	[illegible]	[illegible]	[illegible]	[illegible]	[illegible]	[illegible]	[illegible]	[illegible]	[illegible]	[illegible]	[illegible]	[illegible]	Moate (R.C.)
																				Wexford:
[illegible]	[illegible]	[illegible]	[illegible]	[illegible]	[illegible]	[illegible]	[illegible]	[illegible]	[illegible]	[illegible]	[illegible]	[illegible]	[illegible]	[illegible]	[illegible]	[illegible]	[illegible]	[illegible]	[illegible]	New Ross (R.C.)
[illegible]	[illegible]	[illegible]	[illegible]	[illegible]	[illegible]	[illegible]	[illegible]	[illegible]	[illegible]	[illegible]	[illegible]	[illegible]	[illegible]	[illegible]	[illegible]	[illegible]	[illegible]	[illegible]	[illegible]	Wexford (R.C.)
																				Wicklow:
[illegible]	[illegible]	[illegible]	[illegible]	[illegible]	[illegible]	[illegible]	[illegible]	[illegible]	[illegible]	[illegible]	[illegible]	[illegible]	[illegible]	[illegible]	[illegible]	[illegible]	[illegible]	[illegible]	[illegible]	Bray (Protestant)
[illegible]	[illegible]	[illegible]	[illegible]	[illegible]	[illegible]	[illegible]	[illegible]	[illegible]	[illegible]	[illegible]	[illegible]	[illegible]	[illegible]	[illegible]	[illegible]	[illegible]	[illegible]	[illegible]	[illegible]	Total Girls
																				BOYS.
																				Antrim:
[illegible]	[illegible]	[illegible]	[illegible]	[illegible]	[illegible]	[illegible]	[illegible]	[illegible]	[illegible]	[illegible]	[illegible]	[illegible]	[illegible]	[illegible]	[illegible]	[illegible]	[illegible]	[illegible]	[illegible]	[illegible] (Protestant)
[illegible]	[illegible]	[illegible]	[illegible]	[illegible]	[illegible]	[illegible]	[illegible]	[illegible]	[illegible]	[illegible]	[illegible]	[illegible]	[illegible]	[illegible]	[illegible]	[illegible]	[illegible]	[illegible]	[illegible]	[illegible], Belfast (Protestant)
[illegible]	[illegible]	[illegible]	[illegible]	[illegible]	[illegible]	[illegible]	[illegible]	[illegible]	[illegible]	[illegible]	[illegible]	[illegible]	[illegible]	[illegible]	[illegible]	[illegible]	[illegible]	[illegible]	[illegible]	St. Patrick's (R.C.), Belfast
																				Cork:
[illegible]	[illegible]	[illegible]	[illegible]	[illegible]	[illegible]	[illegible]	[illegible]	[illegible]	[illegible]	[illegible]	[illegible]	[illegible]	[illegible]	[illegible]	[illegible]	[illegible]	[illegible]	[illegible]	[illegible]	Upton
[illegible]	[illegible]	[illegible]	[illegible]	[illegible]	[illegible]	[illegible]	[illegible]	[illegible]	[illegible]	[illegible]	[illegible]	[illegible]	[illegible]	[illegible]	[illegible]	[illegible]	[illegible]	[illegible]	[illegible]	Boys' Home, Cork (Protestant)
[illegible]	[illegible]	[illegible]	[illegible]	[illegible]	[illegible]	[illegible]	[illegible]	[illegible]	[illegible]	[illegible]	[illegible]	[illegible]	[illegible]	[illegible]	[illegible]	[illegible]	[illegible]	[illegible]	[illegible]	Passage West (R.C.)
[illegible]	[illegible]	[illegible]	[illegible]	[illegible]	[illegible]	[illegible]	[illegible]	[illegible]	[illegible]	[illegible]	[illegible]	[illegible]	[illegible]	[illegible]	[illegible]	[illegible]	[illegible]	[illegible]	[illegible]	Baltimore (R.C.)
[illegible]	[illegible]	[illegible]	[illegible]	[illegible]	[illegible]	[illegible]	[illegible]	[illegible]	[illegible]	[illegible]	[illegible]	[illegible]	[illegible]	[illegible]	[illegible]	[illegible]	[illegible]	[illegible]	[illegible]	Greenmount, Cork (R.C.)
																				Donegal:
[illegible]	[illegible]	[illegible]	[illegible]	[illegible]	[illegible]	[illegible]	[illegible]	[illegible]	[illegible]	[illegible]	[illegible]	[illegible]	[illegible]	[illegible]	[illegible]	[illegible]	[illegible]	[illegible]	[illegible]	Killybegs (R.C.)
																				Dublin:
[illegible]	[illegible]	[illegible]	[illegible]	[illegible]	[illegible]	[illegible]	[illegible]	[illegible]	[illegible]	[illegible]	[illegible]	[illegible]	[illegible]	[illegible]	[illegible]	[illegible]	[illegible]	[illegible]	[illegible]	Artane, Dublin (R.C.)
[illegible]	[illegible]	[illegible]	[illegible]	[illegible]	[illegible]	[illegible]	[illegible]	[illegible]	[illegible]	[illegible]	[illegible]	[illegible]	[illegible]	[illegible]	[illegible]	[illegible]	[illegible]	[illegible]	[illegible]	Carriglea (R.C.)
[illegible]	[illegible]	[illegible]	[illegible]	[illegible]	[illegible]	[illegible]	[illegible]	[illegible]	[illegible]	[illegible]	[illegible]	[illegible]	[illegible]	[illegible]	[illegible]	[illegible]	[illegible]	[illegible]	[illegible]	"Meath," [illegible] (Protestant)
																				Galway:
[illegible]	[illegible]	[illegible]	[illegible]	[illegible]	[illegible]	[illegible]	[illegible]	[illegible]	[illegible]	[illegible]	[illegible]	[illegible]	[illegible]	[illegible]	[illegible]	[illegible]	[illegible]	[illegible]	[illegible]	Letterfrack (R.C.)
[illegible]	[illegible]	[illegible]	[illegible]	[illegible]	[illegible]	[illegible]	[illegible]	[illegible]	[illegible]	[illegible]	[illegible]	[illegible]	[illegible]	[illegible]	[illegible]	[illegible]	[illegible]	[illegible]	[illegible]	Salt Hill (R.C.)
																				Kerry:
[illegible]	[illegible]	[illegible]	[illegible]	[illegible]	[illegible]	[illegible]	[illegible]	[illegible]	[illegible]	[illegible]	[illegible]	[illegible]	[illegible]	[illegible]	[illegible]	[illegible]	[illegible]	[illegible]	[illegible]	Killarney (R.C.)
[illegible]	[illegible]	[illegible]	[illegible]	[illegible]	[illegible]	[illegible]	[illegible]	[illegible]	[illegible]	[illegible]	[illegible]	[illegible]	[illegible]	[illegible]	[illegible]	[illegible]	[illegible]	[illegible]	[illegible]	St. Joseph's, Tralee (R.C.)
																				Kilkenny:
[illegible]	[illegible]	[illegible]	[illegible]	[illegible]	[illegible]	[illegible]	[illegible]	[illegible]	[illegible]	[illegible]	[illegible]	[illegible]	[illegible]	[illegible]	[illegible]	[illegible]	[illegible]	[illegible]	[illegible]	Kilkenny (R.C.)
																				Limerick:
[illegible]	[illegible]	[illegible]	[illegible]	[illegible]	[illegible]	[illegible]	[illegible]	[illegible]	[illegible]	[illegible]	[illegible]	[illegible]	[illegible]	[illegible]	[illegible]	[illegible]	[illegible]	[illegible]	[illegible]	Limerick (R.C.)
																				Louth:
[illegible]	[illegible]	[illegible]	[illegible]	[illegible]	[illegible]	[illegible]	[illegible]	[illegible]	[illegible]	[illegible]	[illegible]	[illegible]	[illegible]	[illegible]	[illegible]	[illegible]	[illegible]	[illegible]	[illegible]	Drogheda (R.C.)
																				Tipperary:
[illegible]	[illegible]	[illegible]	[illegible]	[illegible]	[illegible]	[illegible]	[illegible]	[illegible]	[illegible]	[illegible]	[illegible]	[illegible]	[illegible]	[illegible]	[illegible]	[illegible]	[illegible]	[illegible]	[illegible]	Clonmel
																				Waterford:
[illegible]	[illegible]	[illegible]	[illegible]	[illegible]	[illegible]	[illegible]	[illegible]	[illegible]	[illegible]	[illegible]	[illegible]	[illegible]	[illegible]	[illegible]	[illegible]	[illegible]	[illegible]	[illegible]	[illegible]	Cappoquin (R.C.)
																				Co. Wicklow:
[illegible]	[illegible]	[illegible]	[illegible]	[illegible]	[illegible]	[illegible]	[illegible]	[illegible]	[illegible]	[illegible]	[illegible]	[illegible]	[illegible]	[illegible]	[illegible]	[illegible]	[illegible]	[illegible]	[illegible]	St. Kyran's, Rathdrum (R.C.)
[illegible]	[illegible]	[illegible]	[illegible]	[illegible]	[illegible]	[illegible]	[illegible]	[illegible]	[illegible]	[illegible]	[illegible]	[illegible]	[illegible]	[illegible]	[illegible]	[illegible]	[illegible]	[illegible]	[illegible]	Total Boys
[illegible]	[illegible]	[illegible]	[illegible]	[illegible]	[illegible]	[illegible]	[illegible]	[illegible]	[illegible]	[illegible]	[illegible]	[illegible]	[illegible]	[illegible]	[illegible]	[illegible]	[illegible]	[illegible]	[illegible]	Total Girls
[illegible]	[illegible]	[illegible]	[illegible]	[illegible]	[illegible]	[illegible]	[illegible]	[illegible]	[illegible]	[illegible]	[illegible]	[illegible]	[illegible]	[illegible]	[illegible]	[illegible]	[illegible]	[illegible]	[illegible]	Total of Ireland

	[illegible]	[illegible]	[illegible]	[illegible]	[illegible]	[illegible]
	[illegible]	[illegible]	(4)	[illegible]	(6)	[illegible]
[illegible]	[illegible]	[illegible]	[illegible]	[illegible]	[illegible]	[illegible]

Licences, and Terms of Detention actually served.

Dead.	Escaped.	Licences. [illegible]	[illegible]	Number of Licences revoked.	[illegible] Years.	Days.	NAME OF SCHOOL.
[illegible]	[illegible]	[illegible]	[illegible]	[illegible]			
[illegible]	-	[illegible]	-	[illegible]	[illegible]	[illegible]	"[illegible]" Training Ship, Belfast.
-	-	[illegible]	-	[illegible]	[illegible]	[illegible]	[illegible], Belfast.
-	-	[illegible]	-	-	[illegible]	[illegible]	[illegible] House, Belfast.
[illegible]	-	[illegible]	[illegible]	[illegible]	[illegible]	[illegible]	St. Patrick's, [illegible], Belfast.
-	-	[illegible]	-	-	[illegible]	[illegible]	St. Patrick's, Crumlin Road, Belfast.
-	-	-	-	-	-	-	Sacred Heart, [illegible], Belfast.
[illegible]	-	[illegible]	-	-	[illegible]	[illegible]	[illegible] Lodge, Belfast.
[illegible]	-	[illegible]	-	-	[illegible]	[illegible]	Middletown, County Armagh.
-	-	[illegible]	-	-	[illegible]	[illegible]	Lurgan.
-	-	[illegible]	-	-	[illegible]	[illegible]	St. Joseph's, Cavan.
-	-	[illegible]	-	-	[illegible]	[illegible]	Ennis.
-	-	-	[illegible]	-	[illegible]	[illegible]	St. Aloysius', Clonakilty.
-	-	[illegible]	[illegible]	-	[illegible]	[illegible]	St. Colman's, Queenstown.
[illegible]	-	[illegible]	-	[illegible]	[illegible]	[illegible]	Our Lady of Mercy, Kinsale.
[illegible]	[illegible]	[illegible]	[illegible]	-	[illegible]	[illegible]	Upton, County Cork.
-	-	-	-	-	-	-	St. [illegible] House, [illegible] Quay, Cork.
-	[illegible]	-	-	-	-	-	Boys' Home, [illegible] Hill, [illegible], County Cork.
[illegible]	-	[illegible]	-	-	[illegible]	[illegible]	Mallow.
-	-	-	-	-	-	-	Passage West.
-	-	[illegible]	-	-	[illegible]	[illegible]	Baltimore.
[illegible]	-	-	-	-	[illegible]	[illegible]	St. Finbarr's, Sunday's Well, Cork.
-	-	[illegible]	-	-	[illegible]	[illegible]	Greenmount, Cork.
[illegible]	-	[illegible]	[illegible]	[illegible]	[illegible]	[illegible]	Training Home, Union Quay, Cork.
-	-	-	-	-	-	-	St. Columba's, Killybegs.
[illegible]	-	[illegible]	[illegible]	[illegible]	[illegible]	[illegible]	Artane, County Dublin.
[illegible]	-	[illegible]	-	-	[illegible]	-	[illegible], County Dublin.
[illegible]	-	[illegible]	-	-	[illegible]	-	[illegible], County Dublin.
-	-	[illegible]	-	-	[illegible]	[illegible]	Goldenbridge, County Dublin.
[illegible]	[illegible]	[illegible]	-	-	[illegible]	[illegible]	[illegible], County Dublin.
-	-	[illegible]	-	-	[illegible]	[illegible]	Lakelands, Sandymount, Co. Dublin.
[illegible]	-	[illegible]	-	-	[illegible]	[illegible]	[illegible], [illegible], County Dublin.
-	-	[illegible]		[illegible]	[illegible]	[illegible]	Merrion, County Dublin.
-	-	-	-	-	-	-	[illegible]-street, Dublin.
-	-	[illegible]	-	-	[illegible]	[illegible]	St. Brigid's, Loughrea.
[illegible]	-	[illegible]	-	[illegible]	-	[illegible]	Ballinasloe.
-	-	[illegible]	-	-	[illegible]	[illegible]	Clifden, County Galway.
[illegible]	-	[illegible]	-	-	[illegible]	[illegible]	Letterfrack, County Galway.
-	-	-	-	-	-	-	Oughterard, County Galway.
[illegible]	-	[illegible]	-	-	[illegible]	[illegible]	St. Anne's, Galway.
-	-	[illegible]	[illegible]	-	[illegible]	[illegible]	Salthill, Galway.
[illegible]	-	[illegible]	[illegible]	[illegible]	[illegible]	[illegible]	St. Joseph's House, Kilkenny.
-	-	[illegible]		[illegible]	[illegible]	[illegible]	St. Joseph's, Tralee.
-	-	[illegible]	-	-	[illegible]	[illegible]	[illegible] Home, Tralee.
-	-	-	-	-	-	-	Kilkenny Male.
[illegible]	-	[illegible]	-	-	[illegible]	[illegible]	Kilkenny Female.
-	-	[illegible]	[illegible]	-	[illegible]	[illegible]	St. John's, [illegible].
-	-	[illegible]	-	-	[illegible]	[illegible]	St. George's, Limerick.
-	-	[illegible]	[illegible]	-	[illegible]	[illegible]	St. Vincent's, Limerick.
-	-	[illegible]	[illegible]	-	[illegible]	[illegible]	Limerick Male.
-	-	[illegible]	[illegible]	[illegible]	[illegible]	[illegible]	Our Lady of [illegible], [illegible].
[illegible]	-	[illegible]	-	-	[illegible]	[illegible]	House of Charity, Drogheda.
[illegible]	-	[illegible]	-	-	[illegible]	[illegible]	Dundalk.
-	-	[illegible]	-	[illegible]	[illegible]	[illegible]	St. Columba's, Westport.
[illegible]	-	[illegible]	-	[illegible]	[illegible]	[illegible]	Ballaghaderreen.
[illegible]	-	[illegible]	[illegible]		[illegible]	[illegible]	St. Martha's, Monaghan.
[illegible]	-	[illegible]	-	-	[illegible]	[illegible]	St. [illegible]'s, [illegible].
[illegible]	-	[illegible]	[illegible]	[illegible]	[illegible]	[illegible]	[illegible] Abbey.
[illegible]	-	[illegible]	-	[illegible]	[illegible]	-	[illegible] Abbey, [illegible].
-	-	[illegible]	-	-	[illegible]	-	St. Laurence's, Sligo.
-	-	[illegible]	-	-	[illegible]	[illegible]	[illegible].
[illegible]	-	[illegible]	-	-	[illegible]	[illegible]	St. Augustine's, Templemore.
-	-	[illegible]	-	[illegible]	[illegible]	[illegible]	St. Francis', Cashel.
-	-	[illegible]	-	-	[illegible]	[illegible]	St. Louis', Thurles.
-	-	[illegible]	-	[illegible]	[illegible]	[illegible]	Tipperary.
[illegible]	-	[illegible]	[illegible]	-	[illegible]	[illegible]	St. Catherine's, [illegible].
-	-	-	-	-	-	-	[illegible], County Waterford.
[illegible]	-	[illegible]	-	-	[illegible]	[illegible]	St. Dominick's, Waterford.
-	-	[illegible]	-	-	[illegible]	[illegible]	[illegible] Convent, [illegible].
-	-	[illegible]	-	-	[illegible]	[illegible]	St. Aidan's, New Ross.
-	-	[illegible]	-	-	[illegible]	[illegible]	St. Michael's, Wexford.
-	-	[illegible]	-	-	[illegible]	[illegible]	[illegible], Bray.
-	-	[illegible]	-	[illegible]	[illegible]	[illegible]	St. Kyran's, [illegible].
[illegible]	[illegible]	[illegible]	[illegible]	[illegible]	[illegible]	[illegible]	

TABLE 47.—INDUSTRIAL SCHOOLS.—Return showing the Causes for which the
the year ending 31st

SCHOOLS.	[illegible] (1)		[illegible] (2)		[illegible] (3)		[illegible] (4)		[illegible] (5)	
	B.	G.	B.	G.	B.	G.	B.	G.	B.	G.
"Greenmount,"	6	–	1	.	.	.	.	.	1	.
Fox Lodge,	19	–	.	.	.	.	.	.	.	.
Hampton,	.	11	.	.	.	.	.	.	.	1
M'Cleary,	13	–	.	.	.	.	.	.	1	.
Crumlin Road,	.	18	.	.	.	.	.	.	.	1
Abbeyville,	.	9	.	.	.	.	.	.	.	1
Shamrock,	.	7	.	.	.	.	.	.	.	.
Middletown,	.	.	.	.	.	.	.	.	.	1
Lurgan,	.	8	.	.	.	.	.	1	.	9
Cavan,	.	6	.	.	.	.	.	.	.	.
Ennis,	.	6	.	1	.	.	.	.	.	.
Clonakilty,	.	11	.	.	.	.	.	.	.	1
St. Colman's,	.	10	.	.	.	.	.	.	.	.
Kinsale,	.	6	.	7	.	.	.	1	.	8
Upton,	.	–	17	.	.	.	.	.	.	.
St. John's,	.	.	.	.	.	.	.	.	.	.
Cork Protestant,	6	–	.	.	.	.	.	.	.	.
Mallow,	.	6	.	.	.	.	.	.	.	1
Passage,	13	.	.	.	1	.	.	.	.	.
Baltimore,	13	.	.	.	.	.	1	.	8	.
St. Finbar's,	.	.	.	16	.	.	.	.	.	8
Greenmount,	8	.	4	.	.	.	.	.	3	.
Training Home,	.	1	.	.	.	.	.	.	.	.
Killybegs,	10	.	.	.	1	.	.	.	3	.
Artane,	180	.	11	.	.	.	1	.	19	.
Booterstown,	.	14	.	.	.	.	.	.	.	.
Carysfort,	.	12	.	.	.	.	.	.	.	.
Camden Bridge,	.	37	.	.	.	.	.	.	.	.
Carriglea,	.	.	20	.	.	.	.	.	11	.
Lakelands,	.	44	.	.	.	.	.	.	.	.
Westland,	19	.	.	.	.	.	6	.	7	.
Merrion,	.	18	.	.	.	.	.	.	.	1
Cappoquin,	.	5	.	.	.	.	.	.	.	1
Loughrea,	.	37	.	.	.	.	.	.	.	.
Ballinasloe,	.	6	.	.	.	.	.	.	.	.
Clifden,	.	.	.	15	.	.	.	.	.	.
Letterkenny,	14	.	.	.	.	.	.	.	.	.
Castlebar,	.	1	.	.	.	.	.	.	.	.
St. Anne's,	.	5	.	.	.	.	.	.	.	7
[illegible]	29	–	.	.	.	.	.	.	.	.
St. Joseph's,	4	28	.	.	.	.	.	.	3	1
Tralee,	7	.	.	.	.	.	1	.	.	.
Fethard,	.	.	.	.	.	.	.	.	.	1
Kilkenny Male,	40	.	.	.	.	.	.	.	8	.
Do. Female,	.	6	.	.	.	.	.	.	.	6
Parsonstown,	.	8	.	.	.	.	.	.	.	.
St. George's,	.	13	.	.	.	.	.	.	.	1
St. Vincent's,	.	28	.	.	.	.	.	.	.	7
Limerick Male,	23	–	.	.	.	.	.	.	6	.
[illegible]	.	12	.	8	.	4	.	.	.	9
Drogheda,	13	.	.	.	.	.	.	.	5	.
Dundalk,	.	18	.	.	.	5	.	.	.	9
Westport,	.	38	.	.	.	.	.	.	.	.
Ballina,	.	45	.	.	.	5	.	.	.	1
Monaghan,	.	.	.	1	.	.	.	.	.	1
Templemore,	.	9	.	.	.	.	.	.	.	1
Summerhill,	.	28	.	.	.	.	.	.	.	.
[illegible]	.	8	.	.	.	.	.	.	.	.
Sligo,	.	30	.	.	.	.	.	.	.	.

Children were Committed who where admitted into the Industrial School during of December, 1896.

[illegible]		[illegible]		[illegible]		[illegible]		Other Causes.		Total.		[illegible]
M.	F.	M.	F.	M.	F.	M.	F.	M.	F.	M.	F.	
.	.	[illegible]	.	[illegible]	.	[illegible]	.	.	.	[illegible]	.	"[illegible]"
.	.	[illegible]	.	[illegible]	.	1	.	.	.	[illegible]	.	[illegible]
.	.	.	[illegible]	.	[illegible]	.	1	.	.	.	[illegible]	[illegible]
[illegible]	.	[illegible]	.	[illegible]	.	[illegible]	.	.	.	[illegible]	.	[illegible]
.	[illegible]	.	[illegible]	.	[illegible]	.	.	.	.	.	[illegible]	Granite Road.
.	.	.	.	.	.	.	.	.	.	.	[illegible]	[illegible]
.	[illegible]	.	6	.	.	.	.	.	.	.	[illegible]	[illegible]
.	.	.	[illegible]	.	.	.	.	.	.	.	[illegible]	[illegible]
.	[illegible]	.	.	.	[illegible]	.	.	.	.	.	[illegible]	[illegible]
.	.	.	.	.	.	.	.	.	.	.	[illegible]	[illegible]
.	.	.	.	.	.	.	.	.	.	.	[illegible]	[illegible]
.	.	.	7	.	.	.	[illegible]	.	.	.	[illegible]	[illegible]
.	.	.	[illegible]	.	.	.	.	.	.	.	[illegible]	St. [illegible]
.	.	.	[illegible]	.	[illegible]	.	.	.	.	.	[illegible]	[illegible]
[illegible]	.	[illegible]	.	[illegible]	.	[illegible]	.	[illegible]	.	[illegible]	.	[illegible]
.	.	.	.	.	.	.	.	.	.	.	.	St. [illegible]
.	.	.	.	.	.	.	.	.	.	[illegible]	.	Cork Protestant.
.	.	.	[illegible]	.	.	.	.	.	.	.	7	[illegible]
.	.	.	.	[illegible]	.	.	.	.	.	[illegible]	.	[illegible]
[illegible]	.	.	.	[illegible]	.	.	.	.	.	[illegible]	.	[illegible]
.	[illegible]	.	[illegible]	.	.	.	.	.	.	.	[illegible]	[illegible]
[illegible]	.	[illegible]	.	[illegible]	.	.	.	.	.	[illegible]	.	[illegible]
.	.	.	.	.	.	.	.	.	.	.	[illegible]	[illegible]
[illegible]	.	[illegible]	.	[illegible]	.	.	.	[illegible]	.	[illegible]	.	[illegible]
[illegible]	.	[illegible]	.	[illegible]	.	[illegible]	.	6	.	[illegible]	.	Armagh.
.	.	.	[illegible]	.	.	.	.	.	.	.	[illegible]	[illegible]
.	.	.	.	.	.	.	.	.	.	.	[illegible]	[illegible]
.	.	.	.	.	.	.	.	.	.	.	[illegible]	Golden Bridge
[illegible]	.	[illegible]	.	.	.	[illegible]	.	.	.	[illegible]	.	[illegible]
.	.	.	.	.	.	.	.	.	.	.	[illegible]	[illegible]
.	.	.	.	.	.	1	.	.	.	[illegible]	.	[illegible]
.	.	.	.	.	.	.	.	.	.	.	[illegible]	[illegible]
.	.	.	.	.	[illegible]	.	.	.	.	.	[illegible]	[illegible]
.	.	.	.	.	.	.	.	.	.	.	[illegible]	[illegible]
.	.	.	.	.	.	.	.	.	.	.	[illegible]	[illegible]
.	.	.	6	.	.	.	.	.	.	.	[illegible]	[illegible]
.	.	.	.	.	.	.	.	.	.	[illegible]	.	[illegible]
.	.	.	[illegible]	.	.	.	.	.	.	.	[illegible]	[illegible]
.	.	.	.	.	.	.	.	.	.	.	[illegible]	St. Anne's.
[illegible]	.	[illegible]	.	.	.	.	.	.	.	[illegible]	.	Oak Hill.
.	.	.	.	.	.	.	.	.	.	[illegible]	[illegible]	St. Joseph's.
1	.	[illegible]	.	.	.	.	.	.	.	[illegible]	.	Tralee.
.	6	.	[illegible]	.	.	.	.	.	.	.	[illegible]	[illegible]
.	.	1	.	.	.	.	.	.	.	[illegible]	.	Kilkenny Male.
.	[illegible]	.	[illegible]	.	.	.	.	.	.	.	[illegible]	Do. Female.
.	.	.	[illegible]	.	.	.	.	.	.	.	[illegible]	[illegible]
.	[illegible]	.	[illegible]	.	1	.	.	.	.	.	[illegible]	St. George's.
.	[illegible]	.	[illegible]	.	.	.	.	.	.	.	[illegible]	St. Vincent's.
[illegible]	.	.	.	.	.	.	.	.	.	[illegible]	.	Limerick Male.
.	.	.	.	.	.	.	.	.	.	.	[illegible]	[illegible]
.	.	[illegible]	.	.	.	.	.	.	.	[illegible]	.	Drogheda.
.	.	.	[illegible]	.	[illegible]	.	.	.	.	.	[illegible]	Dundalk.
.	.	.	.	.	.	.	.	.	.	.	[illegible]	[illegible]
.	.	.	[illegible]	.	.	.	.	.	.	.	[illegible]	[illegible]
.	1	.	[illegible]	.	[illegible]	.	[illegible]	.	.	.	[illegible]	[illegible]
.	.	.	[illegible]	.	.	.	.	.	.	.	[illegible]	[illegible]
.	.	.	[illegible]	.	.	.	.	.	.	.	[illegible]	[illegible]
.	.	.	[illegible]	.	.	.	.	.	.	.	[illegible]	[illegible]
.	.	.	.	.	.	.	.	.	.	.	[illegible]	[illegible]
.	.	3	.	1	.	.	.	.	.	[illegible]	.	[illegible]
.	.	.	.	.	.	.	.	.	.	.	[illegible]	[illegible]
.	.	.	[illegible]	.	.	.	.	.	.	.	[illegible]	[illegible]
.	.	.	.	.	.	.	1	.	.	.	[illegible]	[illegible]
.	.	.	[illegible]	.	.	.	.	.	.	.	[illegible]	Tipperary.
.	.	.	[illegible]	.	[illegible]	.	.	.	.	.	[illegible]	[illegible]
.	.	[illegible]	.	.	.	.	.	.	.	[illegible]	.	[illegible]
.	.	.	[illegible]	.	[illegible]	.	.	.	.	.	[illegible]	St. Dominick's.
.	.	.	[illegible]	.	.	.	.	.	.	.	[illegible]	[illegible]
.	.	.	[illegible]	.	.	.	.	.	.	.	[illegible]	New Ross.
.	.	.	.	.	.	.	.	.	.	.	[illegible]	Wexford.
.	.	.	.	.	.	.	.	.	.	.	1	Bray.
[illegible]	.	.	.	.	.	.	.	.	.	[illegible]	.	St. Kyran's.
[illegible]	[illegible]	[illegible]	[illegible]	[illegible]	[illegible]	[illegible]	[illegible]	[illegible]	.	[illegible]	[illegible]	Total.

CRIMINAL AND DANGEROUS LUNATICS.

48.—CRIMINAL LUNATICS.—Receptions and Discharges during the Year.

49.—CRIMINAL LUNATICS.—Numbers undergoing Detention on 31st December, 1896.

50.—CRIMINAL LUNATICS.—Offences.

51.—DANGEROUS LUNATICS.—Receptions and Discharges during the Year.

52.—DANGEROUS LUNATICS.—Numbers undergoing detention on 31st December, 1896.

and Discharges during the Year, 1896.

Asylum. (14)	[illegible] (1)	[illegible] (2)	[illegible] (3)	[illegible] (4)	[illegible] (5)	[illegible] (6)	[illegible] (7)	[illegible] (8)	[illegible] (9)	[illegible] (10)
Criminal Asylum.										
Dundrum.	[illegible]	.	[illegible]	[illegible]	.	[illegible]	[illegible]	[illegible]	.	.
District Asylums.										
Armagh.	.	.	.	.	.	.	.	.	.	.
Ballinasloe.	.	[illegible]	.	.	.	.	.	.	.	.
Belfast.	[illegible]	.	.	[illegible]	.	.	.	[illegible]	.	.
Carlow.	.	.	.	.	.	.	.	.	.	.
Castlebar.	[illegible]	.	.	[illegible]	.	.	.	.	.	.
Clonmel.	.	.	.	.	.	.	.	.	.	.
Cork.	.	[illegible]	.	.	.	[illegible]	.	.	.	.
Downpatrick.	.	.	.	.	.	.	.	.	.	.
Ennis.	.	.	.	.	.	.	.	.	.	.
Enniscorthy.	[illegible]	[illegible]	.	.	.	.	.	.	.	.
Kilkenny.	.	.	.	.	.	.	.	.	.	.
Killarney.	.	.	.	[illegible]	.	.	.	.	.	.
Letterkenny.	.	.	.	.	.	.	.	[illegible]	.	.
Limerick.	.	.	.	[illegible]	.	.	1	.	.	.
Londonderry.	.	[illegible]	.	.	.	.	.	.	.	.
Maryborough.	.	.	.	.	.	.	[illegible]	.	.	.
Monaghan.	.	.	.	.	.	.	.	.	.	.
Mullingar.	.	.	.	.	.	.	.	.	.	.
Omagh.	.	.	.	[illegible]	.	.	.	.	.	.
Richmond.	.	[illegible]	.	.	.	.	.	[illegible]	.	.
Sligo.	.	[illegible]	.	.	[illegible]	.	.	.	.	.
Waterford.	[illegible]	[illegible]	.	.	.	.	.	1	.	.
Total.	[illegible]	[illegible]	[illegible]	[illegible]	[illegible]	[illegible]	[illegible]	[illegible]	.	.

TABLE 49.—CRIMINAL LUNATICS.—Numbers

ASYLUM. (1)	Numbers. (2)			[illegible]				
				[illegible]		[illegible]		[illegible]
	Total.	Males.	Females.	[illegible] (3)	[illegible] (4)	[illegible] (5)	[illegible] (6)	(7)
Original Asylum.								
Dundrum,	[illegible]	[illegible]	[illegible]	[illegible]	[illegible]	[illegible]	[illegible]	-
District Asylums.								
Armagh,	[illegible]	[illegible]	[illegible]	-	-	[illegible]	-	-
Ballinasloe,	[illegible]	[illegible]	[illegible]	[illegible]	-	[illegible]	-	-
Belfast,	[illegible]	[illegible]	-	[illegible]	-	[illegible]	[illegible]	-
Carlow,	[illegible]	[illegible]	[illegible]	[illegible]	[illegible]	[illegible]	[illegible]	-
Castlebar,	[illegible]	[illegible]	[illegible]	[illegible]	-	[illegible]	-	-
Clonmel,	[illegible]	[illegible]	-	-	-	-	[illegible]	-
Cork,	[illegible]	[illegible]	[illegible]	-	-	[illegible]	[illegible]	-
Downpatrick,	[illegible]	[illegible]	-	[illegible]	-	-	-	-
Ennis,	[illegible]	[illegible]	-	-	-	[illegible]	-	-
Enniscorthy,	[illegible]	[illegible]	[illegible]	[illegible]	[illegible]	[illegible]	[illegible]	-
Kilkenny,	[illegible]	[illegible]	-	[illegible]	-	-	-	-
Killarney,	[illegible]	[illegible]	[illegible]	[illegible]	[illegible]	[illegible]	-	-
Letterkenny,	[illegible]	[illegible]	[illegible]	[illegible]	[illegible]	[illegible]	-	-
Limerick,	[illegible]	[illegible]	-	[illegible]	-	-	-	-
Londonderry,	[illegible]	[illegible]	[illegible]	[illegible]	[illegible]	[illegible]	-	-
Maryborough,	[illegible]	[illegible]	[illegible]	-	[illegible]	[illegible]	[illegible]	-
Monaghan,	[illegible]	[illegible]	[illegible]	-	[illegible]	[illegible]	-	-
Mullingar,	-	-	-	-	-	-	-	-
Omagh,	[illegible]	[illegible]	-	[illegible]	-	[illegible]	-	-
Richmond,	[illegible]	[illegible]	[illegible]	[illegible]	[illegible]	[illegible]	[illegible]	-
Sligo,	[illegible]	[illegible]	[illegible]	[illegible]	[illegible]	[illegible]	-	-
Waterford,	[illegible]	[illegible]	-	-	-	[illegible]	[illegible]	-
TOTAL,	[illegible]	[illegible]	[illegible]	[illegible]	[illegible]	[illegible]	[illegible]	-

undergoing Detention on 31st December, 1896.

Period of Detention as Criminal Lunatics.								
1 Year and under.	[illegible] Years and above 1.	[illegible] Years and above [illegible].	[illegible] Years and above [illegible].	[illegible] Years and above [illegible].	[illegible] Years and above [illegible].	[illegible] Years and above [illegible].	Above [illegible] Years.	ASYLUM.
(8)	(9)	(10)	(11)	(12)	(13)	(14)	(15)	
								Criminal Asylum.
[illegible]	[illegible]	[illegible]	[illegible]	[illegible]	[illegible]	[illegible]	[illegible]	Dundrum.
								District Asylums.
[illegible]	...	...	[illegible]	...	[illegible]	[illegible]	[illegible]	Armagh.
[illegible]	...	...	[illegible]	[illegible]	...	[illegible]	...	Ballinasloe.
[illegible]	...	...	...	[illegible]	...	...	...	Belfast.
...	...	...	...	...	[illegible]	[illegible]	[illegible]	Carlow.
...	...	...	[illegible]	[illegible]	[illegible]	[illegible]	[illegible]	Castlebar.
[illegible]	...	...	...	...	...	...	...	Clonmel.
[illegible]	...	...	[illegible]	[illegible]	...	...	...	Cork.
...	...	...	...	[illegible]	[illegible]	[illegible]	[illegible]	Downpatrick.
[illegible]	...	...	[illegible]	[illegible]	...	...	...	Ennis.
[illegible]	...	...	...	[illegible]	[illegible]	...	[illegible]	Enniscorthy.
...	...	...	...	...	...	...	[illegible]	Kilkenny.
[illegible]	...	...	...	[illegible]	...	[illegible]	...	Killarney.
[illegible]	...	...	[illegible]	...	[illegible]	[illegible]	[illegible]	Letterkenny.
...	...	...	...	[illegible]	...	...	...	Limerick.
[illegible]	[illegible]	[illegible]	...	...	...	[illegible]	[illegible]	Londonderry.
[illegible]	[illegible]	...	...	[illegible]	[illegible]	[illegible]	[illegible]	Maryborough.
...	...	...	...	[illegible]	[illegible]	[illegible]	...	Monaghan.
...	...	...	...	...	...	...	...	Mullingar.
...	...	[illegible]	...	...	[illegible]	...	[illegible]	Omagh.
[illegible]	[illegible]	...	[illegible]	[illegible]	[illegible]	[illegible]	[illegible]	Richmond.
[illegible]	...	...	...	[illegible]	...	...	...	Sligo.
[illegible]	[illegible]	...	...	[illegible]	...	...	...	Waterford.
[illegible]	[illegible]	14	[illegible]	[illegible]	[illegible]	[illegible]	[illegible]	TOTAL.

TABLE 50.—CRIMINAL

OFFENCE.	Criminals Received during the Year.							Remaining		
	Total.	Males.	Females.	Insane on Arraignment.	[illegible]	[illegible]	[illegible]	From Previous.		
								Total.	Males.	Females.
Murder,	[illegible]	[illegible]	[illegible]	[illegible]	[illegible]	[illegible]	[illegible]	[illegible]	[illegible]	[illegible]
Attempting to Murder,	-	-		-	-	-	-	[illegible]	[illegible]	[illegible]
Threats or Conspiracy to Murder,	-	-		-	-	-	-	[illegible]	[illegible]	-
Manslaughter,	[illegible]	[illegible]	-	[illegible]	-	-	-	[illegible]	[illegible]	[illegible]
Felonious Wounding,	-	-	-		-	-		[illegible]	[illegible]	-
Endangering Safety of Passengers,	[illegible]	[illegible]	[illegible]	[illegible]	-	[illegible]	-	[illegible]	[illegible]	[illegible]
Malicious Wounding,	[illegible]	[illegible]	-	-	-	[illegible]		[illegible]	[illegible]	[illegible]
Unnatural Offences,	-	-	-	-	-	-	-	[illegible]	[illegible]	
Attempts to commit Unnatural Offences,	-	-	-		-	-	-	[illegible]	[illegible]	-
Rape,		-		-	-	-		[illegible]	[illegible]	-
Indecent Assaults,	[illegible]	[illegible]	-	-	-	-	[illegible]	[illegible]	[illegible]	
Cruelty to Children,	[illegible]	-	[illegible]	-	-	-	[illegible]	[illegible]	-	[illegible]
Child Stealing,	-	-	-	-	-	-	-	[illegible]	-	[illegible]
Assaults,	[illegible]	[illegible]	[illegible]	[illegible]	[illegible]	[illegible]	[illegible]	[illegible]	[illegible]	[illegible]
Threatening Language,	[illegible]	[illegible]	[illegible]	-	-	[illegible]	[illegible]	[illegible]	[illegible]	[illegible]
Burglary,	[illegible]	[illegible]	-	[illegible]	[illegible]	-	-	[illegible]	[illegible]	-
Housebreaking,	[illegible]	[illegible]	-	[illegible]	-	-	[illegible]	-	-	-
Entering with Intent,	[illegible]	[illegible]	-		-	-	[illegible]	[illegible]	[illegible]	-
Larceny from Person,	[illegible]	[illegible]	-	-	-	-	[illegible]	[illegible]	[illegible]	[illegible]
Larceny, Simple,	[illegible]	[illegible]	[illegible]	[illegible]	-	[illegible]	[illegible]	[illegible]	[illegible]	[illegible]
Arson,	[illegible]	[illegible]	-	-	-	[illegible]	-	[illegible]	17	[illegible]
Other Malicious Injury,	[illegible]	[illegible]	[illegible]	-	-	-	[illegible]	[illegible]	[illegible]	[illegible]
Indecent Exposure,	[illegible]	[illegible]	-	-	-	-	[illegible]	[illegible]	[illegible]	-
Attempt at Suicide,	[illegible]	[illegible]	[illegible]	[illegible]	[illegible]	[illegible]	[illegible]	14	[illegible]	[illegible]
Misdemeanour by Forgery,	[illegible]	[illegible]	-	-	-	-	[illegible]	-		
Vagrancy—Begging,	[illegible]	[illegible]	[illegible]	-	-	-	[illegible]	-	-	-
Do. Carrying arms,	[illegible]	[illegible]	-	-	-	-	[illegible]	[illegible]	[illegible]	-
Other Larcenies,	[illegible]	[illegible]	[illegible]	-	-	-	[illegible]	-	-	-
Drunkenness,	[illegible]	[illegible]	[illegible]	-	-	-	[illegible]	-	-	-
Trespassing,	-	-		-	-	-	-	-	-	-
Disobeying Prison Rules,	[illegible]	[illegible]	[illegible]	-	-	-	[illegible]	-	-	-
Other Offences,	[illegible]	[illegible]	[illegible]	-	[illegible]	-	[illegible]	[illegible]	[illegible]	[illegible]
TOTAL,	[illegible]	[illegible]	[illegible]	[illegible]	[illegible]	[illegible]	[illegible]	[illegible]	[illegible]	[illegible]

TABLE 51.—DANGEROUS LUNATICS, 1896.—

ASYLUM. (1)	Remaining			Committed by Justices		Admitted under [illegible]	Remaining		
	(2)			(3)		(4)	(5)		
	Total.	Males.	Females.	Males.	Females.	Males.	Total.	Males.	Females.
Armagh,	[illegible]	[illegible]	[illegible]	[illegible]	[illegible]	-	[illegible]	[illegible]	[illegible]
Ballinasloe,	[illegible]	[illegible]	[illegible]	[illegible]	[illegible]	[illegible]	[illegible]	[illegible]	[illegible]
Belfast,	[illegible]	[illegible]	[illegible]	[illegible]	[illegible]	[illegible]	[illegible]	[illegible]	[illegible]
Carlow,	[illegible]	[illegible]	[illegible]	[illegible]	[illegible]	[illegible]	[illegible]	[illegible]	[illegible]
Castlebar,	[illegible]	[illegible]	[illegible]	[illegible]	[illegible]	-	[illegible]	[illegible]	[illegible]
Clonmel,	[illegible]	[illegible]	[illegible]	[illegible]	[illegible]	[illegible]	[illegible]	[illegible]	[illegible]
Cork,	[illegible]	[illegible]	[illegible]	[illegible]	[illegible]	-	[illegible]	[illegible]	[illegible]
Downpatrick,	[illegible]	[illegible]	[illegible]	[illegible]	[illegible]	-	[illegible]	[illegible]	[illegible]
Ennis,	[illegible]	[illegible]	[illegible]	[illegible]	[illegible]	[illegible]	[illegible]	[illegible]	[illegible]
Enniscorthy,	[illegible]	[illegible]	[illegible]	[illegible]	[illegible]	-	[illegible]	[illegible]	[illegible]
Kilkenny,	[illegible]	[illegible]	[illegible]	[illegible]	[illegible]	-	[illegible]	[illegible]	[illegible]
Killarney,	[illegible]	[illegible]	[illegible]	[illegible]	[illegible]	-	[illegible]	[illegible]	[illegible]
Letterkenny,	[illegible]	[illegible]	[illegible]	[illegible]	[illegible]	[illegible]	[illegible]	[illegible]	[illegible]
Limerick,	[illegible]	[illegible]	[illegible]	[illegible]	[illegible]	-	[illegible]	[illegible]	[illegible]
Londonderry,	[illegible]	[illegible]	[illegible]	[illegible]	[illegible]	-	[illegible]	[illegible]	[illegible]
Maryborough,	[illegible]	[illegible]	[illegible]	[illegible]	[illegible]	-	[illegible]	[illegible]	[illegible]
Monaghan,	[illegible]	[illegible]	[illegible]	[illegible]	[illegible]	-	[illegible]	[illegible]	[illegible]
Mullingar,	[illegible]	[illegible]	[illegible]	[illegible]	[illegible]	[illegible]	[illegible]	[illegible]	[illegible]
Omagh,	[illegible]	[illegible]	[illegible]	[illegible]	[illegible]	[illegible]	[illegible]	[illegible]	[illegible]
Richmond,	[illegible]	[illegible]	[illegible]	[illegible]	[illegible]	[illegible]	[illegible]	[illegible]	[illegible]
Sligo,	[illegible]	[illegible]	[illegible]	[illegible]	[illegible]	[illegible]	[illegible]	[illegible]	[illegible]
Waterford,	[illegible]	[illegible]	[illegible]	[illegible]	[illegible]	-	[illegible]	[illegible]	[illegible]
TOTAL,	[illegible]	[illegible]	[illegible]	[illegible]	[illegible]	[illegible]	[illegible]	[illegible]	[illegible]

LUNATICS.—Offences.

[illegible]				[illegible]								
[illegible]	[illegible]	[illegible]	[illegible]	1 year and under	[illegible]	[illegible]	[illegible]	[illegible]	[illegible]	[illegible]	Above 20 years	OFFENCE.
[illegible]	[illegible]	[illegible]	[illegible]	[illegible]	[illegible]	[illegible]	[illegible]	[illegible]	[illegible]	[illegible]	[illegible]	Murder.
[illegible]	[illegible]	[illegible]	[illegible]	[illegible]	[illegible]	[illegible]	[illegible]	[illegible]	[illegible]	[illegible]	[illegible]	Attempting to Murder.
[illegible]	[illegible]	[illegible]	[illegible]	[illegible]	[illegible]	[illegible]	[illegible]	[illegible]	[illegible]	[illegible]	[illegible]	Threat or Conspiracy to Murder.
[illegible]	[illegible]	[illegible]	[illegible]	[illegible]	[illegible]	[illegible]	[illegible]	[illegible]	[illegible]	[illegible]	[illegible]	Manslaughter.
[illegible]	[illegible]	[illegible]	[illegible]	[illegible]	[illegible]	[illegible]	[illegible]	[illegible]	[illegible]	[illegible]	[illegible]	Felonious Wounding.
[illegible]	[illegible]	[illegible]	[illegible]	[illegible]	[illegible]	[illegible]	[illegible]	[illegible]	[illegible]	[illegible]	[illegible]	Endangering Railway Passengers.
[illegible]	[illegible]	[illegible]	[illegible]	[illegible]	[illegible]	[illegible]	[illegible]	[illegible]	[illegible]	[illegible]	[illegible]	Malicious Wounding.
[illegible]	[illegible]	[illegible]	[illegible]	[illegible]	[illegible]	[illegible]	[illegible]	[illegible]	[illegible]	[illegible]	[illegible]	Unnatural Offences.
[illegible]	[illegible]	[illegible]	[illegible]	[illegible]	[illegible]	[illegible]	[illegible]	[illegible]	[illegible]	[illegible]	[illegible]	Attempt to commit Unnatural Offences.
[illegible]	[illegible]	[illegible]	[illegible]	[illegible]	[illegible]	[illegible]	[illegible]	[illegible]	[illegible]	[illegible]	[illegible]	Rape.
[illegible]	[illegible]	[illegible]	[illegible]	[illegible]	[illegible]	[illegible]	[illegible]	[illegible]	[illegible]	[illegible]	[illegible]	Indecent Assault.
[illegible]	[illegible]	[illegible]	[illegible]	[illegible]	[illegible]	[illegible]	[illegible]	[illegible]	[illegible]	[illegible]	[illegible]	Cruelty to Children.
[illegible]	[illegible]	[illegible]	[illegible]	[illegible]	[illegible]	[illegible]	[illegible]	[illegible]	[illegible]	[illegible]	[illegible]	Child Stealing.
[illegible]	[illegible]	[illegible]	[illegible]	[illegible]	[illegible]	[illegible]	[illegible]	[illegible]	[illegible]	[illegible]	[illegible]	Assaults.
[illegible]	[illegible]	[illegible]	[illegible]	[illegible]	[illegible]	[illegible]	[illegible]	[illegible]	[illegible]	[illegible]	[illegible]	Threatening Language.
[illegible]	[illegible]	[illegible]	[illegible]	[illegible]	[illegible]	[illegible]	[illegible]	[illegible]	[illegible]	[illegible]	[illegible]	Burglary.
[illegible]	[illegible]	[illegible]	[illegible]	[illegible]	[illegible]	[illegible]	[illegible]	[illegible]	[illegible]	[illegible]	[illegible]	Housebreaking.
[illegible]	[illegible]	[illegible]	[illegible]	[illegible]	[illegible]	[illegible]	[illegible]	[illegible]	[illegible]	[illegible]	[illegible]	Entering with Intent.
[illegible]	[illegible]	[illegible]	[illegible]	[illegible]	[illegible]	[illegible]	[illegible]	[illegible]	[illegible]	[illegible]	[illegible]	Larceny from Person.
[illegible]	[illegible]	[illegible]	[illegible]	[illegible]	[illegible]	[illegible]	[illegible]	[illegible]	[illegible]	[illegible]	[illegible]	Larceny, Simple.
[illegible]	[illegible]	[illegible]	[illegible]	[illegible]	[illegible]	[illegible]	[illegible]	[illegible]	[illegible]	[illegible]	[illegible]	Arson.
[illegible]	[illegible]	[illegible]	[illegible]	[illegible]	[illegible]	[illegible]	[illegible]	[illegible]	[illegible]	[illegible]	[illegible]	Other Malicious Injury.
[illegible]	[illegible]	[illegible]	[illegible]	[illegible]	[illegible]	[illegible]	[illegible]	[illegible]	[illegible]	[illegible]	[illegible]	[illegible]
[illegible]	[illegible]	[illegible]	[illegible]	[illegible]	[illegible]	[illegible]	[illegible]	[illegible]	[illegible]	[illegible]	[illegible]	Suicide (attempting).
[illegible]	[illegible]	[illegible]	[illegible]	[illegible]	[illegible]	[illegible]	[illegible]	[illegible]	[illegible]	[illegible]	[illegible]	[illegible]
[illegible]	[illegible]	[illegible]	[illegible]	[illegible]	[illegible]	[illegible]	[illegible]	[illegible]	[illegible]	[illegible]	[illegible]	Vagrancy—Begging.
[illegible]	[illegible]	[illegible]	[illegible]	[illegible]	[illegible]	[illegible]	[illegible]	[illegible]	[illegible]	[illegible]	[illegible]	Do. Sleeping out.
[illegible]	[illegible]	[illegible]	[illegible]	[illegible]	[illegible]	[illegible]	[illegible]	[illegible]	[illegible]	[illegible]	[illegible]	Obscene Language.
[illegible]	[illegible]	[illegible]	[illegible]	[illegible]	[illegible]	[illegible]	[illegible]	[illegible]	[illegible]	[illegible]	[illegible]	Drunkenness.
[illegible]	[illegible]	[illegible]	[illegible]	[illegible]	[illegible]	[illegible]	[illegible]	[illegible]	[illegible]	[illegible]	[illegible]	Trespassing.
[illegible]	[illegible]	[illegible]	[illegible]	[illegible]	[illegible]	[illegible]	[illegible]	[illegible]	[illegible]	[illegible]	[illegible]	[illegible]
[illegible]	[illegible]	[illegible]	[illegible]	[illegible]	[illegible]	[illegible]	[illegible]	[illegible]	[illegible]	[illegible]	[illegible]	Other Offences.
[illegible]	[illegible]	[illegible]	[illegible]	[illegible]	[illegible]	[illegible]	[illegible]	[illegible]	[illegible]	[illegible]	[illegible]	Total.

Receptions and Discharges during the Year.

[illegible]												
Recovered.		Relieved.		Not Improved.		Died.		[illegible]		Escaped.		ASYLUM.
Males.	Females.	Males.	Females.	Males.	Females.	Males.	Females.	Males.	Females.	Males.	Females.	
[illegible]	[illegible]	[illegible]	[illegible]	[illegible]	[illegible]	[illegible]	[illegible]	[illegible]	[illegible]	[illegible]	[illegible]	Armagh.
[illegible]	[illegible]	[illegible]	[illegible]	[illegible]	[illegible]	[illegible]	[illegible]	[illegible]	[illegible]	[illegible]	[illegible]	Ballinasloe.
[illegible]	[illegible]	[illegible]	[illegible]	[illegible]	[illegible]	[illegible]	[illegible]	[illegible]	[illegible]	[illegible]	[illegible]	Belfast.
[illegible]	[illegible]	[illegible]	[illegible]	[illegible]	[illegible]	[illegible]	[illegible]	[illegible]	[illegible]	[illegible]	[illegible]	Carlow.
[illegible]	[illegible]	[illegible]	[illegible]	[illegible]	[illegible]	[illegible]	[illegible]	[illegible]	[illegible]	[illegible]	[illegible]	Castlebar.
[illegible]	[illegible]	[illegible]	[illegible]	[illegible]	[illegible]	[illegible]	[illegible]	[illegible]	[illegible]	[illegible]	[illegible]	Clonmel.
[illegible]	[illegible]	[illegible]	[illegible]	[illegible]	[illegible]	[illegible]	[illegible]	[illegible]	[illegible]	[illegible]	[illegible]	Cork.
[illegible]	[illegible]	[illegible]	[illegible]	[illegible]	[illegible]	[illegible]	[illegible]	[illegible]	[illegible]	[illegible]	[illegible]	Downpatrick.
[illegible]	[illegible]	[illegible]	[illegible]	[illegible]	[illegible]	[illegible]	[illegible]	[illegible]	[illegible]	[illegible]	[illegible]	Ennis.
[illegible]	[illegible]	[illegible]	[illegible]	[illegible]	[illegible]	[illegible]	[illegible]	[illegible]	[illegible]	[illegible]	[illegible]	Enniscorthy.
[illegible]	[illegible]	[illegible]	[illegible]	[illegible]	[illegible]	[illegible]	[illegible]	[illegible]	[illegible]	[illegible]	[illegible]	Kilkenny.
[illegible]	[illegible]	[illegible]	[illegible]	[illegible]	[illegible]	[illegible]	[illegible]	[illegible]	[illegible]	[illegible]	[illegible]	Killarney.
[illegible]	[illegible]	[illegible]	[illegible]	[illegible]	[illegible]	[illegible]	[illegible]	[illegible]	[illegible]	[illegible]	[illegible]	Letterkenny.
[illegible]	[illegible]	[illegible]	[illegible]	[illegible]	[illegible]	[illegible]	[illegible]	[illegible]	[illegible]	[illegible]	[illegible]	Limerick.
[illegible]	[illegible]	[illegible]	[illegible]	[illegible]	[illegible]	[illegible]	[illegible]	[illegible]	[illegible]	[illegible]	[illegible]	Londonderry.
[illegible]	[illegible]	[illegible]	[illegible]	[illegible]	[illegible]	[illegible]	[illegible]	[illegible]	[illegible]	[illegible]	[illegible]	Maryborough.
[illegible]	[illegible]	[illegible]	[illegible]	[illegible]	[illegible]	[illegible]	[illegible]	[illegible]	[illegible]	[illegible]	[illegible]	Monaghan.
[illegible]	[illegible]	[illegible]	[illegible]	[illegible]	[illegible]	[illegible]	[illegible]	[illegible]	[illegible]	[illegible]	[illegible]	Mullingar.
[illegible]	[illegible]	[illegible]	[illegible]	[illegible]	[illegible]	[illegible]	[illegible]	[illegible]	[illegible]	[illegible]	[illegible]	Omagh.
[illegible]	[illegible]	[illegible]	[illegible]	[illegible]	[illegible]	[illegible]	[illegible]	[illegible]	[illegible]	[illegible]	[illegible]	Richmond.
[illegible]	[illegible]	[illegible]	[illegible]	[illegible]	[illegible]	[illegible]	[illegible]	[illegible]	[illegible]	[illegible]	[illegible]	Sligo.
[illegible]	[illegible]	[illegible]	[illegible]	[illegible]	[illegible]	[illegible]	[illegible]	[illegible]	[illegible]	[illegible]	[illegible]	Waterford.
[illegible]	[illegible]	[illegible]	[illegible]	[illegible]	[illegible]	[illegible]	[illegible]	[illegible]	[illegible]	[illegible]	[illegible]	TOTAL.

TABLE 52.—DANGEROUS LUNATICS.—Numbers

ASYLUM. (1)	[illegible] (2)			[illegible]			[illegible]			
				[illegible] (3)		[illegible] (4)	[illegible] (5)		[illegible] (6)	
	Total.	Males.	Females.	Males.	Females.	Males.	Males.	Females.	Males.	Females.
Armagh,	[illegible]	[illegible]	[illegible]	[illegible]	[illegible]	-	[illegible]	[illegible]	[illegible]	[illegible]
Ballinasloe,	[illegible]	[illegible]	[illegible]	[illegible]	[illegible]	[illegible]	[illegible]	[illegible]	[illegible]	[illegible]
Belfast,	[illegible]	[illegible]	[illegible]	[illegible]	[illegible]	[illegible]	[illegible]	[illegible]	[illegible]	[illegible]
Carlow,	[illegible]	[illegible]	[illegible]	[illegible]	[illegible]	[illegible]	[illegible]	[illegible]	[illegible]	[illegible]
Castlebar,	[illegible]	[illegible]	[illegible]	[illegible]	[illegible]	[illegible]	[illegible]	[illegible]	[illegible]	[illegible]
Clonmel,	[illegible]	[illegible]	[illegible]	[illegible]	[illegible]	[illegible]	[illegible]	[illegible]	[illegible]	[illegible]
Cork,	[illegible]	[illegible]	[illegible]	[illegible]	[illegible]	[illegible]	[illegible]	[illegible]	[illegible]	[illegible]
Downpatrick,	[illegible]	[illegible]	[illegible]	[illegible]	[illegible]	[illegible]	[illegible]	[illegible]	[illegible]	[illegible]
Ennis,	[illegible]	[illegible]	[illegible]	[illegible]	[illegible]	-	[illegible]	[illegible]	[illegible]	[illegible]
Enniscorthy,	[illegible]	[illegible]	[illegible]	[illegible]	[illegible]	[illegible]	[illegible]	[illegible]	[illegible]	[illegible]
Kilkenny,	[illegible]	[illegible]	[illegible]	[illegible]	[illegible]	[illegible]	[illegible]	[illegible]	[illegible]	[illegible]
Killarney,	[illegible]	[illegible]	[illegible]	[illegible]	[illegible]	[illegible]	[illegible]	[illegible]	[illegible]	[illegible]
Letterkenny,	[illegible]	[illegible]	[illegible]	[illegible]	[illegible]	[illegible]	[illegible]	[illegible]	[illegible]	[illegible]
Limerick,	[illegible]	[illegible]	[illegible]	[illegible]	[illegible]	[illegible]	[illegible]	[illegible]	[illegible]	[illegible]
Londonderry,	[illegible]	[illegible]	[illegible]	[illegible]	[illegible]	-	[illegible]	[illegible]	[illegible]	[illegible]
Maryborough,	[illegible]	[illegible]	[illegible]	[illegible]	[illegible]	[illegible]	[illegible]	[illegible]	[illegible]	[illegible]
Monaghan,	[illegible]	[illegible]	[illegible]	[illegible]	[illegible]	[illegible]	[illegible]	[illegible]	[illegible]	[illegible]
Mullingar,	[illegible]	[illegible]	[illegible]	[illegible]	[illegible]	[illegible]	[illegible]	[illegible]	[illegible]	[illegible]
Omagh,	[illegible]	[illegible]	[illegible]	[illegible]	[illegible]	[illegible]	[illegible]	[illegible]	[illegible]	[illegible]
Richmond,	[illegible]	[illegible]	[illegible]	[illegible]	[illegible]	[illegible]	[illegible]	[illegible]	[illegible]	[illegible]
Sligo,	[illegible]	[illegible]	[illegible]	[illegible]	[illegible]	[illegible]	[illegible]	[illegible]	[illegible]	[illegible]
Waterford,	[illegible]	[illegible]	[illegible]	[illegible]	[illegible]	[illegible]	[illegible]	[illegible]	[illegible]	[illegible]
TOTAL,	[illegible]	[illegible]	[illegible]	[illegible]	[illegible]	[illegible]	[illegible]	[illegible]	[illegible]	[illegible]

IRELAND.

undergoing Detention on 31st December, 1896.

[illegible]

[illegible]		[illegible]		[illegible]		[illegible]		[illegible]		Above [illegible] Years.		ASYLUM.
([illegible])		([illegible])		([illegible])		([illegible])		([illegible])		([illegible])		([illegible])
Males.	Females.	Males.	Females.	Males.	Females.	Males.	Females.	Males.	Females.	Males.	Females.	
[illegible]	[illegible]	[illegible]	[illegible]	[illegible]	[illegible]	[illegible]	[illegible]	[illegible]	[illegible]	[illegible]	[illegible]	Armagh.
[illegible]	[illegible]	[illegible]	[illegible]	[illegible]	[illegible]	[illegible]	[illegible]	[illegible]	[illegible]	[illegible]	[illegible]	Ballinasloe.
[illegible]	[illegible]	[illegible]	[illegible]	[illegible]	[illegible]	[illegible]	[illegible]	[illegible]	[illegible]	[illegible]	[illegible]	Belfast.
[illegible]	[illegible]	[illegible]	[illegible]	[illegible]	[illegible]	[illegible]	[illegible]	[illegible]	[illegible]	[illegible]	[illegible]	Carlow.
[illegible]	[illegible]	[illegible]	[illegible]	[illegible]	[illegible]	[illegible]	[illegible]	[illegible]	[illegible]	[illegible]	[illegible]	Castlebar.
[illegible]	[illegible]	[illegible]	[illegible]	[illegible]	[illegible]	[illegible]	[illegible]	[illegible]	[illegible]	[illegible]	[illegible]	Clonmel.
[illegible]	[illegible]	[illegible]	[illegible]	[illegible]	[illegible]	[illegible]	[illegible]	[illegible]	[illegible]	[illegible]	[illegible]	Cork.
[illegible]	[illegible]	[illegible]	[illegible]	[illegible]	[illegible]	[illegible]	[illegible]	[illegible]	[illegible]	[illegible]	[illegible]	Downpatrick.
[illegible]	[illegible]	[illegible]	[illegible]	[illegible]	[illegible]	[illegible]	[illegible]	[illegible]	[illegible]	[illegible]	[illegible]	Ennis.
[illegible]	[illegible]	[illegible]	[illegible]	[illegible]	[illegible]	[illegible]	[illegible]	[illegible]	[illegible]	[illegible]	[illegible]	Enniscorthy.
[illegible]	[illegible]	[illegible]	[illegible]	[illegible]	[illegible]	[illegible]	[illegible]	[illegible]	[illegible]	[illegible]	[illegible]	Kilkenny.
[illegible]	[illegible]	[illegible]	[illegible]	[illegible]	[illegible]	[illegible]	[illegible]	[illegible]	[illegible]	[illegible]	[illegible]	Killarney.
[illegible]	[illegible]	[illegible]	[illegible]	[illegible]	[illegible]	[illegible]	[illegible]	[illegible]	[illegible]	[illegible]	[illegible]	Letterkenny.
[illegible]	[illegible]	[illegible]	[illegible]	[illegible]	[illegible]	[illegible]	[illegible]	[illegible]	[illegible]	[illegible]	[illegible]	Limerick.
[illegible]	[illegible]	[illegible]	[illegible]	[illegible]	[illegible]	[illegible]	[illegible]	[illegible]	[illegible]	[illegible]	[illegible]	Londonderry.
[illegible]	[illegible]	[illegible]	[illegible]	[illegible]	[illegible]	[illegible]	[illegible]	[illegible]	[illegible]	[illegible]	[illegible]	Maryborough.
[illegible]	[illegible]	[illegible]	[illegible]	[illegible]	[illegible]	[illegible]	[illegible]	[illegible]	[illegible]	[illegible]	[illegible]	Monaghan.
[illegible]	[illegible]	[illegible]	[illegible]	[illegible]	[illegible]	[illegible]	[illegible]	[illegible]	[illegible]	[illegible]	[illegible]	Mullingar.
[illegible]	[illegible]	[illegible]	[illegible]	[illegible]	[illegible]	[illegible]	[illegible]	[illegible]	[illegible]	[illegible]	[illegible]	Omagh.
[illegible]	[illegible]	[illegible]	[illegible]	[illegible]	[illegible]	[illegible]	[illegible]	[illegible]	[illegible]	[illegible]	[illegible]	Richmond.
[illegible]	[illegible]	[illegible]	[illegible]	[illegible]	[illegible]	[illegible]	[illegible]	[illegible]	[illegible]	[illegible]	[illegible]	Sligo.
[illegible]	[illegible]	[illegible]	[illegible]	[illegible]	[illegible]	[illegible]	[illegible]	[illegible]	[illegible]	[illegible]	[illegible]	Waterford.
[illegible]	[illegible]	[illegible]	[illegible]	[illegible]	[illegible]	[illegible]	[illegible]	[illegible]	[illegible]	[illegible]	[illegible]	Total.

DUBLIN CASTLE,

14th *August*, 1899.

SIR,

I have to acknowledge the receipt of your letter of the 12th instant, forwarding, for submission to His Excellency the Lord Lieutenant, Part I. of the Judicial Statistics of Ireland for the Year 1898.

I am,

Sir,

Your obedient Servant.

D. HARREL.

The Registrar-General,

Charlemont House,

Rutland Square

www.ingramcontent.com/pod-product-compliance
Lightning Source LLC
Chambersburg PA
CBHW021807190326
41518CB00007B/485
9783742800053